WORKBOOK

S N A P

Student Notes and Problems

MATH 9 Alberta

Rao, Gautam, 1961 –
STUDENT NOTES AND PROBLEMS – Math 9 Workbook Alberta
(2nd Edition)

1. Mathematics – Juvenile Literature. I. Title

Published by
Castle Rock Research Corp.
2410 Manulife Place
10180 – 101 Street
Edmonton, AB T5J 3S4

2 3 4 MP 13 12 11

Publisher
Gautam Rao

Contributors
Monica Dhaliwal
Angela Naidu

Dedicated to the memory of Dr. V. S. Rao

STUDENT NOTES AND PROBLEMS WORKBOOKS

Student Notes and Problems (SNAP) workbooks are a series of support resources in mathematics for students in grades 3 to 12 and in science for students in grades 9 to 12. SNAP workbooks are 100% aligned with curriculum. The resources are designed to support classroom instructions and provide students with additional examples, practice exercises, and tests. SNAP workbooks are ideal for use all year long at school and at home.

The following is a summary of the key features of all SNAP workbooks.

UNIT OPENER PAGE

- Summarizes the curriculum outcomes addressed in the unit in age-appropriate language
- Identifies the lessons by title
- Lists the prerequisite knowledge and skills the student should know prior to beginning the unit

LESSONS

- Provide essential teaching pieces and explanations of the concepts
- Include example problems and questions with complete, detailed solutions that demonstrate the problem-solving process

NOTES BARS

- Contain key definitions, formulas, reminders, and important steps or procedures
- Provide space for students to add their own notes and helpful reminders

PRACTICE EXERCISES

- Include questions that relate to each of the curriculum outcomes for the unit
- Provide practice in applying the lesson concepts

REVIEW SUMMARY

- Provides a succinct review of the key concepts in the unit

PRACTICE TEST

- Assesses student learning of the unit concepts

ANSWERS AND SOLUTIONS

- Answers and solutions for the odd-numbered questions are provided in each student workbook.

CONTENTS

Linear Relations

Linear Inequalities

Polynomials

Circles and Composite 3-D Objects

Scaling, Similar Triangles, and Polygons

Rotation Symmetry and Transformations of 2-D Shapes

Data Analysis

Answers and Solutions

POWERS

When you are finished this unit, you will be able to…

- demonstrate the differences between the exponent and the base by building models of a given power
- explain, using repeated multiplication, the difference between two given powers in which the exponent and base are interchanged
- express a given power as a repeated multiplication
- express a given repeated multiplication as a power
- explain the role of brackets in powers by evaluating a given set of powers
- evaluate powers with integral bases (excluding base 0) and whole number exponents
- solve a given problem by applying the order of operations with and without the use of technology
- identify the errors in applying the order of operations in a given incorrect solution

PREREQUISITE SKILLS AND KNOWLEDGE

Prior to starting this unit, you should be able to…

- identify mathematical symbols
- identify natural and whole numbers
- complete mathematic operations using paper and pencil
- complete simple mathematical operations on a calculator

Lesson 1 POWERS

NOTES

A power can also be called an exponential expression.

PARTS OF A POWER

Given 10^3, the number 10 represents the base and the number 3 represents the exponent. Together, they represent a power. This expression can also be read as ten exponent three, ten cubed or ten to the power of three.

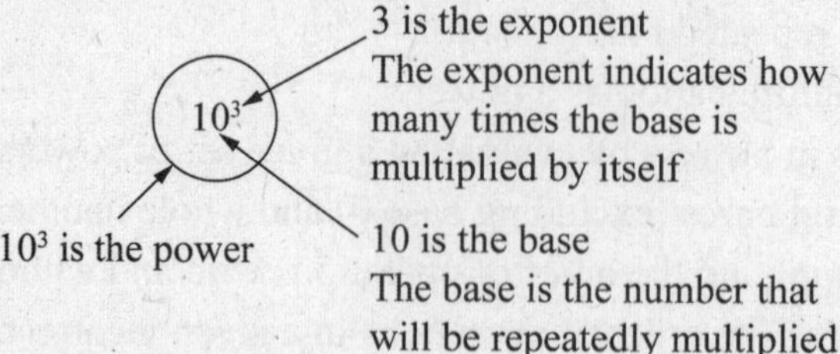

The interchanged expression of the given example is 3^{10}. In this expression, the number 3 represents the base and the number 10 represents the exponent. Together, they represent a power. This expression can also be read as three exponent ten or three to the power of ten.

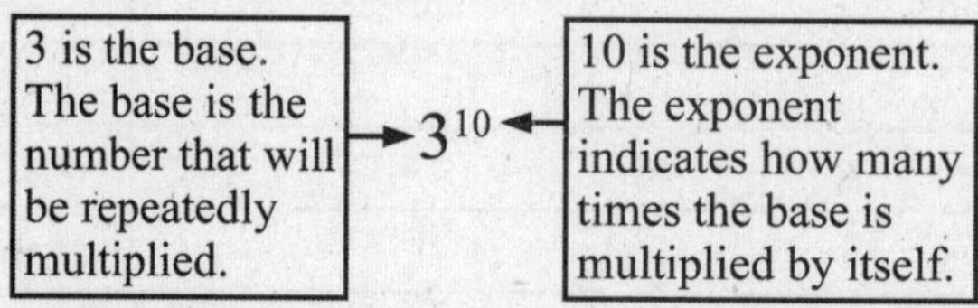

Example

Identify the base and exponent in the expression 9^2.

Solution

The base is 9 and the exponent is 2.

Your Turn 1

Identify the base and the exponent in the expression 6^{12}.

POWER CONVERTED TO EXPANDED FORM

When the base of a power is expanded, the base is multiplied repeatedly. The base is repeated the number of times indicated by the exponent.

Expanded form is shown when a power is multiplied repeatedly.

Example

Given 10^3, the base is 10 and the exponent is 3. The base 10 is multiplied 3 times.

$10^3 = 10 \times 10 \times 10$

Power — Expanded form

NOTES

The interchanged expression of the given example is 3^{10}. The base is 3 and the exponent is 10. The base of 3 is multiplied 10 times.

$$3^{10} = \underbrace{3 \times 3 \times 3 \times 3 \times 3 \times 3 \times 3 \times 3 \times 3 \times 3}_{\text{Expanded form}}$$

Power

Your Turn 2

Convert 7^5 to expanded form.

EXPANDED FORM CONVERTED TO A POWER

If an expression is represented in expanded form, it can be expressed as a power. Count the number of times the given number is multiplied. The number being multiplied represents the base. The number of times it is multiplied represents the exponent.

Example

Convert $5\times5\times5\times5$ to a power.

Solution

The number being multiplied is 5. This value becomes the base. The number 5 is multiplied repeatedly four times. Four becomes the exponent. The power is 5^4.

Your Turn 3

Convert $11\times11\times11\times11\times11\times11$ to a power.

EVALUATING POWERS

Powers can only be evaluated when each term in the expression is represented by a numerical value. When evaluating a power, the final result must be expressed as a number.

Use the following steps to help you evaluate powers.

Step 1
Write the expression in expanded form.

Step 2
Evaluate the expression using repeated multiplication.

NOTES

Example

Evaluate the expression 6^5.

Solution

Step 1

Write the expression in expanded form.

$6^5 = 6 \times 6 \times 6 \times 6 \times 6$

Step 2

Evaluate the expression using repeated multiplication.

$$\begin{aligned} &6 \times 6 \times 6 \times 6 \times 6 \\ &= 36 \times 6 \times 6 \times 6 \\ &= 216 \times 6 \times 6 \\ &= 1\ 296 \times 6 \\ &= 7\ 776 \end{aligned}$$

$6^5 = 7\ 776$

Your Turn 4

Evaluate the expression 8^4.

PRACTICE EXERCISES

Identify the base in the following expressions.

1. 3^5

2. 6^3

3. 7^4

Identify the exponent in the following expressions.

4. 4^2

5. 5^4

6. 2^5

Evaluate the following powers using repeated multiplication.

7. 2^5

8. 6^3

9. 4^2

Express the given expanded forms as powers.

10. $6 \times 6 \times 6 \times 6$

11. $7 \times 7 \times 7$

12. $4 \times 4 \times 4 \times 4 \times 4 \times 4$

Lesson 2 NEGATIVE POWERS

NOTES

BRACKETS IN POWERS

Powers can have positive and negative bases. The placement of brackets in an expression will determine whether the negative sign is grouped with the base or is separated from the base. For example, the expressions -2^4, $(-2)^4$, and $\left(-2^4\right)$ all do not result in the same answer.

Brackets containing a number or power separate their content from the other parts of the expression.

Power	Expanded Form	Standard Form
-2^4	$(-1)\left(2^4\right)=(-1)(2\times2\times2\times2)$	$-2^4=-16$
$(-2)^4$	$(-2)^4=(-2\times-2\times-2\times-2)$	$(-2)^4=16$
$\left(-2^4\right)$	$(-1)\left(2^4\right)=(-1)(2\times2\times2\times2)$	$\left(-2^4\right)=-16$

In this example, the coefficient is the number being multiplied by the base, (–1).

In the expression -2^4, the negative sign actually belongs to the numerical coefficient of 1. This coefficient is invisible in the expression. In this case, since the value of the base is 2, the negative sign is not applied when the power is expanded. It is multiplied by -1 at the last step of the evaluation process.

In the expression $(-2)^4$, the negative sign belongs to the number 2. The exponent 4 applies to everything inside the brackets, including the negative sign. In this case, since the value of the base is -2, the negative sign is used in the expanded form of the power.

Knowing how to apply the negative sign in an expression will mean the difference between a correct answer and an incorrect answer.

Example

Evaluate the expression $(-5)^4$.

Solution

The base of –5 is enclosed in brackets while the exponent 4 is outside the brackets. Since the negative is inside the brackets, it belongs to the number 5. The exponent 4 applies to everything inside the brackets. Solve the expression by multiplying the base, –5, four times.

$$\begin{aligned}(-5)^4&=-5\times-5\times-5\times-5\\&=25\times-5\times-5\\&=-125\times-5\\&=625\end{aligned}$$

NOTES

Your Turn 1

Evaluate the expression $(-3)^2$.

Example

Evaluate the expression $\left(-6^4\right)$.

Solution

The base and exponent are both enclosed in brackets. The exponent 4 only applies to the base of 6. Therefore, the negative sign belongs to the numerical coefficient of 1. Solve the expression by multiplying the base, 6, four times. Then, multiply the result by -1.

$$\begin{aligned}\left(-6^4\right) &= (-1)(6\times6\times6\times6)\\ &= (-1)(36\times6\times6)\\ &= (-1)(216\times6)\\ &= (-1)(1296)\\ &= -1\ 296\end{aligned}$$

Your Turn 2

Evaluate the expression $\left(-8^2\right)$.

NOTES

Example

Evaluate the expression -3^4.

Solution

Since there are no brackets present, the exponent 4 only applies to the base of 3. Multiply the base, 3, four times. Then, multiply the result by -1.

$$\begin{aligned}-3^4 &= (-1)(3\times3\times3\times3)\\ &= (-1)(9\times3\times3)\\ &= (-1)(27\times3)\\ &= (-1)(81)\\ &= -81\end{aligned}$$

Your Turn 3

Evaluate the expression -6^3.

PRACTICE EXERCISES

Evaluate the given expressions.

1. $(-7)^3$

2. $(-2)^6$

3. $(-9)^4$

4. (-1^6)

5. (-9^2)

6. (-7^5)

7. -2^3

8. -4^3

Lesson 3 ORDER OF OPERATIONS

NOTES

BEDMAS

Use the order of operations to solve expressions with more than one operation. The order of operations can be remembered using the acronym BEDMAS. When evaluating expressions involving integers, the operations must be performed in a specific order to get the correct answer.

Brackets	Perform any operations within brackets first. When brackets occur within another set of brackets, start by performing the operations inside the innermost brackets first. Then, work outward.
Exponents	Next, perform operations involving exponents.
Division	Carry out operations as seen in order from left to right.
Multiplication	
Addition	Carry out operations as seen in order from left to right.
Subtraction	

When solving an expression with BEDMAS, you may come across an expression that does not have a particular operation as found in BEDMAS. If that occurs, move to the next letter in the acronym.

USING ORDER OF OPERATIONS WITHOUT A CALCULATOR

Example

Evaluate the expression $5^2 - 4(15-5)$.

Solution

To solve this expression, use the order of operations.

Step 1

Perform the operations located within the brackets.

$5^2 - 4\underline{(15-5)}$

$= 5^2 - 4(10)$

Step 2

Perform any operations involving exponents.

$\underline{5^2} - 4(10)$

$= 25 - 4(10)$

Step 3

Perform any division or multiplication operations from left to right.

$25 - \underline{4(10)}$

$= 25 - 40$

NOTES

Step 4
Perform any addition or subtraction operations from left to right.
$25 - 40$
$= -15$

Your Turn 1

Solve the expression $(15 \div 5 + 11) + 7^2$.

USING ORDER OF OPERATIONS WITH A CALCULATOR

You should be able to use a calculator to solve mathematical problems. Some important keys to remember are

- Brackets [(] [)]
- Fractions [a b/c]
- Exponents [^]
- 10^x, (used in scientific notation) [EXP] or [ee]

Different calculator sequences can be used to obtain the same results.

Example

Identify the keystrokes necessary to solve $\dfrac{31.6 \times 7.3}{(5.2 \times 8.2) - 5.4}$ on a calculator.

Give the answer, rounded to the nearest hundredth.

Solution

When dividing expressions, each expression in the numerator and denominator is treated as a single term. Brackets must be placed around the expressions in the numerator and denominator.

On your calculator, press the keys in the following order:

[(] [3] [1] [.] [6] [×] [7] [.] [3] [)] [÷] [(] [(] [5] [.] [2] [×] [8] [.] [2] [)] [−] [5] [.] [4] [)] [=]

$$\frac{31.6 \times 7.3}{(5.2 \times 8.2) - 5.4} = 6.1944...$$

Rounded to the nearest hundredth, the answer is 6.19.

NOTES

Your Turn 2

Identify the keystrokes required to solve $(21.3-14.7)\times(14.7+3.6)$ and give the answer, rounded to the nearest hundredth.

ERRORS IN BEDMAS OPERATIONS

It is important to follow the order of operations carefully, as a simple misplacement of a bracket can lead to an error in the answer.

Example

Identify the errors in the given solution for the expression $2^2(5+4)-7$.

Step 1	$=4(5+4)-7$
Step 2	$=4(9)-7$
Step 3	$=4(2)$
Step 4	$=8$

Solution

The first error occurred in Step 1, when the exponents were completed before the brackets.

The second error occurred in Step 3, when the subtraction was completed before the multiplication.

The correct solution is

Step 1	$=2^2(9)-7$
Step 2	$=4(9)-7$
Step 3	$=36-7$
Step 4	$=29$

$2^2(5+4)-7=29$

NOTES

Your Turn 3

Identify the errors in the given solution for the expression $30 \div (14-4) \times 4^2 - 2$. Then, give the correct answer.

Given Solution		Error
Step 1	$= 30 \div (14-4) \times 16 - 2$	
Step 2	$= 30 \div (14-4) \times 14$	
Step 3	$= 30 \div (10) \times 14$	
Step 4	$= 30 \div (140)$	
Step 5	$= 0.214$	

PRACTICE EXERCISES

Evaluate the given expressions using the order of operations.

1. $4^2+3^3(2\times9)$

2. $(3^2\times12)-(24\div6)$

3. $5(13-3)^2$

Use your calculator to solve each of the following expressions using as few keystrokes as possible. Record the keying sequence and the answer, rounding your answer to the nearest tenth.

4. $21.4\times(64.1-37.8)$

5. $\dfrac{20.3\times14.5}{15.5}$

6. $(-35.5-13)\div(15.7-21.3)$

7. $\dfrac{311.4}{6.5 \times 22.4} - 101$

8. $\dfrac{14.9 - 8.3}{15.4 - (8.2 \times 4.7)}$

9. Identify the errors in the given solution for the expression $2^2(15+14)-3$. Then, solve the expression using the correct order of operations.

Given Solution		Error
Step 1	$=4(15+14)-3$	
Step 2	$=4(29)-3$	
Step 3	$=4(26)$	
Step 4	$=104$	

REVIEW SUMMARY

- An exponential expression has a base and an exponent. For example, in 2^3, 2 is the base and 3 is the exponent.
- When numbers are multiplied together many times over, it is called repeated multiplication.
- To evaluate a power, convert the power to expanded form and use repeated multiplication to solve.
- The role of brackets in powers is to group the base and exponent together within the brackets or separate the base and exponent by placing the exponent outside the brackets.
- To solve expressions that have many operations, use the order of operations to evaluate the expression.
- The order of operations can be remembered by the acronym BEDMAS. **B**rackets, **E**xponents, **D**ivision, **M**ultiplication, **A**ddition, **S**ubtraction.

PRACTICE TEST

Identify the base and the exponent in the following expressions.

1. 5^2

2. 9^3

3. 4^3

4. 6^4

5. Evaluate the following power using repeated multiplication: 8^2.

6. Express the given expanded form as a power: $9\times9\times9\times9\times9\times9$.

7. Express the given expanded form as a power: $3\times3\times3\times3\times3$.

Evaluate the given expressions.

8. $(-9)^3$

9. $\left(-13^4\right)$

10. -2^3

Evaluate the given expressions using the order of operations.

11. $5^2 + 2^4(12 \times 9)$

12. $(6^2 \times 10) - (25 \div 5)$

Identify the keystrokes needed to evaluate the given expression and then give the answer.

13. $\left(\frac{3}{4} + \frac{3}{8}\right) \times 2^3$

14. $\left(5.1 \times 10^6\right) \times \left(2.34 \times 10^{-2}\right)$

Identify the errors in the given solution for the following expressions.

15. $45 \div (15 - 5) \times 6^3 - 21$

	Given Solution	Error
Step 1	$= 45 \div (15 - 5) \times 216 - 21$	
Step 2	$= 45 \div (15 - 5) \times 195$	
Step 3	$= 45 \div (10) \times 195$	
Step 4	$= 45 \div (1\ 950)$	
Step 5	$= 0.023$	

16. $(215 \div 5) \times 6^3 - 2^2$

Given Solution		Error
Step 1	$=(215 \div 5) \times 216 - 4$	
Step 2	$=(43)216 - 4$	
Step 3	$=43 \times 212$	
Step 4	$=9\ 116$	

NOTES

EXPONENT LAW OF POWERS

When you are finished this unit, you will be able to…

- explain the exponent law of powers with integral bases and whole number exponents using examples
- evaluate expressions by applying the exponent laws
- determine the sum of two given powers
- determine the difference of two given powers
- identify errors in the simplifications of expressions involving powers

PREREQUISITE SKILLS AND KNOWLEDGE

Prior to starting this unit, you should be able to…

- recognize integral and whole numbers
- perform basic mathematical operations
- follow BEDMAS rules
- identify basic mathematical errors

Lesson 1 MULTIPLYING AND DIVIDING POWERS

NOTES

The exponent laws are used to simplify exponents when multiplying or dividing powers.

PRODUCT LAW

To multiply powers with the same base, add the exponents together while keeping the same base.

Product Law: $(a^m)(a^n) = a^{m+n}$

Example

Simplify the expression $2^3 \times 2^2$.

Solution:

Step 1

Verify that the bases of the powers are the same.
The base of both the powers is 2.

Step 2

Add the exponents:

$$\begin{aligned} 2^3 \times 2^2 &= 2^{3+2} \\ &= 2^5 \end{aligned}$$

Your Turn 1

Simplify the expression $6^4 \times 6^2$.

Example

Simplify the expression $3^2 \times 3^5 \times 3^4$.

Solution:

Step 1

Verify that the bases of the powers are the same.
The base of all the powers is 3.

Step 2

Add the exponents:

$$\begin{aligned} 3^2 \times 3^5 \times 3^4 &= 3^{2+5+4} \\ &= 3^{11} \end{aligned}$$

NOTES

Your Turn 2

Simplify the expression $5^5 \times 5^2 \times 5^3$.

The product law also applies to powers with negative bases.

Example

Simplify the expression $(-8)^3 \times (-8)^7$.

Solution

Step 1

Verify that the bases of the powers are the same.

The base of both the powers is -8.

Step 2

Add the exponents:

$$\begin{aligned}(-8)^3 \times (-8)^7 &= (-8)^{3+7} \\ &= (-8)^{10}\end{aligned}$$

Your Turn 3

Simplify the expression $(-4)^2 \times (-4)^{10}$.

Example

Simplify the expression $(-3)^2 \times (-3)^4 \times (-3)^3$.

Solution

Step 1

Verify that the bases of the powers are the same.

The base of both the powers is -3.

Step 2

Add the exponents:

$$\begin{aligned}(-3)^2 \times (-3)^4 \times (-3)^3 &= (-3)^{2+4+3} \\ &= (-3)^9\end{aligned}$$

Your Turn 4

Simplify the expression $(-7)^3 \times (-7)^2 \times (-7)^4$.

NOTES

QUOTIENT LAW

To divide powers with the same base, subtract the exponents while keeping the same base.

Quotient Law: $a^m \div a^n = a^{m-n}$

Example

Simplify the expression $\frac{3^5}{3^3}$.

Solution

Step 1

Verify that the bases of the powers are the same.
The base of both the powers is 3.

Step 2

Subtract the exponents:

$$\frac{3^5}{3^3} = 3^{5-3}$$
$$= 3^2$$

Your Turn 5

Simplify the expression $\frac{10^5}{10^3}$.

Example

Simplify the expression $8^{10} \div 8^7$.

Solution

Step 1

Verify that the bases of the powers are the same.
The base of both powers is 8.

Step 2

Subtract the exponents:

$$8^{10} \div 8^7 = 8^{10-7}$$
$$= 8^3$$

Your Turn 6

Simplify the expression $6^{14} \div 6^8$.

NOTES

The quotient law also applies to powers with a negative base.

Example

Simplify the expression $(-2)^8 \div (-2)^2$.

Solution

Step 1

Verify that the bases of the powers are the same.
The base of both powers is -2.

Step 2

Subtract the exponents:

$$\begin{aligned}(-2)^8 \div (-2)^2 &= (-2)^{8-2}\\ &= (-2)^6\end{aligned}$$

Your Turn 7

Simplify the expression $(-3)^{12} \div (-3)^6$.

Example

Simplify the expression $\frac{(-5)^{12}}{(-5)^3}$.

Solution

Step 1

Verify that the bases of the powers are the same.
The base of both powers is -5.

Step 2

Subtract the exponents:

$$\begin{aligned}\frac{(-5)^{12}}{(-5)^3} &= (-5)^{12-3}\\ &= (-5)^9\end{aligned}$$

Your Turn 8

Simplify the expression $\frac{(-7)^7}{(-7)^4}$.

PRACTICE EXERCISES

Simplify the following expressions by writing them as single powers.

1. $4^4 \times 4^3$

2. $5^3 \times 5^6 \times 5^4$

3. $12^4 \times 12^8$

4. $9^4 \div 9^3$

5. $\frac{10^5}{10^3}$

6. $(-7)^{13} \div (-7)^3$

Simplify the following expressions by applying the product and quotient laws and expressing the result as a single power.

7. $\frac{6^8 \times 6^4}{6^3}$

8. $\frac{10^{14}}{10^3 \times 10^5}$

9. $\frac{2^5 \times 2^3}{2}$

10. $\frac{14^5 \times 14^3}{14^6 \times 14^2}$

Lesson 2 POWER LAWS

NOTES

EXPONENT OF ZERO LAW

Any number with an **exponent of zero** is equal to 1, except for the power 0^0, which is undefined. An expression is undefined when it does not have a value. The following pattern of values demonstrates that a^0 is equal to 1 when a is equal to any number other than 0, $(a \neq 0)$.

Example

Use the expression 10^3 to prove that $a^0 = 1$.

Solution

Start with the fact that $10^3 = 1000$.

Step 1
Divide each side of the equation by 10.

$$10^3 \div 10^1 = 1000 \div 10$$
$$10^{3-1} = 100$$
$$10^2 = 100$$

Step 2
Divide each side of the equation by 10 again.

$$10^2 \div 10^1 = 100 \div 10$$
$$10^{2-1} = 10$$
$$10^1 = 10$$

Step 3
Divide each side of the equation by 10 again.

$$10^1 \div 10^1 = 10 \div 10$$
$$10^{1-1} = 1$$
$$10^0 = 1$$

This pattern verifies the exponent of zero law.

Your Turn 1

Use a pattern to demonstrate the zero exponent law using the exponential expression 5^3.

NOTES

POWER OF A POWER LAW

If a power is raised to another power with the use of brackets, it is called a **power of a power.** For example, $(3^2)^4$ is a power of a power.
The exponent outside the brackets indicates how many times the power inside the brackets is multiplied by itself. The example $(3^2)^4$ can be expanded and simplified as follows:

$$\begin{aligned}(3^2)^4 &= (3^2)(3^2)(3^2)(3^2)\\ &= 3^{2+2+2+2}\\ &= 3^8\end{aligned}$$

This simplification can also be shown as follows:

$$\begin{aligned}(3^2)^4 &= 3^{2\times4}\\ &= 3^8\end{aligned}$$

To take a power to another power, multiply the exponents together while keeping the base the same.

Power of a Power Law: $(a^m)^n = a^{mn}$

Example

Simplify the expression $(5^2)^3$.

Solution

Multiply the exponents to reduce the expression to a single power.

$5^{2\times3} = 5^6$

Your Turn 2

Simplify the expression $(3^4)^3$.

The power of a power law also applies to powers with negative bases.

Example

Simplify the expression $((-9)^2)^4$.

Solution

Multiply the exponents to reduce the expression to a single power.

$(-9)^{2\times4} = (-9)^8$

Your Turn 3

Simplify the expression $((-2)^3)^4$.

NOTES

Remember that when no number is written as the exponent, the value of the exponent is 1.

POWER OF PRODUCTS LAW

To take the power of a product, the exponent of each term inside the brackets must be multiplied by the exponent located outside the brackets.

Power of a Product Law: $(ab)^m = a^m b^m$

Regardless of whether the base in the power is positive or negative, the power of products law is applied.

Example

Evaluate the expression $(3^4 5)^2$.

Solution

Step 1

Distribute the exponent 2 located outside the brackets to each term located inside the brackets.

$(3^4 5)^2 = \left(3^4\right)^2 \left(5\right)^2$

Step 2

Apply the power of a product law.

$(3^4)^2(5)^2$

$= 3^{4\times 2} \times 5^{1\times 2}$

$= 3^8 \times 5^2$

Step 3

Evaluate the expression.

$3^8 \times 5^2$

$= 6\ 561 \times 25$

$= 164\ 025$

Your Turn 4

Evaluate the expression $(2^2 6)^3$.

NOTES

Example

Evaluate the expression $\left((-5)^2 7^3\right)^2$.

Solution

Step 1

Distribute the exponent 2 located outside the brackets to each term located inside the brackets.

$$\left((-5)^2 7^3\right)^2$$
$$=\left((-5)^2\right)^2 \times \left(7^3\right)^2$$

Step 2

Apply the power of a product law.

$$\left((-5)^2\right)^2 \times \left(7^3\right)^2$$
$$=(-5)^{2\times2} \times 7^{3\times2}$$
$$=(-5)^4 \times 7^6$$

Step 3

Evaluate the expression.

$$(-5)^4 \times 7^6$$
$$=625 \times 117\,649$$
$$=73530625$$

Your Turn 5

Evaluate the expression $\left(7^2(-2)^5\right)^2$.

Example

Evaluate the expression $(-4 \times (-2)^3)^3$.

Solution

Step 1

Distribute the exponent 3 located outside the brackets to each term located inside the brackets.

$$(-4 \times (-2)^3)^3 = (-4)^3 \times ((-2)^3)^3$$

Step 2

Apply the power of a product law.

$$(-4)^3 \times ((-2)^3)^3 = (-4)^3 \times (-2)^{3\times3}$$
$$= (-4)^3 \times (-2)^9$$

NOTES

Step 3
Evaluate the expression.
$$(-4)^3 \times (-2)^9 = (-64) \times (-512)$$
$$= 32\ 768$$

Your Turn 6

Evaluate the expression $(-8 \times 10)^4$.

Example

Evaluate the expression $((-9)^2 2^4)^3$.

Solution
Step 1
Distribute the exponent 3 located outside the brackets to each term located inside the brackets.
$$((-9)^2 2^4)^3 = ((-9)^2)^3 (2^4)^3$$

Step 2
Apply the power of a product law.
$$((-9)^2)^3 (2^4)^3 = (-9)^{2\times 3} 2^{4\times 3}$$
$$= (-9)^6 2^{12}$$

Step 3
Evaluate the expression.
$$(-9)^6 2^{12} = 531\ 441 \times 4\ 096$$
$$= 2\ 176\ 782\ 336$$

Your Turn 7

Evaluate the expression $((-13)^2 \times (-4))^2$.

NOTES

When working with the exponent law of powers for power of a quotient, the variable b (the denominator) cannot equal zero because division by zero is undefined.

POWER OF A QUOTIENT LAW

To take the power of a quotient, the exponent of each term inside the brackets must be multiplied by the exponent located outside the brackets.

Power of a Quotient Law: $\left(\frac{a}{b}\right)^n = \frac{a^n}{b^n},\ b \neq 0$

Example

Evaluate the expression $\left(\frac{3}{7}\right)^2$.

Solution

Step 1

Distribute the exponent 2 located outside the brackets to each term located inside the brackets.

$$\left(\frac{3}{7}\right)^2 = \frac{3^2}{7^2}$$

Step 2

Evaluate the expression by using repeated multiplication.

$$\frac{3^2}{7^2} = \frac{3\times3}{7\times7}$$
$$= \frac{9}{49}$$

Your Turn 8

Simplify the expression $\left(\frac{5}{8}\right)^3$ to a fraction expressed in lowest terms.

Example

Evaluate the expression $\left(\frac{3^4}{2^6}\right)^3$ and express the result as a decimal, rounded to the nearest thousandth.

Solution

Step 1

Distribute the exponent 3 located outside the brackets to each term located inside the brackets.

$$\left(\frac{3^4}{2^6}\right)^3 = \frac{(3^4)^3}{(2^6)^3}$$

NOTES

Step 2
Apply the power of a power law.

$$\frac{\left(3^4\right)^3}{\left(2^6\right)^3} = \frac{3^{4\times3}}{2^{6\times3}} = \frac{3^{12}}{2^{18}}$$

Step 3
Evaluate the expression by using repeated multiplication.

$$\frac{3^{12}}{2^{18}} = \frac{3\times3\times3\times3\times3\times3\times3\times3\times3\times3\times3\times3}{2\times2\times2\times2\times2\times2\times2\times2\times2\times2\times2\times2\times2\times2\times2\times2\times2\times2} = \frac{531\ 441}{262\ 144} \doteq 2.027$$

Your Turn 9

Evaluate the expression $\left(\frac{5^2}{9^3}\right)^2$ and express the result as a decimal rounded to the nearest thousandth.

Example

Simplify the expression $\left(\frac{-2}{-5}\right)^6$ to a fraction expressed in lowest terms.

Solution
Step 1
Distribute the exponent 6 located outside the brackets to each term located inside the brackets.

$$\left(\frac{-2}{-5}\right)^6 = \frac{(-2)^6}{(-5)^6}$$

Step 2
Evaluate the expression by using repeated multiplication.

$$\frac{(-2)^6}{(-5)^6} = \frac{-2\times-2\times-2\times-2\times-2\times-2}{-5\times-5\times-5\times-5\times-5\times-5} = \frac{64}{15\ 625}$$

NOTES

Your Turn 10

Simplify the expression $\left(\frac{-5}{-11}\right)^2$ to a fraction expressed in lowest terms.

Example

Evaluate the expression $\left(\frac{(-9)^2}{(-6)^3}\right)^4$ and express the result as a decimal rounded to the nearest thousandth.

Solution

Step 1
Distribute the exponent 4 located outside the brackets to each term located inside the brackets.

$$\left(\frac{(-9)^2}{(-6)^3}\right)^4 = \frac{\left((-9)^2\right)^4}{\left((-6)^3\right)^4}$$

Step 2
Apply the power of a product law.

$$\begin{aligned}\frac{\left((-9)^2\right)^4}{\left((-6)^3\right)^4} &= \frac{(-9)^{2\times 4}}{(-6)^{3\times 4}}\\ &= \frac{(-9)^8}{(-6)^{12}}\end{aligned}$$

Step 3
Evaluate the expression by using repeated multiplication.

$$\begin{aligned}\frac{(-9)^8}{(-6)^{12}} &= \frac{-9\times -9\times -9\times -9\times -9\times -9\times -9\times -9}{-6\times -6\times -6\times -6\times -6\times -6\times -6\times -6\times -6\times -6\times -6\times -6}\\ &= \frac{43\ 046\ 721}{2\ 176\ 782\ 336}\\ &\doteq 0.0198\end{aligned}$$

Your Turn 11

Simplify the expression $\left(\frac{(-3)^2}{(-4)^3}\right)^2$ and express the result as a decimal rounded to the nearest thousandth.

PRACTICE EXERCISES

Simplify the following expressions.

1. $\left(1^2 4^3\right)^4$

2. $\left(3^4\right)^6$

3. $\left(13^4\right)^6$

4. $\left(7^5 \times 7^2\right)^8$

5. $\left(8 \times 2^4\right)^6$

6. $\left(\dfrac{4^3}{10^2}\right)^5$

7. $\left(\dfrac{5}{8^2}\right)^3$

8. $\left(5^{11} \div 5^6\right)^4$

9. $\left((-2)^8 \div (-2)^4\right)^2$

10. $\left(\dfrac{3^5}{3^4}\right)^3$

Lesson 3 SUM AND DIFFERENCE OF POWERS

NOTES

SUM OF TWO POWERS LAW

To determine the sum of two given powers, simplify each of the powers separately and then add the simplified forms together.

Sum of Two Powers Law:
$a^m + a^n$ = simplified a^m + simplified a^n

Example

Evaluate the expression $5^2 + 5^3$.

Solution

Step 1
Solve the first exponential expression using repeated multiplication.

$$\begin{aligned} 5^2 &= 5 \times 5 \\ &= 25 \end{aligned}$$

Step 2
Solve the second exponential expression using repeated multiplication.

$$\begin{aligned} 5^3 &= 5 \times 5 \times 5 \\ &= 125 \end{aligned}$$

Step 3
Add the two values together.

$25 + 125 = 150$

Your Turn 1

Evaluate the expression $3^2 + 8^4$.

When the bases of the powers are negative, the sum of two powers law can still be applied to find the sum.

Example

Evaluate the expression $(-6)^4 + (-7)^2$.

Solution

Step 1
Solve the first exponential expression using repeated multiplication.

$$\begin{aligned} (-6)^4 &= (-6) \times (-6) \times (-6) \times (-6) \\ &= 1\ 296 \end{aligned}$$

Step 2
Solve the second exponential expression using repeated multiplication.

$$\begin{aligned} (-7)^2 &= (-7) \times (-7) \\ &= 49 \end{aligned}$$

NOTES

Step 3
Add the two values together.
$1\ 296 + 49 = 1\ 345$

Your Turn 2

Evaluate the expression $(-8)^3 + (-2)^5$.

DIFFERENCE OF TWO POWERS LAW

To determine the difference of two given powers, simplify the two powers separately and then find the difference between the two simplified values.

> **Difference of Two Powers Law:**
> $a^m - a^n =$ simplified a^m – simplified a^n

Example

Evaluate the expression $7^4 - 7^3$.

Solution

Step 1
Solve the first exponential expression using repeated multiplication.
$7^4 = 7 \times 7 \times 7 \times 7 = 2\ 401$

Step 2
Solve the second exponential expression using repeated multiplication.
$7^3 = 7 \times 7 \times 7 = 343$

Step 3
Subtract the two values.
$2\ 401 - 343 = 2\ 058$

Your Turn 3

Evaluate the expression $4^3 - 2^2$.

NOTES

When the bases of the powers are negative, the difference of two powers law can still be applied to find the difference.

Example

Evaluate the expression $(-12)^3 - (-10)^2$.

Solution

Step 1

Solve the first exponential expression using repeated multiplication.

$$\begin{aligned}(-12)^3 &= (-12)\times(-12)\times(-12)\\ &= -1\ 728\end{aligned}$$

Step 2

Solve the second exponential expression using repeated multiplication.

$$\begin{aligned}(-10)^2 &= (-10)\times(-10)\\ &= 100\end{aligned}$$

Step 3

Subtract the two values

$$(-1\ 728) - (100) = -1\ 828$$

Your Turn 4

Evaluate the expression $(-5)^2 - (-9)^4$.

POSSIBLE ERRORS WITH POWERS

It is important to understand when and how to apply each of the exponent laws when simplifying and evaluating an expression. Remembering when to add versus multiply the exponents is essential because mixing up these two operations can result in the incorrect answer.

Example

Isaiah was asked to simplify the expression $7^2 \times 7^4$ into a single power. These were the steps he took to simplify the expression.

Isaiah's Solution:

Step 1

Verify that the bases are the same.

The base of all powers is 7.

NOTES

Step 2
Multiply the exponents.
$7^{2\times4} = 7^8$
This solution is incorrect because the product law was not applied correctly.

Correct Solution:

Step 1
Verify that the bases are the same.
The base of all powers is 7.

Step 2
Since the powers are being multiplied, add the exponents.
$7^{2+4} = 7^6$

Your Turn 5

Kirk is simplifying the expression $(3^6 + 3^2)^2$ into a single power. He used the following steps to simplify the expression.

$$\begin{aligned}(3^6 + 3^2)^2 &= (3^6)^2 + (3^2)^2 \\ &= 3^{6\times2} + 3^{2\times2} \\ &= 3^{12} + 3^4 \\ &= 3^{12+4} \\ &= 3^{16}\end{aligned}$$

Where did Kirk make his mistakes?

PRACTICE EXERCISES

Evaluate the given expressions.

1. $(-3)^4 + (-4)^2$

2. $6^2 + 9^4$

3. $8^5 + 7^4$

4. $6^3 - 6^2$

5. $5^5 - 3^2$

6. $(-4)^3 - 9^2$

7. $(2^4 - 3^2) + (5^3 + 4^2)$

8. $(7^2 - 5^2) - (8^3 + 6^2)$

9. Jana got a result of 4^8 when she simplified the given expression: $4^2 \times 4^4$. Determine if this solution is correct or incorrect. If it is incorrect, explain where the mistake occurred.

10. Cam got a result of 6^2 when he simplified the given expression $6^5 \div 6^3$. Determine if this solution is correct or incorrect. If it is incorrect, explain where the mistake occurred.

REVIEW SUMMARY

- The product law is $(a^m)(a^n) = a^{m+n}$
- The quotient law is $a^m \div a^n = a^{m-n}$
- The power of a power law is $(a^m)^n = a^{mn}$
- The power of a product law is $(ab)^m = a^m b^m$
- The power of a quotient law is $\left(\frac{a}{b}\right)^n = \frac{a^n}{b^n},\ b \neq 0$
- The sum of two powers law is $a^m + a^n =$ simplified a^m + simplified a^n
- The difference of two powers law is $a^m - a^n =$ simplified a^m − simplified a^n

PRACTICE TEST

Simplify the given expressions.

1. $\left(5^2\right)^3$

2. $\left(\dfrac{10^4}{10^3}\right)^5$

3. $\dfrac{5^3}{5^2}\times\dfrac{4^6\times4^3}{\left(4^2\right)^2}$

4. $\left(12^2\right)^3\left(12^6\right)^2$

5. $\left(\dfrac{15^4}{11^6}\right)^3$

6. $21^5\times21^9$

7. $(-8)^7\times(-8)^6$

8. $\dfrac{17^3}{17}$

9. $\dfrac{16^4\times16^8}{16^3}$

Evaluate the given expressions.

10. $\left(1\times 6^{2}\times 9\right)^{3}$.

11. $\left(4\times 6^{2}\right)^{3}$

12. $\left(2^{8}\div 2^{4}\right)^{3}$

13. $-3(5)^{2}\times 4(5)^{3}$

14. $-(4^{8}\div 4^{2})$

15. $\dfrac{11^{5}}{11}$

16. $-\dfrac{35(2)^{4}}{7(2)^{2}}$

17. $\dfrac{10^{5}}{10^{2}}\times\dfrac{\left(3^{2}\times 3^{3}\right)^{3}}{\left(3^{2}\right)^{7}}$

18. $\left(10^4 \times 2^2\right)\left(10^3 \times 2^3\right)$.

19. $\dfrac{42(4)^7(5)^5}{6(4)^4(5)}$

20. $\dfrac{5 \times 10^6 \times 12^3}{6 \times 12^2 \times 10^4 \times 2}$

RATIONAL NUMBERS AND SQUARE ROOTS

When you are finished this unit, you will be able to…

- order rational numbers on a number line
- solve problems using rational numbers
- identify square numbers
- determine the square root of a positive rational number
- identify errors in a square root calculation
- determine the value of a number given its square root
- identify non-perfect squares
- estimate the approximate square root of rational numbers that are not perfect squares using benchmarks
- estimate the approximate square root of rational numbers that are not perfect squares using technology
- identify a number with a square that is between two given numbers

PREREQUISITE SKILL AND KNOWLEDGE

Prior to starting this unit, you should be able to…

- identify natural numbers, whole numbers, and integers
- recognize the square root sign
- identify an exponent
- perform simple mathematical operations

Lesson 1 COMPARE AND ORDER RATIONAL NUMBERS

NOTES

Terminating decimals are decimal numbers that end; e.g., 5.687 is a terminating decimal.

Repeating decimal numbers are decimal numbers in which one or more numbers repeat indefinitely; e.g., $0.\overline{6}$. The bar over one or more numbers indicates that the number repeats.

Rational numbers are defined as numbers written as the quotient of two integers in the form of $\frac{a}{b}$, where b is any value **except** 0.

The set of rational numbers includes the set of integers {…–4, –3, –2, –1, 0, 1, 2, 3, 4 …}, all fractions and mixed numbers, and all terminating and repeating decimal numbers.

The following numbers are examples of rational numbers:

$\frac{5}{6}, 3\frac{1}{2}, \frac{43}{3}, -12, 0, 17, 0.813, 0.4545..., -2.\overline{379}$

COMPARING RATIONAL NUMBERS

When comparing rational numbers, first change them both to the same format.

This can be done in one of two ways:

- convert all the decimals into fractions by placing the number over a denominator of 10, 100, 1 000, etc., depending on the place value of the last decimal number
- convert all the fractions into decimals by dividing the numerator by the denominator

If the numbers are being expressed as fractions, make equivalent fractions and compare the numbers using the numerators of the fractions.

If the numbers are being expressed as decimals, compare the numbers based on the place value of each decimal value in the number.

Example

Replace the □ with >, <, or = to make the statement $\frac{14}{5}$ □ 2.6 true.

Solution

Step 1

First, express the rational numbers in the same format. In this case, convert the fraction into a decimal.

$$\begin{aligned}\frac{14}{5} &= 14 \div 5 \\ &= 2.8\end{aligned}$$

Now the statement becomes 2.8 □ 2.6.

NOTES

Step 2
Compare the decimal numbers by comparing the decimals based on their place values in each number. The number 2.8 has an 8 in its tenths position, and 2.6 has a 6 in its tenths position. Since 8 is greater than 6, the statement becomes $2.8 > 2.6$ or $\frac{14}{5} > 2.6$.

Your Turn 1

Replace the □ with >, <, or = to make the statement $\frac{21}{4}$ □ 5.29 true.

Example

Replace the □ with >, <, or = to make the statement $1\frac{3}{8}$ □ 1.75 true.

Solution
Step 1
First, express the rational numbers in the same format.
In this case, convert the decimal into a fraction.

$$\begin{aligned}1.75 &= 1\frac{75}{100}\\ &= 1\frac{3}{4}\end{aligned}$$

Now the statement becomes $1\frac{3}{8}$ □ $1\frac{3}{4}$.

Make equivalent fractions using a lowest common denominator of 16.

$1\frac{3}{8} = 1\frac{6}{16}$, $1\frac{3}{4} = 1\frac{12}{16}$

Step 2
Compare the fractions by looking at the numerators of each fraction.
Since 12 is greater than 6, the statement becomes $1\frac{6}{16} < 1\frac{12}{16}$

or $1\frac{3}{8} < 1.75$.

NOTES

Your Turn 2

Replace the □ with >, <, or = to make the statement $3\frac{3}{4}$ □ 3.8 true.

ORDERING RATIONAL NUMBERS

One method of ordering rational numbers is to place them on a number line.

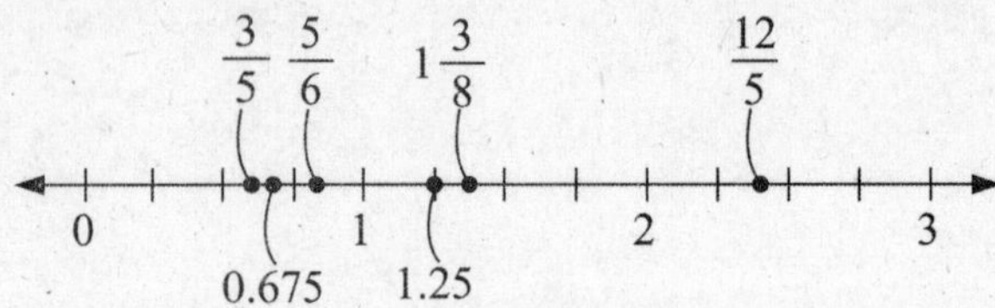

When ordering rational numbers, convert all the numbers to the same format. This can be done in one of two ways:

- convert all the decimals into fractions by placing the number over a denominator of 10, 100, 1 000, etc., depending on the place value of the last decimal number
- convert all the fractions into decimals by dividing the numerator by the denominator

Having numbers in the same format helps order the numbers and place them on a number line.

Example

Place the following rational numbers on a number line:

$0.311, \frac{9}{18}, 1, 0.43, \frac{5}{11}$

Solution

Step 1

Change the fractions to decimals.

$\frac{9}{18} = 0.5$

$\frac{5}{11} = 0.\overline{45}$

Step 2

Arrange the numbers in ascending order.

$0.311,\ 0.43,\ 0.\overline{45},\ 0.5,\ 1$

NOTES

Step 3
Arrange the numbers on the number line. The original form of fractions can be used.

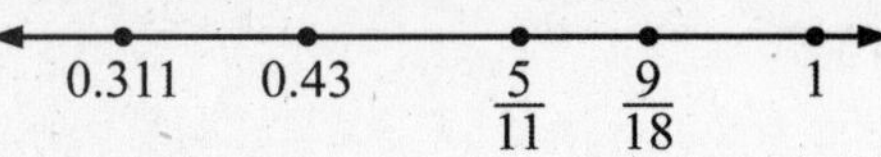

Your Turn 3

Place the given rational numbers on a number line:

$0.217,\ 0.573,\ 2,\ \frac{3}{11},\ \frac{4}{11}$

PRACTICE EXERCISES

Are the following numbers rational numbers? Explain why or why not.

1. 0.371 59

2. 0.4213

3. $\sqrt{5}$

4. $0.0\overline{3}$

5. Convert the following decimals into fraction form and then arrange them on a number line.
$0.2,\ 0.\overline{11},\ 1.035$

6. Convert the following fractions into decimal form and then arrange them on a number line.
$2\frac{2}{9},\ \frac{15}{36},\ \frac{24}{30}$

Lesson 2 PROBLEM SOLVING WITH RATIONAL NUMBERS IN DECIMAL FORM

NOTES

ADDING RATIONAL NUMBERS IN DECIMAL FORM

When adding decimal numbers, apply the following sign rules:

- If the signs are the same, add the numbers, keeping the sign of the original numbers.
- If the signs are different, ignore the signs. Subtract the smaller number from the larger number. The sign in the answer will be the same as the sign of the larger number.

Remember, when adding or subtracting numbers with decimals, line up the decimals.

Example

Evaluate $-4.21+(-6.9)$.

Solution

Since both signs are the same, the answer will be negative.
$4.21+6.9=11.11$, so $-4.21+(-6.9)=-11.11$

Example

Evaluate $-10.3+6.42$.

Solution

Both signs are different, so subtract the smaller number from the larger number. The sign in the answer will be the same as the sign of the larger number, which means it will be negative.

$10.3-6.42=3.88$, so $-10.3+6.42=-3.88$

Your Turn 1

Evaluate $-189.13+(-32.62)$.

SUBTRACTING RATIONAL NUMBERS IN DECIMAL FORM

When subtracting decimals, the additive inverse is used. The additive inverse of a number is the number's opposite value. For example, the additive inverse of 8 is –8. The same sign rules that apply to adding decimal numbers apply to subtracting decimal numbers.

The sum of a number and its additive inverse is 0.

Example

Evaluate $-1.13-(-18.4)$.

Solution

Step 1

Rewrite the expression using the additive inverse of the second term.
$-1.13+(+18.4)$

NOTES

Step 2
Both signs are different, so subtract the smaller number from the larger number. The sign of the answer will be the same as the sign of the larger number, which means the answer will be positive.
$18.4-1.13=17.27$, so $-1.13-(-18.4)=17.27$

Example

Evaluate $-6.99-3.44$.

Solution
Step 1
Rewrite the expression using the additive inverse of the second term.
$-6.99+(-3.44)$.

Step 2
Since both signs are the same, the answer will be negative.
$6.99+3.44=10.43$, so $-6.99-3.44=-10.43$

Your Turn 2

Evaluate $68.13-(-17.87)$.

MULTIPLYING & DIVIDING RATIONAL NUMBERS IN DECIMAL FORM

When multiplying or dividing decimal numbers, first multiply or divide the numbers and then apply the following sign rules:
- If there is an *odd* number of negative signs in the expression, the answer will be negative.
- If there is an *even* number of negative signs in the expression, the answer will be positive.

Example

Evaluate $(-4.6)\times(-3.2)$.

Solution
Step 1
Multiply the decimal numbers.
$4.6\times3.2=14.72$

Step 2
Determine the sign of the answer. The answer will be positive because there is an even number of negative signs.

The answer is 14.72.

NOTES

Example

Evaluate $5.83\times(-1.9)$.

Solution

Step 1
Multiply the decimal numbers.
$5.83\times1.9=11.077$

Step 2
Determine the sign of the answer. The answer will be negative because there is an odd number of negative signs.

The answer is -11.077.

Your Turn 3

Evaluate $(-3.68)\times(-12.7)$.

Example

Evaluate $-18.2\div(-0.7)$.

Solution

Step 1
Divide the decimal numbers.
$18.2\div0.7=26$

Step 2
Determine the sign of the answer. The answer will be positive because there is an even number of negative signs.

The answer is 26.

Example

Evaluate $-3.74\div0.22$.

Solution

Step 1
Divide the decimal numbers.
$3.74\div0.22=17$

Step 2
Determine the sign of the answer. The answer will be negative because there is an odd number of negative signs.

The answer is -17.

NOTES

Your Turn 4

Evaluate $19.215 \div (-9.15)$.

PROBLEM SOLVING WITH RATIONAL NUMBERS IN DECIMAL FORM

To solve word problems involving rational numbers expressed in decimal form, first translate the words in the problem into a mathematical expression.

Carefully read the question, underlining any keywords that tell you which operation to perform or which integer sign to apply to the number. Some examples of keywords are listed in the given table.

Add	sum, total, altogether, more than
Subtract	difference, less than, take away, taken from, left, left over
Multiply	above, increased, gain higher, rise, up, over, more
Divide	below, lower, decreased, down, under, loss

Then, evaluate the numerical expression by applying the order of operations.

The order of operations always applies when solving any problem involving rational numbers.

Example

Mindy goes to a store that is having a "Get Ready for Winter" sale. She has a coupon that discounts her total purchase by $5.00. There is no GST on any of the products. The items are priced as follows:

- Scarf—$7.49
- Mittens—$14.99
- Toque—$12.49

If Mindy chooses to buy 2 toques and 3 scarves and decides to use the coupon, how much will she spend altogether?

Solution

Step 1

Translate the words in the problem into a mathematical expression.

The problem is asking how much it will cost for the toques and scarves after using the coupon.

The price of the toque is $12.49.
The price of the scarf is $7.49.
The coupon is worth $5.00.

NOTES

The keyword "altogether" implies addition. The keyword "discounts" implies subtraction.
The expression that represents this problem is
$2(12.49) + 3(7.49) - 5.00$.

Step 2
Evaluate the expression by applying the order of operations.
$2(12.49) + 3(7.49) - 5.00$
$= 24.98 + 22.47 - 5.00$
$= 42.45$

Mindy's total purchase will cost her $42.45.

Your Turn 5

Justin buys a magazine for $2.55 and a bag of chips for $1.25. He pays with a $10.00 bill. How much change should Justin get back?

PRACTICE EXERCISES

Evaluate each of the following expressions.

1. $3.13+(-19.16)$

2. $-1.2+3.16$

3. $-6.17-(-21.4)$

4. $1.19\times(-2.4)$

5. $-25.16\times(-6.3)$

6. $-33.58\div(-4.6)$

7. $5.992\div(-0.7)$

Solve each of the following problems.

8. A submarine is put into the water and descends to a depth of –19.4 m. If it then rises 7.2 m, what is its new depth?

9. Bob bought 12 pencils at $0.28 each. What was the total cost?

10. At 6 P.M., the temperature outside is –4°C. If it drops 1.2°C/h, what will the temperature be after 7 hours?

11. Matt builds a tower that is 15 building blocks high. If each block is 1.6 cm high, how tall is his tower?

12. A hot-air balloon is 33.5 m above the ground. From this point, it rises 2.8 m more and then falls 14.6 m. How far above the ground is the hot-air balloon now?

Lesson 3 OPERATIONS WITH RATIONAL NUMBERS IN FRACTION FORM

NOTES

Fractions can be added, subtracted, multiplied, or divided in the same way that whole numbers and integers are.

ADDING & SUBTRACTING RATIONAL NUMBERS IN FRACTION FORM

To add or subtract fractions and mixed numbers, follow these steps.

Step 1
Change any mixed numbers into improper fractions.

Step 2
Find the lowest common denominator (LCD) of the fractions. Write new fractions with the new denominator.

Step 3
Add or subtract the numerators of the fractions, keeping the denominators the same.

Step 4
Reduce the fraction to lowest terms. Change any improper fractions into mixed numbers.

If one or more of the fractions is negative, apply the same sign rules as you did when adding or subtracting decimal numbers.

Example

Evaluate $-\frac{2}{3}+\frac{1}{4}$.

Solution

Step 1
There are no mixed numbers to change into improper fractions.

Step 2
Find the lowest common denominator (LCD) of the fractions.
The lowest common denominator of 3 and 4 is 12.

$$-\frac{2}{3}+\frac{1}{4}=-\frac{8}{12}+\frac{3}{12}$$

Step 3
Evaluate the numerators of the fractions.

$$\begin{aligned}-\frac{8}{12}+\frac{3}{12}&=\frac{-8+3}{12}\\&=\frac{-5}{12}\end{aligned}$$

NOTES

Step 4
Reduce the fraction to lowest terms. The fraction is in lowest terms.

The answer is $-\frac{2}{3}+\frac{1}{4}=-\frac{5}{12}$.

Example

Evaluate $4\frac{3}{10}-1\frac{1}{5}$.

Solution
Step 1
Change the mixed numbers into improper fractions.
$4\frac{3}{10}=\frac{43}{10},\ 1\frac{1}{5}=\frac{6}{5}$

Step 2
Find the lowest common denominator (LCD) of the fractions.
The lowest common denominator of 10 and 5 is 10.
$\frac{43}{10}-\frac{6}{5}=\frac{43}{10}-\frac{12}{10}$

Step 3
Evaluate the numerators of the fractions.
$$\begin{aligned}\frac{43}{10}-\frac{12}{10}&=\frac{43-12}{10}\\&=\frac{31}{10}\end{aligned}$$

Step 4
Reduce the fraction to lowest terms. Rewrite $\frac{31}{10}$ as a mixed number.

$\frac{31}{10}=3\frac{1}{10}$

The final answer is $4\frac{3}{10}-1\frac{1}{5}=3\frac{1}{10}$.

Your Turn 1

Evaluate $3\frac{5}{9}-2\frac{1}{2}$.

NOTES

MULTIPLYING RATIONAL NUMBERS IN FRACTION FORM

To multiply fractions and mixed numbers, follow these steps:

Step 1
Change any mixed numbers to improper fractions.

Step 2
Multiply numerator by numerator and denominator by denominator.

Step 3
Reduce the fraction to lowest terms. Change any improper fractions to mixed numbers.

If one or more of the fractions is negative, then apply the same sign rules as you did when multiplying decimal numbers.

- If there is an *odd* number of negative signs in the expression, the answer will be negative.
- If there is an *even* number of negative signs in the expression, the answer will be positive.

Example

Evaluate $-\frac{1}{2}\times-\frac{3}{4}$.

Solution

Step 1
There are no mixed numbers to change into improper fractions.

Step 2
Multiply numerator by numerator and denominator by denominator.

$$-\frac{1}{2}\times-\frac{3}{4}=\frac{(-1)\times(-3)}{2\times4}$$

$$=\frac{3}{8}$$

Step 3
Reduce the fraction to lowest terms.

Since $\frac{3}{8}$ is already in lowest terms, this is the answer.

Your Turn 2

Evaluate $-3\frac{2}{3}\times5\frac{4}{5}$.

DIVIDING RATIONAL NUMBERS IN FRACTION FORM

NOTES

For a given fraction, a related fraction known as the **reciprocal** can be formed by switching the placement of the numerator and denominator or "flipping" the fraction.

For example, the reciprocal of $\frac{2}{3}$ is $\frac{3}{2}$.

If given a mixed number, such as $1\frac{4}{7}$, first change it into an improper fraction. It becomes $\frac{11}{7}$, and the reciprocal of that fraction is $\frac{7}{11}$.

The product of a number and its reciprocal is always equal to 1.

For example, $\frac{5}{7}\times\frac{7}{5}=\frac{35}{35}$
$=1$

To divide fractions and mixed numbers, follow these steps:

Step 1
Change any mixed numbers to improper fractions.

Step 2
Find the reciprocal of the second fraction.
Do this by switching the numerator and the denominator.

Use the reciprocal of the second fraction only. The first fraction always stays as it is.

Step 3
Rewrite the expression by changing the ÷ sign to a × sign.

Step 4
Multiply the fractions, and then reduce the product into lowest terms.
Change any improper fractions to mixed numbers.

If one or more of the fractions is negative, then apply the same sign rules as you did when dividing decimal numbers.

- If there is an *odd* number of negative signs in the expression, the answer will be negative.
- If there is an *even* number of negative signs in the expression, the answer will be positive.

Example

Evaluate $\left(-\frac{7}{8}\right)\div\left(-1\frac{1}{6}\right)$.

Solution

Step 1
Change any mixed numbers to improper fractions.

$-1\frac{1}{6}=-\frac{7}{6}$

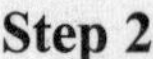

NOTES

Step 2
Find the reciprocal of the second fraction.

The reciprocal of $-\frac{7}{6} \rightarrow -\frac{6}{7}$.

Step 3
Rewrite the expression by changing the ÷ sign to a × sign.

$$\left(-\frac{7}{8}\right) \div \left(-\frac{6}{7}\right) \rightarrow \left(-\frac{7}{8}\right) \times \left(-\frac{6}{7}\right)$$

Step 4
Multiply the fractions, and then reduce the product into lowest terms.

$$\begin{aligned}\left(-\frac{7}{8}\right) \times \left(-\frac{6}{7}\right) &= \frac{(-7)\times(-6)}{8\times 7} \\ &= \frac{42}{56} \\ &= \frac{3}{4}\end{aligned}$$

Therefore, $\left(-\frac{7}{8}\right) \div \left(-1\frac{1}{6}\right) = \frac{3}{4}$

Your Turn 3

Evaluate $\frac{6}{15} \div \left(-3\frac{4}{7}\right)$.

PROBLEM SOLVING WITH RATIONAL NUMBERS IN FRACTION FORM

To solve word problems involving rational numbers expressed in fraction form, first translate the words in the problem into a mathematical expression.

Carefully read the question, underlining any keywords that tell you which operation to perform or which integer sign to apply to the number. Some examples of keywords are listed in the given table.

Add	sum, total, altogether, more than
Subtract	difference, less than, take away, taken from, left, left over
Multiply	above, increased, gain higher, rise, up, over, more
Divide	below, lower, decreased, down, under, loss

Then, evaluate the numerical expression by applying the order of operations.

NOTES

The order of operations always applies when solving any problem involving rational numbers.

Example

James owns $2\frac{3}{5}$ acres of land and his brother Art owns $3\frac{1}{5}$ acres of land that they farm together. One day, Sheila offers to buy $1\frac{2}{5}$ acres of the brothers' combined land.

If the brothers decide to sell the land to Sheila, how much land will they still own?

Solution

Step 1

Translate the words in the problem into a mathematical expression.

James owns $2\frac{3}{5}$ acres of land.

Art owns $3\frac{1}{5}$ acres of land.

Sheila wants to buy $1\frac{2}{5}$ acres of land.

The keyword "together" means addition.
The keywords "how much land will they still own" mean subtraction.

The expression that represents the problem is $\left(2\frac{3}{5}+3\frac{1}{5}\right)-1\frac{2}{5}$.

Step 2

Evaluate the numerical expression.

Follow the order of operations.
Change the mixed numbers into improper fractions.

$$\left(2\frac{3}{5}+3\frac{1}{5}\right)-1\frac{2}{5}=\left(\frac{13}{5}+\frac{16}{5}\right)-\frac{7}{5}$$

Calculate the brackets first.

$$\left(\frac{13}{5}+\frac{16}{5}\right)-\frac{7}{5}$$
$$=\left(\frac{13+16}{5}\right)-\frac{7}{5}$$
$$=\frac{29}{5}-\frac{7}{5}$$

Complete the subtraction.

$$\frac{29-7}{5}$$
$$=\frac{22}{5}$$

NOTES

Convert to a mixed number.

$\frac{22}{5}=4\frac{2}{5}$

The brothers will have $4\frac{2}{5}$ acres of land left if they decide to sell some to Sheila.

Your Turn 4

To raise funds, an equestrian club runs thoroughbred horse races. If a race is $4\frac{1}{2}$ km long and the track is $\frac{7}{8}$ km long, how many times will the horses have to run around the track to complete the race?

PRACTICE EXERCISES

Evaluate each of the following expressions.

1. $\left(-\frac{1}{6}\right)-5\frac{1}{2}$

2. $\left(-\frac{9}{10}\right)+\left(-\frac{3}{4}\right)$

3. $3\frac{6}{7}-\left(-1\frac{5}{8}\right)$

4. $\frac{3}{5}+\left(-\frac{4}{10}\right)$

5. $5\frac{2}{3}\times\left(-8\frac{1}{5}\right)$

6. $\left(-3\frac{1}{8}\right)\times\left(-\frac{4}{6}\right)$

7. $-\frac{2}{7}\div\frac{5}{6}$

8. $6\frac{7}{10}\div(-3)$

9. $\left(-8\frac{2}{3}\right)\div\left(-5\frac{1}{4}\right)$

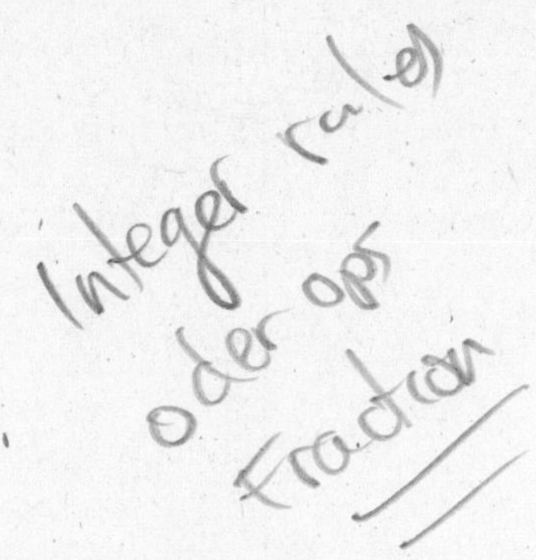

Solve each of the following problems.

10. Carmen is moving. On Monday, she packed $\frac{1}{8}$ of the total dishes in her kitchen. On Tuesday, she packed $\frac{1}{4}$ of the total dishes. What amount of dishes does Carmen still have left to pack?

11. Danielle needs $1\frac{3}{5}$ sheets of plywood to make a doghouse. How many identical doghouses could she make with 10 sheets of plywood?

12. A sum of \$5 000 is shared between Alisha, Maria, Jennifer, and Enrique. If Alisha gets $\frac{1}{4}$ of the sum and Maria and Jennifer each get $\frac{3}{10}$ of the sum, how much does Enrique get?

Lesson 4 RATIONAL NUMBERS AND PERFECT SQUARES

The square root of a number is a value that when multiplied by itself gives the original number. The mathematical symbol used to calculate square roots is $\sqrt{\ }$.

$\sqrt{36}$ is asking for a number that when multiplied by itself gives you 36. The answer is –6 and 6 because $-6\times-6=36$ and $6\times6=36$.

The square root of any number will result both a positive and a negative answer. The positive answer is most commonly used in calculations and is called the **principal square root.**

Any number that has a square root that is a whole number is called a **perfect square.**

The first 9 perfect squares are:
1 because $1\times1=1$
4 because $2\times2=4$
9 because $3\times3=9$
16 because $4\times4=16$
25 because $5\times5=25$
36 because $6\times6=36$
49 because $7\times7=49$
64 because $8\times8=64$
81 because $9\times9=81$

Example

Determine whether the rational number 169 is a square number.

Solution

To determine if 169 is a square number, identify a whole number that when multiplied by itself results in 169.
The rational number 169 is a square number because $13\times13=169$.

Your Turn 1

Determine whether the rational number 324 is a square number.

NOTES

$\sqrt{\ }$ is also referred to as a radical sign.

A whole number is any number from zero to infinity.

A square number is the same as a perfect square.

NOTES

To determine the principal square root of a given rational number, you can use one of two methods: mental calculation or technology.

Mental calculation is used primarily when working with the commonly used perfect squares, which are the perfect squares located between 1 and 100.

When given a rational number that does not look familiar, it is best to use technology to calculate the square root.
Most calculators will have a button that looks like [√]. Use this button to calculate the square root of any given rational number.
Depending on your calculator, you may have to press the [√] button before entering the rational number or after entering the rational number.

Example

Determine the principal square root of 529.

Solution

To calculate the positive square root of 529, determine what number multiplied by itself results in 529. When 23 is multiplied by itself, the result is 529.

This result can be determined using a calculator. Type in the following sequence:

[√] [5] [2] [9] or [5] [2] [9] [√] depending on your calculator.

The result of 23 will appear in your calculator screen.

Your Turn 2

Determine the prinicpal square root of 289.

You can also determine the value of a positive rational number if given its square root. Simply multiply the square root by itself to determine the value of the rational number.

NOTES

Example

Evaluate $\sqrt{?} = 0.5$

Solution

To solve for the unknown number, multiply the square root by itself.
The square root is 0.5 so $0.5 \times 0.5 = 0.25$.
The unknown value is 0.25.

Your Turn 3

Evaluate $\sqrt{?} = 0.12$

ERRORS IN CALCULATING SQUARE ROOTS

The square root of a number is a value that when multiplied by itself gives the original number. The square root of a decimal number can also be calculated. Sometimes, you can use mental calculations to find the square root of a number, or you can use technology. In both instances, there may be errors that occur during the calculation process.

When checking for errors in square roots, use the following relationships:
$\sqrt{a} = b$ or $b^2 = a$.

Example

Is the following calculation correct?
$\sqrt{6.4} = 3.2$

Solution

To verify the calculation, use the relationship $b^2 = a$. Multiply the square root by itself.
$3.2 \times 3.2 = 10.24$

Since $10.24 \neq 6.4$, the calculation is incorrect.

The correct calculation is $\sqrt{6.4} \doteq 2.53$.

Your Turn 4

Is the following calculation correct?
$\sqrt{9.61} = 1.45$

PRACTICE EXERCISES

From the given sequence of rational numbers, identify which numbers are square numbers.

1. 121, 98, 100, 48, 64

2. 47, 220, 196, 81, 55

Determine the square root of each of the following perfect squares.

3. $\sqrt{144}$

4. $\sqrt{9}$

5. $\sqrt{81}$

Determine if the following calculations are correct. Explain why or why not.

6. $\sqrt{3.44} = 2.12$

7. $\sqrt{37} = 7.21$

8. $\sqrt{44} = 5.43$

Determine the value of the rational number that results in each of the given square roots.

9. $\sqrt{?} = 5.48$

10. $\sqrt{?} = 6.71$

Lesson 5 RATIONAL NUMBERS AND NON-PERFECT SQUARES

NOTES

Knowing the values of perfect squares allows you to estimate approximate square roots of other positive rational numbers that have rational square roots.

Example

Find the approximate square root of 52 using the roots of perfect squares as a benchmark.

Solution

There is no whole number when multiplied by itself that equals 52. Estimation is required.

$\sqrt{49} = 7$ because $7 \times 7 = 49$, $\sqrt{64} = 8$ because $8 \times 8 = 64$.

Since 52 is in between 49 and 64, its square root is between 7 and 8.

Since 52 is a little closer to 49 than 64, the decimal portion of the square root will be less than 0.5.

Estimate that the decimal number is around 2 or 3. The estimate is $\sqrt{52} \doteq 7.2$ or 7.3.

Your Turn 1

Find the approximate square root of 110 using the roots of perfect squares as a benchmark.

DETERMINING APPROXIMATE SQUARE ROOTS USING A CALCULATOR

Since each calculator is different, determining the approximate square roots using a calculator can be done in one of two ways.

1. Type the number, then press the $\boxed{\sqrt{\ }}$ sign.
2. Press the $\boxed{\sqrt{\ }}$ sign, type the number, then press $\boxed{=}$.

If the given rational number is a non-perfect square, then its square root will not be a rational number. Since the decimal number does not terminate in a predictable manner, the result that is given on the calculator screen is an approximation of the square root of the given rational number.

A rational number is a number that can be expressed as $\frac{a}{b}$, where b cannot equal zero.

NOTES

When using technology to calculate the square root of a non-perfect square, you must round the answer to a reasonable decimal value.

Example

On your calculator, calculate $\sqrt{21}$ to the nearest thousandth.

Solution

Method 1: type in the following sequence of keys:

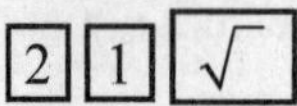

Method 2: type in the following sequence of keys:

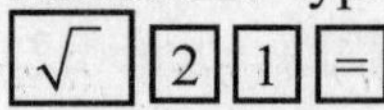

Either of these methods will result in an answer of 4.582 575 695….
The approximate square root is 4.583.

Your Turn 2

Using a calculator, calculate $\sqrt{98}$ to the nearest tenth.

Example

Identify a number that has a square root between 7 and 8.

Solution

Identify any rational number between 7 and 8.

In this case, you can choose 7.5.

To determine the square of 7.5, multiply 7.5 by itself using the relationship of $b^2 = a$.

$$\begin{aligned}7.5^2 &= 7.5 \times 7.5\\ &= 56.25\end{aligned}$$

Therefore, 56.25 is one number that has a square root between 7 and 8.

Your Turn 3

Identify a number that has a square root between 3 and 4.

PRACTICE EXERCISES

Estimate the square root of each given rational number using the roots of perfect squares as a benchmark.

1. $\sqrt{150}$

2. $\sqrt{72}$

Calculate the principal square root of each of the given numbers. Round your answers to the nearest tenth.

3. $\sqrt{125}$

4. $\sqrt{1.57}$

5. $\sqrt{\frac{13}{27}}$

6. $\sqrt{289}$

Each of the following numbers represents the area of a square. Calculate the side length of each square, rounded to the nearest tenth of a centimetre.

7. 90 cm^2

8. 165 cm^2

9. 0.36 cm^2

10. 8 000 cm^2

REVIEW SUMMARY

- Rational numbers are defined as numbers written as the quotient of two integers in the form of $\frac{a}{b}$, where b is any value *except* 0.
- Rational numbers include the set of integers, all fractions and mixed numbers, and all terminating and repeating decimal numbers.
- A number line is a straight line in which numbers are placed in their correct position.
- Adding Decimals: if the signs are the same, add the numbers, keeping the sign of the original numbers. If the signs are different, ignore the signs and subtract the smaller number from the larger number.
- Subtracting Decimals: use the additive inverse. The additive inverse of a number is the number's opposite value. The same sign rules apply when subtracting decimals.
- Multiplying and Dividing Decimals: multiply or divide the numbers and then place the correct sign in front of the answer. Use the following sign rules:
  - if there is an *odd* number of negative signs in the expression, the answer will be negative
  - if there is an *even* number of negative signs in the expression, the answer will be positive
- When adding or subtracting rational numbers in fraction form, follow these steps:
  - change mixed numbers to improper fractions
  - find the lowest common denominator and rewrite new fractions
  - add or subtract numerators, but keep denominators the same
  - reduce: change improper fractions to mixed numbers
- When multiplying rational numbers in fraction form, follow these steps:
  - change mixed numbers to improper fractions
  - multiply numerator by numerator and denominator by denominator
  - reduce: change improper fractions to mixed numbers
- When dividing rational numbers in fraction form, follow these steps:
  - change any mixed numbers to improper fractions
  - find the reciprocal of the fraction to the right of the ÷ sign. Do this by switching the numerator and the denominator
  - rewrite the question by changing the ÷ sign to a × sign
  - multiply the fractions, and then reduce the product into lowest terms
  - change any improper fractions to mixed numbers
- The square root of a number is a value that when multiplied by itself gives the original number.
- Any number that has a square root that is a whole number is called a perfect square.
- When checking for errors in square roots, use the following relationships: $\sqrt{a} = b$ or $b^2 = a$.
- Knowing the values of perfect squares allows you to estimate approximate square roots of other positive rational numbers that have rational square roots.

PRACTICE TEST

Which of the following rational numbers are square numbers?

1. 0.16

2. 2.34

3. 5.29

4. 400

5. 6.4

6. 36.1

Evaluate the following expressions.

7. $4.68+(-1.2)$

8. $2.19-5.92$

9. $3.27\times(-22.4)$

10. $(-10.6)\times(-7.99)$

11. $-24.4\div 6.4$

12. $-6\frac{4}{5}+2\frac{1}{3}$

13. $3+\left(-4\frac{1}{2}\right)$

14. $-7\frac{1}{6}-\frac{3}{8}$

15. $3\frac{1}{3}-2\frac{1}{8}$

16. $-\frac{2}{7}\div\frac{5}{6}$

17. $\frac{7}{10}\div(-5)$

18. $\left(-4\frac{1}{2}\right)\div\left(-3\frac{2}{3}\right)$

Estimate the square root of the given numbers using square roots of perfect squares as benchmarks.

19. $\sqrt{20}$

20. $\sqrt{90}$

Use the following information to answer the next 2 questions.

Ben has a square garden with an area of 200 m^2.

21. How long is each side of Ben's garden, rounded to the nearest tenth?

22. How much fence would Ben need to enclose his garden?

LINEAR RELATIONS

When you are finished this unit, you will be able to…

- write linear equations to represent a given context
- describe a context for a given linear equation
- solve a given problem using a linear equation that involves linear patterns
- write linear equations from given tables of values
- describe patterns in a graph
- graph linear relations
- match given linear equations with their corresponding graphs
- interpolate and extrapolate graphical findings
- solve linear equations of different forms
- identify errors in a solution of a linear equation

PREREQUISITE SKILLS AND KNOWLEDGE

Prior to starting this unit, you should be able to…

- identify patterns from simple problems
- create a table of values for a given equation
- create simple equations for given word problems
- solve problems using equations
- multiply, divide, add, and subtract integers

Lesson 1 LINEAR EQUATIONS

NOTES

Algebraic equations are made up of numbers and variables and can be expressed using words. The most common operations can be represented by the following keywords:

- **Addition:** add, increased by, sum, total, altogether, more than
- **Subtraction:** minus, decreased by, difference, less than, take away, taken from
- **Multiplication:** of, times, product, by
- **Division:** quotient, times greater than, times less than, groups

The words used to represent an equal sign are *equal to*, *is*, *same*, and *result*.

When writing equations using words, numbers should be written out in their word form. Variables are written as "a number" because the variable is replacing a numerical value in the equation. Any letter or symbol can represent the variable. The most commonly used letter is x.

Example

Describe a context for the equation $x+2=9$.

Solution

Step 1
Write the equation in words.
Two is being added to a number to equal nine.

Step 2
Write a context.

Two possible contexts are:

- In two years, Olivia will be nine years old.
- After Yostina gets her two dollars allowance, she will have nine dollars.

Your Turn 1

Describe a context for the equation $r-5=12$.

NOTES

Example

Describe a context for the equation $7p = 21$.

Solution

Step 1
Write the equation in words.
Seven is multiplied by a number to equal twenty-one.

Step 2
Write a context.

One context could be:
Kiana buys a number of books for seven dollars each. She spends a total of twenty-one dollars.

Your Turn 2

Describe an equation for $\frac{c}{9} = 4$.

Sometimes, you may need to write an equation based on a given word problem.

A linear equation is an equation whose graph consists of points that lay on a straight, non-vertical line. These points may or may not be joined. Linear equations are equations that have x as the input variable and x is raised to the power of 1.

To write an equation that represents a given context with more than one part, follow these general rules:

Step 1
Identify a variable to represent the unknown value.

Step 2
Write an expression that represents each part of the situation.

Step 3
Write the equation.

NOTES

Example

Connor is two years older than Kathy, and the sum of their ages is eighteen. Write an equation that represents this situation.

Solution

Step 1
Identify a variable to represent the unknown value.
In this case, Kathy's age is the unknown value.
Let x represent Kathy's age.

Step 2
Write an expression that represents each part of the situation.
Connor is two years older than Kathy, so Connor's age is represented by $x+2$.
The sum of their ages is eighteen and is represented by $=18$.

Step 3
Write the equation.
$x+x+2=18$

Like terms are terms that have the same variable and the same exponent

Because x and x are like terms, they can be combined. The equation that represents this situation is $2x+2=18$.

Your Turn 3

Shannon is three years older than Matt, and the sum of their ages is thirty. Write an equation that represents this situation.

NOTES

LINEAR RELATIONS

A linear equation shows the relationship of the x and y variables in a linear relation.

A **linear relation** is a set of ordered pairs that form a straight line when they are connected.

Before graphing a linear relation, understand how the variables in the equation are related, or, in other words, understand the **relation** between the variables.

A table of values organizes the values of each of the variables found in a linear relation in a clear and concise manner.
A table of values for the linear relation $y = x + 1$ is given.

x	y
1	2
2	3
3	4
4	5
5	6

When given a table of values, a relationship among the variables can be determined.

To express this relationship as a linear equation, follow these steps:

Step 1
Determine the relationship between the first set of ordered pairs.

Step 2
Determine the relationship between the second set of ordered pairs.

Step 3
If the relationship is the same, write the linear equation. If the relationship is different, then a linear equation does not exist for the given table of values.

Step 4
Verify the equation by substituting ordered pairs from the table of values.

NOTES

Example

Write a linear equation that represents the pattern found in the given table of values and verify the equation.

x	y
5	2
6	3
7	4
8	5
9	6

Solution

Step 1

Determine the relationship between the first set of ordered pairs.
The value of x is 5 and the value of y is 2.
The y-value is 3 less than the x-value.

Step 2

Determine the relationship between the second set of ordered pairs.
The value of x is 6 and the value of y is 3.
The y-value is 3 less than the x-value.

Step 3

Write the linear equation.
Since the y-value is consistently 3 less than the x-value, the equation that represents the given table of values is $y = x - 3$.

Step 4

Verify the equation by substituting ordered pairs from the table of values.

Choose an ordered pair and substitute them into the linear equation and solve.

$$y = x - 3$$
$$(4) = (7) - 3$$
$$4 = 4$$

Since both sides of the linear equation are equal, the linear equation has been verified.

Your Turn 4

Write a linear equation that represents the pattern found in the given table of values and verify the equation.

x	y
2	7
1	4
0	1
−1	−2
−2	−5

PRACTICE EXERCISES

1. Write an equation for a situation in which a number is increased by 3 and the result is 21.

$x + 3 = 21$

2. Write an equation for a situation where half of a number reduced by 5 results in 12.

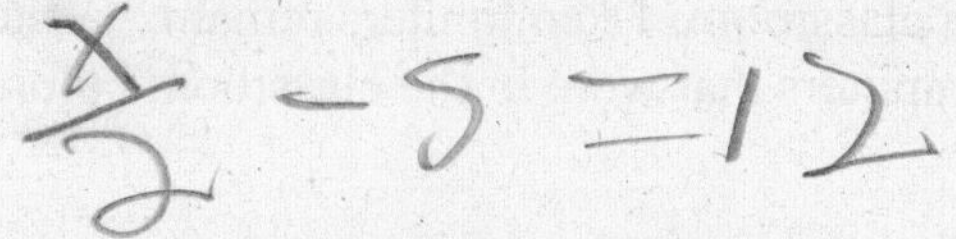

3. The cost to rent a DVD player is $5 per day, plus a $15 deposit. Bill paid $30 for his DVD player rental. Write an equation to find the number of days he rented the DVD player.

$5x + 15 = 30$

4. Maaz mows lawns on the weekends. He charges ten dollars per hour plus a commitment fee of five dollars. He charged one of his neighbours sixty-five dollars to mow his lawn. Write an equation that can be used to calculate the number of hours he spent mowing this neighbour's lawn.

$10x + 5 = 65$

5. Myra goes down thirty-four stories in an elevator and ends up on the sixth floor. Write an equation that can be used to calculate which floor she started on.

$x - 34 = 6$

6. Harpaul is purchasing a number of cupcakes for three dollars each. When he gets to the cashier, he receives a discount of seven dollars. In total, Harpaul pays twenty-nine dollars for the cupcakes. Write an equation that can be used to calculate the number of cupcakes purchased.

$3x - 7 = 29$

7. Danielle has $45 more in her bank account than in her pocket. Danielle has a total of $105. Write an equation that can be used to calculate the money in Danielle's pocket.

$x + 45 + x = 105$

8. The flying distance from Edmonton to Winnipeg is 4 times the flying distance from Edmonton to Calgary. The sum of these two distances is 1 550 km. Write an equation that can be used to calculate the distance from Edmonton to Calgary.

9. After 3 computers are removed from a classroom, 18 computers remain. Write an equation that can be used to calculate the number of computers that were in the classroom before the 3 were removed.

Write the linear equation that represents each of the following tables of values and verify the equation.

10.

x	y
2	4
3	6
4	8
5	10
6	12

11.

x	y
4	−3
5	−2
6	−1
7	0
8	1

12.

x	y
3	9
6	15
9	21
12	27
15	33

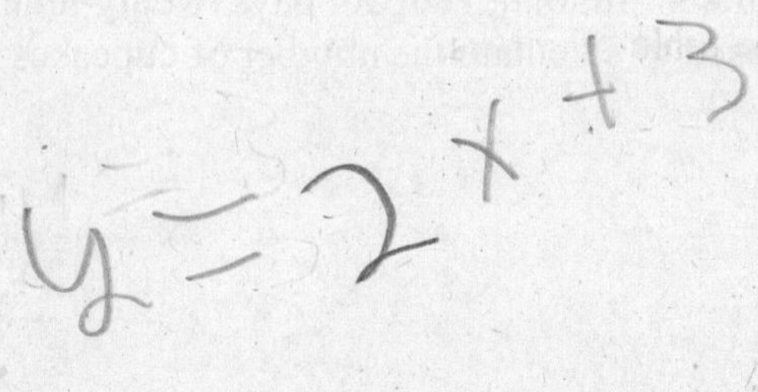

Lesson 2 ANALYSIS OF LINEAR RELATIONS

NOTES

The graph of a linear relation is always a straight line. There are an infinite number of points that make the relation true, not just the few that are included in a table of values. Graphs are useful when plotting gathered data, identifying patterns in the data, and making predictions from these patterns.

To graph a linear relation, follow the steps below:

Step 1
Make a table of values.

Step 2
Write the ordered pairs from the table of values.

Step 3
Plot the ordered pairs on the Cartesian plane.

Step 4
Join the points.

Step 5
Label the graph.

Example

Draw the graph of $y = x + 2$ and describe the pattern found in the graph.

Solution

Step 1
Make a table of values.

x	y
0	2
1	3
2	4
3	5

Step 2
Write the ordered pairs from the table of values.
Ordered pairs are written as (x, y).
(0, 2), (1, 3), (2, 4), (3, 5)

An easy way to remember the correct order of the variables x and y in an ordered pair is that x comes before y in the alphabet.

NOTES

Step 3
Plot the ordered pairs on the Cartesian plane.
Start at the origin (0, 0). Move horizontally to the value of the x-coordinate. Then, move vertically to the value of the y-coordinate and plot the point.

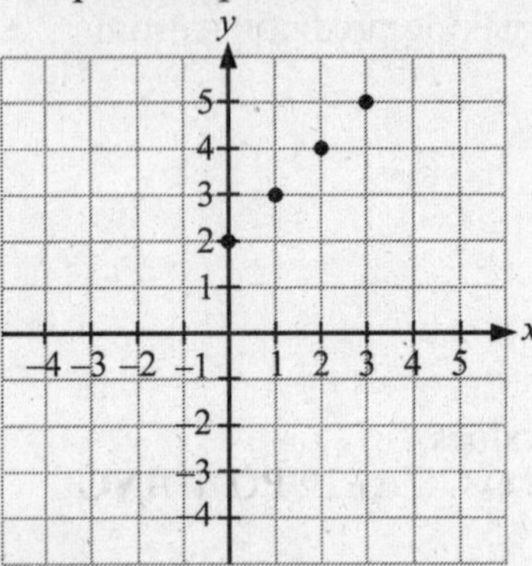

There are many other points that could be used in a relation other than the ones in a table of values. Any x- and y-value found on the line would make the equation true.

Step 4
Join the points with a straight line.
Go beyond the two end points and place arrows on both ends of the line to indicate that this line does not just stop at the end points and continues in both directions.

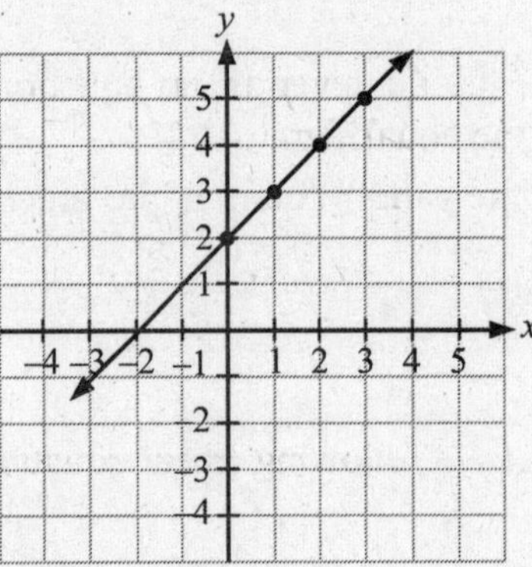

Step 5
Write the equation beside the line.

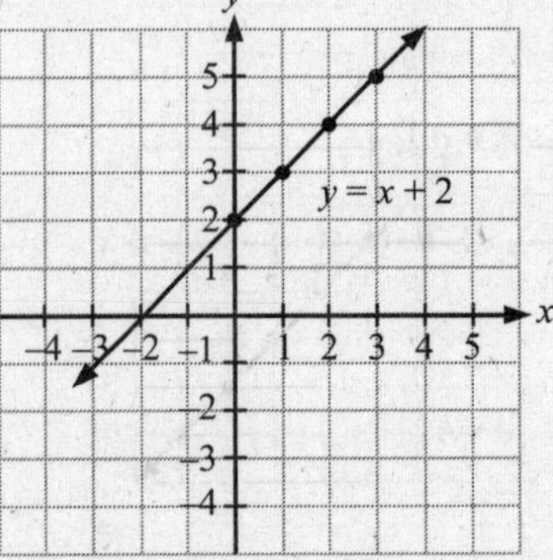

The pattern in the graph is such that the line is moving up in the positive direction. For every unit the x-value increases, the y-value increases by 1 unit as well.

NOTES

Your Turn 1

Draw a graph of $y = -x + 3$ and describe the pattern found in the graph.

MATCHING LINEAR EQUATIONS TO CORRESPONDING GRAPHS OF LINEAR RELATIONS

When given a set of linear equations and asked to match them to their corresponding graphs, follow these steps:

Step 1
List the ordered pairs as plotted on the graph.

Step 2
Substitute one or two sets of ordered pairs into the given linear equations and look for equivalence on both sides of the equal sign.

Step 3
Label each graph with the correct equation.

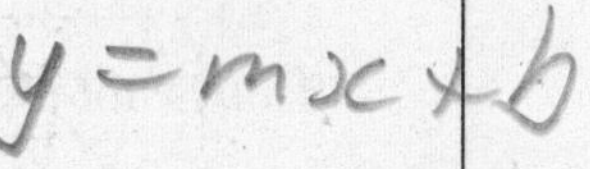

Example

Match each of the given graphs with one of the following linear equations: $y = 1 - x$, $y = 3x - 2$, $y = x - 1$.

Graph A

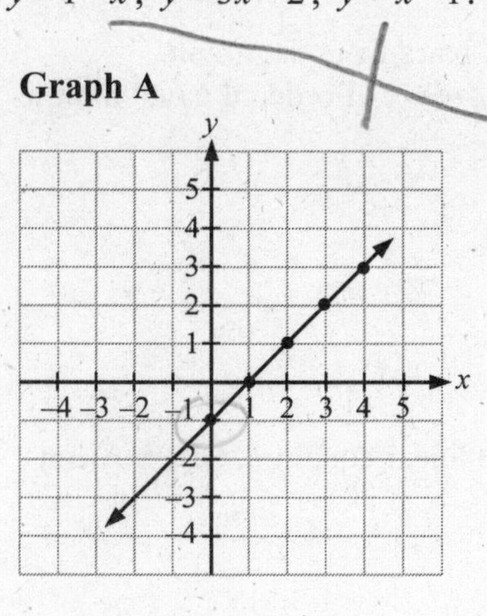

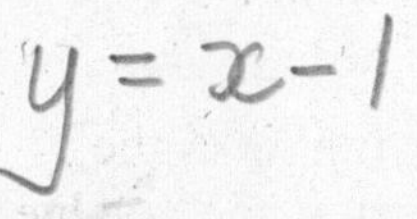

Graph B

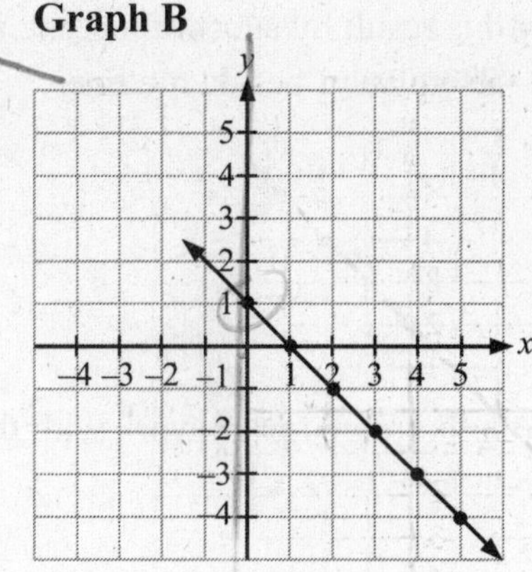

NOTES

Graph C

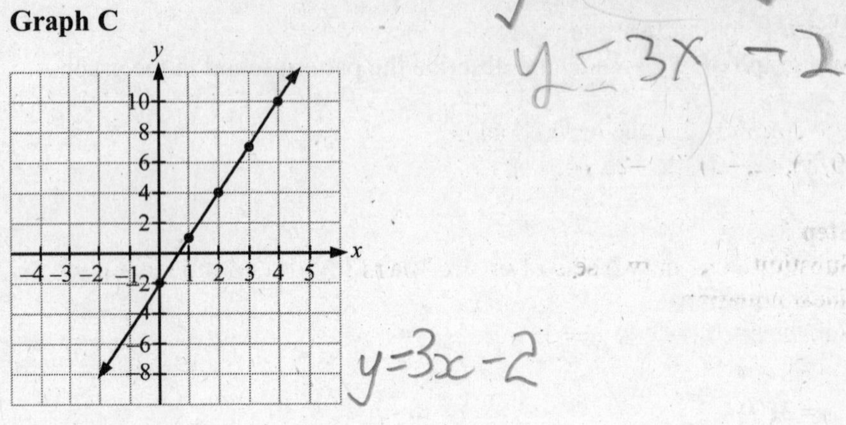

Solution

Step 1

For Graph A, list the ordered pairs.
(0, –1), (1, 0), (2, 1), (3, 2), (4, 3)

Step 2

Substitute one or two sets of ordered pairs into the given linear equations.

Substitute (0, –1) into $y = 1 - x$:

$$y = 1 - x$$
$$(-1) = 1 - 0$$
$$-1 \neq 1$$

This is not the correct equation.

Substitute (0, –1) into $y = x - 1$:

$$y = x - 1$$
$$(-1) = (0) - 1$$
$$-1 = -1$$

This is correct according to the ordered pairs from the graph. Verify this result by substituting one more set of ordered pairs into this linear equation.

Substitute (1, 0) into $y = x - 1$:

$$y = x - 1$$
$$(0) = (1) - 1$$
$$0 = 0$$

Since these ordered pairs work with the linear equation, Graph A can be labelled as $y = x - 1$.

NOTES

Continue with the next graph.

Step 1
For Graph B, list the ordered pairs.
(0, 1), (2, –1), (3, –2), (4, –3), (5, –4),

Step 2
Substitute one or two sets of ordered pairs into one of the remaining linear equations.
Substitute (0, 1) into $y = 3x - 2$:

$$
\begin{aligned}
y &= 3x - 2\\
(1) &= 3(0) - 2\\
1 &= 0 - 2\\
1 &\neq -2
\end{aligned}
$$

This is not the correct equation.

Substitute (0, 1) into $y = 1 - x$:

$$
\begin{aligned}
y &= 1 - x\\
(1) &= 1 - (0)\\
1 &= 1
\end{aligned}
$$

This is correct according to the ordered pairs from the graph.
Verify this result by substituting one more set of ordered pairs into this linear equation.

Substitute (2, –1) into $y = 1 - x$:

$$
\begin{aligned}
y &= 1 - x\\
(-1) &= 1 - (2)\\
-1 &= -1
\end{aligned}
$$

Since these ordered pairs work with the linear equation, Graph B can be labelled as $y = 1 - x$.

According to the process of elimination, Graph C must correspond to the linear equation $y = 3x - 2$.

PRACTICE EXERCISES

Using the linear relation $y = x + 6$, fill in the missing coordinates in the following ordered pairs.

1. (2, __)

2. (__ , 0)

3. (10, __)

4. (__ , 3)

For the following graphs, write three ordered pairs, make a table of values with at least five values, and find the equation.

5.

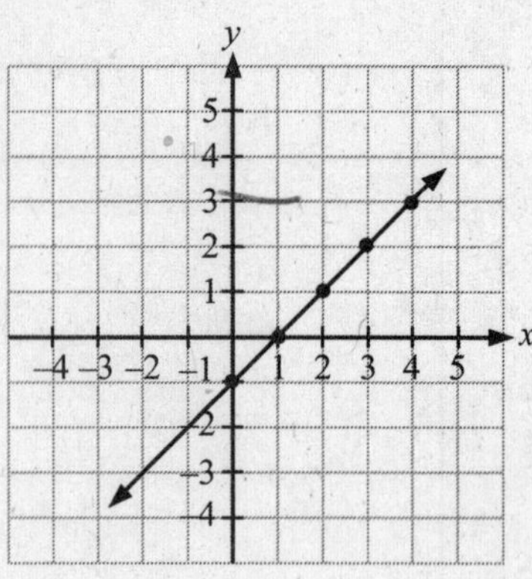

6.

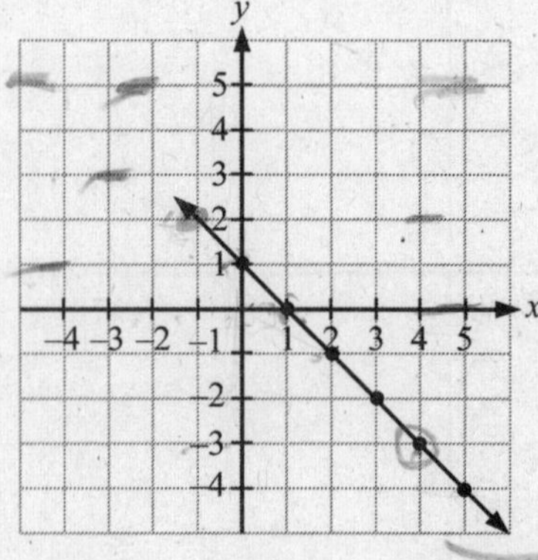

7.

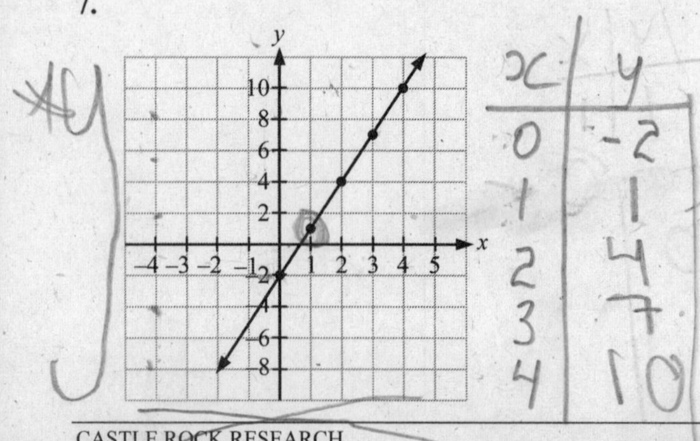

Lesson 3 EXTRAPOLATE AND INTERPOLATE FROM A GRAPH

A graph is helpful in identifying patterns and making predictions. The graph can be used as a tool to **interpolate** information such as approximate values of a particular variable when given the value of other variables on a graph.

A graph can also be used to **extrapolate** information. Extending a given graph to determine particular values that may not be displayed on the graph is a way to extrapolate information.

These are all ways of analysing a graph, answering questions, and forming conclusions given information on the graph. Examples of how to interpolate and extrapolate information from a graph are outlined below.

NOTES

Interpolate: to estimate the values of new data within a set of known data.

Extrapolate: to estimate the values of new data beyond a set of known data. This is usually done by extending a line on a linear graph.

Example

Susan hired a computer technician to repair her laptop. He charged a fee of $30.00/hour.

a) Draw a graph that illustrates the cost of hiring the computer technician.

Solution

To hire him for one hour would cost $30, so the ordered pair is (1, 30). To hire him for two hours would cost $60, so the ordered pair is (2, 60).

Continue adding the cost of another hour to $60 to determine the next ordered pairs. Then, plot the points and draw the graph.

The relation between the cost and the number of hours the computer technician worked is $C = 30t$, where C represents cost and t represents the number of hours worked.

The graph would look like this:

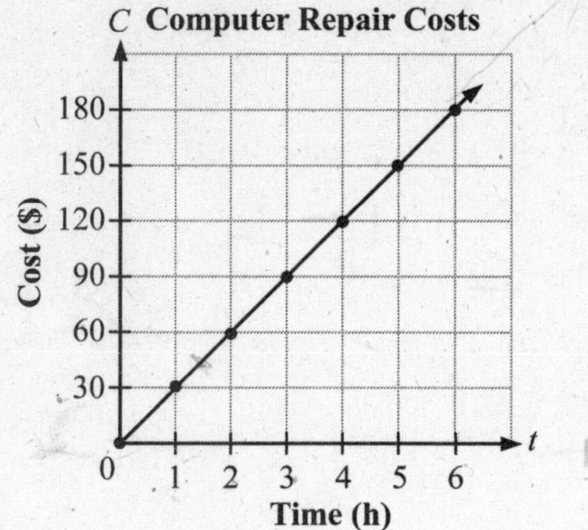

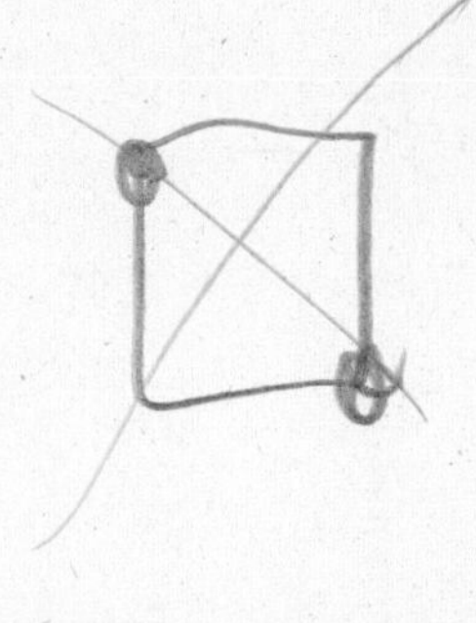

NOTES

b) How much will Susan have to pay if she hires the computer technician for 2.5 hours?

Solution

To determine the cost of hiring the computer technician for 2.5 hours, you must interpolate from the given data.
Look on the graph for $t = 2.5$, and draw a dotted line vertically upward until you reach the line of the graph. Then, draw another dotted line horizontally left until you reach the *C*-axis.

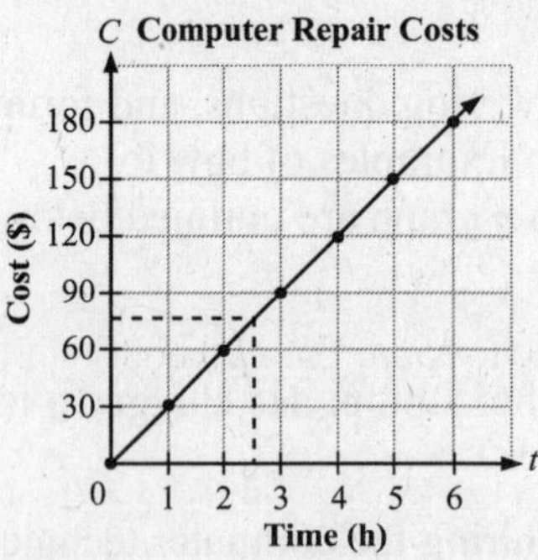

The point where the dotted line touches the *C*-axis is the cost of hiring the computer technician for 2.5 hours.
The dotted line touches the *C*-axis at approximately 75. Therefore, the cost of hiring him for 2.5 hours is about $75.00.

c) How much will Susan have to pay if she hires the computer technician for 7 hours?

Solution

To determine the cost of hiring the computer technician for 7 hours, you must extrapolate from the given data.
Extend the line on the graph by following its pattern. Look on the graph for $t = 7$, and draw a dotted line vertically upward until you reach the line of the graph. Then, draw another dotted line horizontally left until you reach the *C*-axis.

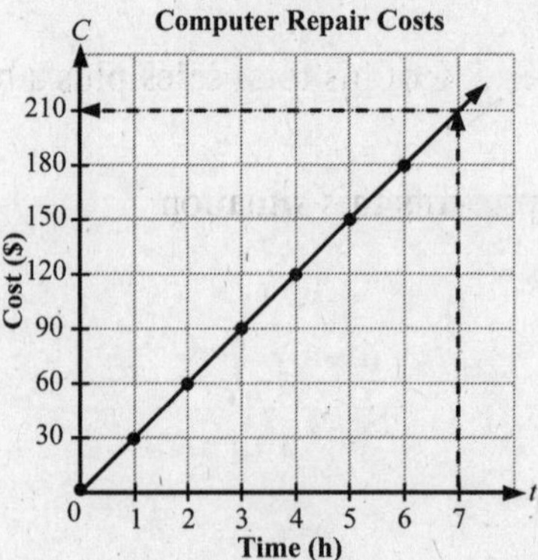

The point where the dotted line touches the *C*-axis is the cost of hiring the computer technician for 7 hours.
The dotted line touches the *C*-axis at approximately 210.
Therefore, the cost of hiring him for 7 hours is about $210.00.

NOTES

Your Turn 1

The graph below shows the relation between the length of a long distance call and the cost.

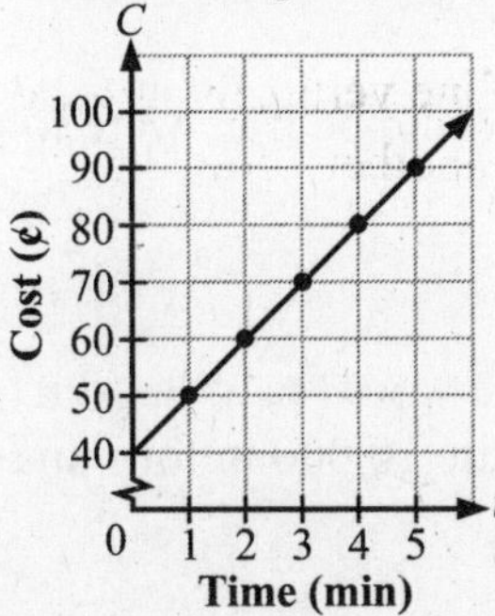

a) If Becca talked for 3.5 minutes, how much would the call cost?

b) If she talked for 8 minutes, how much would the call cost?

By making use of interpolating and/or extrapolating from a graph, you can use that information to solve problems regarding a particular situation. The conclusions that are reached after a graph has been analyzed can be useful, particularly when making important decisions about something.

If a linear equation is known for a linear relation, then it can be used to solve for values of unknown variables. To do this, substitute the given value of a variable into the linear equation and solve for the unknown variable.

Example

Roger is a furniture salesman. He receives 5% of his total sales plus a base monthly salary of \$1 500.

a) Determine the linear equation that represents this situation.

$$5\% \text{ of } 1\,000 = 0.05 \times 1\,000 = 50$$

Solution

Step 1
Make a table of values.

x	y
0	1 500
1 000	1 550
2 000	1 600
3 000	1 650
4 000	1 700

NOTES

Step 2
Let I represent Roger's total income for the month and s represent the furniture sales he made that month. The base rate is $1 500 plus 5% commission on his sales. The equation that represents this situation is $I = 1\ 500 + 0.05s$.

b) Determine how much Roger's monthly income would be if he were to sell $10 000 worth of furniture in a month.

Solution
To determine how much Roger's monthly income would be if he sold $10 000 worth of furniture in that month, substitute 10 000 in for s and solve for I.

$$\begin{aligned} I &= 1\ 500 + 0.05s \\ &= 1\ 500 + 0.05(10000) \\ &= 1\ 500 + 500 \\ &= 2\ 000 \end{aligned}$$

Roger would earn an income of $2 000 that month.

Your Turn 2

The following graph represents the rate at which Rahim rows his boat across a lake.

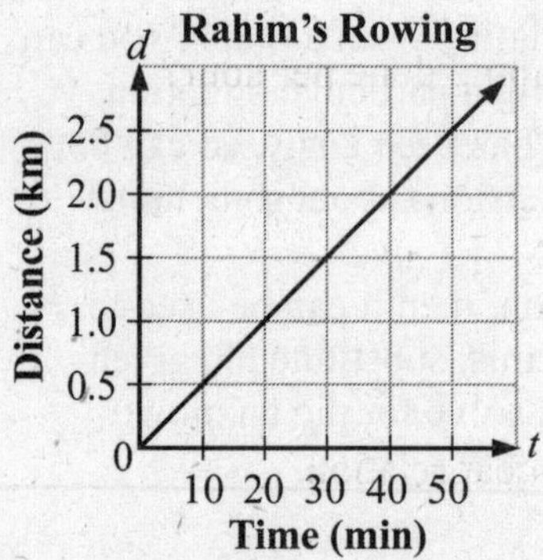

a) Write the relation representing Rahim's rowing rate.

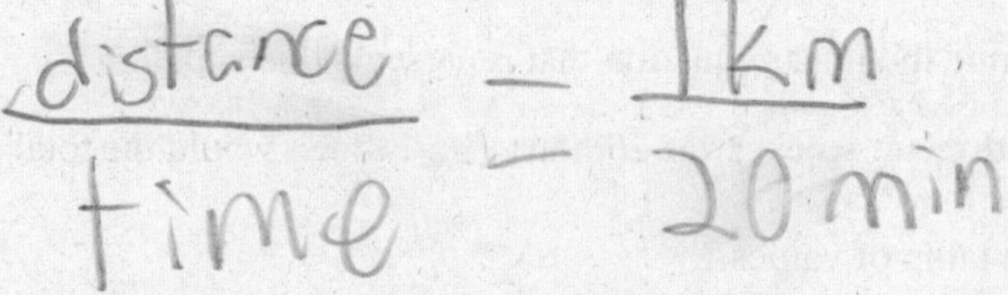

b) In an hour and a half, how far will Rahim row?

4.5 km / 90 min

PRACTICE EXERCISES

Use the following information to answer the next four questions.

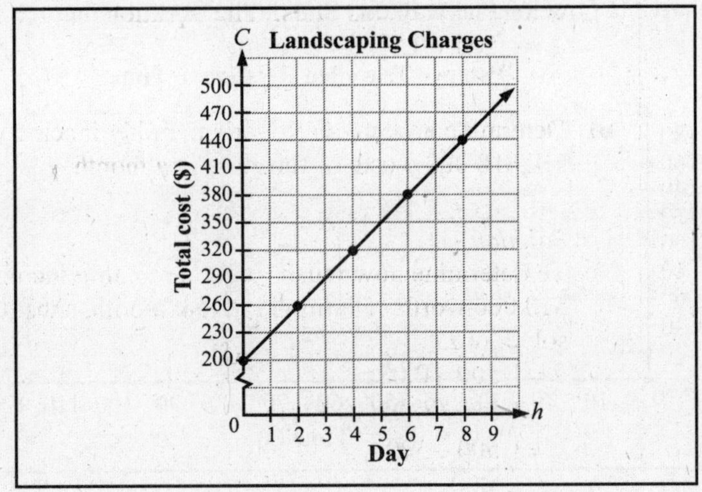

1. Determine what variables are being graphed.

2. How much does it cost to have the landscaping done per hour?

3. Identify the equation that represents this linear relation.

4. If a landscaper worked for 25 hours, how much would the total landscaping cost come to?

Use the following information to answer the next three questions.

One day, Sandy decided to make a graph that represented the distance her son walked relative to how long he walked. She plotted four points.

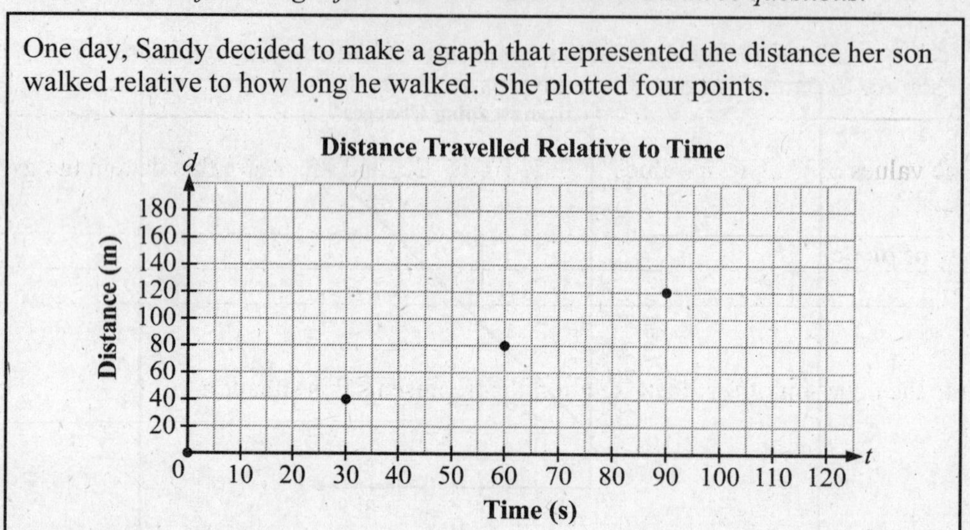

5. How long did it take Sandy's son to walk 40 m?

6. After 90 s, how far had Sandy's son walked?

7. According to the pattern of the data in this graph, how far would Sandy's son walk in 2 min?

Use the following information to answer the next three questions.

The cost, C, in dollars, of producing a number of books of photographs, n, is $50 for the initial production setup plus $5 per book.

8. Determine values of C using n-values of 0, 5, 10, 15, 20, and 25. Enter this data in the given table of values.

Number of books						
Cost ($)						

9. Determine the equation of the linear relation that represents this situation.

10. Given this pattern, what is the cost of producing 29 books?

Lesson 4 SOLVING LINEAR EQUATIONS OF DIFFERENT FORMS

NOTES

Algebra is used to solve linear equations and can be used to solve problems that occur in real life situations. A variable is used to represent an unknown value in an equation.

When solving equations, the goal is to isolate the variable. Only when the variable is isolated can its value be determined.

SOLVING EQUATIONS USING ALGEBRA TILES

Algebra tiles can be used to assist in solving equations. If you do not have a set of tiles, draw a diagram of how the tiles are used to solve equations. Below is the legend for algebra tiles. Shaded symbols represent positive numbers and variables. Unshaded symbols represent negative numbers and variables.

$= +x$

$= -x$

$= +1$

$= -1$

Manipulate the equation by performing the inverse operations as you work toward isolating the variable on one side of the equation and moving the numbers to the opposite side of the equation. The two sides of the equation are separated by an equal sign.

When the same number of positive tiles and negative tiles of the same type are on one side of the equation, they cancel each other out. This cancelling out is known as the *zero principle*. The zero principle states that an equal number of positives and an equal number of negatives equal zero.

Example

Use algebra tiles to solve $3x - 2 = 6 - x$.

Solution

Step 1

Draw the tiles to represent the equation.

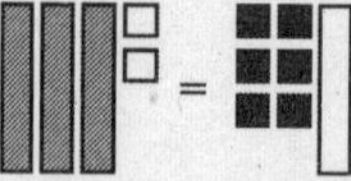

Step 2

Use inverse operations to isolate the variable.

Add two positive number tiles to both sides of the equation to cancel out the negative tiles on the left side of the equation.

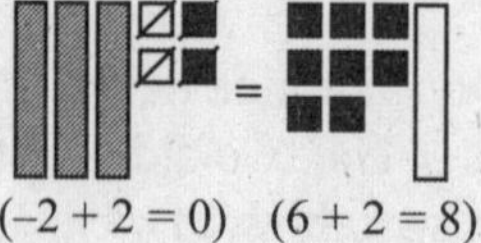

$(-2 + 2 = 0)$ $(6 + 2 = 8)$

Now, all the numbers are on the right side of the equation.

$3x = 8 - x$

NOTES

Step 3
Add a positive x-tile to both sides of the equation to cancel out the negative x-tile on the right side of the equation.

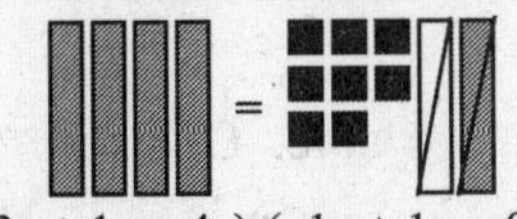

$(3x + 1x = 4x)$ $(-1x + 1x = 0)$

Now, all the variables are on the left side of the equation.
$4x = 8$

Step 4
Share each variable tile with an equal number of number tiles.
This represents dividing both sides of the equation by 4.

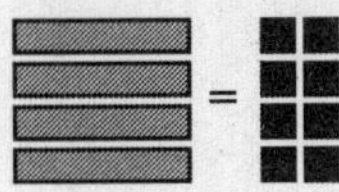

Notice each variable tile (x) equals two number tiles.
The solution is $x = 2$.

Your Turn 1

Solve $3 + 4x = 9 - 2x$ by drawing algebra tiles.

To "isolate the variable" means to get the variable on one side of the equation by itself and the numbers on the other side. The two sides of the equation are separated by an equal sign. To isolate variables, always perform the opposite operation of what is given.

NOTES

SOLVING LINEAR EQUATIONS OF THE FORM $ax = b$

To solve equations of the form $ax = b$, perform the inverse operation by dividing both sides of the equation by the value of a.

Example

Solve the equation $4x = 32$. Verify the solution.

Solution

The x is being multiplied by 4. The inverse of multiplying by 4 is dividing by 4.

$$\frac{4x}{4} = \frac{32}{4}$$

Solve for x.

$$\frac{\not{4}x}{\not{4}} = \frac{32}{4}$$
$$x = 8$$

To verify the answer, substitute $x = 8$ into the original equation. If both sides of the equation are equal, then the result is correct.

$$4x = 32$$
$$4(8) = 32$$
$$32 = 32$$

The solution has been verified.

Your Turn 2

Solve the equation $6x = 54$. Verify the solution.

NOTES

SOLVING LINEAR EQUATIONS OF THE FORM $\frac{x}{a} = b$

To solve equations of the form $\frac{x}{a} = b$, perform the inverse operation by multiplying both sides of the equation by the value of a.

Example

Solve the equation $\frac{x}{5} = 125$. Verify the solution.

Solution
The x is being divided by 5. The inverse of dividing by 5 is multiplying by 5.

$$5\left(\frac{x}{5}\right) = (125)5$$

Solve for x.

$$\cancel{5}\left(\frac{x}{\cancel{5}}\right) = (125)5$$
$$x = 625$$

To verify the answer, substitute $x = 625$ into the original equation. If both sides of the equation are equal, then the result is correct.

$$\frac{x}{5} = 125$$
$$\frac{(625)}{5} = 125$$
$$125 = 125$$

The solution has been verified.

Your Turn 3

Solve the equation $\frac{x}{3} = 12$. Verify the solution.

NOTES

Two-step equations require two operations to isolate the variable.

SOLVING LINEAR EQUATIONS OF THE FORM $ax + b = c$

Solving equations with two terms, one a variable with a numerical coefficient (ax) and one a constant $(+b)$, means that two operations will be necessary to isolate the variable.

To solve these equations, use the following steps:

Step 1
Remove the constant from both sides of the equation using the inverse operation of addition or subtraction.

Step 2
Isolate the variable by dividing both sides of the equation by the value of *a*.

Example

Solve the equation $2x + 4 = 10$. Verify the solution.

Solution

Step 1
Remove the constant by completing the inverse operation.
The constant is 4. The inverse of adding 4 is subtracting 4.

$$2x + 4 - 4 = 10 - 4$$
$$2x = 6$$

Step 2
Isolate the variable by dividing both sides of the equation by the value of *a*.
The value of *a* is 2, so divide both sides of the equation by 2.

$$\frac{2x}{2} = \frac{6}{2}$$
$$x = 3$$

Step 3
To verify the answer, substitute $x = 3$ into the original equation.
If both sides of the equation are equal, then the result is correct.

$$2x + 4 = 10$$
$$2(3) + 4 = 10$$
$$6 + 4 = 10$$
$$10 = 10$$

The solution has been verified.

Your Turn 4

Solve the equation $-5w - 7 = 23$. Verify the solution.

NOTES

SOLVING LINEAR EQUATIONS OF THE FORM $\frac{x}{a}+b=c$

Equations of the form $\frac{x}{a}+b=c$ require two inverse operations in order to solve for the variable *x*:

Step 1
Remove the constant from both sides of the equation using the inverse operation of addition or subtraction.

Step 2
Isolate the variable by multiplying both sides of the equation by the value of *a*.

Example

Solve the equation $\frac{h}{8}+6=-11$. Verify the solution.

Solution

Step 1
Remove the constant by completing the inverse operation.
The constant is 6. The inverse of adding 6 is subtracting 6.

$$\frac{h}{8}+6-6=-11-6$$
$$\frac{h}{8}=-17$$

Step 2
Isolate the variable by multiplying both sides of the equation by the value of *a*.
The value of *a* is 8, so multiply both sides of the equation by 8.

$$8\left(\frac{h}{8}\right)=(-17)8$$
$$h=-136$$

Step 3
To verify the answer, substitute $h=-136$ into the original equation. If both sides of the equation are equal, then the result is correct.

$$\frac{h}{8}+6=-11$$
$$\frac{(-136)}{8}+6=-11$$
$$-17+6=-11$$
$$-11=-11$$

The solution has been verified.

NOTES

Your Turn 5

Solve the equation $\frac{r}{3}-2=-1$. Verify the solution.

SOLVING LINEAR EQUATIONS OF THE FORM $ax=b+cx$

Equations of the form $ax=b+cx$ require two inverse operations in order to solve for the variable x:

Step 1
Move all the variables to the left side of the equal sign by using an operation of addition or subtraction.

Step 2
Isolate the variable by dividing both sides of the equation by the numerical coefficient of x.

Example

Solve the equation $15x=63+6x$. Verify the solution.

Solution

Step 1
Move all the variables to the same side of the equation.
In this case, move $6x$ to the left side of the equation by subtracting $6x$ from both sides.

$$15x-6x=63+6x-6x$$
$$9x=63$$

Step 2
Isolate the variable.
Divide both sides of the equation by 9.

$$\frac{\cancel{9}x}{\cancel{9}}=\frac{63}{9}$$
$$x=7$$

Step 3
To verify the answer, substitute $x=7$ into the original equation.
If both sides of the equation are equal, then the result is correct.

$$15x=63+6x$$
$$15(7)=63+6(7)$$
$$105=63+42$$
$$105=105$$

The solution has been verified.

NOTES

Your Turn 6

Solve the equation $12x = 48 + 9x$. Verify the solution.

SOLVING LINEAR EQUATIONS OF THE FORM $ax + b = cx + d$

Equations of the form $ax + b = cx + d$ require three inverse operations in order to solve for the variable x:

Step 1
Move all the terms with *x*-variables to the left side of the equation by completing the inverse operation.

Step 2
Move the constant term, *b*, to the right side of the equation sign by completing the inverse operation (*d* and *b* will now both be on the right side of the equation).

Step 3
Isolate the variable by dividing both sides of the equation by the numerical coefficient of *x*.

Example

Solve the equation $3x + 5 = 6x + 2$. Verify the solution.

Solution

Step 1
Move all the terms with *x*-variables to the left side by subtracting 6*x* from both sides of the equation.

$$3x - 6x + 5 = 6x - 6x + 2$$
$$-3x + 5 = 2$$

Step 2
Move the constant term to the right side of the equation by subtracting 5 from both sides of the equation.

$$-3x + 5 - 5 = 2 - 5$$
$$-3x = -3$$

Step 3
Isolate the variable by dividing both sides of the equation by -3.

$$\frac{-3x}{-3} = \frac{-3}{-3}$$
$$x = 1$$

NOTES

Step 4
To verify the answer, substitute $x=1$ into the original equation. If both sides of the equation are equal, then the result is correct.

$$\begin{aligned} 3x+5&=6x+2 \\ 3(1)+5&=6(1)+2 \\ 3+5&=6+2 \\ 8&=8 \end{aligned}$$

The solution has been verified.

Your Turn 7

Solve the equation $9x+15=18x+6$. Verify the solution.

SOLVING LINEAR EQUATIONS OF THE FORM $a(x+b)=c$

The **distributive property** is often used to simplify an equation. When using this property, the term located outside of the brackets is multiplied by each term located inside the brackets.

The distributive property states: $a(b+c)=ab+ac$

For example, the equation $2(x+4)=7$ is simplified to $2x+8=7$ by applying the distributive property.

To solve for the variable in equations in the form $a(x+b)=c$, follow these steps:

Step 1
Apply the distributive property to simplify the equation.

Step 2
Move the constant to the opposite side of the equation by using the inverse operation of addition or subtraction.

Step 3
Isolate the variable by dividing both sides of the equation by the numerical coefficient of x.

NOTES

Example

Solve the equation $3(x+5)=126$. Verify the solution.

Solution

Step 1

Apply the distributive property to simplify the equation.

$$3(x+5)=126$$
$$3x+15=126$$

Step 2

Move the constant to the opposite side of the equation by subtracting 15 from both sides of the equation.

$$3x+15-15=126-15$$
$$3x=111$$

Step 3

Isolate the variable by dividing both sides of the equation by the numerical coefficient of x, which is 3.

$$\frac{\cancel{3}x}{\cancel{3}}=\frac{111}{3}$$
$$x=37$$

Step 4

To verify the answer, substitute $x=37$ into the original equation. If both sides of the equation are equal, then the result is correct.

$$3(x+5)=126$$
$$3(37+5)=126$$
$$3(42)=126$$
$$126=126$$

The solution has been verified.

Your Turn 8

Solve the equation $8(x+4)=72$. Verify the solution.

NOTES

SOLVING LINEAR EQUATIONS OF THE FORM $a(bx+c)=d(ex+f)$

To solve for the variable in equations of the form $a(bx+c)=d(ex+f)$, follow these steps:

Step 1
Apply the distributive property to simplify the equation.

Step 2
Move all the variables to one side of the equation by completing the inverse operation.

Step 3
Move all the constants to the opposite side of the equation by completing the inverse operation.

Step 4
Isolate the variable by dividing both sides of the equation by the numerical coefficient of x.

Example

Solve the equation $-2(3x-1)=2(-4x+3)$. Verify the solution.

Solution

Step 1
Apply the distributive property to simplify the equation.

$$-2(3x-1)=2(-4x+3)$$
$$-6x+2=-8x+6$$

Step 2
Move all the variables to one side of the equation by adding $8x$ to both sides of the equation.

$$-6x+2=-8x+6$$
$$-6x+8x+2=-8x+8x+6$$
$$2x+2=6$$

Step 3
Move all the constants to the opposite side of the equation by subtracting 2 from both sides of the equation.

$$2x+2=6$$
$$2x+2-2=6-2$$
$$2x=4$$

Step 4
Isolate the variable by dividing both sides of the equation by the numerical coefficient of x, which is 2.

$$2x=4$$
$$\frac{2x}{2}=\frac{4}{2}$$
$$x=2$$

NOTES

Step 5
To verify the answer, substitute $x = 2$ into the original equation. If both sides of the equation are equal, then the result is correct.

$$\begin{aligned} -2(3x-1) &= 2(-4x+3) \\ -2(3(2)-1) &= 2(-4(2)+3) \\ -2(6-1) &= 2(-8+3) \\ -2(5) &= 2(-5) \\ -10 &= -10 \end{aligned}$$

The solution has been verified.

Your Turn 9

Solve the equation $3(2x+5) = -2(-4x+7)$. Verify the solution.

SOLVING LINEAR EQUATIONS OF THE FORM $\frac{a}{x} = b$

To solve for the variable in equations of the form $\frac{a}{x} = b$, follow these steps:

Step 1
Multiply both sides of the equation by x.

Step 2
Isolate the variable by dividing both sides of the equation by the numerical coefficient of x.

Example

Solve the equation $\frac{96}{x} = 12$. Verify the solution.

Solution
Step 1
Multiply both sides of the equation by x.

$$\begin{aligned} x\left(\frac{96}{x}\right) &= (12)x \\ 96 &= 12x \end{aligned}$$

Step 2
Isolate the variable by dividing both sides of the equation by the numerical coefficient of x, which is 12.

$$\begin{aligned} 96 &= 12x \\ \frac{96}{12} &= \frac{12x}{12} \\ 8 &= x \end{aligned}$$

NOTES

Step 3
To verify the answer, substitute $x=8$ into the original equation.
If both sides of the equation are equal, then the result is correct.

$$\frac{96}{x}=12$$
$$\frac{96}{(8)}=12$$
$$12=12$$

The solution has been verified.

Your Turn 10

Solve the equation $\frac{-49.2}{x}=24.6$. Verify the solution.

IDENTIFYING ERRORS IN SOLVING LINEAR EQUATIONS

When solving linear equations, remember that the goal is to isolate the variable because only then can its numerical value be determined. The process of isolating the variable involves a series of inverse operations. Knowing when and how to apply inverse operations will determine the difference between a correct answer and an incorrect answer.

Example

Keith solved the linear equation $5x-156=-21x$ using the following steps.

Step 1	$5x+5x-156=-21x+5x$
Step 2	$-156=-16x$
Step 3	$\frac{-156}{-16}=\frac{-16x}{-16}$
Step 4	$9.75=x$

However, when he went to verify his answer, the left side of the equation was not equivalent to the right side of the equation.
In which step did Keith make his mistake?

Explain your reasoning and solve the equation correctly.

NOTES

Solution

Keith made his mistake in Step 1. He did not apply the inverse operations correctly.

In Step 1, $5x$ needs to move over to the right side of the equation. In order to do that, Keith must subtract $5x$ from both sides of the equation, not add $5x$ to both sides of the equation.

The correct solution is:

$$\begin{aligned} 5x-156&=-21x \\ 5x-5x-156&=-21x-5x \\ -156&=-26x \\ \frac{-156}{-26}&=\frac{-26x}{-26} \\ 6&=x \end{aligned}$$

Your Turn 11

Shamit solved the linear equation $-4(x-18)=14x$ using the following steps.

Step 1	$-4x+72=14x$
Step 2	$-4x+4x+72=14x+4x$
Step 3	$72=18x$
Step 4	$72=\frac{18x}{18}$
Step 5	$72=x$

In which step did Shamit make his mistake? Explain your reasoning and solve the equation correctly.

PRACTICE EXERCISES

Solve each of the following equations using algebra tiles.

1. $5x - 2 = 3x - 4$

2. $-4x + 3 = -11 + 3x$

Solve each of the following equations and verify your answers.

3. $3x + x = 5x - 6$

4. $-6x + 9 = 3x$

5. $5 - 6x = 2x + 5$

6. $2(x + 1) = 3(x - 1)$

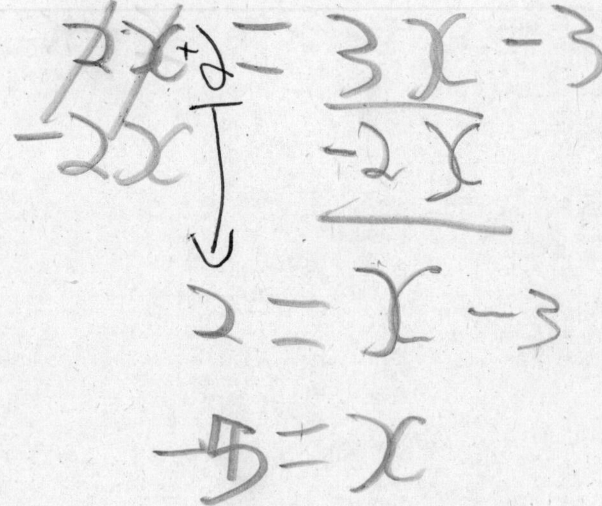

7. $41 = 0.5x + 0.7x - 7$

Solve each of the following equations, rounding answers to the nearest tenth.

8. $2.5x - 4 + 1.3x = 3$

9. $1.2x + 3.5(2.5 - x) = 41$

10. $5.9 - (3x + 2.5) = 0.4x$

Solve each of the following equations. Express your answer as a fraction in lowest terms.

11. $14 = \dfrac{-3}{x}$

12. $\dfrac{5x}{3} - 3 = 8 + \dfrac{x}{2}$

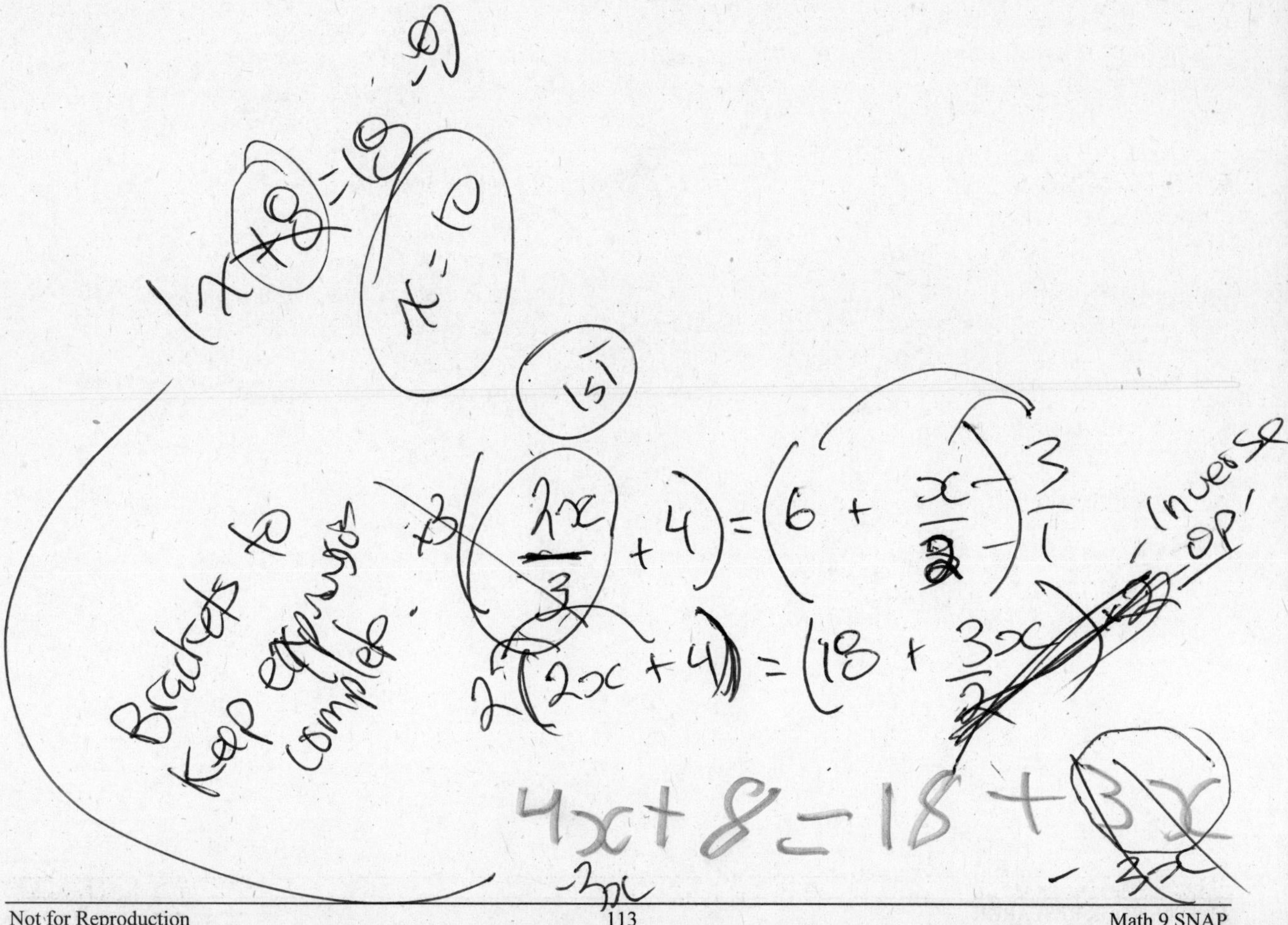

REVIEW SUMMARY

- Numbers and variables (a letter or symbol that represents an unknown value) are used to make up algebraic equations.
- A linear equation is an equation whose graph consists of points on a straight, non-vertical line.
- The standard form of a linear relation in two variables, x and y, is $Ax + By + C = 0$, where A, B, and C can be any numbers but A and B cannot both be zero.
- A table of values can be used to find the relationship between x and y for a linear relation.
- If the x-coordinate is positive, move to the right of the origin. If it is negative, move to the left of the origin.
- If the y-coordinate is positive, move up from the origin. If it is negative, move down from the origin.
- In order to match a given graph with its corresponding linear equation, identify ordered pairs in the given graphs and substitute those values into the given linear equations. If both sides of the equation are equivalent to one another, than that linear equation corresponds to the given graph.
- A graph is a great way to interpolate information such as approximate values of a particular variable when given the value of other variables on a graph.
- You can use a graph to extrapolate information, which means that by extending a given graph, you can predict particular values that may not be displayed on the graph.
- To "isolate the variable" means to get the variable on one side of the equation and the numerical values on the opposite side of the equation.
- The distributive property is often used to simplify an equation. When using this property, the term located outside of the brackets is multiplied by each term located inside of the brackets.

PRACTICE TEST

Write the equation that represents the following situations.

1. Mr. Binns is dividing up his land amongst his family. He wants to give his eight children equal portions of the land and save four acres for his wife. In total, he has twenty acres of land. Write an equation that can be used to determine how much land each one of his children receives.

2. Roopali goes to the store and buys three pairs of earrings that are on sale for seven dollars off each pair. In total, she pays fourteen dollars for her entire purchase. Write an equation that can be used to calculate the cost of each pair of earrings.

Write the following equations in words. Then provide a context for the linear equation.

3. $3(x+4)=21$

4. $-4+x=29$

Solve each of the following equations and verify your answers.

5. $\frac{j}{5.5}=-8.1$

6. $15x=105$

Solve each of the following equations.

7. $3g-9=33$

8. $-5u+45=95$

9. $18=\frac{n}{4}+3$

10. $\frac{b}{-10}-1=-1$

Solve each of the following equations and verify your answers.

11. $2q-35=16q$

12. $-7(d-12)=-21$

13. $-9.2x-16.2=3.4x+53.1$

14. $6(8m+11)=9(2m-23)$

Solve each of the following equations.

15. $\frac{222}{c} = 74$

16. $\frac{36}{z} + 4 = 10$

Write the equation, and then solve it.

17. The product of ten and a number decreased by seven gives a result of forty-three.

18. A quarter of a number increased by eight is twenty-one.

19. One-seventh of Jason's movies are comedies. If he has 6 comedies, how many movies does he have?

20. Cheri has seven more dollars in her pocket than Shawn. If together they have forty-seven dollars, how much does each person have?

NOTES

LINEAR INEQUALITIES

When you are finished this unit, you will be able to…

- translate a given problem into a single variable linear inequality
- determine if a given rational number is a possible solution of a linear inequality
- solve a given linear inequality algebraically
- verify the solution of a given linear inequality
- add and subtract positive and negative numbers to determine the solution of a given inequality
- multiply and divide positive and negative numbers to determine the solution of a given inequality
- graph the solution of a given linear inequality on a number line
- solve a given problem involving a linear inequality and graph it

PREREQUISITE SKILLS AND KNOWLEDGE

Prior to starting this unit, you should be able to…

- create simple equations from given word problems
- evaluate algebraic expressions
- apply the order of operations
- add, subtract, multiply, and divide, integers

Lesson 1 SOLVING LINEAR INEQUALITIES

NOTES

The symbol > means greater than and ≥ means greater than or equal to, < means less than and ≤ means less than or equal to, and ≠ means not equal to.

Inequalities are equations that use >, <, ≥, ≤, or ≠ in place of the equal sign.

The following examples illustrate how to translate a given word problem into a single variable linear inequality.

Example

Write the following word problem as a single variable linear inequality.

Charlene received a $500.00 gift card for her birthday to a local sporting goods store. She knows that she wants to buy a pair of basketball shoes that cost $250.00. She would like to spend the rest of the money on track suits, which are on sale for $20.00 each. What is the maximum number of track suits can she buy?

Solution

A linear inequality can be set up using the information in the question:

Let x represent the number of track suits Charlene can buy.

The basketball shoes cost $250.00.
The track suits cost $20.00 each.
The maximum amount she has to spend is $500.00.
The equation can be set up like this:
cost of basketball shoes + cost of the track suits × number of track suits she can buy ≤ amount of the gift card

The algebraic expression becomes $250 + 20x \leq 500$.

Your Turn 1

Write the following word problem as a single variable linear inequality.

Lindsay has to go to a workshop for a project she is working on in school. She has to park her car underground for the day. The cost of parking underground is $3.00 for the first hour and $1.25 for each additional hour or portion of the hour. She has $20.00 to spend on parking. What is the maximum number of extra hours she can park?

NOTES

RULES FOR SOLVING LINEAR INEQUALITIES

Inequalities are solved in the same way that equations are solved: all the variables are moved to one side of the equation and all of the numbers are moved to the other side by applying inverse operations.

The distinct difference between the solution to a linear equation and the solution to a linear inequality is that in a linear equation, the unknown variable can only have one numerical value. However, in a linear inequality, the unknown variable can have multiple numerical values, as long as the linear inequality statement is true when the solution is verified.

Example

Solve for x in the following linear inequality: $x+4\le 10$.

Solution

Isolate the variable by applying inverse operations.

$$x+4\le 10$$
$$x+4-4\le 10-4$$
$$x\le 6$$

Therefore, all numbers less than or equal to 6 will make the linear inequality a true statement.

Your Turn 2

Solve for x in the following linear inequality: $x-7\ge 25$.

Example

Solve for x in the following linear inequality: $15x\ge 125$.

Solution

Isolate the variable by applying inverse operations.

$$15x\ge 125$$
$$\frac{15x}{15}\ge\frac{125}{15}$$
$$x\ge 8.\overline{3}$$

Therefore, all the numbers greater than or equal to $8.\overline{3}$ will make the linear inequality a true statement.

NOTES

Your Turn 3

Solve for x in the following linear inequality: $\frac{x}{9} \geq 36$.

So far, you have seen that inequalities are solved in the same way that equations are solved—by isolating the variable. However, the rules change if you are multiplying or dividing by a negative number.

When you multiply or divide both sides of an inequality by a negative number, *reverse* the inequality sign.

Example

Solve for x in the following linear inequality: $-9x \geq 12$.

Solution

Isolate the variable by applying inverse operations.
When you divide by a negative, the inequality sign is reversed.

$$-9x \geq 12$$
$$\frac{-9x}{-9} \leq \frac{12}{-9}$$
$$x \leq 1.\overline{3}$$

Therefore, all numbers less than or equal to $1.\overline{3}$ will make the linear inequality a true statement.

Your Turn 4

Solve for x in the following linear inequality: $\frac{x}{-3} \leq 27$.

When solving linear inequalities algebraically, it is best to verify the solution with multiple elements. This means that you should substitute at least two values into the given linear inequality and check for a true statement.

The first value should be the **boundary point**. The boundary point is the number that will make the two sides of the linear inequality equal to each other. The second value should be part of the solution set of the given linear inequality.

NOTES

Example

Solve the linear inequality $6-4x \geq 30$ and verify the solution with multiple elements.

Solution

Step 1

Isolate the variable by applying inverse operations.
Subtract 6 from each side of the inequality.

$$6-4x \geq 30$$
$$6-6-4x \geq 30-6$$
$$-4x \geq 24$$

Step 2

Divide each side of the inequality by -4.

$$-4x \geq 24$$
$$\frac{-4x}{-4} \leq \frac{24}{-4}$$
$$x \leq -6$$

Step 3

Verify the solution by substituting the boundary point into the inequality.
The boundary point is -6.

$$6-4x = 30$$
$$6-4(-6) = 30$$
$$6+24 = 30$$
$$30 = 30$$

Step 4

Verify the solution by substituting a value from the solution set into the inequality.

Use any number less than -6.
Use -10.

$$6-4x \geq 30$$
$$6-4(-10) \geq 30$$
$$6+40 \geq 30$$
$$46 \geq 30$$

Your Turn 5

Solve the linear inequality $15-12x \geq 63$ and verify the solution with multiple elements.

NOTES

Example

Solve the linear inequality $6x-6\geq 2x+2$ and verify the solution with multiple elements.

Solution

Step 1

Isolate the variable by applying inverse operations.
Add 6 to each side of the inequality.

$$\begin{aligned}6x-6&\geq 2x+2\\6x-6+6&\geq 2x+2+6\\6x&\geq 2x+8\end{aligned}$$

Subtract $2x$ from both sides of the inequality.

$$\begin{aligned}6x-2x&\geq 2x-2x+8\\4x&\geq 8\end{aligned}$$

Divide each side by 4.

$$\frac{4x}{4}\geq\frac{8}{4}$$
$$x\geq 2$$

Step 2

Verify the solution by substituting the boundary point into the inequality.
The boundary point is 2.

$$\begin{aligned}6x-6&=2x+2\\6(2)-6&=2(2)+2\\12-6&=4+2\\6&=6\end{aligned}$$

Step 3

Verify the solution by substituting a value from the solution set into the inequality.

Use any number greater than 2.
Use 5.

$$\begin{aligned}6x-6&\geq 2x+2\\6(5)-6&\geq 2(5)+2\\30-6&\geq 10+2\\24&\geq 12\end{aligned}$$

Your Turn 6

Solve the linear inequality $8x-4\leq 6x+2$ and verify the solution with multiple elements.

PRACTICE EXERCISES

Use the following information to answer the next question.

Sandy received a $400.00 gift card to a local hair salon for Mother's Day. She knows that she wants to get a pedicure that costs $60.00. She would like to spend the rest of the money on monthly hair treatments, which are $120.00 each. What is the maximum number of hair treatments she can buy?

1. Write the given problem as a single variable linear inequality.

Solve the following linear inequalities.

2. $x+5\leq 16$

3. $x-8>24$

4. $5x\geq 135$

5. $\frac{x}{7}>24$

6. $-12x+4\geq 12$

7. $\frac{x}{-6}+10<24$

Solve the following linear inequalities algebraically and verify the solution with multiple elements.

8. $3x+3\le -6$

9. $12-8x\ge 60$

10. $36-15x\le 66$

Lesson 2 GRAPHING LINEAR INEQUALITIES

NOTES

Since the solutions to a linear inequality can have multiple numerical values, the result of solving a linear inequality is creating a **solution set**.

A solution set consists of all the possible values that make a linear inequality true.

A visual representation of the solution set can be shown by graphing the solution set on a number line.

When creating your number line, start by placing the boundary point in the middle of the line. Then, write the next three numbers in the sequence on either side of that number.

Draw a circle at the boundary point. If you shade in the circle, you are indicating that the boundary point is part of the solution. If you do not shade in the circle, you are indicating that the solution begins at the boundary point but does not include it.

Next, draw your arrow in the direction of the numbers that satisfy your solution set. You can check to make sure your arrow goes in the proper direction by taking numbers from either side of the boundary point and substituting them for x in the linear inequality.

The following number line shows the solution set for $x \leq -1$. If the solution set to a given linear inequality is $x \leq -1$, that means the solution can have any value that is less than or equal to -1.

Since -1 is included in the solution set, this is represented by a shaded circle, followed by all numbers less than -1.

If the solution for a given linear inequality is $x < -1$, then the number line would look like the following:

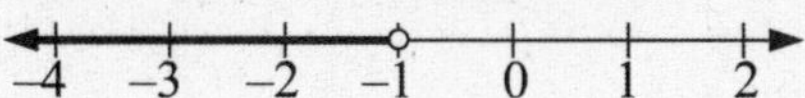

Since -1 is not included in the solution set, this is represented by an unshaded circle, followed by all numbers less than -1.

NOTES

Example

Solve the following linear inequality and graph the solution set for $2x < 8$.

Solution

Step 1

Isolate the variable by applying inverse operations.
To solve this linear inequality, divide each side by 2.

$$2x < 8$$
$$\frac{2x}{2} < \frac{8}{2}$$
$$x < 4$$

The solution set consists of all the values of x that are less than but not equal to 4.

Step 2

Represent the solution set on a graph.
Since the solution set consists of all the values of x that are less than but not equal to 4, the 4 is not included in the graph. This is represented by an unshaded circle, followed by all the numbers less than 4.

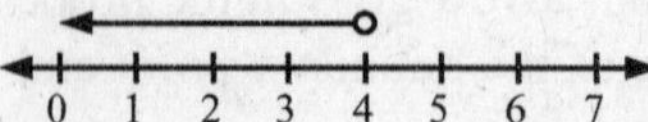

Your Turn 1

Solve the following linear inequality and graph the solution set for $9x \leq 135$.

NOTES

Example

Solve the following linear inequality and graph the solution set for $\frac{x}{-7} > 3$.

Solution

Step 1

To solve this linear inequality, multiply each side by -7.

$$\frac{x}{-7} > 3$$
$$(-7)\left(\frac{x}{-7}\right) < (3)(-7)$$
$$x < -21$$

The solution set consists of all the values of x that are less than -21.

Step 2

Represent the solution set on a graph.

Since the solution set consists of all the values of x that are less than but not equal to -21, the -21 is not included in the graph. This is represented by an unshaded circle, followed by all the numbers less than -21.

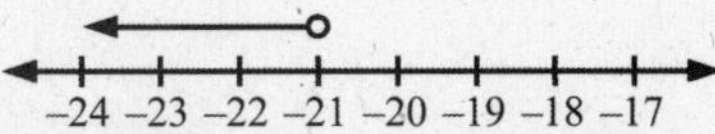

Your Turn 2

Solve the following linear inequality and graph the solution set for $\frac{x}{-3} < 6$.

PRACTICE EXERCISES

Solve the following inequalities and then graph them on a number line.

1. $-4x > 4$

2. $-6 \geq 3 - x$

3. $2x + 2 > x + 4$

4. Identify which of the numbers 0, 2, –6, and –10 belong to the solution set of $-3 < x + 2$.

5. Identify which of the numbers 5, –7, –6, and 4 belong to the solution set of $4x + 16 \leq 36$.

REVIEW SUMMARY

- Inequalities are equations that use >, <, ≥, ≤, or ≠ in place of the equal sign.
- Solving inequalities is done in nearly the same way as solving equations. One difference is if you multiply or divide both sides of an inequality by a negative number, the direction of the inequality sign is reversed. The second difference is that there are multiple solutions to a linear inequality.
- Linear inequalities are graphed on a number line.
- If the solution of a linear inequality is < or >, the graph has an unshaded circle followed by a line.
- If the solution of a linear inequality is ≤ or ≥, the graph has a shaded circle followed by a line.

PRACTICE TEST

Solve the following linear inequalities.

1. $\frac{x}{-9} \leq 81$

2. $-6x > 42$

3. $12x - 6 < 30$

4. $3e + 6 \geq 72$

5. $8.2f + 1.2 \geq 79.1$

6. $-\frac{4t}{5} + 6 > 13$

Solve the following linear inequalities algebraically and verify the solution with multiple elements.

7. $19x - 5.22 \leq 32.78$

8. $15 + \frac{5x}{6} > -10$

Write an inequality to represent the following graphs.

9.

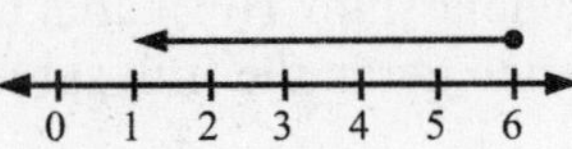

10.

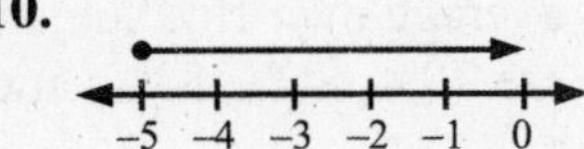

11.

10 11 12 13 14

12.

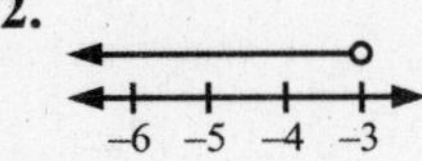

Solve the following inequalities and then graph them on a number line.

13. $2x-2\leq 3x+1$

14. $-3x<2x+10$

15. $4x-7\geq 5x-9$

Write the following word problems as inequalities, solve them, and then graph them on a number line.

16. Enrico needs an 80% average over five subjects in order to qualify for a scholarship. His marks for the first four subjects are 79%, 86%, 83%, and 77%. What mark must Enrico get in the fifth subject to earn the scholarship?

17. Molly is saving for a new mountain bike that costs $584.00, including taxes. She has $62.00 saved and can save an additional $8.70 for every hour that she works. What is the minimum number of hours of work that it will take her to reach her goal?

POLYNOMIALS

When you are finished this unit, you will be able to…

- identify parts of a polynomial: variables, degree, terms, and coefficients
- determine the degree of a polynomial
- create pictorial representations of polynomial expressions
- write polynomial expressions
- describe a situation for a first degree polynomial expression
- identify equivalent polynomial expressions
- identify like terms in a given polynomial expression
- add and subtract two given polynomial expressions
- multiply and divide two given polynomial expressions

PREREQUISITE SKILLS AND KNOWLEDGE

Prior to starting this unit, you should be able to…

- identify natural numbers and integers
- identify exponents
- apply algebraic operations
- apply BEDMAS rules
- create equations from word problems
- solve problems using equations

Lesson 1 MODELLING AND CREATING POLYNOMIAL EXPRESSIONS

NOTES

Polynomials are algebraic expressions that are formed by combining numbers, variables, and exponents into algebraic terms. An example of an algebraic term is $3x^2$.

In algebraic expressions, **terms** are separated by addition and subtraction signs. The expression $-4xz$ is just one term because there are no addition or subtraction signs present.

A number that stands alone without any variables connected to it is called a **constant**. Examples of a constant are 8 and $\frac{2}{3}$. Notice that there are no variables connected to either of them.

Polynomials with one term, two terms, and three terms have special names.

A polynomial with one term is called a **monomial**.
Examples are $8y$, $\frac{2}{7}$, and $-9yz$.

A polynomial with two terms is called a **binomial**.
Examples are $2x+3$ and $4c^2-7c$.

For negative terms, remember to include the sign in front of the number when identifying the coefficient.

A polynomial with three terms is called a **trinomial**.
Examples are x^2+3x-5 and $2xy+5x+9$.

An algebraic expression with four or more terms is simply referred to as a **polynomial**.
An example is $4x^2+3x-7xy+2$.

The **degree of a term** is equivalent to the sum of the exponents found on the variables.

For example, the degree of the term $7ab$ is 2 since the exponent on each variable is 1, $7a^1b^1$, and $1+1=2$.

The **degree of a polynomial** is not found by adding the degrees of each of the terms. Instead, the degree of a polynomial is equal to the degree of the highest-degree monomial.

If the polynomial in question is a monomial, then the polynomial has the same degree as that monomial.

For example, in the polynomial $12xy-4y$, the degree of the first term is 2 and the degree of the second term is 1. The highest degree is 2; therefore, the degree of the polynomial is 2.

NOTES

Example

Identify the coefficients, variables, and constants of the polynomial $2x-7$. Name the polynomial and determine its degree.

Solution

The coefficient is 2.
The variable is x.
The constant is -7.
This polynomial is a binomial because there are two terms: $2x$ and -7.
The degree of the polynomial is 1.

Your Turn 1

Identify the coefficients, variables, and constants of the polynomial $5x+8$. Name the polynomial and determine its degree.

Example

Identify the coefficients, variables, and constants of the polynomial $3n^2-4n+7$. Name the polynomial and determine its degree.

Solution

The coefficients are 3 and -4.
The variable is n.
The constant is 7.
This polynomial is a trinomial because there are three terms: $3n^2$, $-4n$, and 7.
The degree of the polynomial is 2.

Your Turn 2

Identify the coefficients, variables, and constants of the polynomial $-9r+3r^3+2$. Name the polynomial and determine its degree.

NOTES

REPRESENTING POLYNOMIALS USING ALGEBRA TILES

Algebra tiles can be used to represent a polynomial expression. The following chart shows the tiles and what they represent.

	Positive tile	**Negative tile**
Unit tile		
***x*-tile**		
x^2-tile		

To represent a given polynomial expression, determine which tiles you need and lay or draw them out side by side.

For the polynomial $2x^2 - 3x + 3$, you will need 2 positive x^2-tiles, 3 negative x-tiles, and 3 positive unit tiles.

The given arrangement of algebra tiles represents the polynomial $2x^2 - 3x + 3$.

Example

Draw a pictorial representation of the polynomial expression $3x^2 - 2x + 4$.

Solution

Determine which tiles you need and draw them out side by side. You need 3 positive x^2-tiles, 2 negative x-tiles, and 4 positive unit tiles.

$3x^2 - 2x + 4$ can be represented as

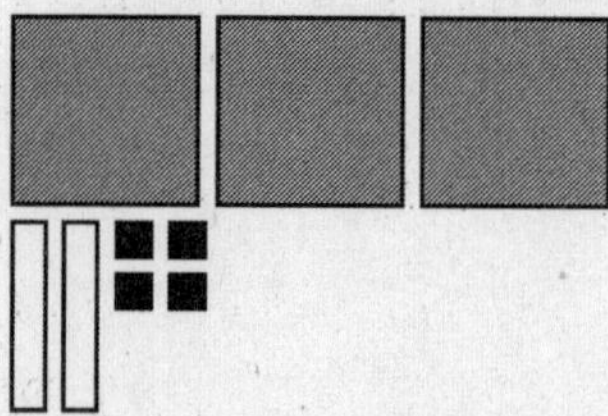

NOTES

Your Turn 3

Draw a pictorial representation of the polynomial expression $-3x^2+2x+5$.

When given a pictorial representation of a polynomial, you can determine its algebraic equivalent by identifying what tiles are given. Then, you can arrange the terms into an algebraic expression.

Example

Determine the polynomial expression that represents the following arrangement of algebra tiles.

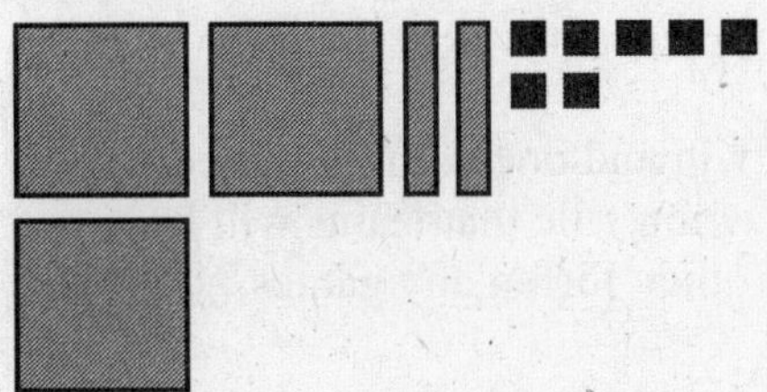

Solution

Identify the algebra tiles that are given.
You have 3 positive x^2-tiles, 2 positive x-tiles, and 7 positive unit tiles.

The polynomial expression that represents this arrangement of algebra tiles is $3x^2+2x+7$.

Your Turn 4

Determine the polynomial expression that represents the following arrangement of algebra tiles.

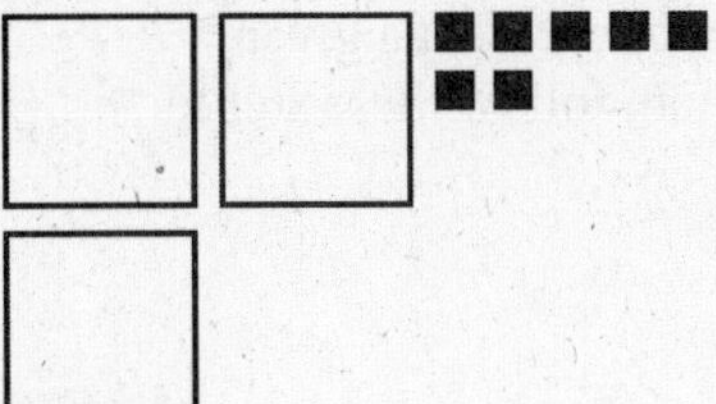

NOTES

Polynomial expressions can be used to represent word problems. This is a useful tool because then the expressions can be evaluated and used to solve problems.

To do this, define the unknown variable and translate the keywords found in the word problem into mathematical operators.

Example

A pizza store sells pizza at a rate of \$8 per pizza and charges a fixed fee of \$5 per delivery. Determine an algebraic expression that can be used to determine the total cost of ordering a pizza.

Solution

Let p represent the number of pizzas ordered.
The cost of the pizza itself is eight times the number of pizzas ordered. This can be represented as $8p$.
The additional fixed fee of \$5 for delivery is a constant in the algebraic expression; it must be separated from the variable with an addition sign.
The polynomial expression becomes $8p+5$.

Your Turn 5

In soccer, three points are awarded for a win and one point is earned for a tie game. A league director implements a new rule that teams will be deducted two points from the standings if they forfeit any games.

Determine an algebraic expression that could be used to represent the number of points a team holds in the league standings.

It is also possible to create a real life situation to represent a given expression. To write a context for an expression, follow these steps:

Step 1
Determine what the first term could represent.

Step 2
Determine what the constant could mean.

Step 3
Create a context that fits within those terms.

NOTES

Example

Give a possible context for the polynomial expression $20p + 50$.

Solution

Step 1

Determine what the first term could represent.
Assuming the variable is meaningful, p could represent person and 20 multiplies p.

Step 2

Determine what the constant could mean.
A constant 50 is added to $20p$.
This could represent a $50 fee.

Step 3

Create a context that fits within those terms.
The school is having a party. The caterer charges $20 a person plus a $50 booking fee.

Your Turn 6

Give a possible context for the polynomial expression $17.5h - 10$.

PRACTICE EXERCISES

Identify the coefficients, variables, and constants of each of the following polynomials. Name each polynomial and determine its degree.

1. $6t^2 - 4t$

2. $-2a - 6 + t$

3. $-xy + 2x$

4. $5 - d + 3c - p$

5. $\frac{7}{8}x$

6. $x - \frac{3}{5}$

Use the legend below to answer the next 3 questions.

	Positive tile	**Negative tile**
Unit tile	■	□
***x*-tile**		
x^2-tile		

Represent the following polynomial expression using algebra tiles.

7. $x^2 + 3x - 2$

8. $-5x^2 + 4x + 4$

9. $4x^2 + 6x + 3$

10. Give a possible context for the polynomial expression $50 + 0.30m$.

Lesson 2 IDENTIFYING EQUIVALENT POLYNOMIALS

NOTES

When terms in a polynomial expression are rearranged in a different order, the value of the expression stays the same. The two polynomial expressions are called *equivalent polynomials*. Familiarity with parts of a polynomial is effective in identifying equivalent polynomial expressions.

The polynomial expression $2x^2 - 3xy - z$ can be rewritten as any one of the following:

- $-3xy + 2x^2 - z$
- $-3xy - z + 2x^2$
- $2x^2 - z - 3xy$
- $-z + 2x^2 - 3xy$
- $-z - 3xy + 2x^2$

Notice how the signs stay with the numerical coefficient they belong to.

As long as the signs stay with the numerical coefficient, the terms can be written in any order.

Your Turn 1

Write equivalent polynomial expressions for each of the following polynomial expressions:

a) $-8x^2 + 2$ **b)** $3x^2 + 4x + 2$

Example

Using the following polynomials lettered *A* to *H*, identify the equivalent polynomials. Each polynomial has one equivalent polynomial.

A $3x^2 + 4x - 6$ *E* $-3x + 2 + x^2$

B $3x^2 - 7x + 6$ *F* $-x + x^2 + 3$

C $x^2 - 3x + 2$ *G* $-6 + 4x + 3x^2$

D $x^2 - x + 3$ *H* $-7x + 6 + 3x^2$

Solution

The polynomial *A* has the terms $3x^2$, $4x$, and -6. To find the equivalent polynomial for this expression, start by identifying another polynomial that has a constant of -6. The only other polynomial with a constant of -6 is *G*. Therefore, *A* and *G* are equivalent.

NOTES

The polynomial *B* has the terms $3x^2$, $-7x$, and 6. To find the equivalent polynomial for this expression, identify another polynomial with a term of $-7x$. The only other polynomial with a $-7x$ is *H*. Therefore, *B* and *H* are equivalent.

The polynomial *C* has the terms x^2, $-3x$, and 2. To find the equivalent polynomial for this expression, identify another polynomial with a term of $-3x$. The only other polynomial with a $-3x$ is *E*. Therefore, *C* and *E* are equivalent.

The polynomial *D* has the terms x^2, $-x$, and 3. To find the equivalent polynomial for this expression, identify another polynomial with a term of $-x$. The only other polynomial with a $-x$ is *F*. Therefore, *D* and *F* are equivalent.

Your Turn 2

Using the following polynomials lettered *A* to *H*, identify the equivalent polynomials. Each polynomial has one equivalent polynomial.

A $-8x^2-2x+6$

B $-12x^2+6x+2$

C $2x^2+9x+12$

D $x^2-5x+23$

E $9x+12+2x^2$

F $x^2+23-5x$

G $6-8x^2-2x$

H $-12x^2+2+6x$

IDENTIFYING LIKE TERMS

Terms with the *exact* same variables with *identical* exponents are called **like terms**. Like terms always have the same degree.

For example, $2x^2$ and $-3x^2$ are like terms because they both have the same variable *x* with the identical exponent of 2, so they have the same degree. Constants, such as 2, −5, and 12, are like terms since they all have a degree of 0.

Unlike terms are terms that cannot be combined. This may be because the variables are different or the exponents on the variables are not the same.

For example, $2y^2$ and $2x^2$ are unlike terms because, although they have the same exponent, the variables are different. Similarly, $3y$ and $-2y^2$ are unlike terms because, although they have the same variable, the exponents are different.

NOTES

Example

Rearrange each term in the right-hand column so that the terms line up with a like term in the left-hand column.

$2x$	-3
$-4yz$	$-6y$
23	x^2
$2x^2$	yz
$2y^2$	$-2x$
y	$9y^2$

Solution

The list below shows the like terms.

$2x$	$-2x$
$-4yz$	yz
23	-3
$2x^2$	x^2
$2y^2$	$9y^2$
y	$-6y$

Your Turn 3

Rearrange each term in the right-hand column so that the terms line up with a like term in the left-hand column.

$3x$	-5
$-2xy$	$7xz$
21	z^2
$4y$	$-3x$
$3xz$	xy
z^2	$2y$

COMBINING LIKE TERMS

Like terms can be combined by addition or subtraction.
To add or subtract like terms, follow these steps:

Step 1
Identify the like terms by underlining or circling them.

Step 2
Add or subtract the like terms.

Example

Simplify the following polynomial expression by combing like terms:
$4x^2 - 9y + 6x^2 + 13x - 7y$.

Solution

Step 1

Identify the like terms. You can underline or circle the like terms.

$\underline{4x^2} \underbrace{-9y} \underline{+6x^2} + 13x \underbrace{-7y}$

Step 2

Add or subtract the like terms.

$$\begin{aligned} &4x^2 - 9y + 6x^2 + 13x - 7y \\ &= 4x^2 + 6x^2 - 9y - 7y + 13x \\ &= 10x^2 - 16y + 13x \end{aligned}$$

Your Turn 4

Simplify the following polynomial expression by combing like terms:
$-12z + 8y^2 + 10 - y^2 + 14z - 7$..

NOTES

Notice how the operators become the signs of the numerical coefficient that follows.

Rearranging the expression so that like terms appear side by side may make it easier to add or subtract them.

PRACTICE EXERCISES

Write the equivalent expression to the given polynomial.

1. $2n-8$

2. $2x^2-2+3x$

3. $-4+5x$

4. $5y+3y^2$

5. $-23+7x^2$

6. $3x^2+6$

7. A binomial with no like terms is added to a trinomial with no like terms (and there are no like terms between the two polynomials). How many terms will there be in the resulting polynomial?

Simplify each of the following polynomial expressions. Then state the degree of the resulting polynomial.

8. $2x^2+7y-x^2+10y+1$

9. $3y^2-y^2+5y-9-18$

10. $4x-3y-5x^2+12x$

Lesson 3 ADDING AND SUBTRACTING POLYNOMIALS

NOTES

You can add or subtract polynomials concretely or pictorially using algebra tiles or algebraically.

ADDING POLYNOMIALS USING ALGEBRA TILES

Algebra tiles can help you understand the addition of polynomials.

The following chart shows the tiles and what they represent.

	Positive tile	**Negative tile**
Unit tile		
***x*-tile**		
x^2-tile		

Follow these steps when adding polynomials using algebra tiles:

Step 1
Model the polynomials with tiles.

Step 2
Simplify the equation by cancelling negative and positive tiles of the same size.

Step 3
Determine the solution by counting up the remaining tiles.

Example

Simplify the polynomial $(2x^2-3x+4)+(x^2+5x-6)$ using algebra tiles.

Solution

Step 1
Model the polynomials with tiles.

Step 2
Simplify the equation by cancelling negative and positive tiles of the same size.

=

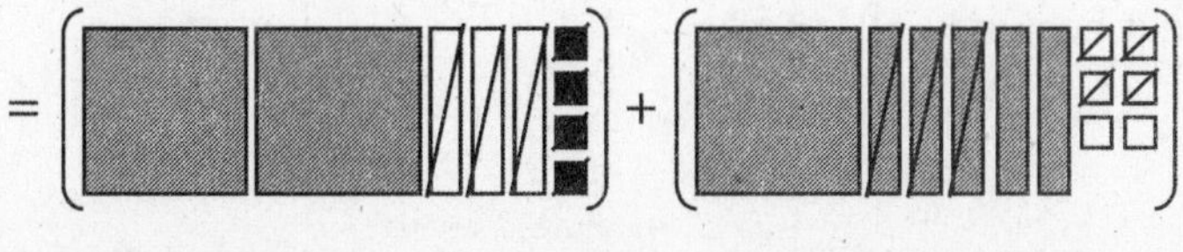

NOTES

Step 3
Write the remaining tiles as the solution.

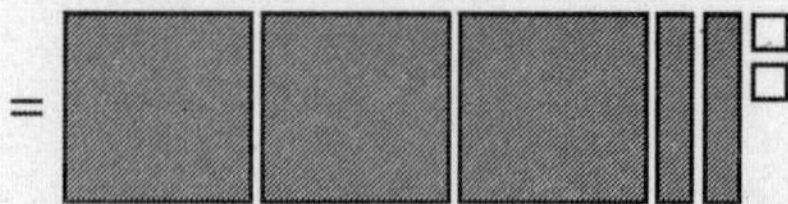

The answer is $3x^2 + 2x - 2$.

Your Turn 1

Simplify the polynomial $(x^2 + x + 1) + (-2x + 2)$ using algebra tiles.

ADDING POLYNOMIALS ALGEBRAICALLY

To add polynomials algebraically, follow these steps:

Step 1
Rewrite the polynomial by removing the brackets.

Step 2
Gather the like terms in descending order.

Step 3
Add the numerical coefficients of the like terms.

Recall that like terms have the same variable and the same exponent.

Descending order means highest degree terms are followed by lower degree terms. For example, the polynomial $1 + x^2 - x$ written in descending order becomes $x^2 - x + 1$.

NOTES

Example

Add the following polynomials by combining like terms:
$(-x^2 - 7x - 4) + (5x^2 + 8x - 1)$.

Solution

Step 1
Rewrite the polynomial without the brackets.
$= -x^2 - 7x - 4 + 5x^2 + 8x - 1$

Step 2
Gather the like terms in descending order.
$= -x^2 + 5x^2 - 7x + 8x - 4 - 1$

Step 3
Add the numerical coefficients of the like terms.
$= 4x^2 + x - 5$

Your Turn 2

Add the following polynomials by combining like terms:
$(2x^2 + 3x - 5) + (9x^2 + 4x + 2)$

Example

Add the following polynomials by combining like terms:
$(x^2 + 3x - 8) + (-2x^2 + 5x - 2) + (x^2 + 2x + 12)$

Solution

Step 1
Rewrite the polynomial without the brackets.
$(x^2 + 3x - 8) + (-2x^2 + 5x - 2) + (x^2 + 2x + 12)$
$= x^2 + 3x - 8 - 2x^2 + 5x - 2 + x^2 + 2x + 12$

Step 2
Gather the like terms in descending order.
$x^2 + 3x - 8 - 2x^2 + 5x - 2 + x^2 + 2x + 12$
$= x^2 - 2x^2 + x^2 + 3x + 5x + 2x - 8 - 2 + 12$

Step 3
Add the numerical coefficients of the like terms.
$x^2 - 2x^2 + x^2 + 3x + 5x + 2x - 8 - 2 + 12$
$= 10x + 2$

NOTES

Your Turn 3

Add the following polynomials by combining like terms:
$(-2x^2 + 2x + 4) + (-8x^2 + 9x - 3) + (5x^2 + 7x + 4)$

SUBTRACTING POLYNOMIALS USING ALGEBRA TILES

Algebra tiles can help you understand the subtraction of polynomials. When subtracting polynomials, change the subtraction sign between the polynomials to an addition sign. Then, for every term inside the polynomial that was being subtracted, switch the sign to its opposite sign. This process is called *adding the additive inverse.*

If the additive inverse is not performed, the solution will be full of errors and will be incorrect.

Follow these steps when subtracting polynomials using algebra tiles:

Step 1
Model the polynomials with tiles.

Step 2
Change the tiles of the second polynomial to the opposite colour (its additive inverse).

Step 3
Simplify the equation by cancelling negative and positive tiles of the same size.

Step 4
Determine the solution by counting up the remaining tiles.

Example

Simplify the polynomial $\left(2x^2 - 3x + 4\right) - \left(x^2 + 5x - 6\right)$ using algebra tiles.

Solution

Step 1
Model the polynomials with tiles.

NOTES

Step 2
Add the opposite when subtracting polynomials. To do this, change the tiles of the second polynomial to the opposite colour.

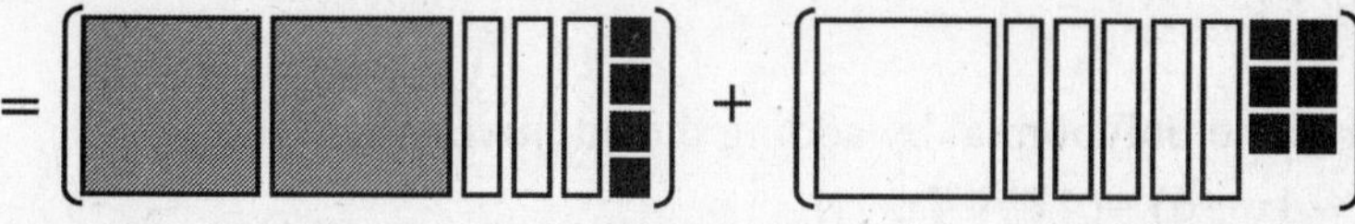

Step 3
Simplify the equation by cancelling negative and positive tiles of the same size.

Step 4
Determine the solution by counting up the remaining tiles.

The answer is $x^2 - 8x + 10$.

Your Turn 4

Simplify the polynomial $\left(2x^2 - 3x - 2\right) - \left(-x^2 + 2x - 1\right)$ using algebra tiles.

SUBTRACTING POLYNOMIALS ALGEBRAICALLY

To subtract polynomials algebraically, follow these steps:

Step 1
Rewrite the polynomial by adding the additive inverse.

Step 2
Rewrite the polynomial without the brackets.

Step 3
Gather the like terms in descending order.

Step 4
Add the numerical coefficients of the like terms.

NOTES

Example

Subtract the following polynomials: $(2x^2 - 4x + 6) - (4x^2 - 4x + 1)$

Solution

Step 1

Rewrite the polynomial by adding the additive inverse.

$(2x^2 - 4x + 6) - (4x^2 - 4x + 1)$
$= (2x^2 - 4x + 6) + (-4x^2 + 4x - 1)$

Step 2

Rewrite the polynomial without the brackets.

$(2x^2 - 4x + 6) + (-4x^2 - 4x + 1)$
$= 2x^2 - 4x + 6 - 4x^2 + 4x - 1$

Step 3

Gather the like terms in descending order.

$2x^2 - 4x + 6 - 4x^2 + 4x - 1$
$= 2x^2 - 4x^2 - 4x + 4x + 6 - 1$

Step 4

Add the numerical coefficients of the like terms.

$2x^2 - 4x^2 - 4x + 4x + 6 - 1$
$= -2x^2 + 5$

Your Turn 5

Subtract the following polynomials: $(-2x^2 + x - 2) - (x + 3 - 3x^2)$

Example

Subtract the following polynomials:
$(6x^2 - 5x + 7) - (-2x^2 - 4x - 6) - (x - 5)$

Solution

Step 1
Rewrite the polynomial by adding the additive inverse.
$(6x^2 - 5 + 7) - (-2x^2 - 4x - 6) - (x - 5)$
$= (6x^2 - 5x + 7) + (2x^2 + 4x + 6) + (-x + 5)$

Step 2
Rewrite the polynomial without the brackets.
$(6x^2 - 5x + 7) + (2x^2 \_ + 4x + 6) + (-x + 5)$
$6x^2 - 5x + 7 + 2x^2 + 4x + 6 - x + 5$

Step 3
Gather the like terms in descending order.
$6x^2 - 5x + 7 + 2x^2 + 4x + 6 - x + 5$
$= 6x^2 + 2x^2 - 5x + 4x - x + 7 + 6 + 5$

Step 4
Add the numerical coefficients of the like terms.
$6x^2 - 2x^2 - 5x + 4x - x + 7 + 6 + 5$
$= -8x^2 - 2x + 18$

Your Turn 6

Subtract the following polynomials:
$(3x^2 - 2x + 2) - (-12x^2 - 2x - 9) - (x - 3)$

NOTES

PRACTICE EXERCISES

Simplify each of the following polynomials using algebra tiles.

1. $\left(2x^2+3x+1\right)+\left(-x^2+2x-5\right)$

2. $\left(3x^2-2\right)+\left(-x^2+6\right)$

3. $\left(-x^2+2x\right)-\left(-3x^2-6\right)$

4. $\left(-2x^2+x-3\right)-\left(x^2+x-5\right)$

5. $(5x+2)-(x^2-1)+(-2x-3)$

Add or subtract each set of polynomials using algebraic processes.

6. $(3x^2+4x-8)+(-2x^2+8x-9)$

7. $(x^2-7x-3)+(-2x+11)$

8. $(3x-4x^2)-(5+3x^2)$

9. $\left(-5x^2-6x+1\right)-\left(-2x^2+7-8x\right)$

10. $(3x-5)+(3-6x)+(8x-7)$

Lesson 4 MULTIPLYING AND DIVIDING POLYNOMIALS

NOTES

You can multiply or divide polynomials concretely and pictorially using algebra tiles and algebraically.

MULTIPLYING POLYNOMIALS USING ALGEBRA TILES

Multiplying polynomials using algebra tiles is similar to finding the area of a rectangle.

To multiply polynomials with algebra tiles, follow these steps:

Step 1
Set up a grid using the value of the factors in the expression to represent the width and length of a rectangle.

Step 2
Carry out the multiplication by filling in the area of the rectangle using algebra tiles.

Step 3
Obtain the product by collecting like terms.

Step 4
Write the resulting polynomial expression in degree order: write the highest degree term first, followed by the rest of the terms in descending order of degree and ending with the constant term (if any).

Example

Expand and simplify $2(x+2)$ using algebra tiles.

Solution

Step 1
Set up a grid using the value of the multiplicand and the multiplier in the expression to represent the width and length of a rectangle. Drawing the dotted lines shows the shape of the tile that is the product of the two outside tiles.

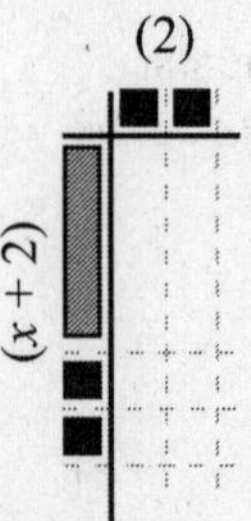

NOTES

Step 2
Carry out the multiplication by filling in the area of the rectangle using algebra tiles.

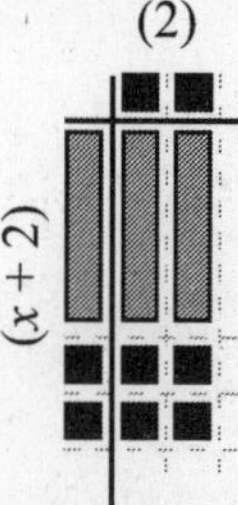

Step 3
Obtain the product by collecting like terms.

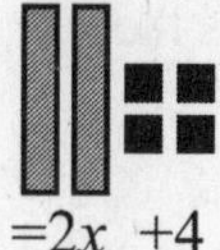

$=2x$ $+4$

Step 4
Write the resulting polynomial expression in degree order.
The answer is $2x+4$.

Your Turn 1

Expand and simplify $2x(x+6)$ using algebra tiles.

MULTIPLYING POLYNOMIALS ALGEBRAICALLY

To multiply monomials, first multiply the numerical coefficients. Next, multiply the variables together by adding the exponents of the variables with the same base.

A numerical coefficient is the number in front of the variable.

Example

Multiply the following monomials: $(2x)(3x)$

When multiplying terms with the same base, as the exponents.

Solution

Multiply the numerical coefficients and then the variables together.

$(2)(3)(x)(x)$
$=6(x)(x)$
$=6x^{1+1}$
$=6x^2$

NOTES

A numerical coefficient is the number in front of the variable.

When multiplying terms with the same base, add the exponents.

Your Turn 2

Multiply the following monomials: $(3x)(5x)$

When determining the product of a monomial and a polynomial that is within brackets, the monomial multiplies with each term of the polynomial in the brackets. This process is referred to as the **distributive property**. The distributive property states that a product can be written as the sum of two or more products.

Example

Simplify the following polynomial expression: $3(2x^2 - 6x + 4)$

Solution

Multiply the term outside the brackets by each term inside the brackets.

$3(2x^2 - 6x + 4)$
$= (3)(2x^2) + (3)(-6x) + (3)(4)$

Notice that addition signs are written between each group that is being multiplied.

Now, multiply the numerical coefficients together.

$(3)(2x^2) + (3)(-6x) + (3)(4)$
$= 6x^2 - 18x + 12$

Your Turn 3

Simplify the following polynomial expression: $2(4x^2 + 3x - 6)$

Example

Simplify the following polynomial expression: $2x(x+3)$

Solution

Multiply the monomial by each term of the binomial inside the brackets.

$$\begin{aligned}&2x(x+3)\\&=(2x)(x)+(2x)(3)\end{aligned}$$

Now, multiply the numerical coefficients and variables together.

$$\begin{aligned}&2x^{1+1}+(2)(3)(x)\\&=2x^2+6x\end{aligned}$$

Your Turn 4

Simplify the following polynomial expression: $5x(x+2)$

NOTES

DIVIDING POLYNOMIALS USING ALGEBRA TILES

When multiplying polynomials using algebra tiles, the solution is found by determining the area of a rectangle.

For example, 4×2 can be represented by the following arrangement of algebra tiles:

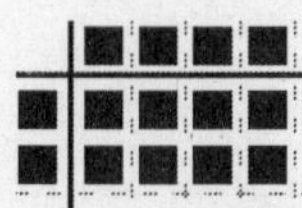

When dividing polynomials using algebra tiles, the area of a rectangle and the length of one side are given. The length of the second side needs to be determined.

The dividend is the number being divided into smaller units. The quotient is the answer to the division question.

For example, $8\div 2$ can be represented by the following arrangement of algebra tiles:

To divide polynomials with algebra tiles, follow these steps:

Step 1

Set up the multiplication grid with the divisor on the side.

NOTES

Step 2
Arrange the dividend into a rectangle.

Step 3
Determine the quotient.

Example

Simplify the polynomial expression $\frac{2x^2+8x}{2x}$ using algebra tiles.

Solution
Step 1
Set up the grid with the divisor on the side.

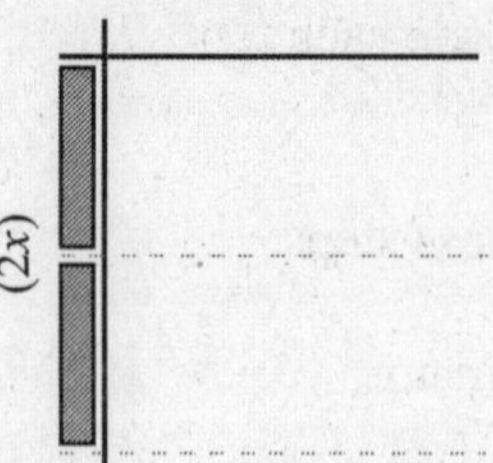

Step 2
Arrange the dividend into a rectangle. There are a few rules for how the tiles are displayed in the rectangle.

- Only equal length sides may touch.
- Big squares cannot touch little squares.
- Little squares must all be together.

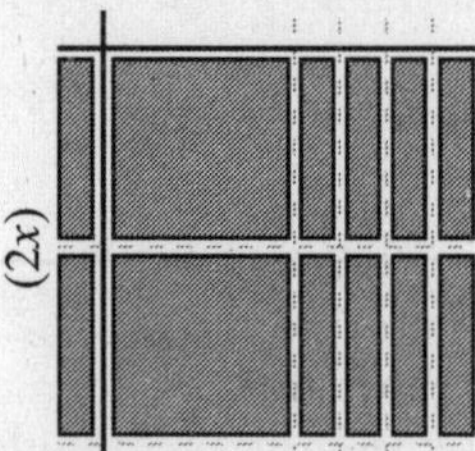

Step 3
Determine the quotient.
The quotient is the side length of each of the tiles.

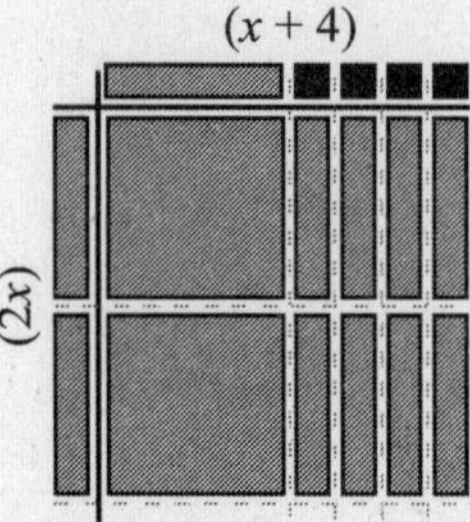

The answer is $x+4$.

NOTES

Your Turn 5

Simplify the polynomial expression $\frac{3x^2 + 9x}{3x}$ using algebra tiles.

DIVIDING POLYNOMIALS ALGEBRAICALLY

When dividing a polynomial by a monomial, divide each term of the polynomial by the monomial. In other words, divide each term in the numerator by the denominator.

To divide a polynomial by a monomial, follow these steps:

Step 1
Divide each term of the numerator by the denominator.

Step 2
Divide the numerical coefficients.

Step 3
Divide the variables by subtracting the exponents of the variables with the same base.

Example

Find the quotient of $\frac{4x^2 - 8x}{-2x}$.

Solution

Step 1
Divide each term of the numerator by the denominator.

$$\frac{4x^2}{-2x} - \frac{8x}{-2x}$$

Step 2
Divide the numerical coefficients.

$$\frac{4x^2}{-2x} - \frac{8x}{-2x}$$
$$= -2\frac{x^2}{x} + 4\frac{x}{x}$$

Step 3
Divide the variables.

$$-2\frac{x^2}{x} + 4\frac{x}{x}$$
$$= -2x + 4$$

NOTES

Your Turn 6

Find the quotient of $\frac{15x^2+3x}{3x}$.

Example

Find the quotient of $\frac{4n^2+12n-20}{-4}$.

Solution

Step 1

Divide each term of the numerator by the denominator.

$$\frac{4n^2+12n-20}{-4}$$
$$=\frac{4n^2}{-4}+\frac{12n}{-4}-\frac{20}{-4}$$

Step 2

Divide the numerical coefficients.

$$\frac{4n^2}{-4}+\frac{12n}{-4}-\frac{20}{-4}$$
$$=-n^2-3n+5$$

Your Turn 7

Find the quotient of $\frac{8n^2+16n-20}{-2}$.

PRACTICE EXERCISES

Simplify the following expressions.

1. $(3x)(-4x)$

2. $(5x)(4y)$

3. $(-2)(x^2 - x - 6)$

4. $(3)(4x^2 - 2x - 3)$

5. $5x(x + 6)$

6. $3x(-2x - 5)$

7. $\dfrac{12x^2 - 8x}{4x}$

8. $\dfrac{12x^2 - 20x}{-2x}$

9. $\dfrac{-28 + 14x}{-7}$

10. $\dfrac{15x^2 - 30xy + 35x}{5x}$

REVIEW SUMMARY

- Polynomials are algebraic expressions that are formed by combining numbers, variables, and exponents into algebraic terms.
- Terms in algebraic expressions are separated by addition and subtraction signs.
- A number that stands alone without any variables connected to it is called a constant.
- A polynomial with one term is called a monomial.
- A polynomial with two terms is called a binomial.
- A polynomial with three terms is called a trinomial.
- A polynomial with four or more terms is simply referred to as a polynomial
- The degree of a term is equivalent to the sum of the exponents found on the variables.
- The degree of a polynomial is equal to the degree of the highest-degree monomial.
- Pictorial representations can be used to write polynomial expressions.
- Polynomials are such that if the terms are rearranged, the expression can still mean the same thing; this is called equivalent polynomials.
- Like terms are terms that have the exact same variables with identical exponents.
- When adding polynomials algebraically, gather like terms in descending order of degree, and add the like terms.
- When subtracting polynomials, change the subtraction sign between the polynomials to an addition sign. This process is called adding the additive inverse.
- To multiply monomials, first multiply the numerical coefficients together and then multiply the variables together by adding the exponents of the variables with the same base.
- To determine the product of a monomial and a polynomial, use the distributive property.
- When dividing a polynomial by a monomial, divide each term of the polynomial by the monomial.

PRACTICE TEST

Determine the degree of each of the following polynomials.

1. $5y$

2. 6^2x^2

3. $2x^2 - 6x + 10$

4. $4xy + 3x + y$

Add or subtract each of the following polynomials.

5. $(3x + 7) + (2x + 9)$

6. $(2x^2 - 3x - 6) + (-x^2 + 3x + 12)$

7. $(6x^2 + 5x + 8) - (2x^2 + 3x + 7)$

8. $(2x^2 - 4x + 5) - (-4x^2 - 7 + 2x)$

Multiply each of the following polynomial expressions.

9. $5(10x)$

10. $(3x)(10x)$

11. $3(2x^2 - 6x + 5)$

12. $4x(-3x + 5)$

Identify the coefficients, variables, and constants of the following polynomial expressions.

13. $-6x^2 + 3y - 8$

14. $z^2 + 4z + 20$

15. $12 + 10s^2 - 7t$

Simplifythe following expressions.

16. $-4\left(5g^2-9g+\frac{3}{4}\right)$

17. $-5x^2(x-4)$

18. $-2(-x^2+8x)$

19. $2(4x)(3x+2)$

20. $\frac{4n^2-10n-5}{5}$

21. $\frac{2a^2+15-3a}{-3}$

NOTES

CIRCLES AND COMPOSITE 3-D OBJECTS

When you are finished this unit, you will be able to…

- identify questions that illustrate circle properties
- solve problems involving the application of one or more of the circle properties
- determine the measure of a given angle inscribed in a semicircle using the circle properties
- explain the relationship between the centre of a circle, a chord, and the perpendicular bisector of the chord
- determine the area of overlap in a given composite 3-D object, and explain the effect on determining the total surface area
- solve a given problem involving surface area

PREREQUISITE SKILLS AND KNOWLEDGE

Prior to starting this unit, you should be able to…

- measure angles and line segments
- apply the Pythagorean theorem
- perform simple mathematical calculations
- draw 3-D objects
- solve problems involving calculating area and surface area
- understand the relationship between the diameter and radius of a circle

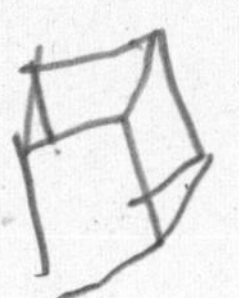

Lesson 1 CIRCLE PROPERTIES

NOTES

BASIC CIRCLE TERMINOLOGY

Perpendicular lines are lines that intersect at right angles.
A perpendicular bisector is a line that bisects a line segment at 90°.

CIRCLE

A circle is a set of points in a plane equidistant from a given point. The given point is called the centre of the circle, and the distance from the centre to any point on the circumference of the circle is called the radius of the circle.

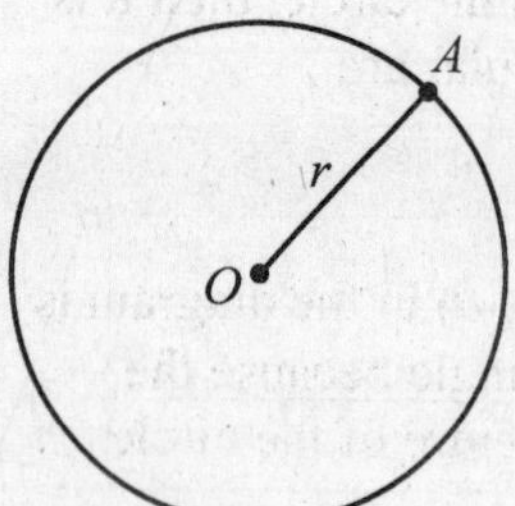

A is any point on the circumference of the circle, and *A* is always the same distance from the centre, *O*.

RADIUS

The term radius may refer to the:

- distance from the centre to any point on the circumference of the circle (distance *OA* in the diagram above)
- line segment connecting the centre to any point on the circumference of the circle (the line segment *OA* in the diagram above)

CHORD

A chord of a circle is a line segment with endpoints on the circumference of the circle. For example, in the following diagram, line segment *AB* is a chord.

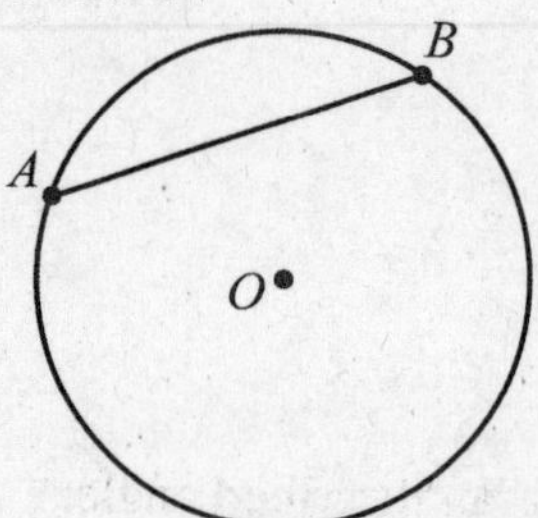

NOTES

ARC

An arc is part of the circumference of a circle. There are two arcs that make up the circumference: the major arc and the minor arc. In the following diagram, points A and B divide the circle into two arcs: minor arc AB and major arc ATB.

Three letters are required to represent a major arc in order to distinguish it from a minor arc.

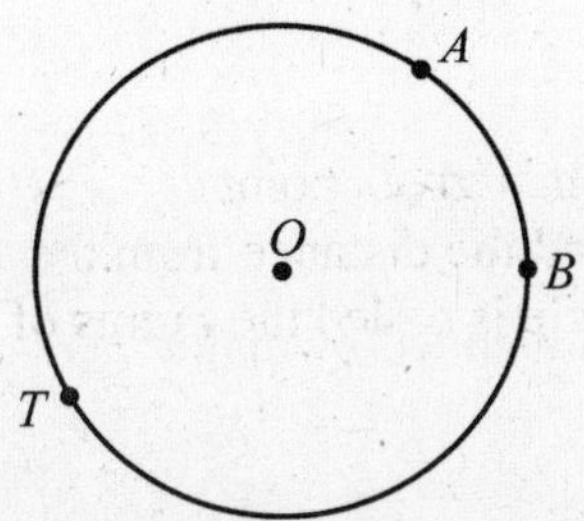

A minor arc is always less than half of the circumference of the circle and a major arc is always more than half of the circumference of the circle.

If the arc is exactly half of the circumference of the circle, then it is called a semicircular arc.

CENTRAL OR SECTOR ANGLE

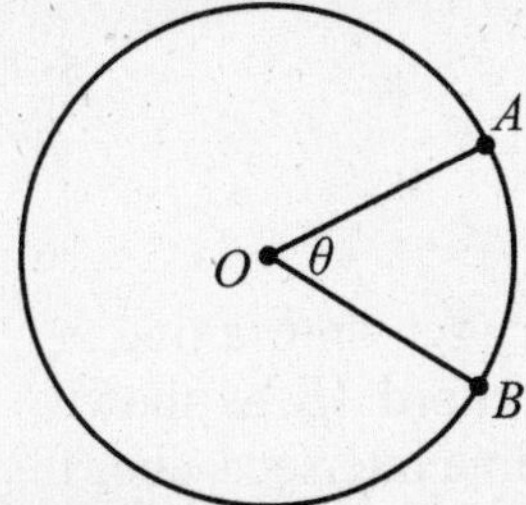

$\angle AOB$ (or angle θ) in the diagram is called a central angle because the vertex is at the centre of the circle.

The measure of angle θ is defined by the size of arc AB. Thus, angle θ is subtended by an arc.

The word "subtend" means to extend under or be opposite to.

Note that arc AB actually subtends two central angles, one using minor arc AB (shown above) and one using the major arc ATB (shown below).

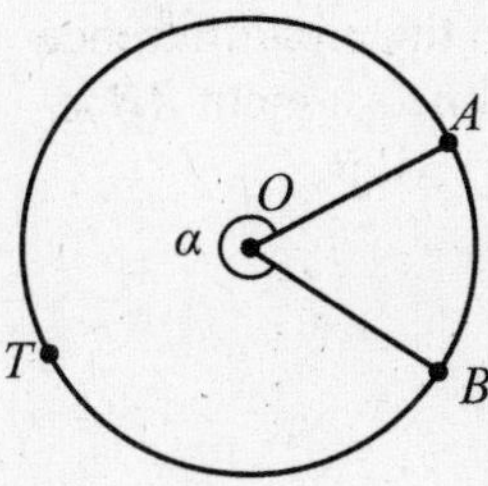

The angle denoted by α is also a central angle subtended by major arc ATB.

INSCRIBED ANGLE

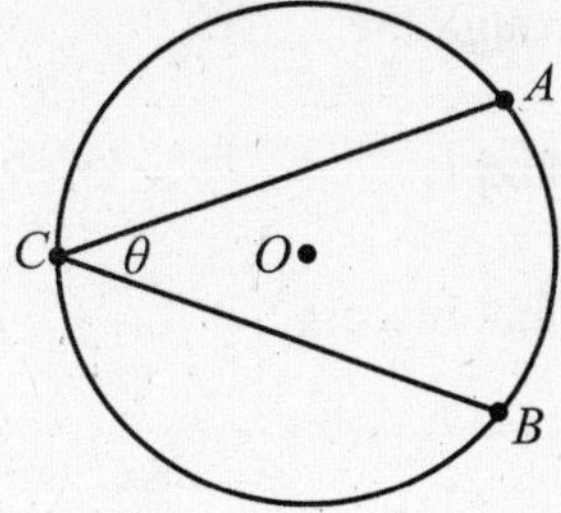

$\angle ACB$ (or angle θ) is an inscribed angle. The vertex of an inscribed angle is on the circumference of the circle and the arms of the angle are chords.

NOTES

Inscribed angles can be subtended by minor and major arcs.

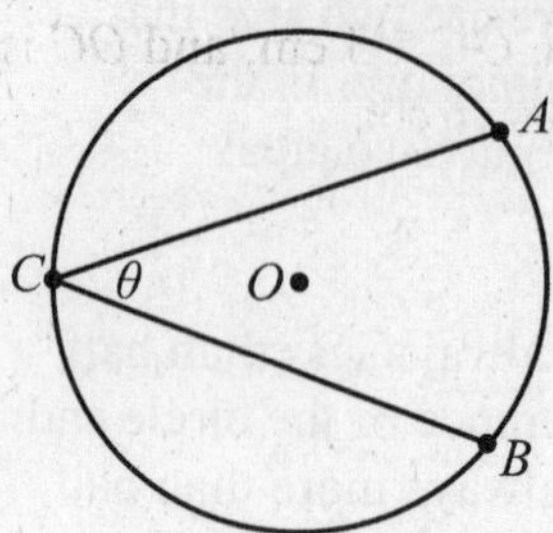

Angle θ is also said to be subtended by minor arc AB.

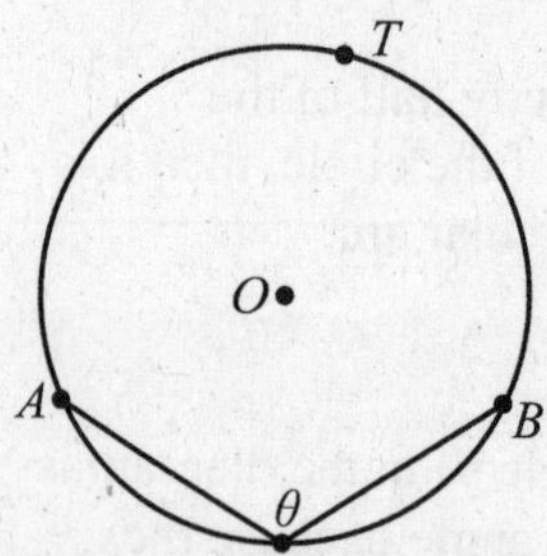

Angle θ is subtended by major arc ATB.

PROPERTIES OF CHORDS

Using the appropriate instruments from your geometry set, draw a line through point O such that the line is perpendicular to chord AB, as shown in the following diagram. Label the point where the line intersects chord AB as point C. Measure the length of line segment AC and line segment BC. What do you notice? Measure $\angle ACO$ and $\angle BCO$. What do you notice?

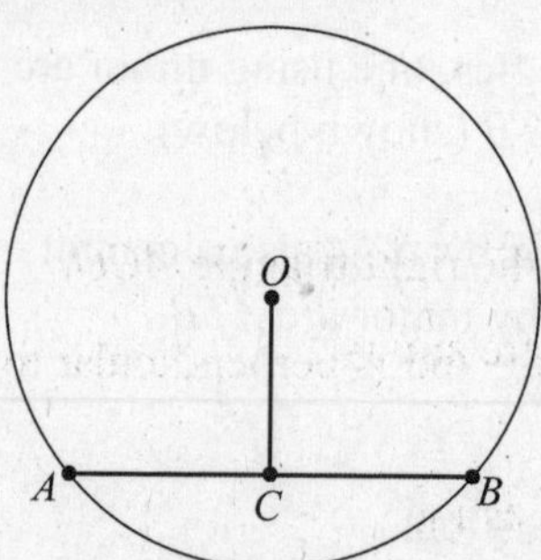

O is the centre of the circle.

OC is perpendicular to AB

$$AB = BC$$
$$\angle ACO = \angle BCO = 90°$$

THEOREM:

- The perpendicular bisector of a chord passes through the centre of the circle.
- A line that passes through the centre of a circle and is perpendicular to a chord bisects the chord.
- A line that passes through the centre of a circle that bisects a chord is perpendicular to the chord.

NOTES

Example

A circle with centre O, chord AB, where $AB = 8$ cm, $OC = 3$ cm, and OC is perpendicular to AB, is given. Find the radius of this circle.

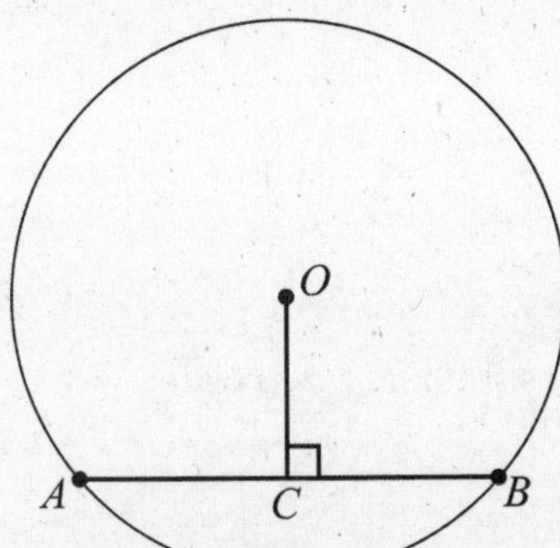

Solution

Step 1

Draw a radius OB on the diagram and label it r.

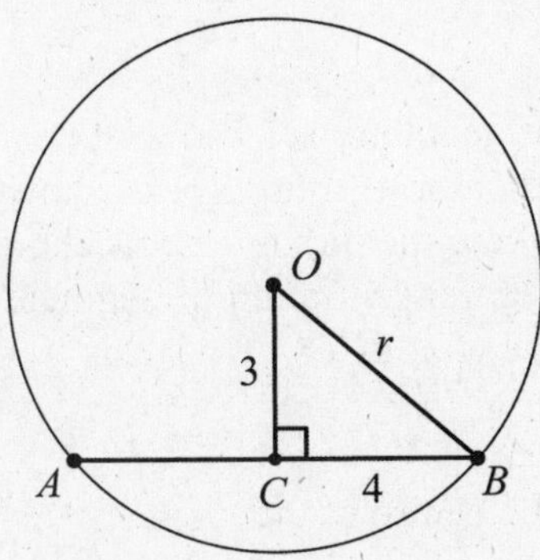

Step 2

Determine the measures of the other sides of the right triangle BCO.

$CB = \frac{8}{2} = 4$ since OC passes through the centre and is perpendicular to chord AB.

$OC = 3$ as this information is given in the question.

Step 3

Apply the Pythagorean Theorem to right triangle BCO to solve for r.

$r^2 = 4^2 + 3^2$

$r^2 = 16 + 9$

$r^2 = 25$

Take the positive square root of both sides

$\sqrt{r^2} = \sqrt{25}$

Solve for r

$r = 5$

The radius of the circle is 5 cm.

NOTES

Your Turn 1

Given a circle with centre O and the lengths of the line segments as shown, find the length of chord AB.

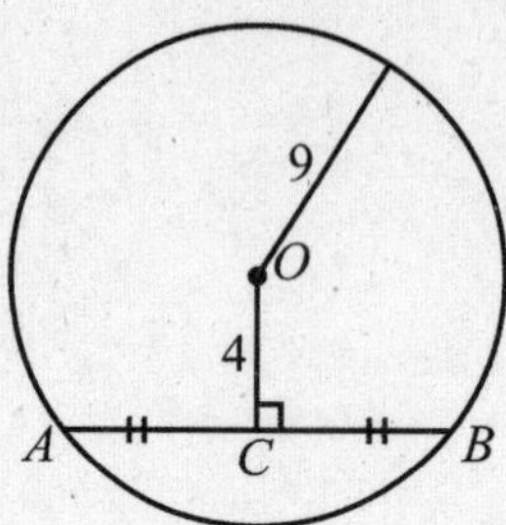

ANGLES INSCRIBED IN A CIRCLE

Using your protractor, determine the measure of $\angle ACB$ and the measure of $\angle AOB$ in the following diagram. What do you notice?

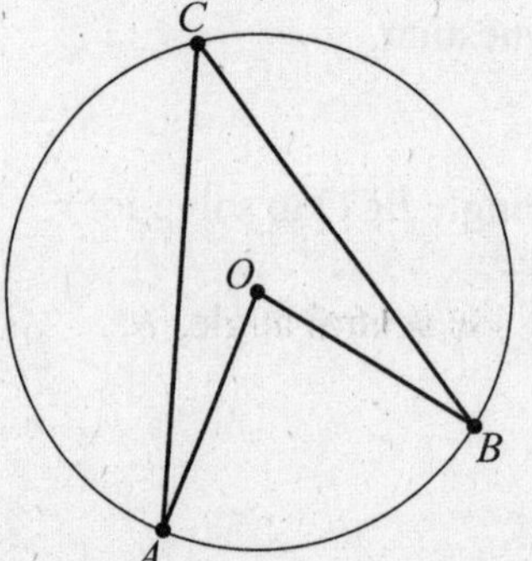

O is the centre of the circle.

$\angle AOB = 2 \times \angle ACB$

or

$\frac{1}{2} \times \angle AOB = \angle ACB$

THEOREM:

The measure of the central angle is twice the measure of the inscribed angle subtended by the same arc.

NOTES

Example

In the given diagram, if O is the centre of the circle and $\angle AOB = 80°$, what is the measure of $\angle ACB$?

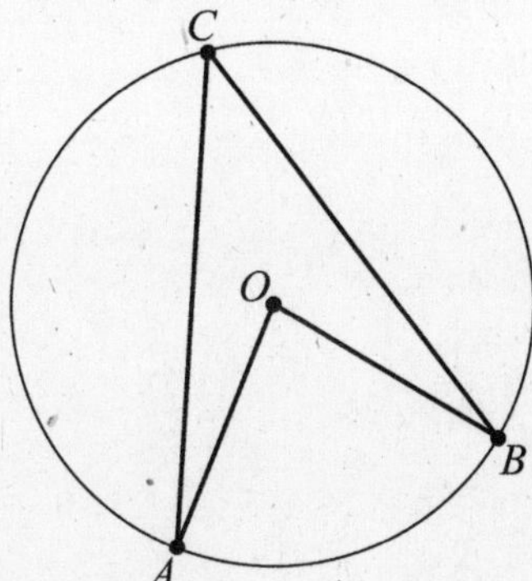

Solution

The measure of $\angle ACB$ is $\frac{1}{2}$ the measure of $\angle AOB$.

Therefore,

$$\angle ACB = \frac{1}{2} \times 80° \\ = 40°$$

Example

Find the measure of $\angle ACB$ if $\angle \theta = 300°$ in the following diagram.

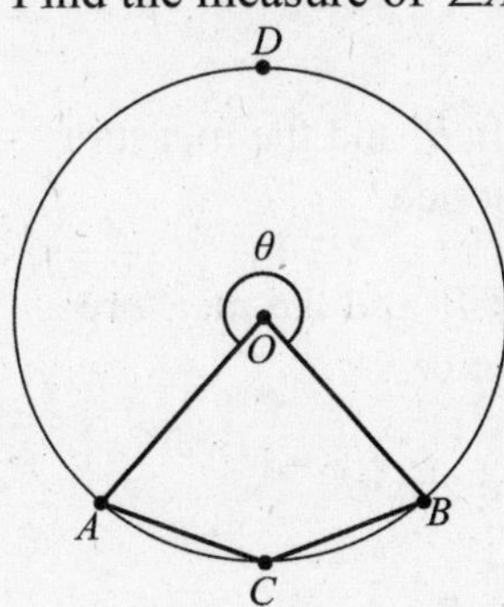

Solution

The measure of $\angle ACB$ is $\frac{1}{2}$ the measure of the central angle, θ, which is 300°. Therefore:

$$\angle ACB = \frac{1}{2} \times 300° \\ = 150°$$

NOTES

Your Turn 2

Find the measure of θ if $\angle ACB = 114°$ in the following diagram.

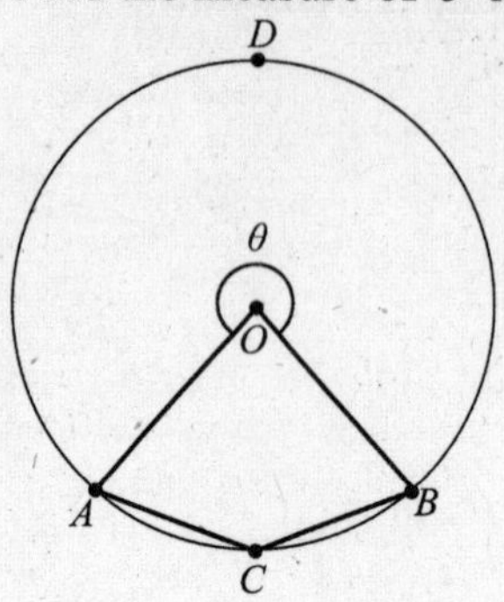

ANGLES SUBTENDED BY THE SAME ARC

Using your protractor, determine the measure of $\angle ACB$ and the measure of $\angle ADB$ in the following diagram. What do you notice?

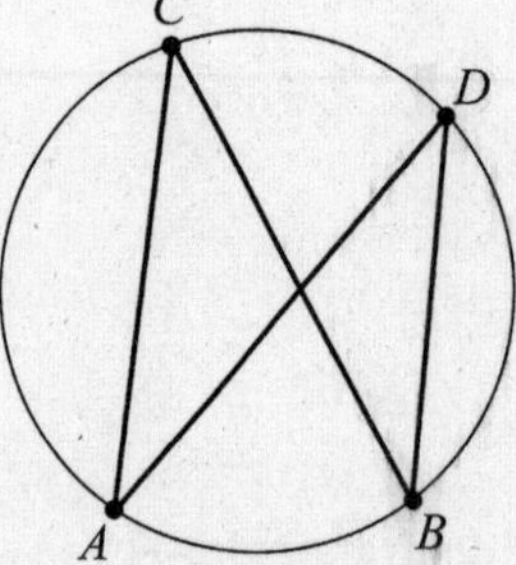

$\angle ACB = 35°$
$\angle ADB = 35°$

$\angle ACB = \angle ADB$
or simply $\angle C = \angle D$

THEOREM:
Inscribed angles subtended by the same arc (or chord) are congruent.

NOTES

Example

Find the measure of $\angle D$ given the following diagram.

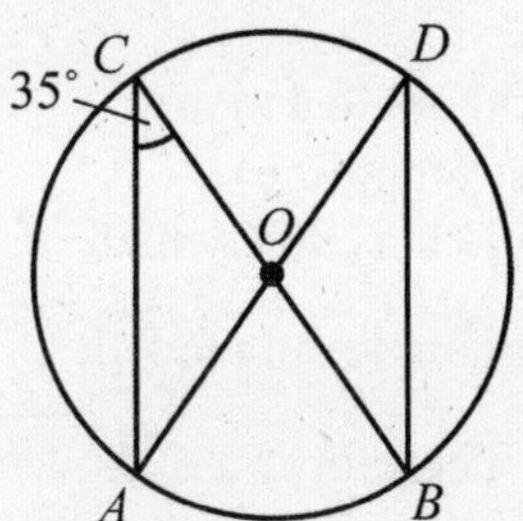

Solution

Inscribed angles *C* and *D* are both subtended by arc *AB*.
Therefore, $\angle C = \angle D$ and $\angle D = 35°$.

Your Turn 3

If the measure of $\angle D = 27°$, find the measure of $\angle C$ in the following diagram.

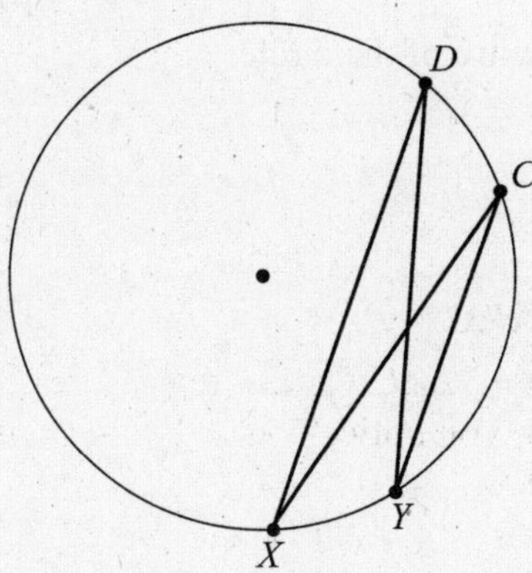

NOTES

ANGLE INSCRIBED IN A SEMICIRCLE

Using your protractor, determine the measure of $\angle ABC$ in the following diagram. What do you notice?

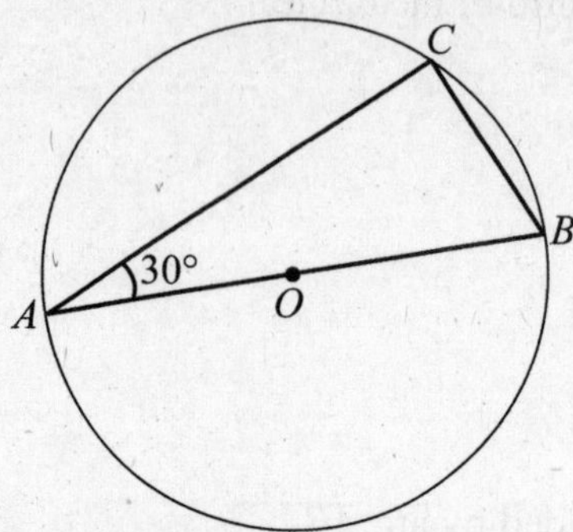

$\angle AOB$ is a central angle and is equal to 180° (a straight line). The inscribed angle C is 90°, which is $\frac{1}{2}$ of the central angle subtended by the same arc. Therefore, $\angle C$ is a right angle.

THEOREM:
An angle inscribed in a semicircle is a right angle.

Example

Find the measures of $\angle x$ and $\angle y$ in the following diagram.

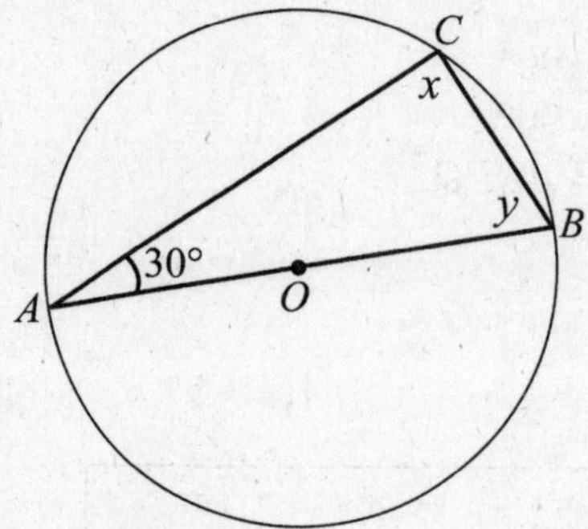

O is the centre of the circle.

Solution

Step 1

Determine the measure of $\angle x$.

$$\begin{aligned}\angle x &= \frac{180°}{2}\\ &= 90°\end{aligned}$$

Step 2

Determine the measure of $\angle y$.

The sum of the measures of the angles in a triangle equals 180°.

$$\begin{aligned}30° + \angle y + 90° &= 180°\\ \angle y + 120° &= 180°\\ \angle y &= 180° - 120°\\ &= 60°\end{aligned}$$

NOTES

Your Turn 4

If $\angle A = 45°$, find the measures of $\angle C$ and $\angle B$ in the following diagram.

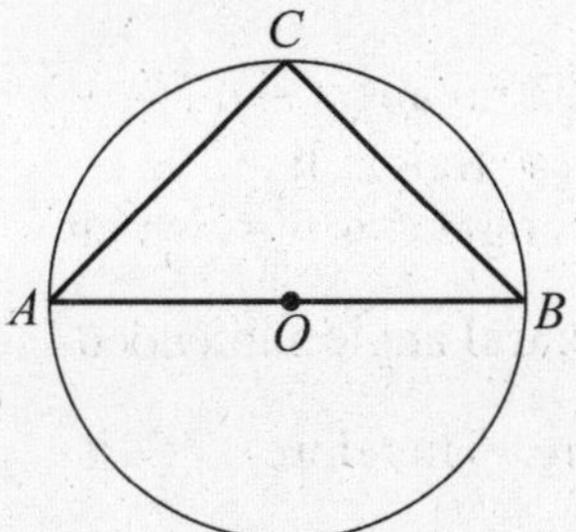

O is the centre of the circle.

TANGENTS TO A CIRCLE

In the following diagram, using your ruler, connect point *O* to point *P*. Next, using your protractor, measure $\angle APO$ and $\angle BPO$. What do you notice?

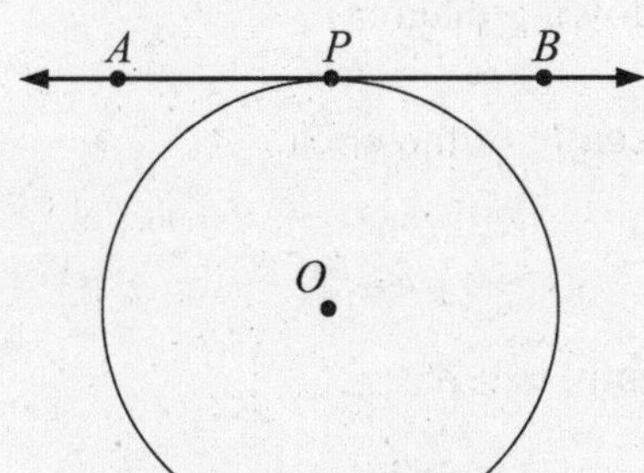

O is the centre of the circle.

$\angle APO = 90°$
$\angle BPO = 90°$
$\angle APO = \angle BPO$

A line or line segment is tangent to a circle if it intersects the circle in exactly one location.

TANGENT-RADIUS THEOREM:
A tangent to a circle is perpendicular to the radius at the point of tangency.

NOTES

Example

If line segment TA is a tangent segment, calculate the length of x, rounded to the nearest tenth.

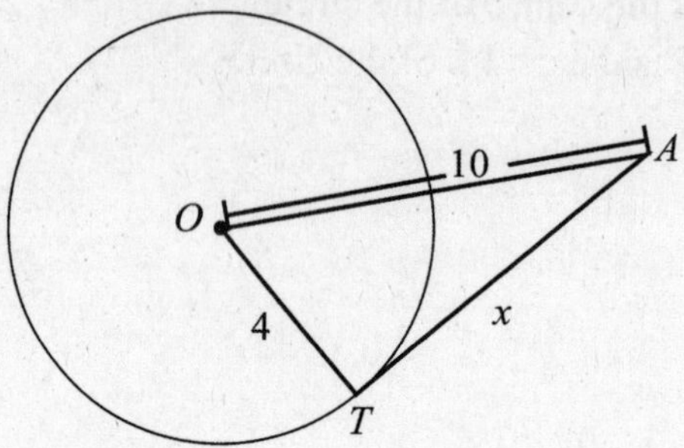

Solution

$\angle T$ is a right angle since TA is a tangent segment to the circle, apply the Pythagorean Theorem.

$(OA)^2 = (AT)^2 + (OT)^2$

Substitute 10 for OA, x for AT, 4 for OT, and then solve for x.

$$10^2 = x^2 + 4^2$$
$$100 = x^2 + 16$$
$$84 = x^2$$
$$\sqrt{84} = x$$
$$9.17 \doteq x$$

The value of x, rounded to the nearest tenth, is 9.2.

Your Turn 5

If line segment TA is a tangent segment, calculate the length of r, rounded to the nearest tenth.

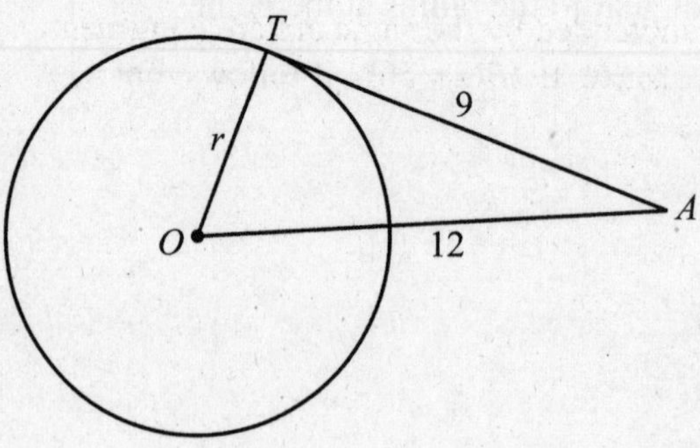

APPLICATION OF CIRCLE PROPERTIES

NOTES

Example

Determine the measure of $\angle ADC$ in the following diagram.

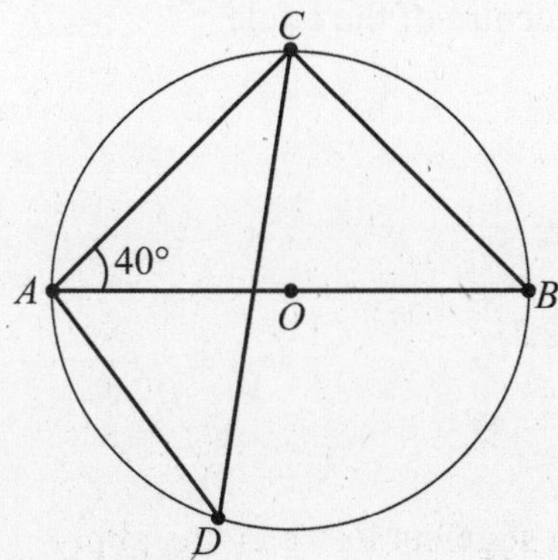

O is the centre of the circle.

Solution

Step 1

Determine the measure of $\angle ACB$.
Since $\angle ACB$ is inscribed in a semicircle, the measure of $\angle ACB = 90°$.

Step 2

Determine the measure of $\angle ABC$.
The sum of the measures of the angles in a triangle is equal to 180°.
Therefore for triangle ABC, $\angle BAC + \angle ACB + \angle ABC = 180°$.

Substitute 40° for $\angle BAC$, 90° for $\angle ACB$ and solve for $\angle ABC$.

$$\begin{aligned} 40° + 90° + \angle ABC &= 180° \\ 130° + \angle ABC &= 180° \\ \angle ABC &= 180° - 130° \\ &= 50° \end{aligned}$$

Recall that inscribed angles subtended by the same arc are congruent. Therefore, $\angle ABC = \angle ADC$. Since $\angle ABC = 50°$, it follows that $\angle ADC = 50°$.

NOTES

Your Turn 6

Determine the measure of $\angle DPB$ (y) in the following diagram if line CD is tangent to the circle at point P.

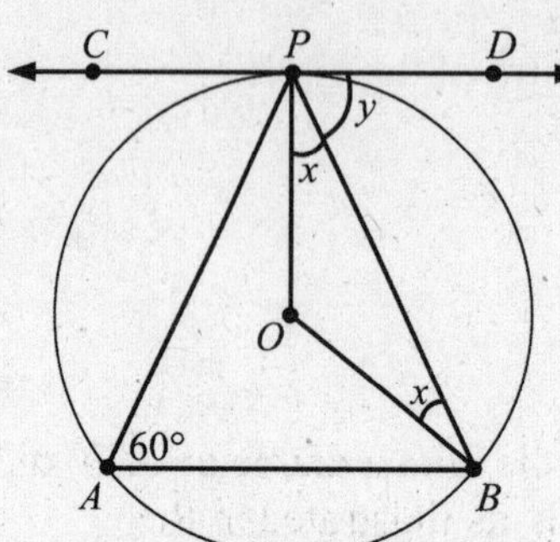

O is the centre of the circle.

Example

A circular water pipe is horizontal with water flowing through it below the half-full mark. The width of the water's surface in the pipe is 32 cm, and the maximum depth of the water in the pipe is 10 cm. What is the diameter of the water pipe?

Solution

Step 1

Draw a diagram of the situation.

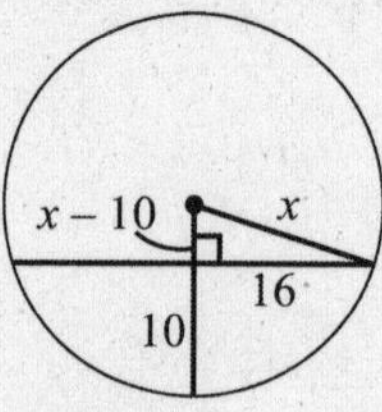

Step 2

Apply the Pythagorean Theorem.

$a^2 + b^2 = c^2$

Substitute $(x-10)$ for a, 16 for b, and x for c.

$$\begin{aligned}(x-10)^2 + 16^2 &= x^2 \\ x^2 - 20x + 100 + 256 &= x^2 \\ -20x &= -356 \\ x &= 17.8 \text{ cm}\end{aligned}$$

NOTES

Step 3
Calculate the diameter of the pipe.
The diameter is twice the measure of the radius. The radius of the pipe was calculated to be 17.8 cm.

$$\begin{aligned} d &= 2r \\ &= 2(17.8) \\ &= 35.6 \text{ cm} \end{aligned}$$

The diameter of the pipe is 35.6 cm.

Your Turn 7

The base of a large hemispherical dome is a circle with a diameter of 70 m. Two parallel support beams each 30 m in length, as illustrated in the following diagram, are used to support the base of the dome.

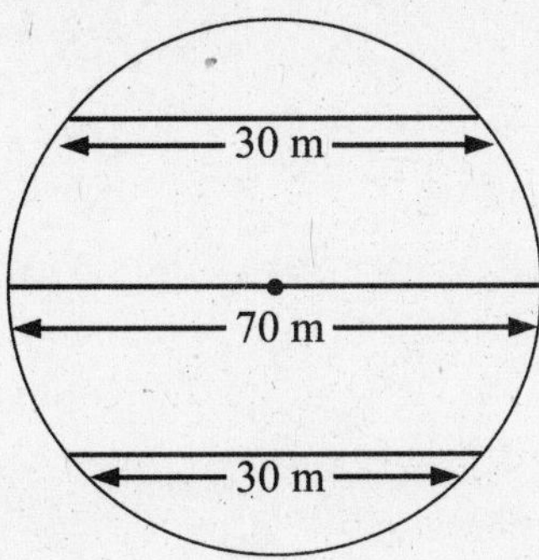

Rounded to the nearest tenth of a metre, how far apart are the two support beams?

PRACTICE EXERCISES

Solve for the variable x in each of the following diagrams. Letter O is the centre of the circle.

1.

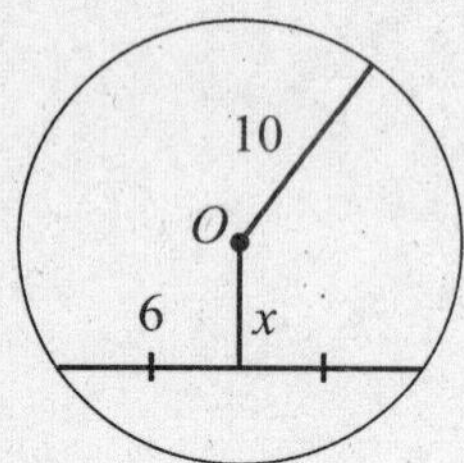

2.

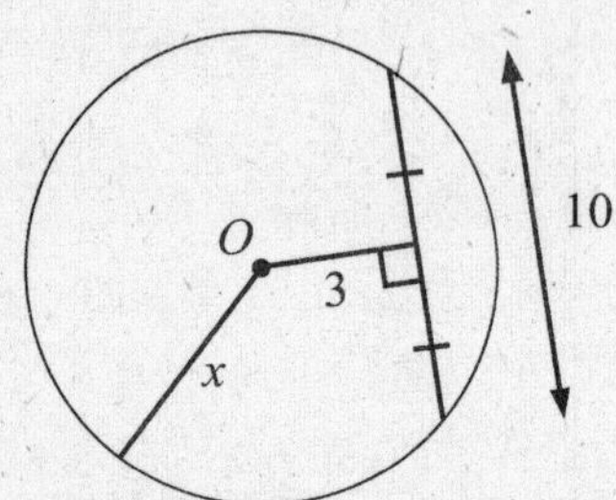

3.

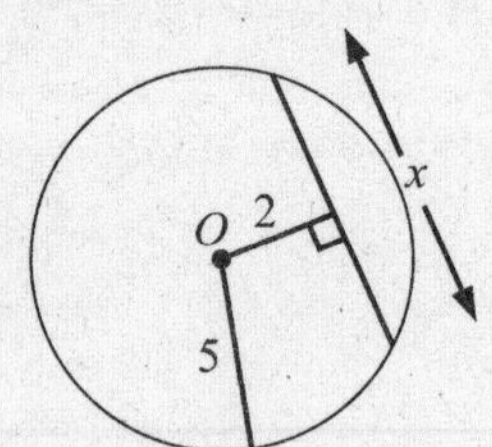

4. A circle contains a chord 14 cm long that is 3 cm from the centre of the circle. What is the diameter of the circle?

5. Two parallel chords are drawn on the same side of the centre in a circle with a diameter of 16 cm. The chords are 8 cm long and 4 cm long. What is the shortest distance between the chords?

Find the value of the variable in each of the following diagrams.

6.

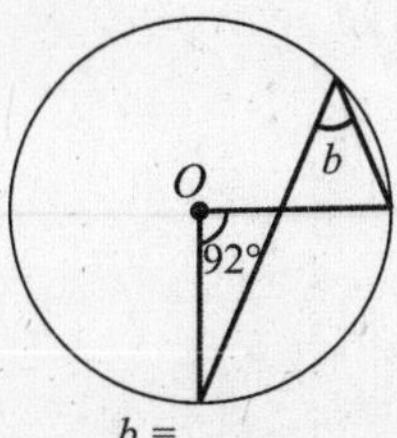

$b =$ ____

7.

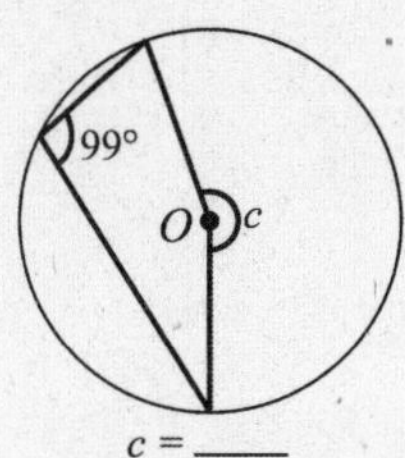

$c =$ ____

8.

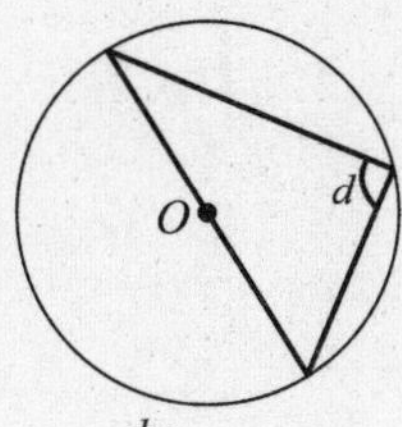

$d =$ ____

9.

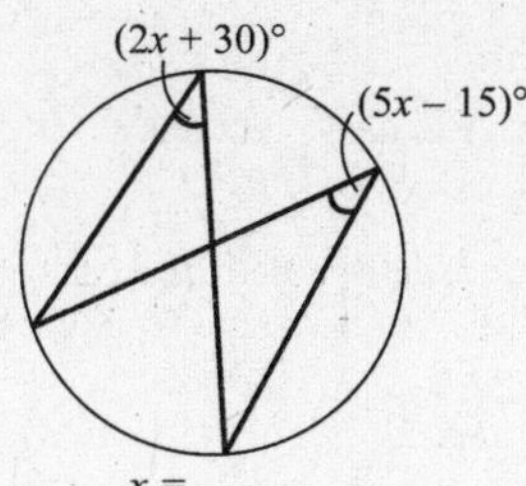

$x =$ ____

10. **Determine the value of x in the following diagram, rounded to the nearest hundredth. The lines that touch the circles are tangent lines.**

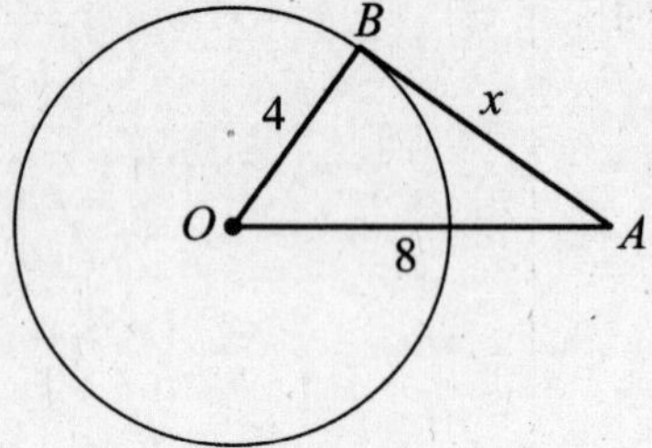

Lesson 2 SURFACE AREA OF COMPOSITE 3-D OBJECTS

NOTES

The area of any shape is the measure of the number of square units contained within it. The surface area of a 3-D object is the combined area of all of its exposed faces.

When two or more 3-D objects are placed together to build a single 3-D object, it is called a composite 3-D object.

The total surface area can be calculated using one of the following two methods:

- Calculate the surface area of only the exposed faces of each individual prism. Then, add up all the surface areas together.
- Calculate the complete surface area of each individual prism and then subtract the overlapped regions from the final sum of all the areas.

Example

Calculate the total surface area of the following composite 3-D object by adding only the exposed faces of each individual prism.

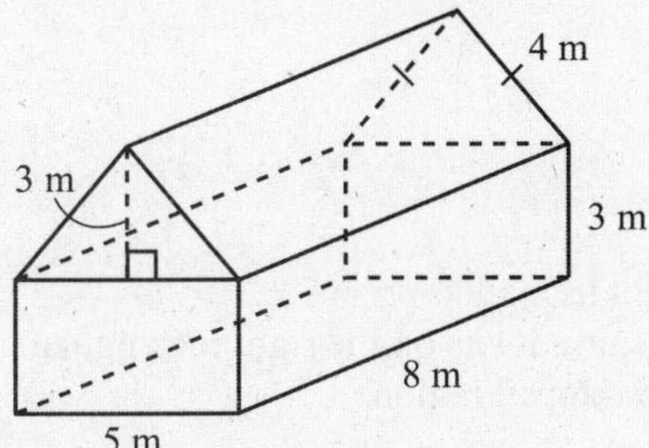

Solution

Find the surface area of each exposed face and then add them together.

Step 1

Break the 3-D composite object into a right rectangular prism and a right triangular prism.

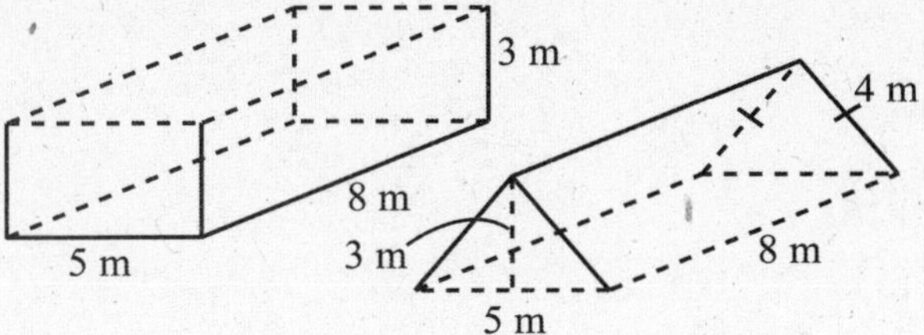

NOTES

Step 2
Calculate the surface area of the right rectangular prism.
There is no top to the right rectangular prism because the right triangular prism sits on top of it. The top is part of the overlapped region.

$$\begin{aligned} A_{\text{front and back}} &= 2(lw) \\ &= 2(5\times 3) \\ &= 2\times 15 \\ &= 30\ \text{m}^2 \end{aligned}$$

$$\begin{aligned} A_{\text{bottom}} &= lw \\ &= 5\times 8 \\ &= 40\ \text{m}^2 \end{aligned}$$

$$\begin{aligned} A_{\text{sides}} &= 2(lw) \\ &= 2(8\times 3) \\ &= 2\times 24 \\ &= 48\ \text{m}^2 \end{aligned}$$

$$\begin{aligned} SA_{\text{rectangular prism}} &= 30+40+48 \\ &= 118\ \text{m}^2 \end{aligned}$$

Step 3
Calculate the surface area of the right triangular prism.
There is no bottom to this figure because it sits on the right rectangular prism. The bottom is part of the overlapped region.

$$\begin{aligned} A_{\text{lateral faces}} &= 2(lw) \\ &= 2(8\times 4) \\ &= 2\times 32 \\ &= 64\ \text{m}^2 \end{aligned}$$

$$\begin{aligned} A_{\text{triangular faces}} &= 2\left(\frac{bh}{2}\right) \\ &= b\times h \\ &= 5\times 3 \\ &= 15\ \text{m}^2 \end{aligned}$$

$$\begin{aligned} SA_{\text{triangular prism}} &= 64+15 \\ &= 79\ \text{m}^2 \end{aligned}$$

Step 4
Calculate the total surface area of the composite 3-D object.
Add the surface areas of the rectangular prism and the triangular prism together.

$$\begin{aligned} SA_{\text{composite object}} &= SA_{\text{rectangular prism}} + SA_{\text{triangular prism}} \\ &= 118+79 \\ &= 197\ \text{m}^2 \end{aligned}$$

NOTES

Your Turn 1

Calculate the total surface area of the following composite 3-D object by adding only the exposed faces of each individual prism.

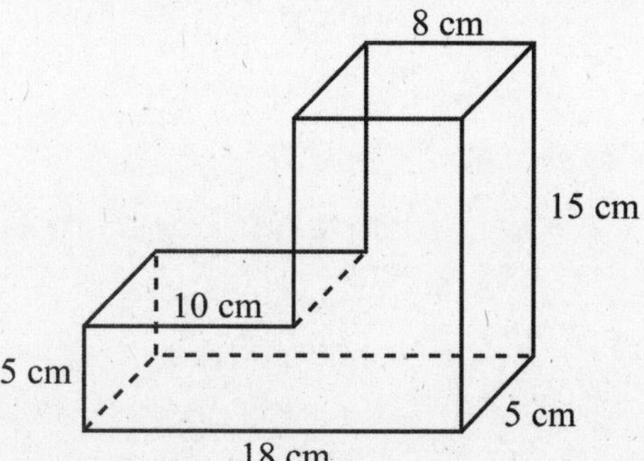

Example

Jason wants to build a miniature version of a design for a skateboard ramp proposed for his local skate park. He needs to calculate the surface area of the structure. Given the composite 3-D object, calculate the total surface area of the structure by subtracting any overlap.

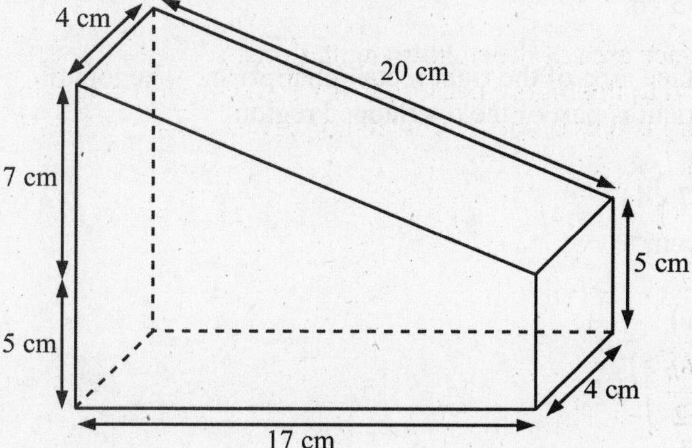

Solution

Step 1

Break the composite 3-D object into a right triangular prism and right rectangular prism.

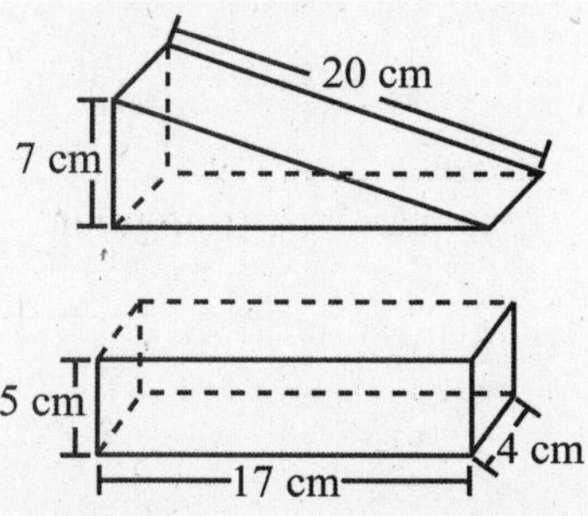

NOTES

Step 2
Calculate the surface area of the right triangular prism. The bottom of the triangular prism is part of the overlapped region.

$$\begin{aligned} A_{\text{front and back}} &= 2\left(\frac{bh}{2}\right) \\ &= 2\left(\frac{17 \times 7}{2}\right) \\ &= 119 \text{ cm}^2 \end{aligned}$$

$$\begin{aligned} A_{\text{side}} &= lw \\ &= 4 \times 7 \\ &= 28 \text{ cm}^2 \end{aligned}$$

$$\begin{aligned} A_{\text{top}} &= lw \\ &= 4 \times 20 \\ &= 80 \text{ cm}^2 \end{aligned}$$

$$\begin{aligned} A_{\text{bottom}} &= lw \\ &= 17 \times 4 \\ &= 68 \text{ cm}^2 \end{aligned}$$

$$\begin{aligned} SA_{\text{triangular prism}} &= 119 + 28 + 80 + 68 \\ &= 295 \text{ cm}^2 \end{aligned}$$

Step 3
Calculate the surface area of the right rectangular prism. The top of the rectangular prism is part of the overlapped region

$$\begin{aligned} A_{\text{top and bottom}} &= 2(lw) \\ &= 2(17 \times 4) \\ &= 136 \text{ cm}^2 \end{aligned}$$

$$\begin{aligned} A_{\text{front and back}} &= 2(lw) \\ &= 2(17 \times 5) \\ &= 2(85) \\ &= 170 \text{ cm}^2 \end{aligned}$$

$$\begin{aligned} A_{\text{left and right}} &= 2(lw) \\ &= 2(4 \times 5) \\ &= 2(20) \\ &= 40 \text{ cm}^2 \end{aligned}$$

$$\begin{aligned} SA_{\text{rectangular prism}} &= 136 + 170 + 40 \\ &= 346 \text{ cm}^2 \end{aligned}$$

NOTES

Step 4
Calculate the areas of the overlapped regions.
The pieces that overlap are the top of the rectangular prism and the bottom of the right triangular prism. This region is rectangular in shape.

$$\begin{aligned} A_{\text{overlap}} &= 2(lw) \\ &= 2(17 \times 4) \\ &= 2(68) \\ &= 136 \text{ cm}^2 \end{aligned}$$

Step 5
Calculate the total surface area of the composite 3-D object.
Add the surface areas of the two prisms and subtract the area of overlap.

$$\begin{aligned} SA_{\text{composite object}} &= SA_{\text{triangular prism}} + SA_{\text{rectangular prism}} - A_{\text{overlap}} \\ &= 295 + 346 - 136 \\ &= 505 \text{ cm}^2 \end{aligned}$$

Your Turn 2

Given the composite 3-D object, calculate the total surface area of the structure by subtracting any overlap.

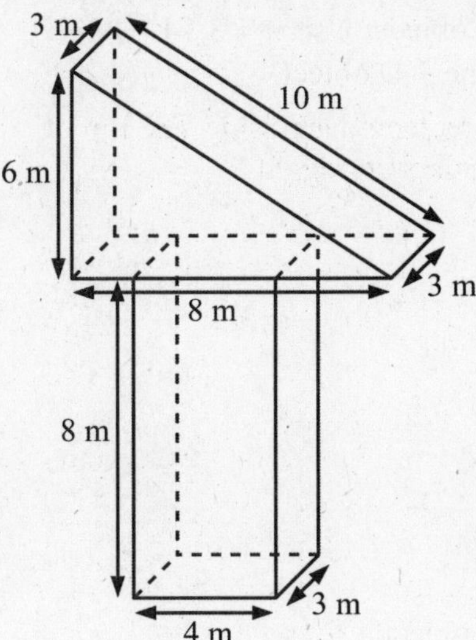

NOTES

When a composite 3-D object contains a missing piece (that is in the shape of a recognizable 3-D object), the surface area must be calculated using a slightly different method. Think of surface area as anything that air can touch. Air can go right through the centre of this object. So, the entire centre surface must be included in the surface area.

Follow these steps to calculate the total surface area of a composite 3-D object that contains a missing piece:

Step 1
Calculate the surface area of the larger object.

Step 2
Calculate the area of the bases of the missing object.

Step 3
Calculate the area of the lateral faces of the missing object.

Step 4
Subtract the area of the bases and add the area of the lateral faces of the missing object to the surface area of the entire object that was calculated in Step 1.

Example

Calculate the surface area of the given 3-D object. Use $\pi = 3.14$. The inner cylinder is a missing portion of the 3-D object.

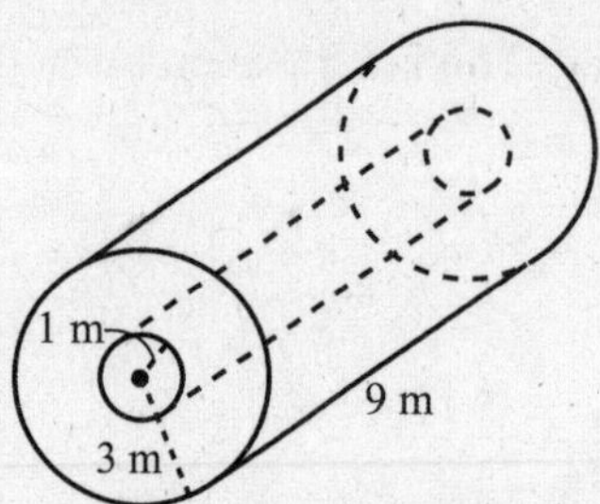

Solution

Step 1
Calculate the surface area of the larger object.
The larger object is a cylinder.

$$\begin{aligned} SA_{\text{large cylinder}} &= 2\pi r^2 + 2\pi rh \\ &= 2(3.14 \times 3^2) + 2(3.14 \times 3 \times 9) \\ &= 2(3.14 \times 9) + 2(84.78) \\ &= 2(28.26) + 2(84.78) \\ &= 56.52 + 169.56 \\ &= 226.08 \text{ m}^2 \end{aligned}$$

NOTES

Step 2
Calculate the area of the bases of the missing object.
The bases of the smaller cylinder are circular in shape.

$$\begin{aligned} A_{\text{bases}} &= 2\pi r^2 \\ &= 2(3.14)(1^2) \\ &= 6.28 \text{ m}^2 \end{aligned}$$

Step 3
Calculate the area of the lateral face of the missing object.
The length of the cylinder is rectangular in shape.

$$\begin{aligned} A_{\text{lateral face}} &= 2\pi rh \\ &= 2(3.14)(1)(9) \\ &= 56.52 \text{ m}^2 \end{aligned}$$

Step 4
Calculate the surface area of the entire 3-D object including the missing piece.

Subtract the area of the bases and add the area of the lateral faces of the missing object to the surface area of the entire object.

$$\begin{aligned} SA_{\text{entire object}} &= SA_{\text{large cylinder}} - A_{\text{bases}} + A_{\text{lateral face}} \\ &= 226.08 - 6.28 + 56.52 \\ &= 276.32 \text{ m}^2 \end{aligned}$$

Your Turn 3

Calculate the surface area of the given 3-D object. The inner prism is a missing portion of the 3-D object.

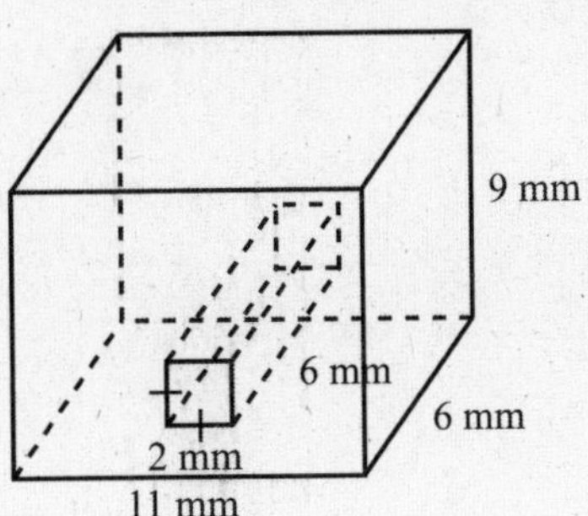

PRACTICE EXERCISES

Calculate the surface area of the given composite 3-D objects by adding only the exposed faces of each individual prism.

1.

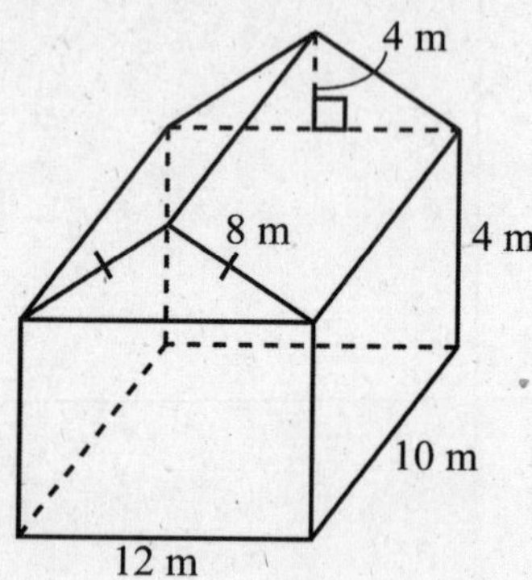

2.

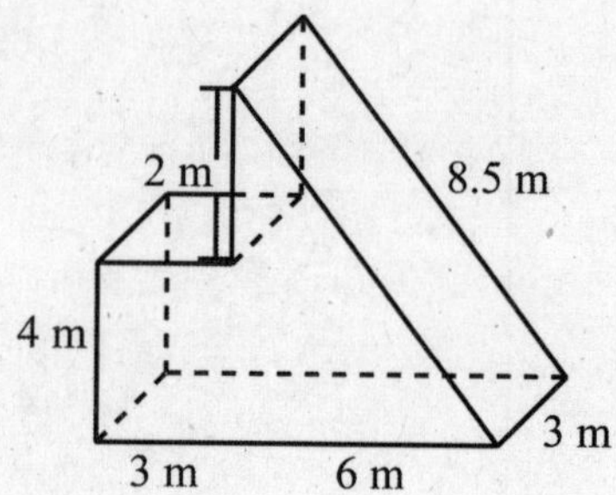

3.

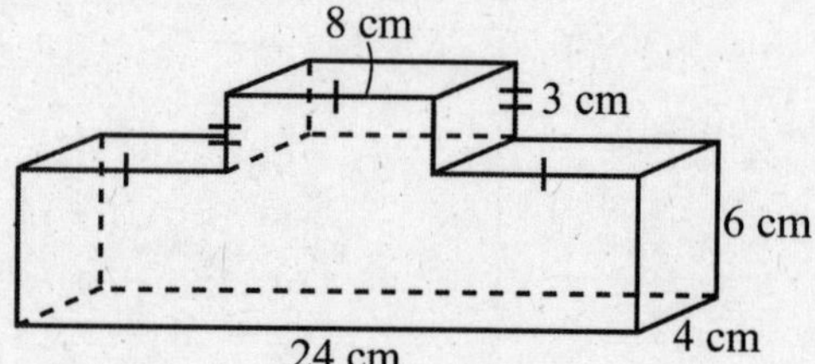

Calculate the surface area of the given composite 3-D objects by subtracting any overlap.

4.

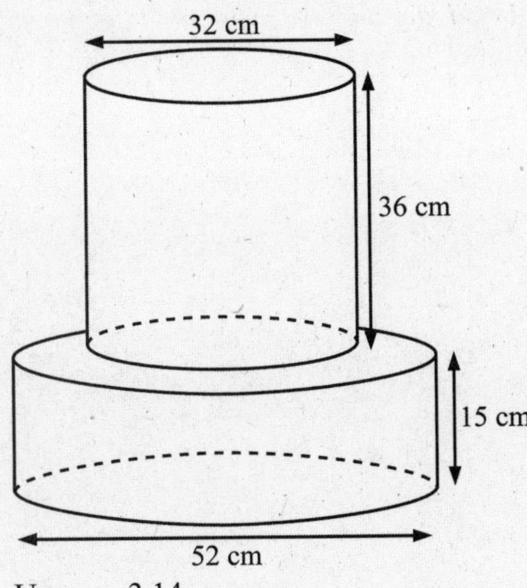

Use $\pi = 3.14$.

5.

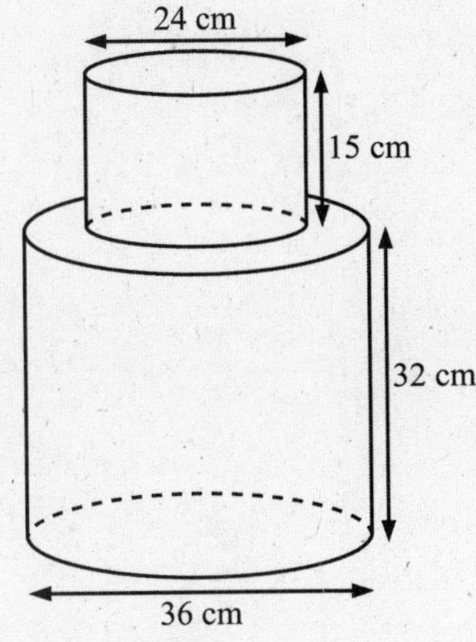

Use $\pi = 3.14$.

Find the total surface area of the given 3-D objects. The inner prism is a missing portion of the 3-D object.

6.

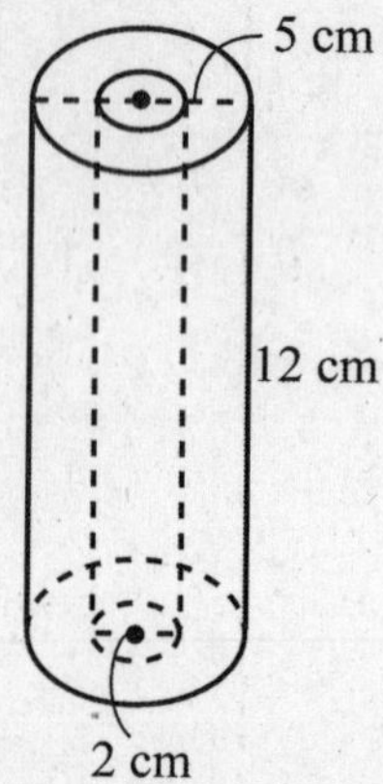

7.

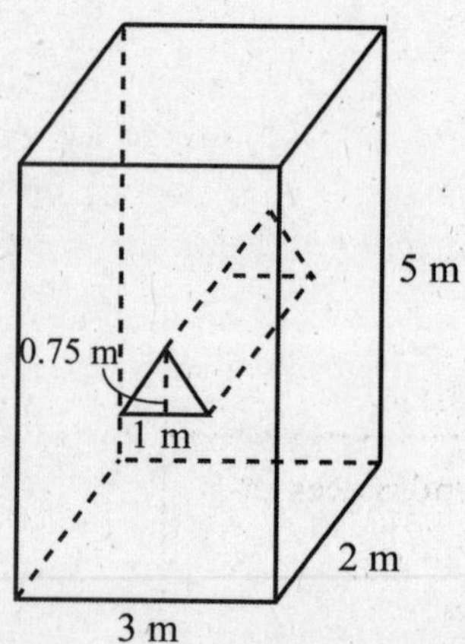

(The base of the right triangular prism is an equilateral triangle.)

Use the following information to answer the next question.

A table in the fast-food section of a shopping mall is constructed by using three right cylinders, as illustrated in the following diagram.

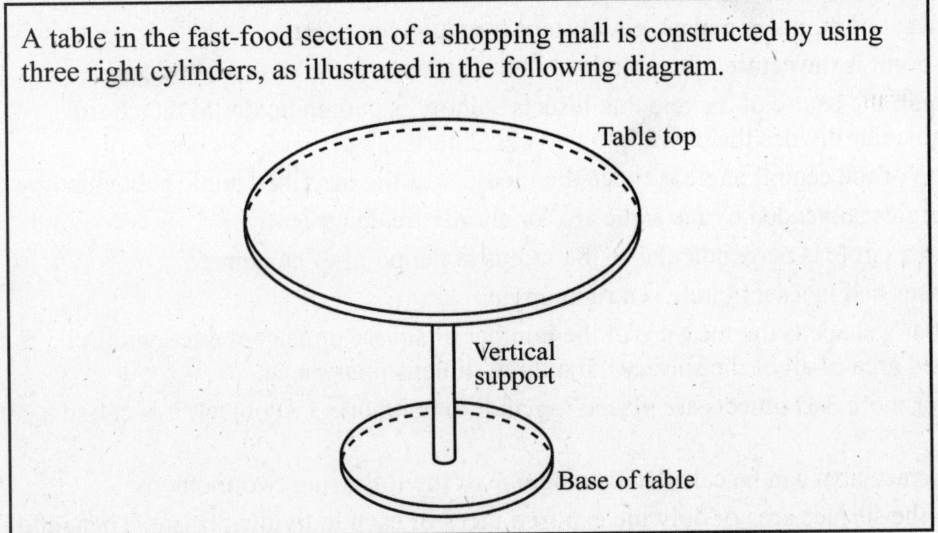

8. The table top is 150 cm in diameter and has a height of 3 cm. The vertical support is 8 cm in diameter and has a height of 90 cm. The base of the table is 80 cm in diameter and has a height of 4 cm. To the nearest whole number, what is the surface area of the table? Use $\pi = 3.14$.

Use the following information to answer the next question.

A device used for weight training has a cylindrical handle and end pieces in the shape of square based right prisms, as shown.

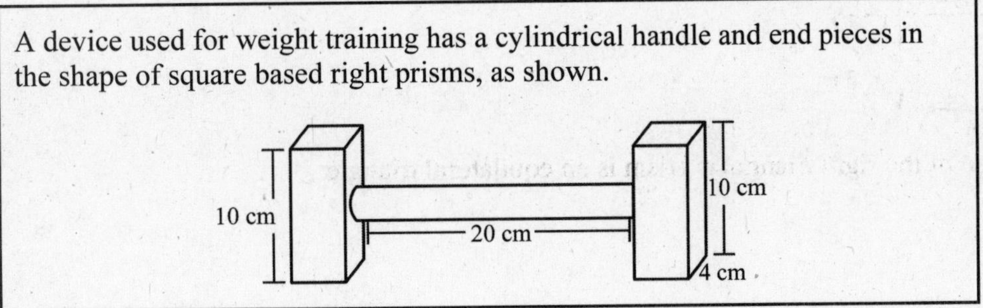

9. The handle is 2 cm in diameter and the base of each end piece has a side length of 4 cm. What is the surface area of the weight-training device, rounded to the nearest tenth of a centimetre? Use $\pi = 3.14$.

REVIEW SUMMARY

- A circle is a set of points in a plane equidistant from a given point.
- This given point is the centre of the circle, and the distance is the radius of the circle.
- A line through the centre of a circle that bisects a chord is perpendicular to the chord. The perpendicular divides the chord into two equal parts.
- The measure of the central angle is twice the measure of the inscribed angle subtended by the same arc.
- Inscribed angles subtended by the same arc (or chord) are congruent.
- A tangent to a circle is perpendicular to the radius at the point of tangency.
- An angle inscribed in a semicircle is a right angle.
- The area of any shape is the measure of the number of square units contained within it. Surface area is the combined area of all of the surfaces of a three-dimensional shape.
- When two or more 3-D objects are placed together to build one 3-D object, it is called a composite 3-D object.
- The total surface area can be calculated using one of the following two methods:
  - Calculate the surface area of only the exposed faces of each individual prism. Then, add up all the surface areas together.
  - Calculate the complete surface area of each individual prism and then subtract the overlapped regions from the final sum of all the areas.

PRACTICE TEST

Throughout the test, letter O indicates the centre of the circle.

1. Use the diagram to give examples of the following.

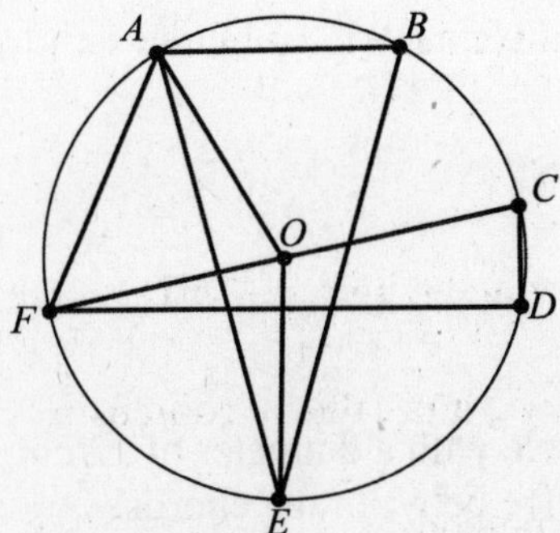

a) one radii

b) two chords

c) one major arc

d) one minor arc

e) one inscribed angle

f) one inscribed angle subtended by arc *CD*

g) one central angle subtended by arc *AE*

h) one central angle subtended by arc *ABE*

Solve for the variable x in each of the following diagrams. Round the answers to the nearest tenth of a unit.

2.

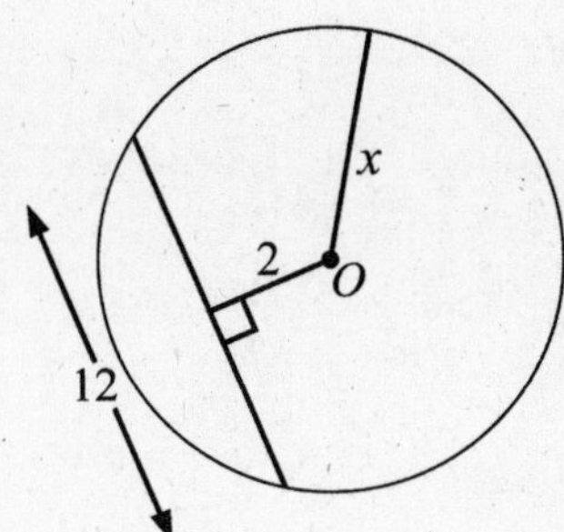

3.

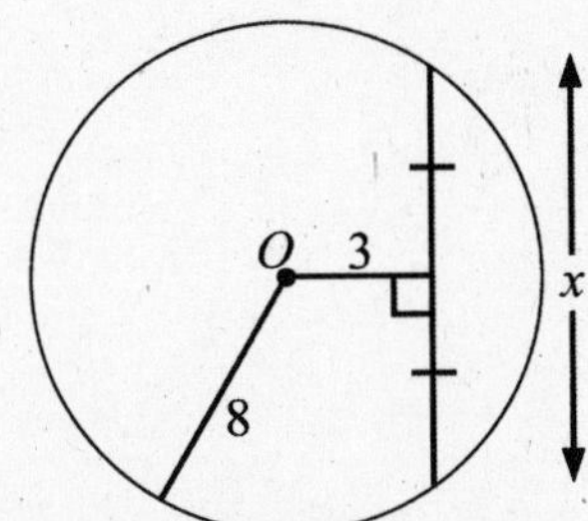

4. A circle has a diameter of 10 cm. A chord is 2 cm from the centre of the circle. Rounded to the nearest hundredth, how long is the chord?

5. Two parallel chords are drawn on opposite sides of the centre in a circle with a diameter of 12 cm. The chords are 6 cm long and 10 cm long. What is the shortest distance between the chords?

6. In the following diagram, $\angle ACB = 165°$. What is the measure of angle θ?

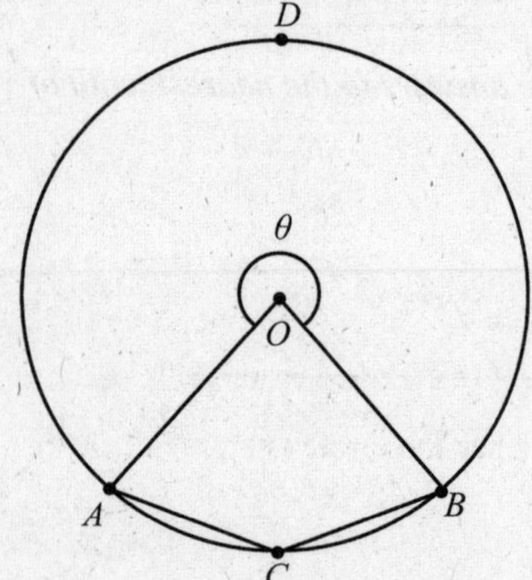

Use the following information to answer the next question.

OM is perpendicular to chord *AB*. The radius of the circle is 7 cm, and the length of chord *AB* is 10 cm.

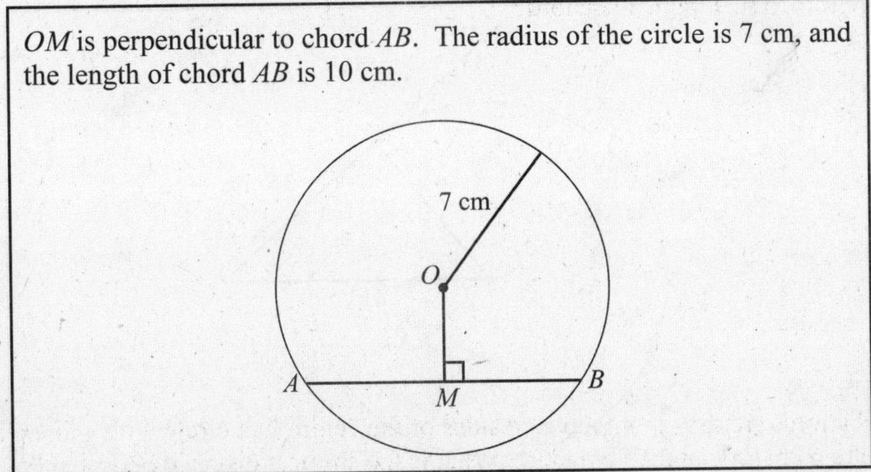

7. Determine the length of line segment *OM* as shown in the given diagram, rounded to the nearest tenth of a centimetre.

Use the following information to answer the next question.

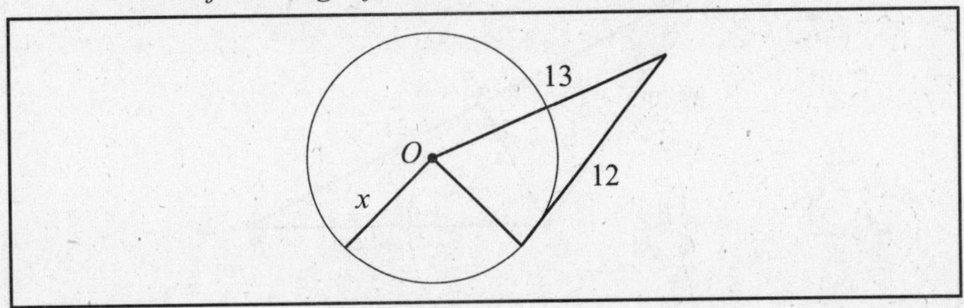

8. Determine the value of x in the given diagram. The line that touches the circle is a tangent line.

Use the following information to answer the next question.

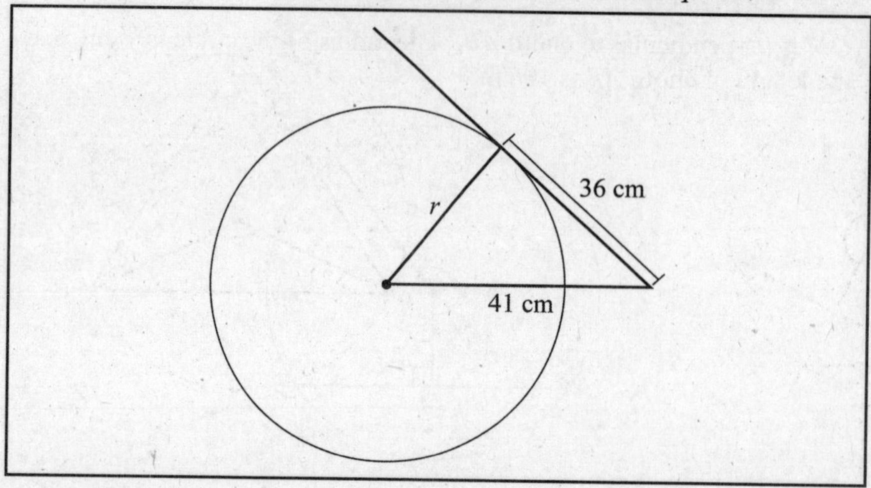

9. The given diagram represents a circle and a tangent line to the circle. To the nearest tenth of a centimetre, what is the length of radius r?

Use the following information to answer the next question.

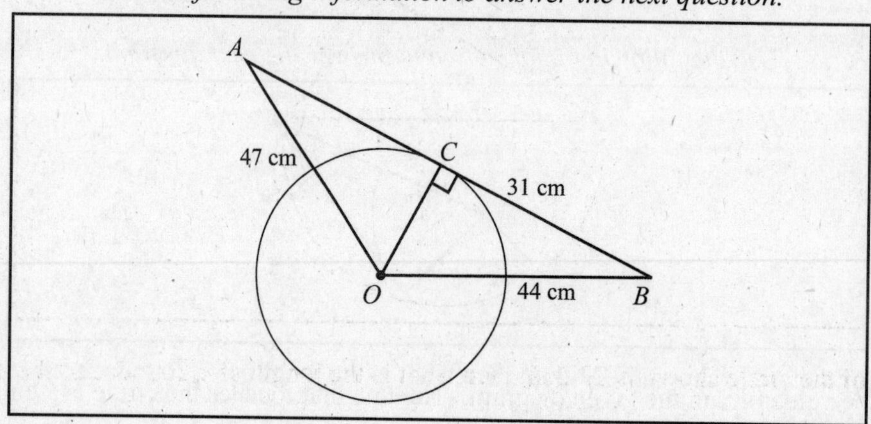

10. Rounded to the nearest tenth of a centimetre, what is the area of ΔAOB ? Line AB is tangent to the circle.

Determine the measure of angle x in the following diagrams.

11.

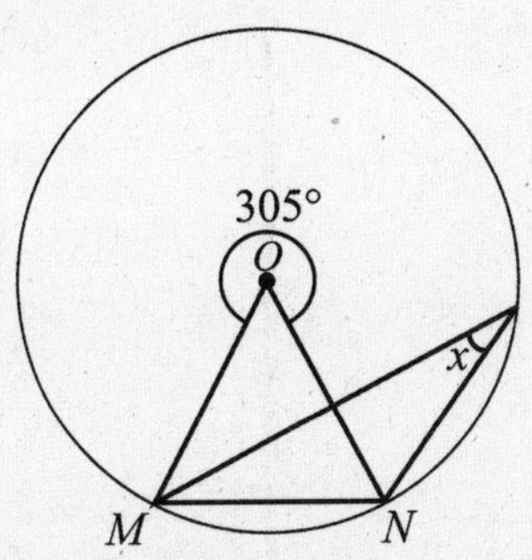

12.

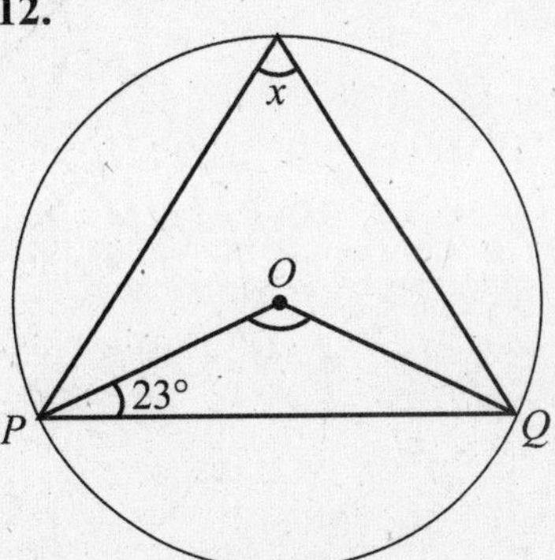

Use the following information to answer the next question.

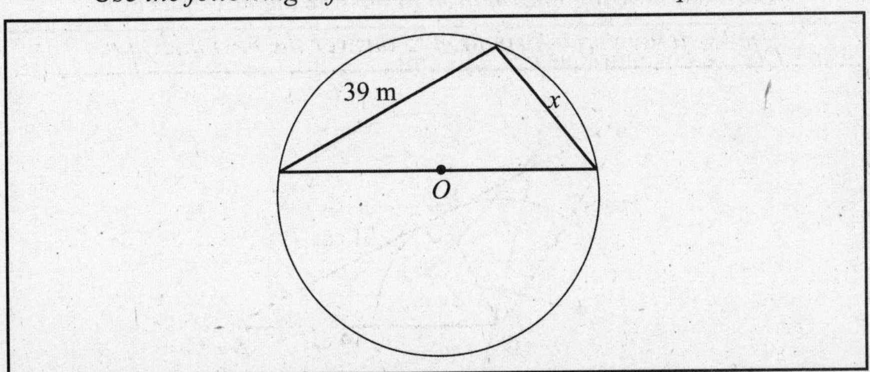

13. If the radius of the circle shown is 23.2 m, then what is the length of x, rounded to the nearest tenth of a metre?

Use the following information to answer the next question.

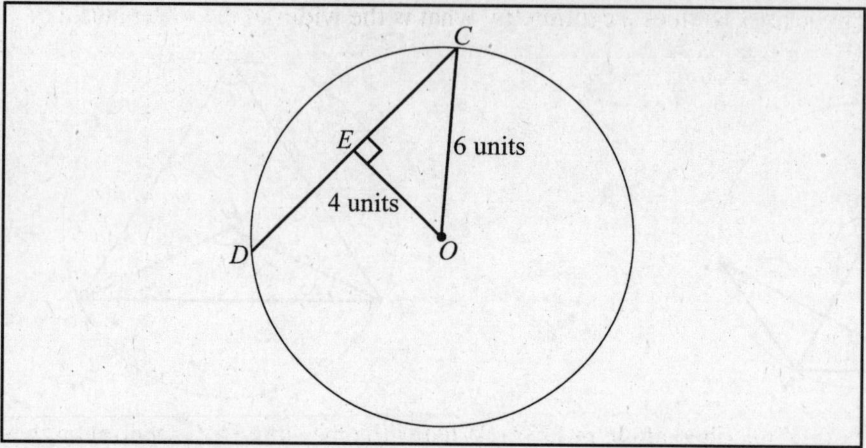

14. What is the measure of chord *DC*?

Use the following information to answer the next question.

Line $OC = 8$ cm and line $CB = 13$ cm.

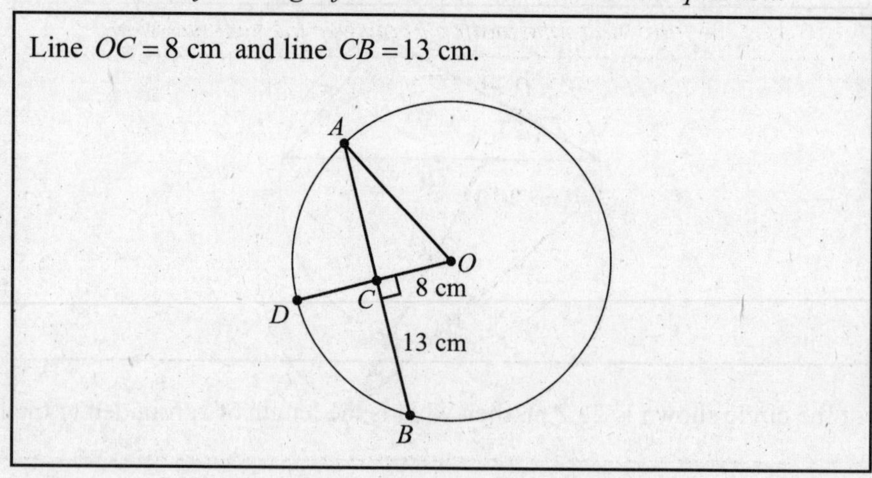

15. What is the length of *CD*, to the nearest tenth of a centimetre?

16. A circular water pipe has a radius of 15 cm. The maximum depth of the water in the pipe is 24 cm. Rounded to the nearest tenth of a centimetre, what is the width of the water surface?

17. The measure of an inscribed angle is $123°$. What is the measure of the central angle subtended by the same arc?

Use the following information to answer the next question.

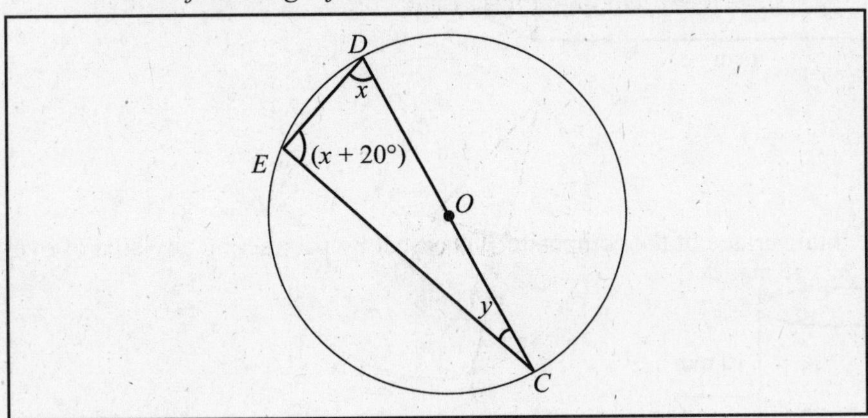

18. What are the values of x and y in the given diagram?

Use the following information to answer the next question.

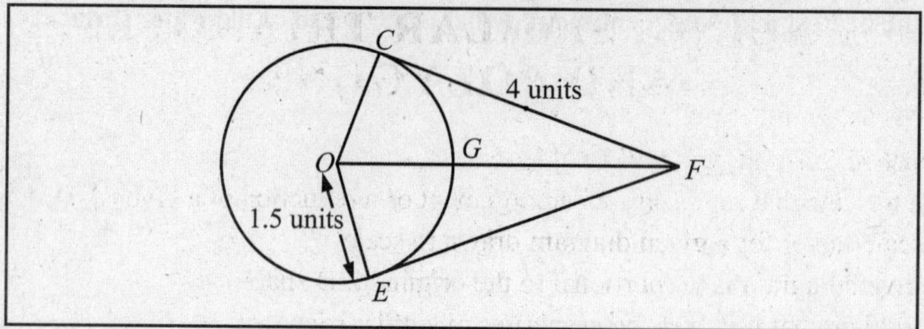

19. To the nearest tenth, what is the length of segment FG?

20. Calculate the surface area of the composite 3-D object by adding only the exposed faces of each individual prism.

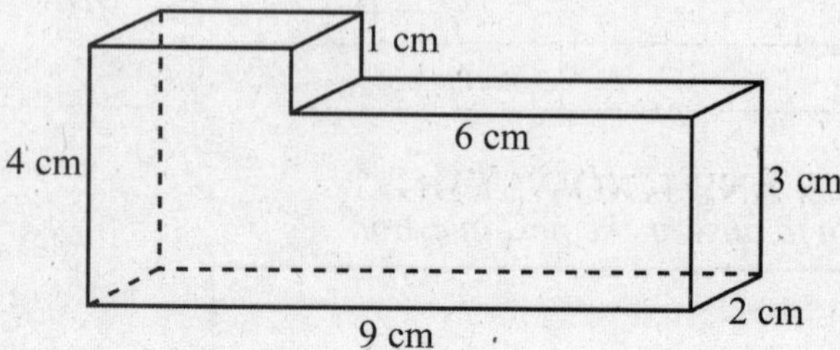

21. Calculate the total surface of the composite 3-D object by subtracting any area of overlap.

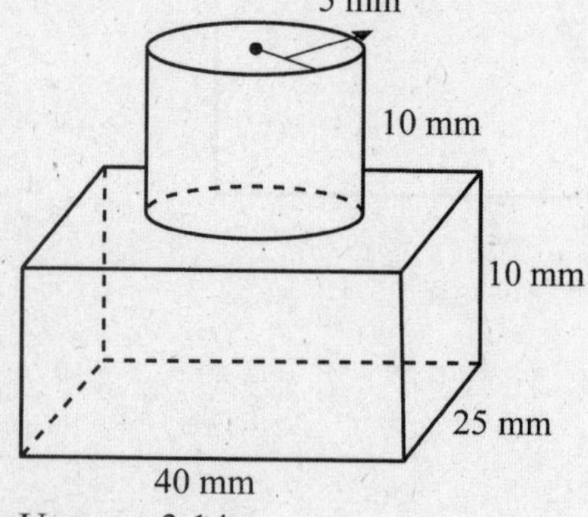

Use $\pi = 3.14$.

SCALING, SIMILAR TRIANGLES, AND POLYGONS

When you are finished this unit, you will be able to…

- draw a diagram to scale that represents an enlargement or a reduction of a given 2-D shape
- determine the scale factor for a given diagram drawn to scale
- determine if a given diagram is proportional to the original 2-D shape
- solve a given problem that involves the properties of similar triangles
- determine if the polygons in a given pre-sorted set are similar and explain why they are similar
- solve a given problem using the properties of similar polygons

PREREQUISITE SKILLS AND KNOWLEDGE

Prior to starting this unit, you should be able to…

- measure angles and line segments
- identify different shapes
- compute simple mathematical operations
- draw shapes
- use cross-products

Lesson 1 SCALING

NOTES

ENLARGEMENTS AND REDUCTIONS

An enlargement or a reduction of a 2-D shape involves taking the shape and making it larger or smaller respectively. The scale factor between the original shape and the new image is a number that tells you how much larger or smaller the shape was made.

If the scale factor is a number greater than one, the shape was made larger. If the scale factor is a number less than one, the shape was made smaller. Consider the following diagram of a triangle that has been enlarged.

$$\text{scale factor} = \frac{\text{image length}}{\text{original length}}$$

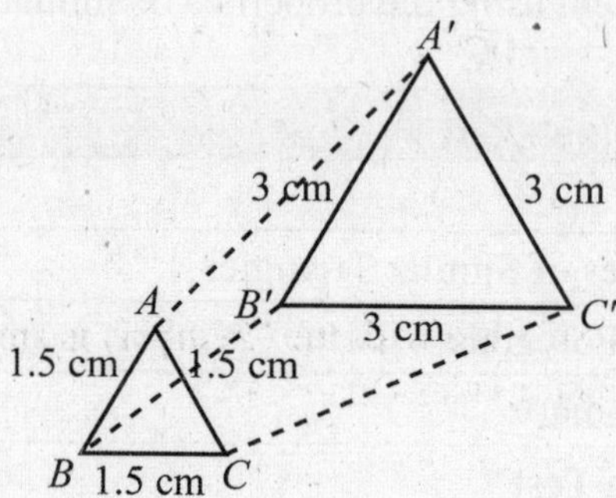

The ′ symbol is called the prime symbol. It is used to show the vertex on an image that corresponds with a vertex on the original diagram. Vertex *A* on the original diagram would be labelled as *A*′ ("A prime") on the image diagram after an enlargement or reduction. Similarly, segment *A*′*B*′ is "A prime, B prime."

The image of the triangle is larger than the original, so the scale factor must be a number greater than 1.

In the original triangle, line segment *AB* is 1.5 cm in length. In the image, line segment *A*′*B*′ is 3 cm in length. The size of the triangle has been doubled, so the scale factor of the diagram is 2.

Use the following steps to find the scale factor of any enlargement or reduction:

Step 1
Pick one known length in the image diagram.

Step 2
Find the corresponding known length in the original diagram.

Step 3
Use the general formula to calculate the scale factor. Divide the known length in the image diagram by the corresponding length in the original diagram.

NOTES

Example

Determine the scale factor used in the following diagram.

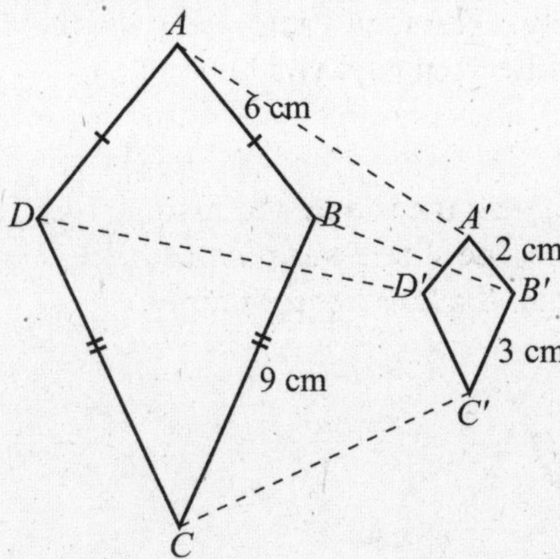

Notice that the image (labelled with the ′ symbol) is smaller than the original, so the scale factor is less than one.

Solution

Step 1
Pick one known length in the image diagram.
Segment $A'B'$ is 2 cm long.

Step 2
Find the corresponding length in the original diagram.
Segment AB is 6 cm long.

Step 3
Use the general formula to calculate the scale factor.

$$\begin{aligned}\text{scale factor} &= \frac{\text{image length}}{\text{original length}}\\ &= \frac{2}{6}\\ &= \frac{1}{3}\end{aligned}$$

Since the scale factor for the diagram is $\frac{1}{3}$, the image diagram is $\frac{1}{3}$ the size of the original diagram.

If the scale factor of a diagram is given and you are asked to find the length of a missing side in the image diagram, take the length of the corresponding side in the original diagram and multiply its length by the scale factor.

NOTES

Your Turn 1

Determine the scale factor used in the following diagram.

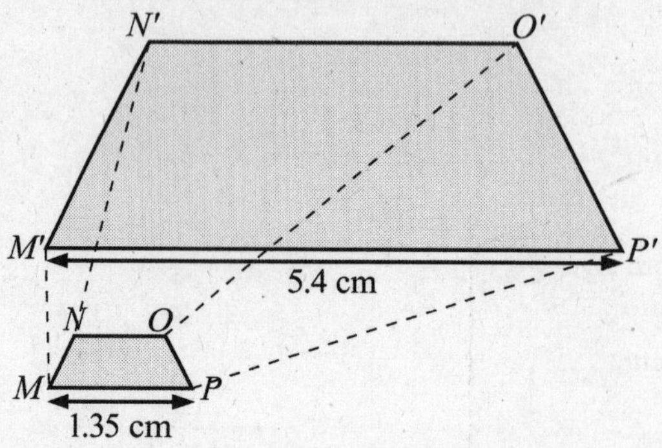

Example

What is the length of side $B'C'$ in the given image?

Scale factor = 2.5

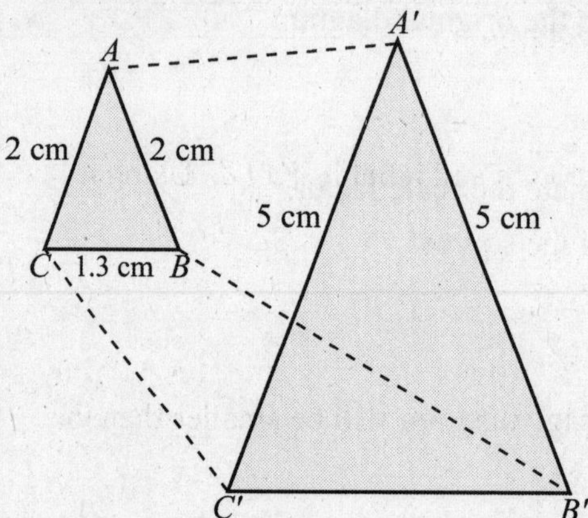

Solution

Side $B'C'$ in the image diagram corresponds to side BC in the original diagram. The length of side BC is 1.3 cm and the scale factor of the image is 2.5.

Multiply 1.3 by 2.5 to determine the length of side $B'C'$.
$1.3 \times 2.5 = 3.25$ cm

The length of side $B'C'$ is 3.25 cm.

NOTES

Your Turn 2

What is the length of side $P'Q'$ in the given image?

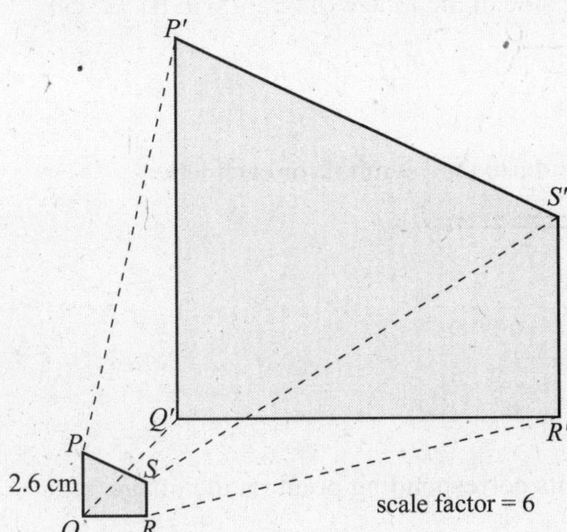

Knowing the scale factor also allows you to draw the image diagram or go backwards and draw the original diagram.

Example

Draw a square with sides measuring 3 cm and label it *WXYZ*. Using a scale factor of $\frac{1}{2}$, draw an image of the square.

Solution

The scale factor is $\frac{1}{2}$, so the image diagram will be smaller than the original diagram.
This is a reduction.

Step 1
Draw and label the original square.

NOTES

Step 2
Determine the length of each side in the image diagram.

Since $3\times\frac{1}{2}=1.5$ cm, each side in the image diagram will be 1.5 cm long.

Step 3
Draw the image diagram and use the ′ symbol for each letter.

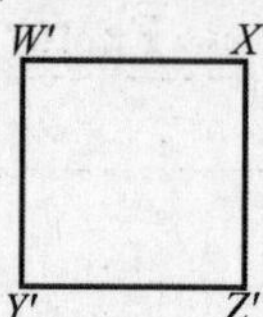

Step 4
Join each original point to its corresponding point on the image, and write the scale factor.

Scale factor $=\frac{1}{2}$

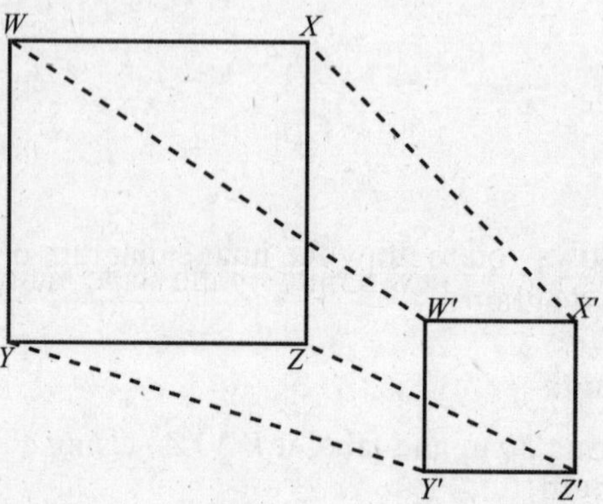

Your Turn 3

Draw a rectangle with a height of 3.5 cm and a length of 1.5 cm. Label it *RSTU*. Using a scale factor of 4, draw an image of the rectangle.

NOTES

Given two of the three relevant numbers, you can find the remaining number, either the original length, the new length, or the scale factor by manipulating the general formula: $\text{scale factor} = \frac{\text{image length}}{\text{original length}}$.

Example

Complete the following table.

	Original Length (cm)	Image Length (cm)	Scale Factor
1.	7	14	
2.		27	$4\frac{1}{2}$
3.	11		0.5

Solution

Row 1

To find the scale factor, divide the new length by the original length.

$$\begin{aligned}\text{scale factor} &= \frac{\text{image length}}{\text{original length}}\\ &= \frac{14}{7}\\ &= 2\end{aligned}$$

Row 2

To find the original length, divide the new length by the scale factor.

$$\begin{aligned}\text{scale factor} &= \frac{\text{image length}}{\text{original length}}\\ 4\frac{1}{2} &= \frac{27}{\text{original length}}\\ \frac{9}{2} &= \frac{27}{\text{original length}}\\ \text{original length} &= \frac{27}{\frac{9}{2}}\\ &= 27\times\frac{2}{9}\\ &= 6\end{aligned}$$

Row 3

To find the new length, multiply the original length by the scale factor.

$$\begin{aligned}\text{scale factor} &= \frac{\text{image length}}{\text{original length}}\\ 0.5 &= \frac{\text{image length}}{11}\\ \text{image length} &= 11\times 0.5\\ &= 5.5\end{aligned}$$

NOTES

The completed table will look as shown:

	Original Length (cm)	Image Length (cm)	Scale Factor
1.	7	14	2
2.	6	27	$4\frac{1}{2}$
3.	11	5.5	0.5

Your Turn 4

Complete the following table.

	Original Length (cm)	Image Length (cm)	Scale Factor
1.	7		32
2.	75	15	
3.		8.1	2.7
4.	14.2		0.4
5.	0.93	93	

SCALE DIAGRAMS

Scale drawings are used when objects are either too large or too small to be drawn on a sheet of paper. Something drawn to a scale means the original object has been reduced or enlarged by a scale factor.

When a scale factor is expressed as a ratio, such as 1:50, it can also be written as a fraction, $\frac{1}{50}$. What this fraction says is that every 1 unit drawn in the image represents 50 units in real-life.

To apply cross products, multiply the numbers that are diagonally across from each other, and divide by the remaining number.

Expressing scale factors as fractions allows you to solve problems involving scale drawings. You may be asked to determine the measure of a particular shape in a drawing or the measure of a particular object in real life.

To solve problems involving scale drawings, set up a proportion and apply cross products in order to calculate the new length.

NOTES

Example

Find the original length of a car that is drawn on a sheet of paper as 6 cm long with a scale factor of 1:35.

Solution

Step 1

Express the scale factor as a fraction.

$$1{:}35 = \frac{1}{35}$$

Step 2

Set up a proportion that represents the situation.
Let *a* represent the length of the original car.

Since 6 is the length of the car in the drawing, it will represent the numerator in the second fraction.

Since *a* represents the length of the original car, it will be the denominator in the second fraction.

$$\frac{1}{35} = \frac{6}{a}$$

Step 3

Solve for *a* by applying cross products.

$$1 \times a = 6 \times 35$$
$$a = 210$$

The car is originally 210 cm in length.

Your Turn 5

A building that is 37 m tall is to be drawn on a sheet of paper. If the scale factor is 1:2 000, how tall is the building in the drawing? Express the result in centimetres.

PRACTICE EXERCISES

1. Complete the following table.

	Original Length (cm)	Image Length (cm)	Scale Factor
a)	10	30	
b)	15		$\frac{1}{2}$
c)		15	$2\frac{1}{2}$

Use the following information to answer the next question.

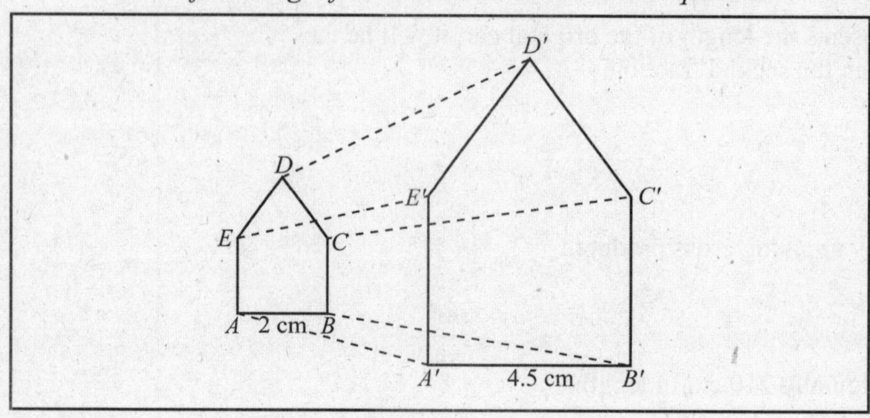

2. What is the scale factor of the given diagram?

Use the following information to answer the next question.

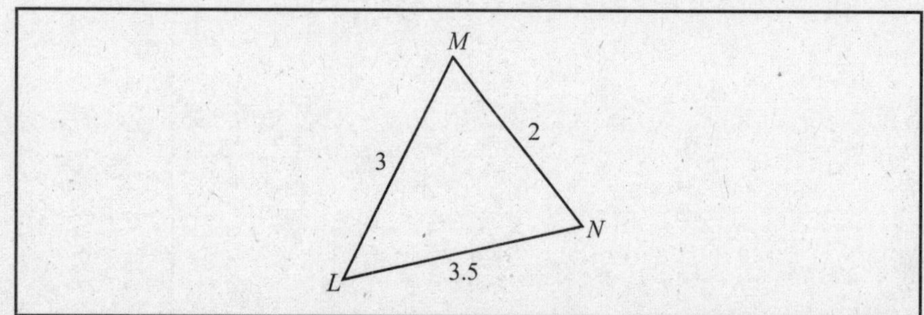

3. If the scale factor is 1:2, what are the lengths of $L'M'$, $M'N'$, and $N'L'$?

4. Draw a rectangle 1 cm by 2 cm and label it *JKLM.* Using a scale factor of 2.5, draw and label the image diagram.

5. If a calf is 0.75 m tall and its mother is 1.5 m tall, what is the scale factor of the height of the calf to the height of the mother?

6. In a drawing, a lamp is 2 cm tall. If the scale factor is 1:125, what is the actual height of the lamp in metres?

7. The scale factor of a drawing of a mosquito is 4:1. If the mosquito is actually 0.75 cm long, how long is it on the drawing?

8. Before being burned, a candle was 40 cm tall. After burning, it was 6 cm tall. What is the scale of the reduction in the height of the candle?

9. Ottawa and Toronto are 363 km apart. If a map has a scale of 1:7 000 000, how far apart are they on the map? Express your answer in centimetres rounded to the nearest tenth.

10. What is the actual height of a tree if it is 3.5 cm tall on a drawing that has a scale factor of 1:255? Express the result in metres rounded to the nearest tenth.

11. A picture is 4.5 cm by 18 cm. If it is enlarged to 27 cm by 108 cm, what is the scale factor of the enlargement?

12. A tulip is 75 cm tall in real life. What is the height of the tulip in a diagram that has a scale factor of 1:25?

13. Edmonton is about 1 500 km from Yellowknife. How far apart are these cities on a map with a scale of 1:20 000 000? Express the result in centimetres rounded to the nearest tenth.

14. Jasper and Lethbridge are 2.6 cm apart on a map with a scale factor of 1:22 000 000. How far is it from Jasper to Lethbridge? Express the result in kilometres.

Lesson 2 PROPERTIES OF SIMILAR TRIANGLES

NOTES

A property is an attribute, quality, or characteristic of something.

PROPERTIES OF SIMILAR TRIANGLES

- All corresponding angles are equal.
- All corresponding sides are proportionately equal in length.

In other words, similar triangles have the same shape, but are not necessarily the same size.

In triangles, corresponding angles refer to the matching pairs of angles that are found in the same place in both triangles. The corresponding sides are the matching pairs of sides found in the same place in both triangles.

For example, consider the following diagram:

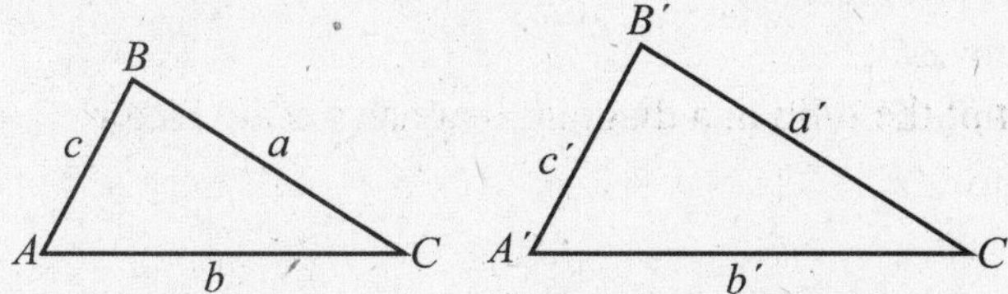

- Angles A and A' are corresponding angles.
- Angles B and B' are corresponding angles.
- Angles C and C' are corresponding angles.

- Sides a and a' are corresponding sides.
- Sides b and b' are corresponding sides.
- Sides c and c' are corresponding sides.

For these two triangles to be similar, it is necessary to prove that the

- corresponding angles are equal, meaning $\angle A = \angle A'$, $\angle B = \angle B'$, and $\angle C = \angle C'$

or

- corresponding sides are proportional, meaning $\frac{a}{a'} = \frac{b}{b'} = \frac{c}{c'}$.

NOTES

Example

Determine whether the following triangles are similar using the property of corresponding angles.

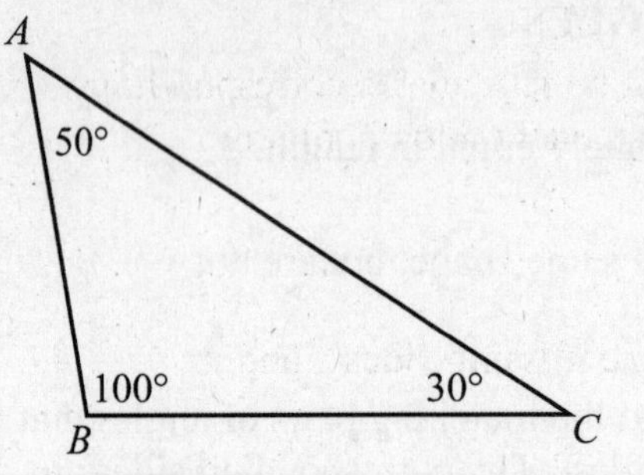

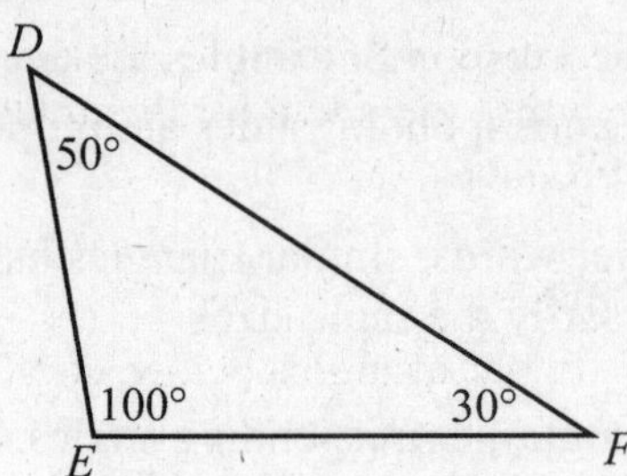

Solution

Identify the corresponding angles.

Corresponding angles are the matching pair of angles that are found in the same place in both triangles.

- $\angle A$ corresponds to $\angle D$.
- $\angle B$ corresponds to $\angle E$.
- $\angle C$ corresponds to $\angle F$.

Since $\angle A$ and $\angle D$ are each $50°$, $\angle A = \angle D$.

Also, $\angle B$ and $\angle E$ are each $100°$, therefore $\angle B = \angle E$.

Finally, $\angle C$ and $\angle F$ are each $30°$, therefore $\angle C = \angle F$.

The corresponding angles are equal; therefore ΔABC is similar to ΔDEF, which can be written as $\Delta ABC \sim \Delta DEF$.

Your Turn 1

Determine whether the following triangles are similar using the property of corresponding sides.

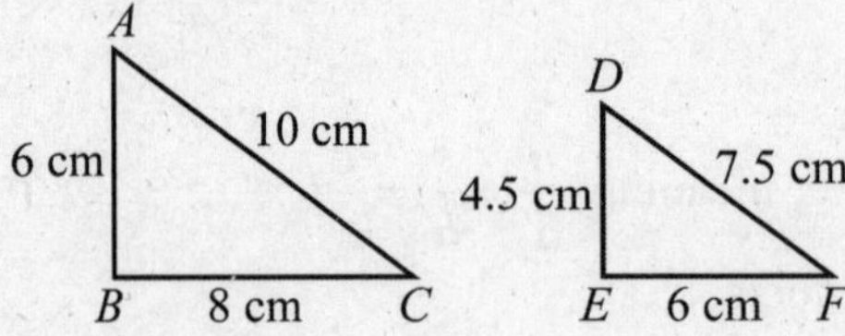

NOTES

PROBLEM SOLVING WITH SIMILAR TRIANGLES

When solving problems involving similar triangles, you may be given a triangle and asked to calculate the unknown sides of another triangle that is similar to the given triangle.

In these cases, you must set up a proportion that equates corresponding side lengths, and solve for the unknown side length by applying cross products.

Example

In the similar triangles below, solve for the missing sides x and y.

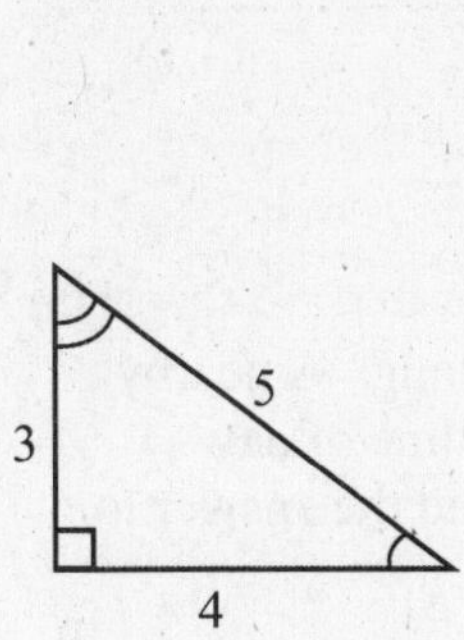

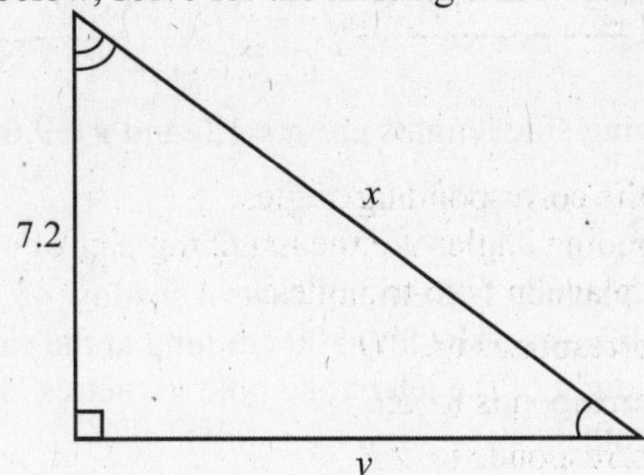

Solution

Step 1

Identify the corresponding sides in both triangles.
Corresponding sides are the matching pair of sides that have the same place in both triangles. The pairs of equivalent angles indicate the pairs of corresponding sides.

- 3 corresponds to 7.2
- 5 corresponds to x
- 4 corresponds to y

Step 2

Write a proportion that represents the ratio of each pair of corresponding sides.

$$\frac{7.2}{3}=\frac{x}{5}=\frac{y}{4}$$

Step 3

Solve for x by applying cross products.
Set up a proportion that involves a ratio where both the numerator and denominator of the fraction are known and where the fraction involves the variable x.

$$\begin{aligned}\frac{7.2}{3}&=\frac{x}{5}\\7.2\times5&=3x\\36&=3x\\\frac{36}{3}&=\frac{3x}{3}\\12&=x\end{aligned}$$

NOTES

Step 4
Solve for y by applying cross products.
Set up a proportion that involves a ratio where both the numerator and denominator of the fraction are known and where the fraction involves the variable y.

$$\frac{7.2}{3}=\frac{y}{4}$$
$$7.2\times 4=3y$$
$$28.8=3y$$
$$\frac{28.8}{3}=\frac{3y}{3}$$
$$9.6=y$$

The missing side lengths are $x=12$ and $y=9.6$.

Your Turn 2

A person who stands 180 cm tall casts a shadow 45 cm long. A nearby telephone pole casts a shadow 300 cm long at the same time of day. What is the height of the telephone pole in metres? Round the answer to the nearest tenth.

PRACTICE EXERCISES

Use the following information to answer the next question.

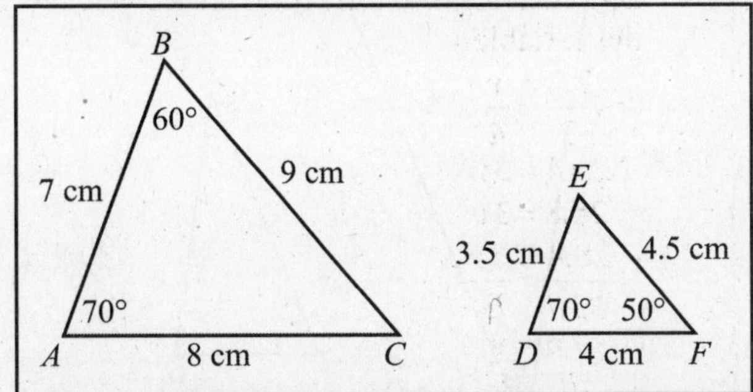

1. Triangle *ABC* and triangle *DEF* are as shown. Is triangle *ABC* similar to triangle *DEF*? Explain your answer.

Use the following information to answer the next question.

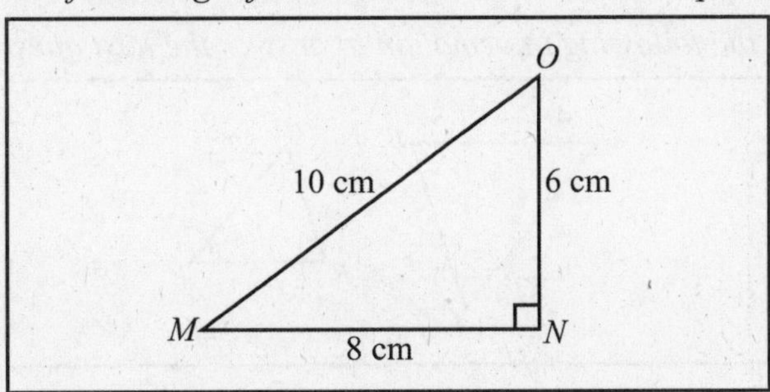

2. Triangle *MNO* is as shown. Draw triangle *PQR* such that triangle *PQR* is similar to triangle *MNO*.

Use the following information to answer the next question.

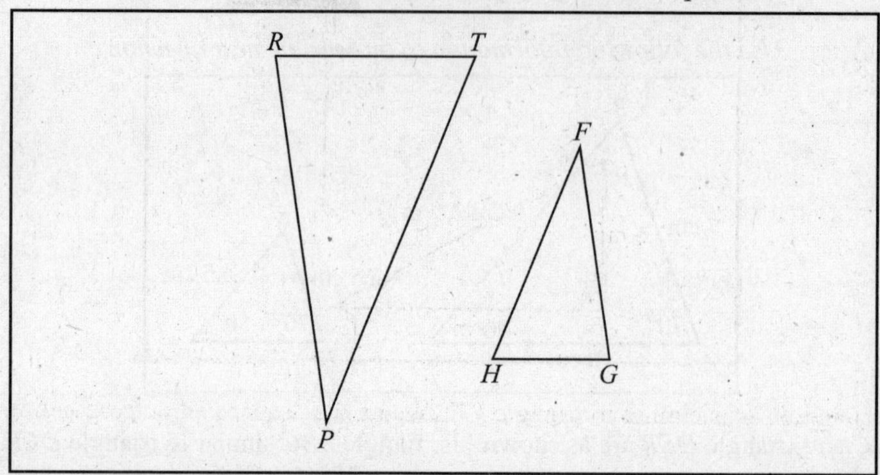

3. If triangle *PRT* is similar to triangle *FGH*, then side *RT* corresponds to which side in triangle *FGH*?

Use the following information to answer the next question.

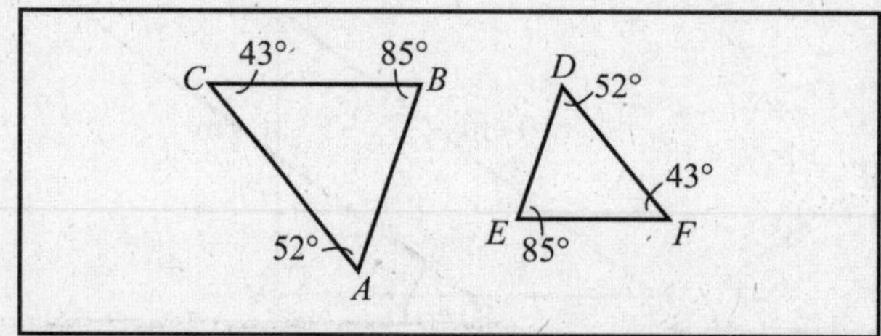

4. Determine whether triangles ΔABC and ΔDEF are similar using the property of corresponding angles.

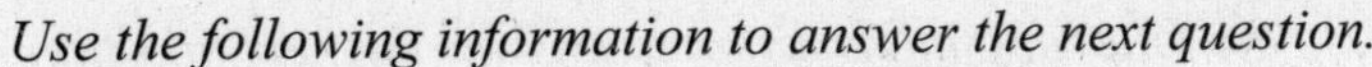

Use the following information to answer the next question.

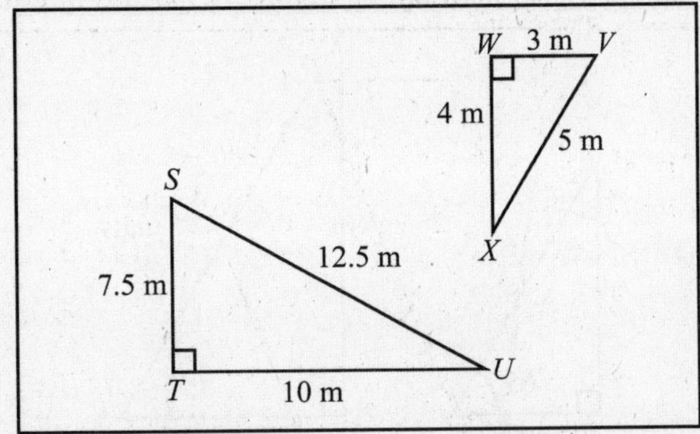

5. Prove that triangle STU is similar to triangle VWX using the property of corresponding sides.

Use the following information to answer the next question.

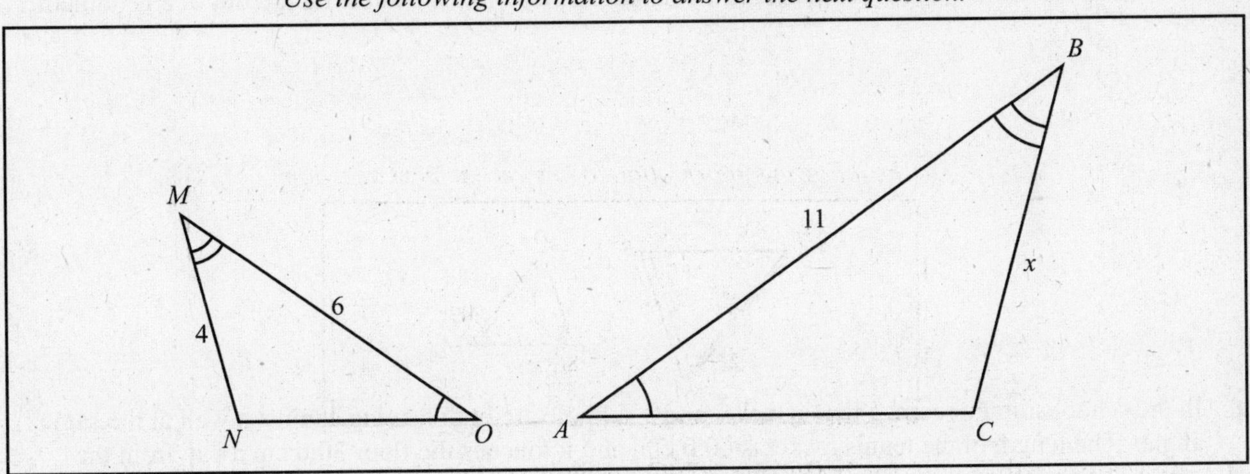

6. For the set of similar triangles, calculate the length of side x to the nearest tenth of a unit.

Use the following information to answer the next question.

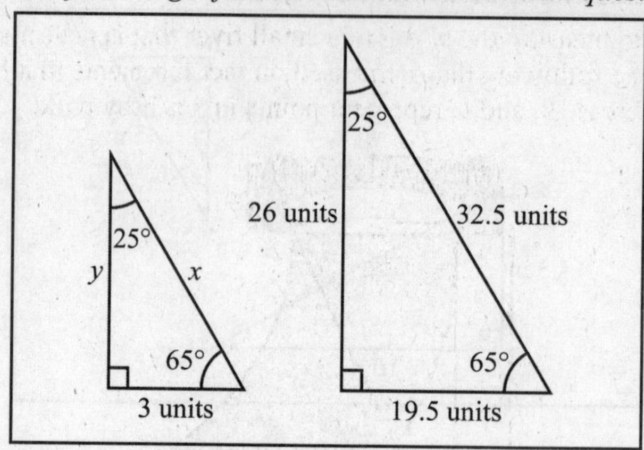

7. What is the length of side x?

8. During an afternoon soccer game, Samira casts a 62 cm shadow and Leah casts a 77 cm shadow. If Leah is 158 cm tall, then what is Samira's height rounded to the nearest hundredth of a centimetre?

9. In the school storage room, a tennis racket and a ski pole are both leaning against a wall at the same angle. The length of the tennis racket is 60.0 cm, and it touches the floor 30.0 cm away from the wall. The ski pole touches the floor 67.5 cm away from the wall. What is the length of the ski pole?

Use the following information to answer the next question.

Jim wants to measure the width of a small river that is near his house. He draws the following diagram based on measurements that he knows, where *A*, *B*, and *C* represent points in a nearby park.

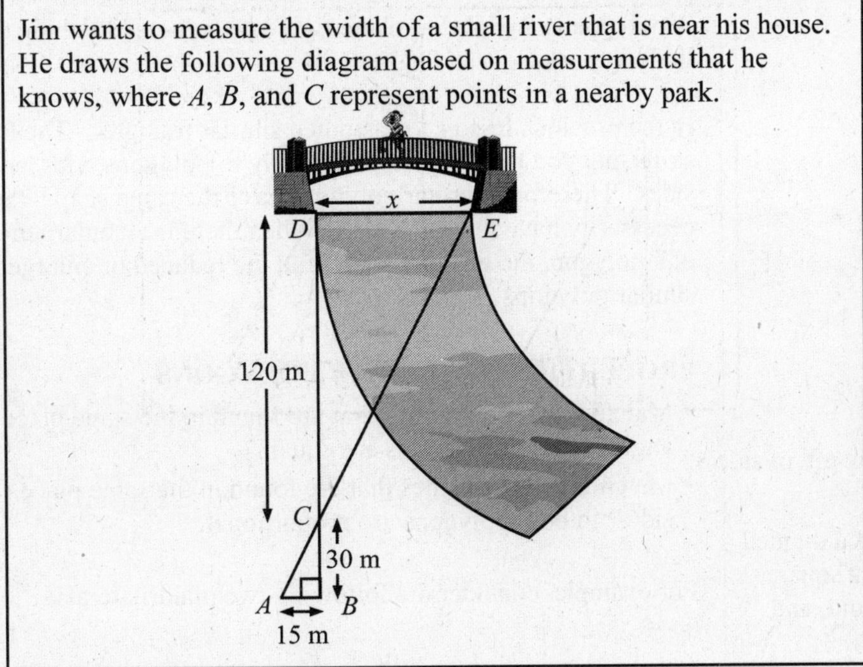

10. What is the width of the river?

Lesson 3 SIMILAR POLYGONS

NOTES

A polygon is any closed plane figure constructed by three or more line segments.

In the previous lesson, you studied similar triangles. The knowledge and skills that you have learned also apply to polygons with more than three sides. Therefore, similar polygons have the same shape, though do not necessarily have the same size. When there is an enlargement or reduction of a polygon, the original shape and the reduced or enlarged shape are the similar polygons.

PROPERTIES OF SIMILAR POLYGONS

- Matching pairs of angles that are found in the same place (corresponding angles) in both polygons are equal.
- Matching pairs of sides that are found in the same place (corresponding sides) in both polygons are proportional.

A quadrilateral is a 4-sided polygon such as a square, rectangle, trapezoid, and parallelogram.

For example, consider the following two quadrilaterals.

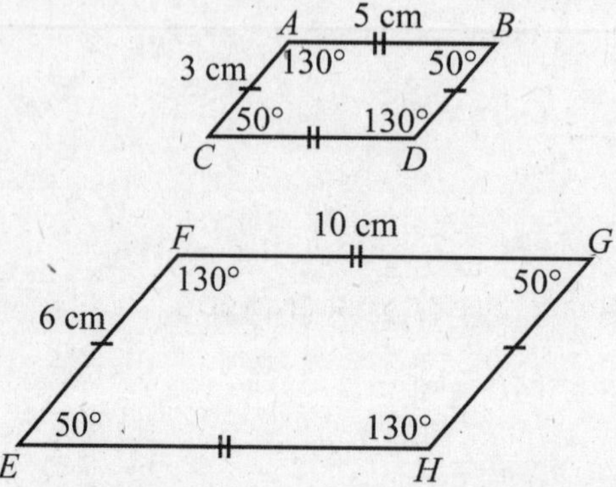

If quadrilateral *ABCD* is similar to quadrilateral *EFGH*, then the corresponding angles of the two quadrilaterals are equal and the corresponding sides are proportional. In particular,

$\angle A = \angle F$
$\angle B = \angle G$
$\angle C = \angle E$
$\angle D = \angle H$

- Side *AB* is proportional to side *FG*
- Side *BD* is proportional to side *GH*
- Side *CD* is proportional to side *EH*
- Side *AC* is proportional to side *FE*

NOTES

Example

Draw a similar polygon to the polygon shown. State the scale factor that you used.

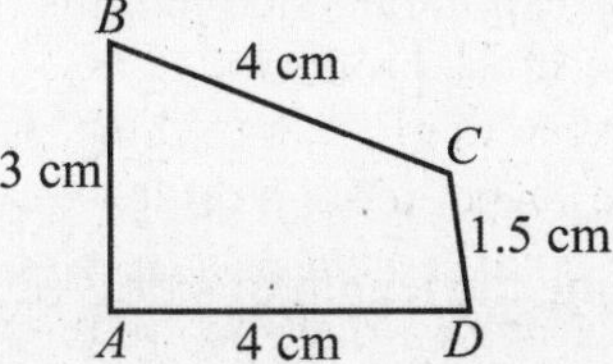

Solution

One possible polygon similar to the given polygon is as shown.
A scale factor of 2 was used.

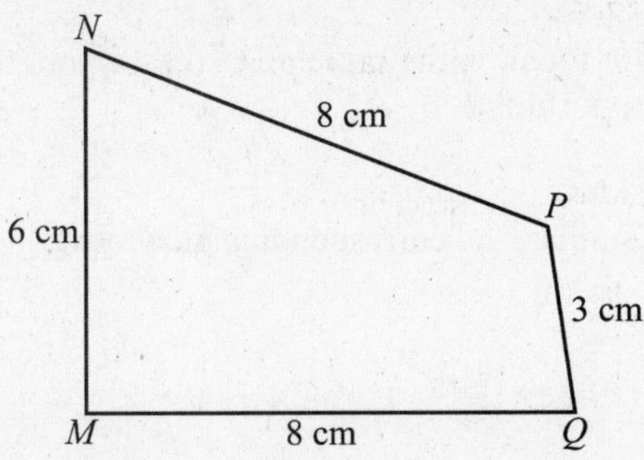

Your Turn 1

Are the following two polygons similar? Justify your answer.

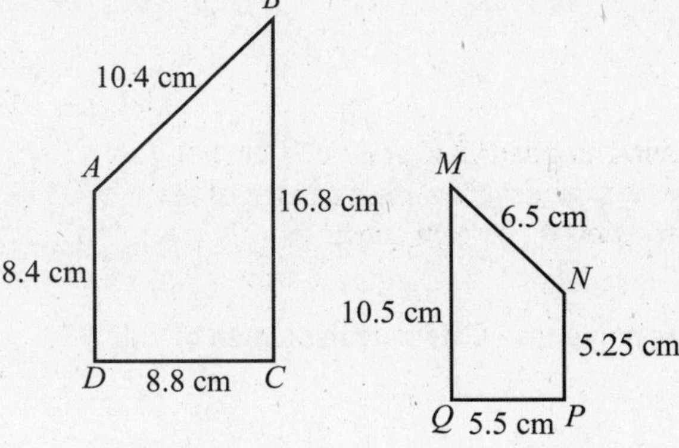

NOTES

When solving problems involving similar polygons, you may be given a polygon and asked to calculate the unknown sides of another polygon that is similar to the given one.

In these cases, set up a proportion that equates corresponding side lengths and solve for the unknown side length by applying cross products.

Example

If the following two polygons are similar, determine the length of side *FG*.

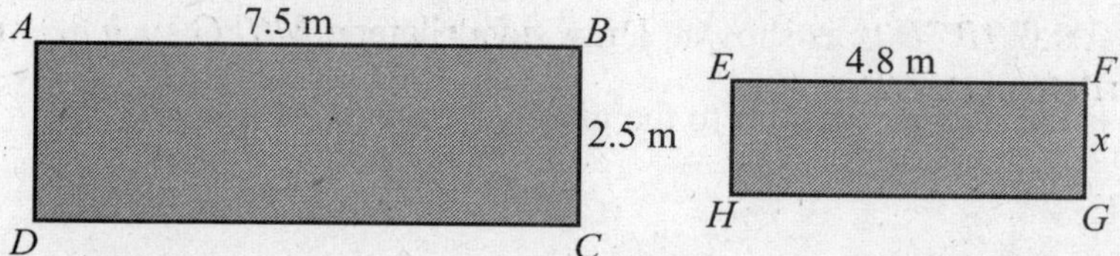

Solution

Step 1

Identify the corresponding sides.

Since the two polygons are similar, the corresponding side must be proportional.

$$\frac{AB}{EF}=\frac{BC}{FG}$$

Step 2

Set up a proportion and solve by applying cross products.

Substitute 7.5 for *AB*, 4.8 for *EF*, and 2.5 for *BC* and solve.

$$\frac{7.5}{4.8}=\frac{2.5}{FG}$$
$$7.5\times FG=2.5\times 4.8$$
$$7.5(FG)=12$$
$$\frac{7.5(FG)}{7.5}=\frac{12}{7.5}$$
$$FG=1.6\text{ cm}$$

Your Turn 2

These two shapes are similar polygons. Calculate the length of side *SR*.

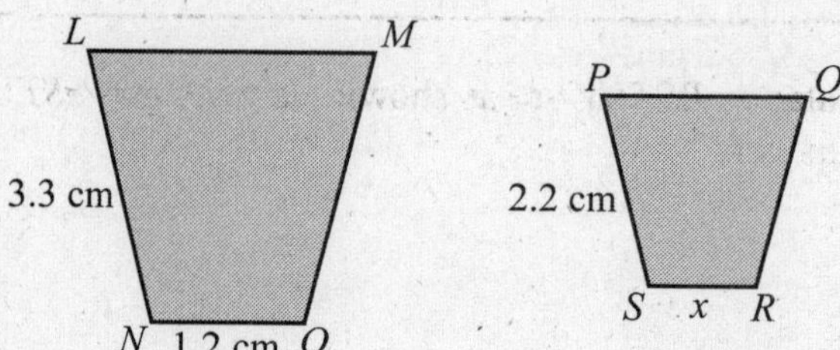

PRACTICE EXERCISES

Use the following to answer the next question.

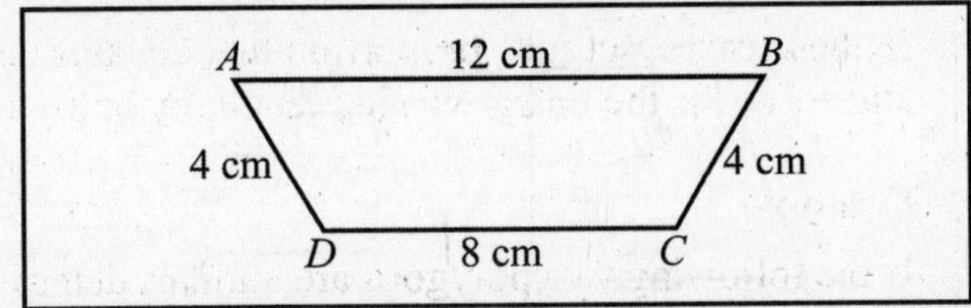

1. Quadrilateral *ABCD* is as shown. Draw quadrilateral *MNPQ* such that quadrilateral *MNPQ* is similar to quadrilateral *ABCD*.

Use the following to answer the next question.

G K 90° $x°$ 110° J 130° H 100° I

V R $y°$ 100° U 110° 130° S 95° T

2. Pentagon *GHIJK* and pentagon *RSTUV* are as shown. Is pentagon *RSTUV* similar to pentagon *GHIJK*? Explain your answer.

Use the following information to answer the next question.

Two similar polygons are as shown.

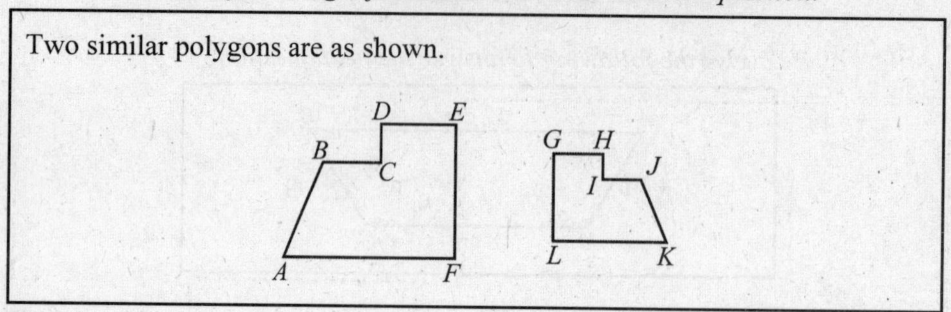

3. Which side in polygon *ABCDEF* does side *HI* correspond to and which angle corresponds to $\angle K$?

4. Polygon *ABCDEF* is similar to polygon *MNPQRS*. If $AB = 24$ cm , $BC = 28$ cm , and $MN = 36$ cm , then what is the length of side *NP* given that side *AB* corresponds to side *MN*, side *BC* corresponds to side *NP*, and a scale factor of 1.5 is used to draw polygon *MNPQRS*?

Use the following information to answer the next question.

Two similar rectangles are as shown.

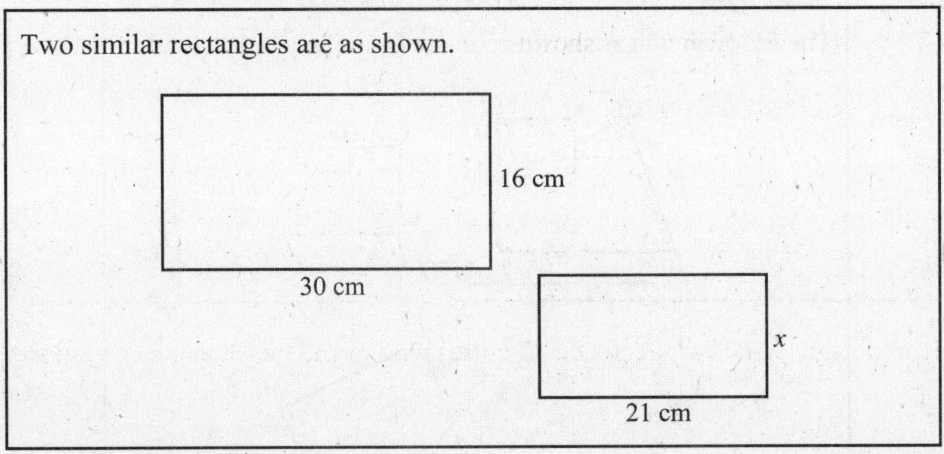

5. What is the length of side x?

Use the following information to answer the next question.

The following diagram illustrates two stained glass windows of similar shape in a church.

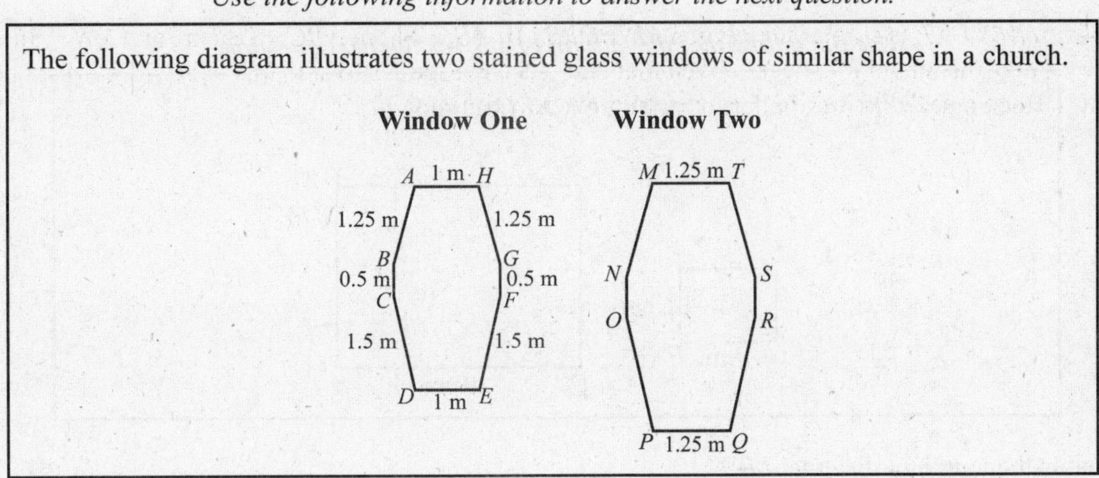

6. The measures of the sides of Window One are known. What is the length of the two shortest sides of Window Two?

Use the following information to answer the next question.

The following diagram illustrates two similar quadrilaterals.

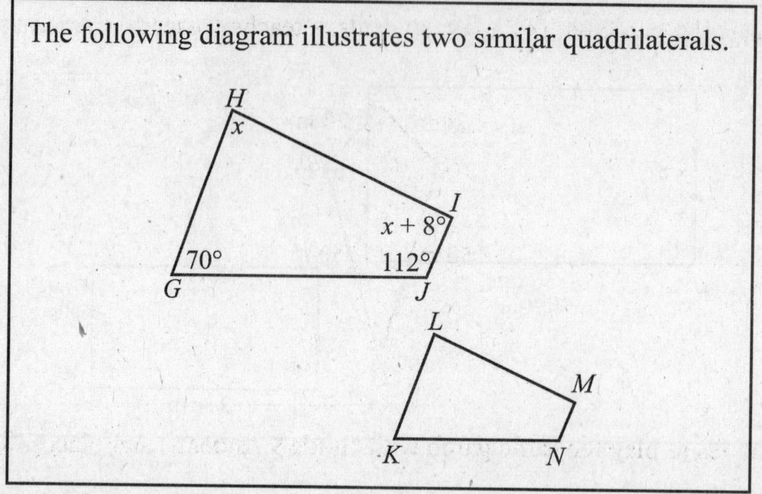

7. Given that the sum of the measures of the angles in a quadrilateral is $360°$, what is the measure of $\angle M$?

Use the following information to answer the next question.

Rectangle *DEFG* is similar to rectangle *MNPQ* as shown.

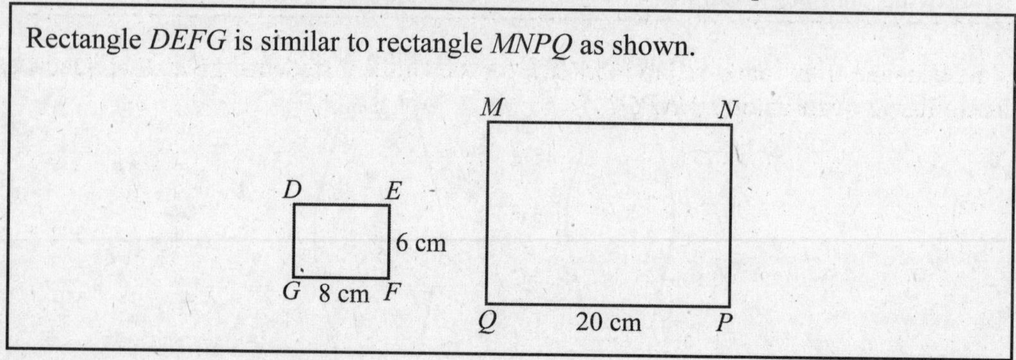

8. What is the length of diagonal *MP*?

Use the following information to answer the next question.

In order to play a particular game with Grade 6 students, a teacher places 4 markers as shown.

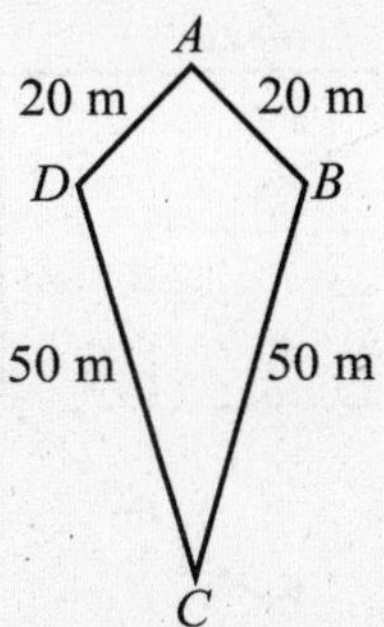

The teacher then decides to play the same game with Grade 9 students, and places the 4 markers as shown.

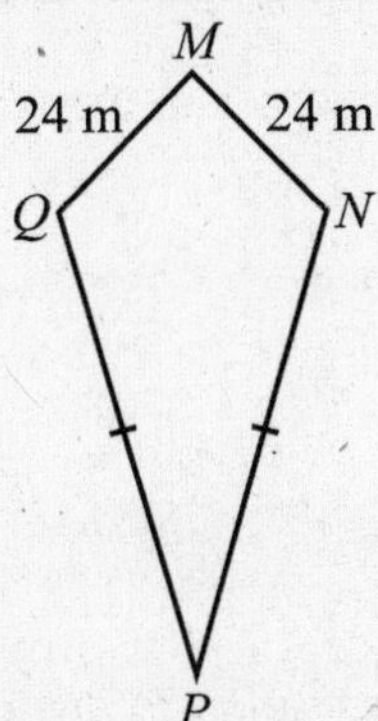

9. What is the distance from marker Q to marker P for the Grade 9 students, given that quadrilateral $ABCD$ is similar to quadrilateral $MNPQ$?

Use the following information to answer the next question.

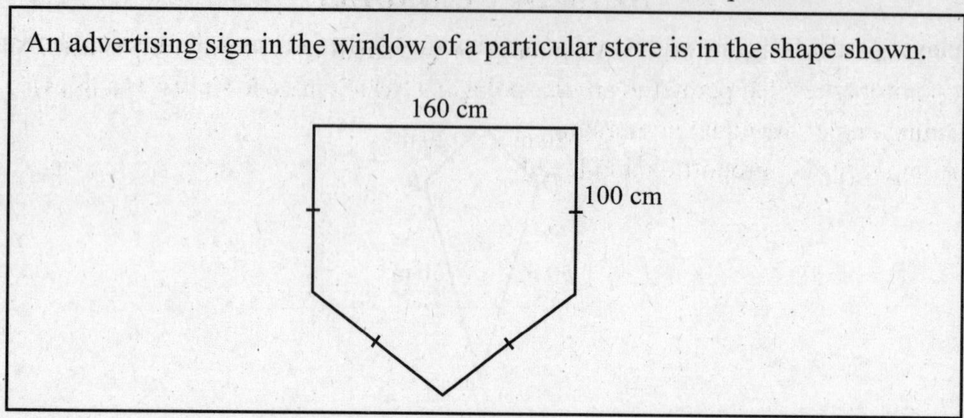

10. In order to attract more attention to the sign, the store owner decides to enlarge the sign. If the owner uses a scale factor of 1.4, what would be the length of the longest side in a sign of similar shape?

REVIEW SUMMARY

- Scale drawings are used when objects are too large or two small to be drawn on a sheet of paper.
- There are two properties that pertain to similar polygons (which include similar triangles):
  - corresponding angles are equal in measure
  - corresponding sides are proportional in length

PRACTICE TEST

1. Complete the following table.

	Original Length (cm)	Image Length (cm)	Scale Factor
a)		32.5	6.5
b)	18		$\frac{1}{3}$
c)	770	77	

Use the following information to answer the next question.

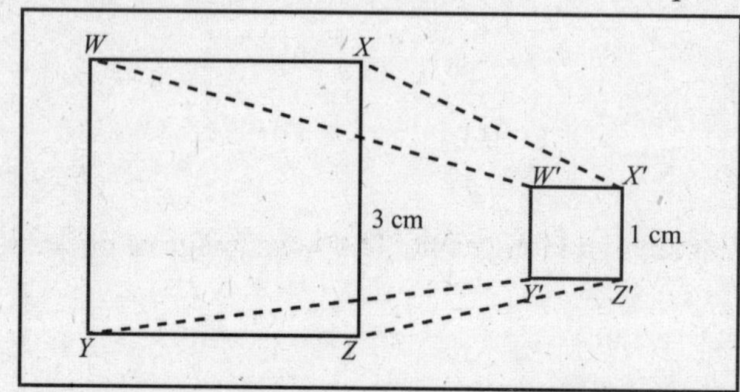

2. What is the scale factor of the given diagram

Use the following information to answer the next question.

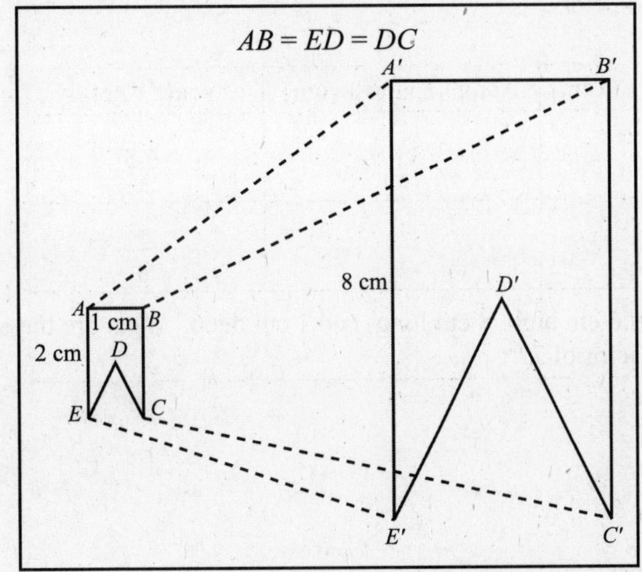

3. For the given diagram, state the scale factor and write the lengths of the sides of the image.

4. Triangle *CAT* has sides that are 6 cm long each. Draw the image of the triangle after a scale factor of $\frac{1}{3}$ is applied.

5. In a drawing, a sofa is 7 cm in length. If the scale factor is 1:50, what is the actual length of the sofa in metres?

6. Winnipeg and Calgary are 7.45 cm apart on a map. If the scale is 1:16 000 000, how far apart are the cities, expressed in kilometers?

7. A drawing of a piano is 6 cm high, 8 cm long, and 1 cm deep. What are the actual dimensions of the piano if it has a scale factor of 7?

8. A person is 162 cm tall in real life. What is the person's height in a picture that has a scale factor of 1:9?

Use the following information to answer the next question.

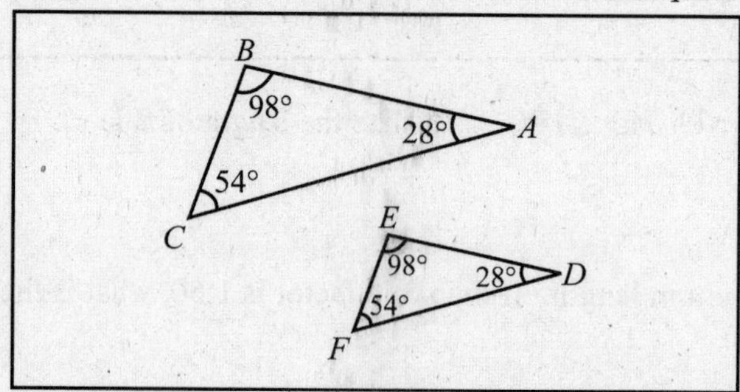

9. Prove that triangle *ABC* is similar to triangle *DEF* using the property of corresponding angles.

Use the following information to answer the next question.

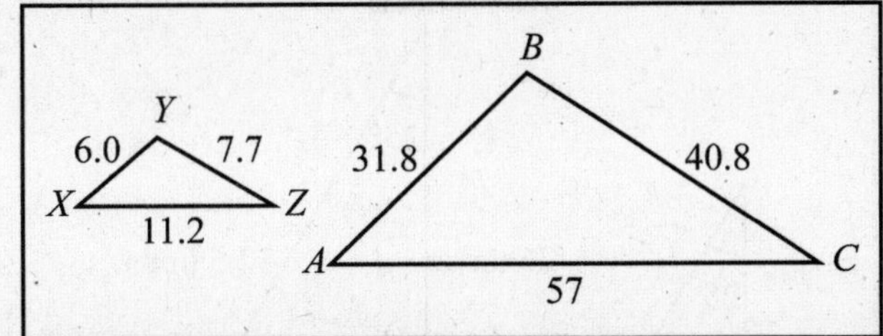

10. Determine whether ΔABC and ΔXYZ are similar using the property of corresponding sides.

Use the following information to answer the next question.

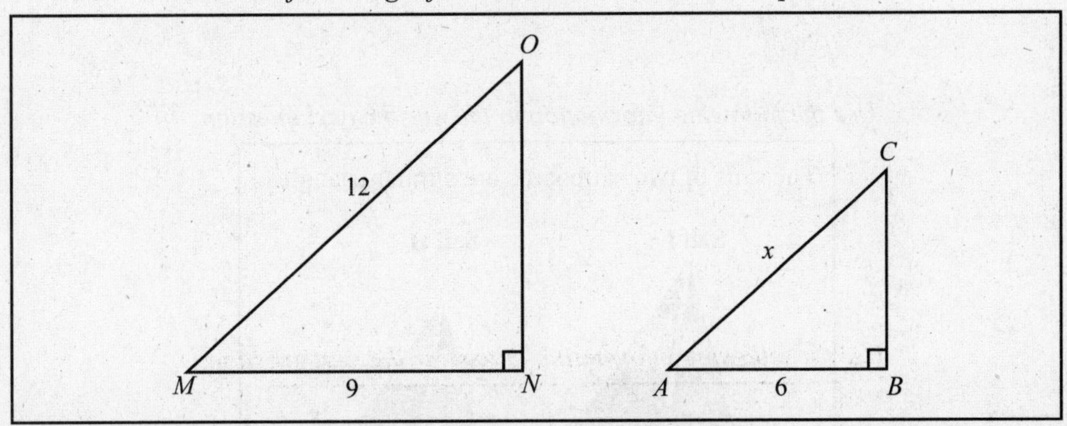

11. For similar triangles ΔMNO and ΔABC, calculate the length of side x.

Use the following information to answer the next question.

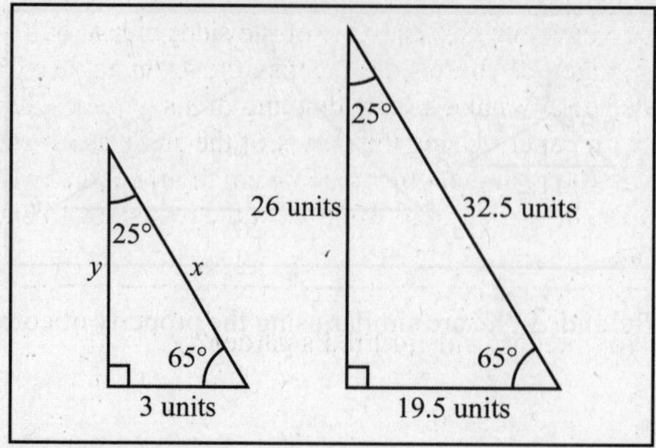

12. What is the length of side y?

Use the following information to answer the next question.

The sails of two sailboards are similar triangles.

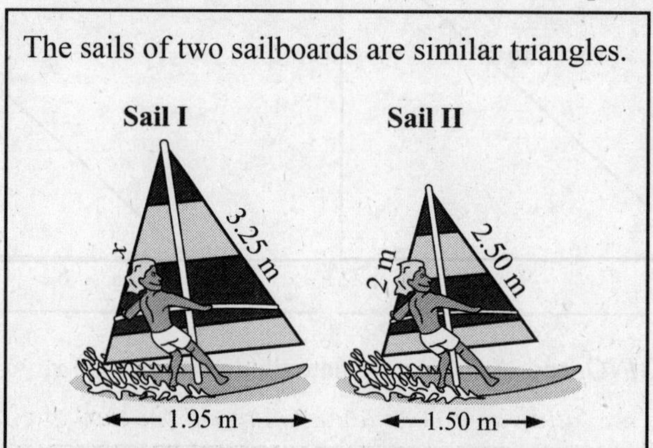

13. What is the length of side x?

Use the following information to answer the next question.

Fred has a triangular vegetable garden. One of the sides measures 10 m and another side measures 12 m; together, these sides meet and form an angle of 50°. To prepare for planting, Fred decides to make a scale drawing of his garden. He begins by drawing a 50° angle on paper. Using the vertex of the angle as his starting point, he marks off one side of 20 cm and another side 24 cm to model the two sides of the actual garden. Finally, he draws a line to connect the two sides. This third line measures 19 cm long.

14. What is the actual length of the third side of Fred's garden?

Use the following information to answer the next question.

A ladder is 6 m long. When it is resting against a wall, the first rung is 30 cm from the bottom of the ladder and 24 cm above the ground.

15. How far up the wall does the ladder reach?

Use the following information to answer the next question.

In parallelogram *ABCD*, $AB = DC = 30$ cm, $BC = AD = 40$ cm, $\angle A = \angle C = 60°$, and $\angle B = \angle D = 120°$. In parallelogram *RSTU*, $RS = UT = 15$ cm and $ST = RU = 20$ cm.

16. What is the measure of $\angle U$ in parallelogram *RSTU*?

The following diagram illustrates two similar polygons.

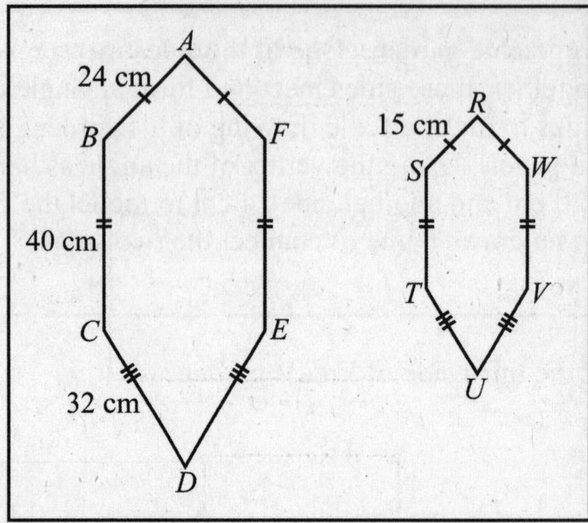

17. What is the length of side ST?

Use the following information to answer the next question.

Quadrilaterals $WXYZ$ is similar to quadrilateral $JKLM$ as shown.

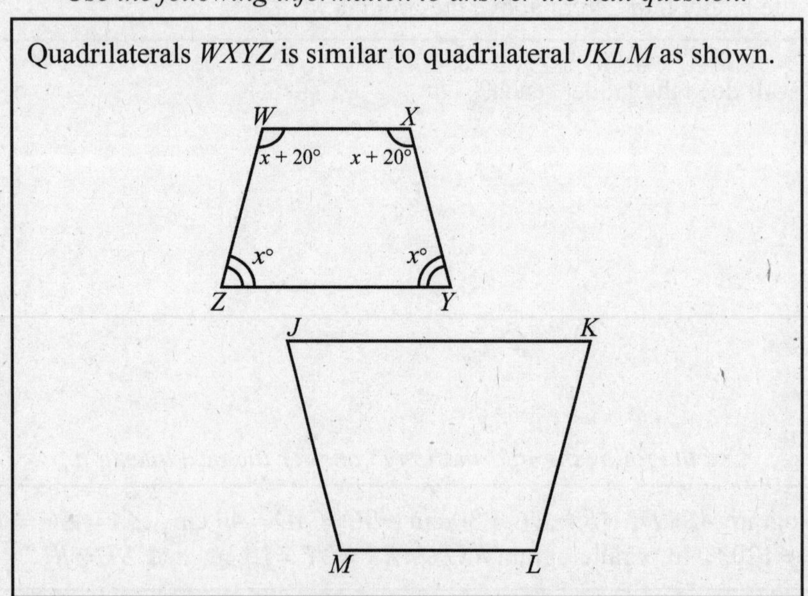

18. What is the measure of $\angle J$, given that the sum of the angle measures in a quadrilateral is equal to 360°?

Use the following information to answer the next question.

Two pieces to a jigsaw puzzle are as shown.

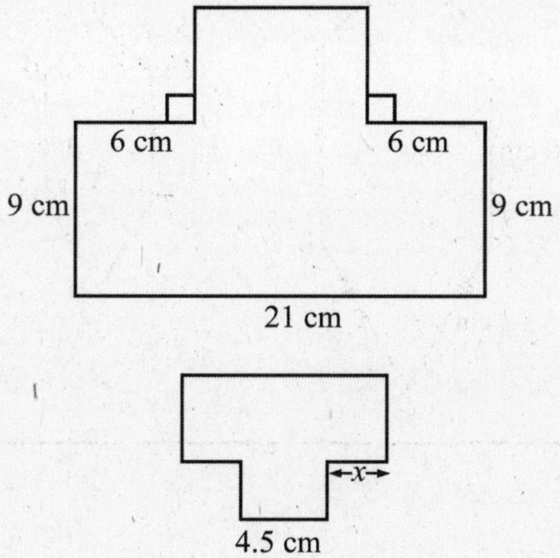

6 cm
6 cm
9 cm
9 cm
21 cm
x
4.5 cm

19. If the top piece is similar to the bottom piece, then what is the length of side x in the bottom piece?

NOTES

ROTATION SYMMETRY AND TRANSFORMATIONS OF 2-D SHAPES

When you are finished this unit, you will be able to…

- classify a given set of 2-D shapes or designs according to the number of lines of symmetry
- complete a 2-D shape or design, given one half of the shape or design and a line of symmetry
- determine if a given 2-D shape or design has rotation symmetry about the point at its centre
- rotate a given 2-D shape about a vertex and draw the resulting image
- identify a line of symmetry or the order and angle of rotation symmetry in a given tessellation
- identify the type of symmetry that arises from a given transformation on a Cartesian plane
- complete, concretely or pictorially, a given transformation of a 2-D shape on a Cartesian plane, record the coordinates, and describe the type of symmetry that results
- determine whether or not two given 2-D shapes on a Cartesian plane are related by either rotation or line symmetry

PREREQUISITE SKILLS AND KNOWLEDGE

Prior to starting this unit, you should be able to…

- perform simple mathematic operations
- describe the characteristics of a Cartesian plane
- define and label the quadrants of a Cartesian plane
- plot points on a Cartesian plane according to their coordinates
- draw shapes on a Cartesian plane
- identify the properties of simple polygons

Lesson 1 CLASSIFY AND COMPLETE 2-D SHAPES

NOTES

2-D shapes can be classified according to the number of lines of symmetry that they have. A shape is symmetrical if both sides are the same size and shape when a line is drawn through it. That is, the image on one side of the line is identical to the image on the other side of the line. This line is called a line of symmetry.

To test if a shape is symmetrical, imagine folding it in half. If it can be folded in half so that one half folds exactly on top of the other half, then the shape is symmetrical and the fold line is a line of symmetry.

Another way to test for symmetry is to use a mirror. If a mirror is used, the right triangle shown on the left will appear as the right triangle shown on the right. In other words, the triangle on the right is the mirror image of the triangle on the left.

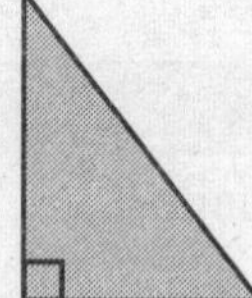

When the two images are placed side by side, the following 2-D shape results.

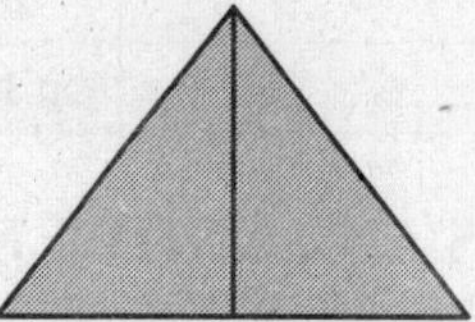

In this case, the line drawn through the side that the two right triangles share is called the **line of symmetry.**

Example

The line of symmetry can also be referred to as the line of reflection.

Draw one line of symmetry for the given pentagon.

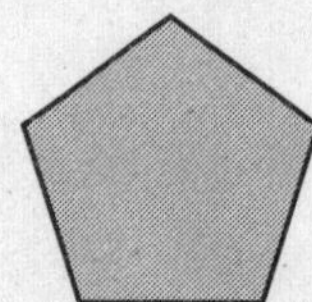

Solution

One line of symmetry or line of reflection is shown in the given diagram.

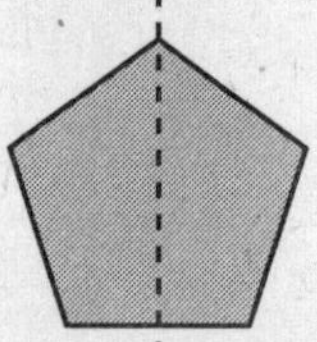

NOTES

Your Turn 1

Draw two lines of symmetry for the following shape.

A **regular polygon** is a polygon where all of the sides are congruent and all of the interior angles are congruent. There is a relationship between regular polygons and lines of symmetry. The number of lines of symmetry equals the number of congruent sides of a regular polygon.

Example

From the set of 2-D shapes given, classify the shapes according to the number of lines of symmetry.

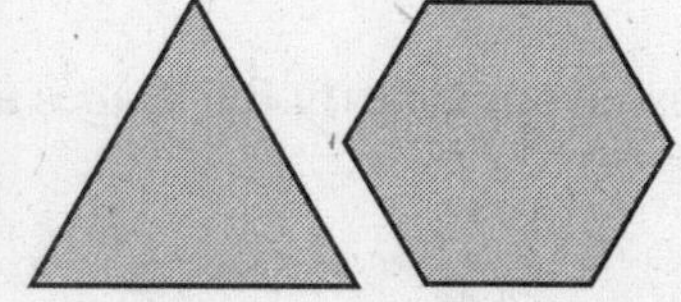

Solution

This shape has one line of symmetry.

This shape has 3 lines of symmetry.

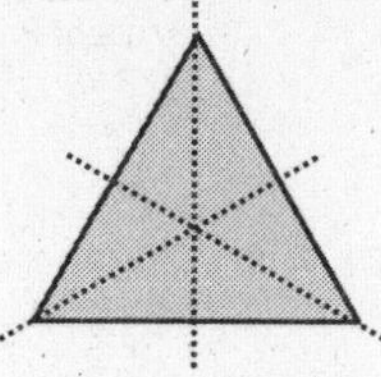

NOTES

This shape has 4 lines of symmetry.

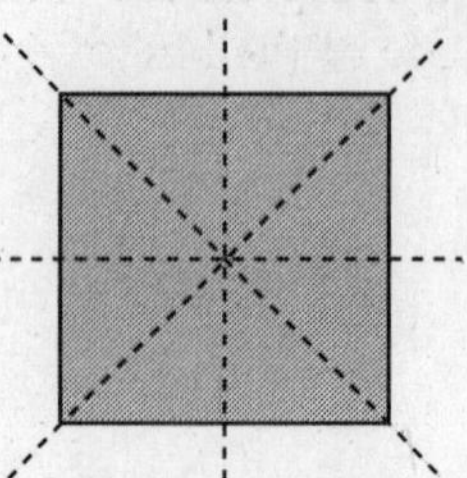

This shape has 6 lines of symmetry.

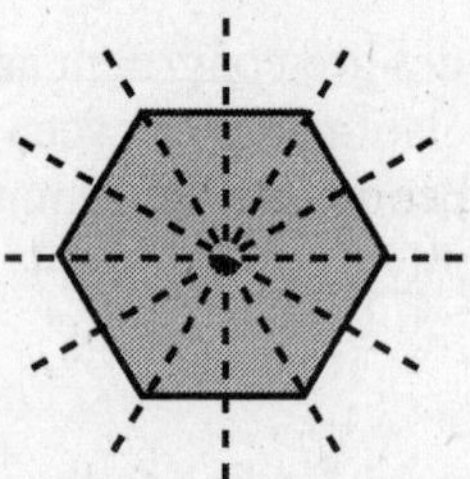

Your Turn 2

From the set of 2-D shapes given, classify the shapes according to the number of lines of symmetry.

NOTES

COMPLETING 2-D SHAPES

When given one-half of a 2-D shape, it is possible to complete the entire shape by drawing the identical image on the other side of the line of symmetry.

Example

Given one-half of a shape and its line of symmetry, complete the entire shape.

Solution

Draw the identical image on the other side of the line of symmetry.

Your Turn 3

Given one-half of a shape and its line of symmetry, complete the entire shape.

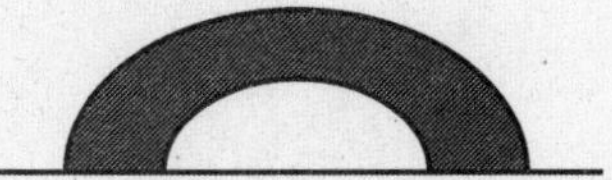

PRACTICE EXERCISES

1. Which of the following diagrams represents a shape and its mirror image as reflected through a line of symmetry?

A.

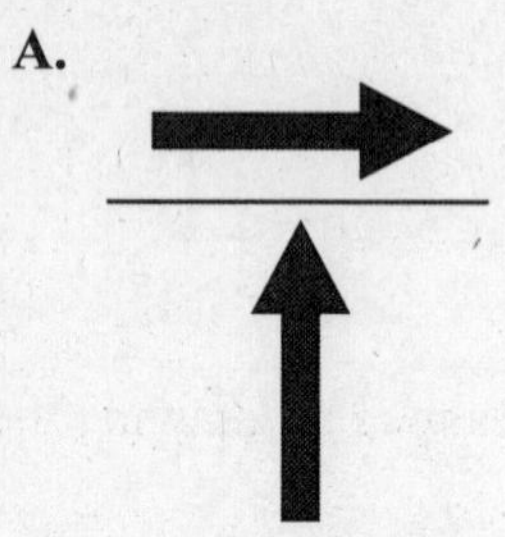

B.

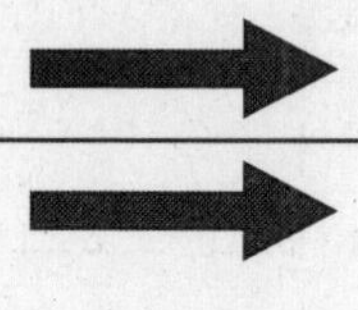

C.

D.

2. Which of the following diagrams represents a shape and its mirror image as reflected through a line of symmetry?

A.

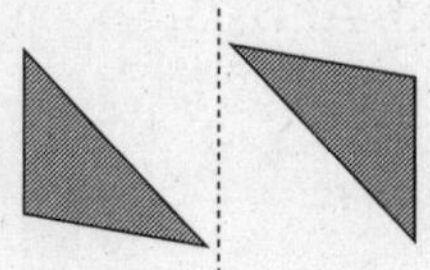

B.

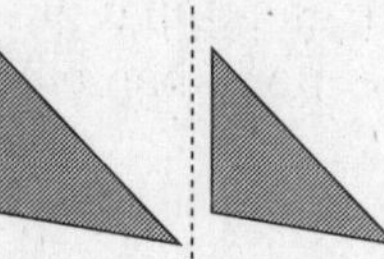

C.

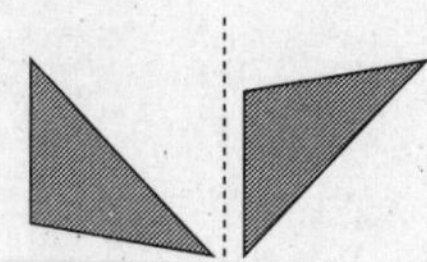

D.

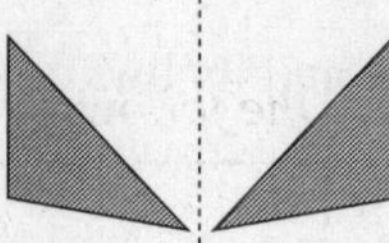

Use the following information to answer the next question.

3. If all the sides of the yield sign shown are equal lengths, how many lines of symmetry does the yield sign have?

Use the following information to answer the next question.

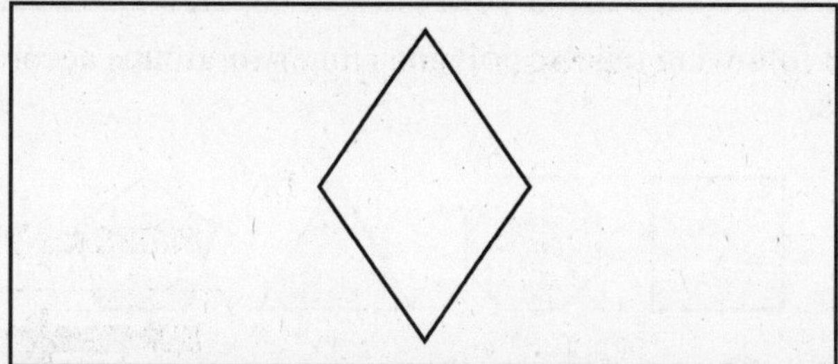

4. How many lines of symmetry does the given quadrilateral have? Show your answer by drawing the lines of symmetry on the shape.

Use the following information to answer the next question.

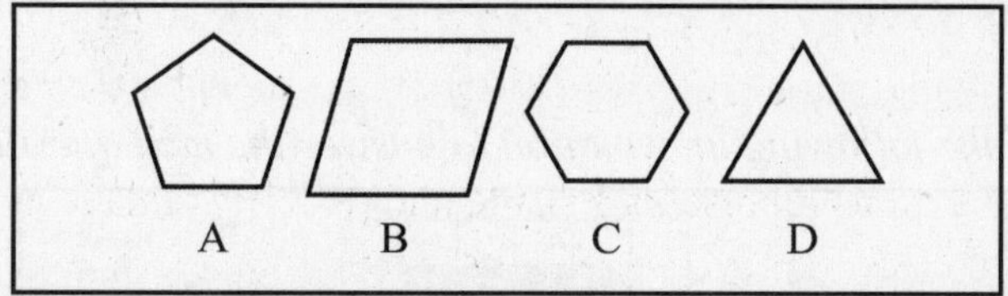

5. A teacher drew the given regular polygons on the whiteboard and labelled them A, B, C, and D. Which polygons have more than two lines of symmetry?

Use the following information to answer the next question.

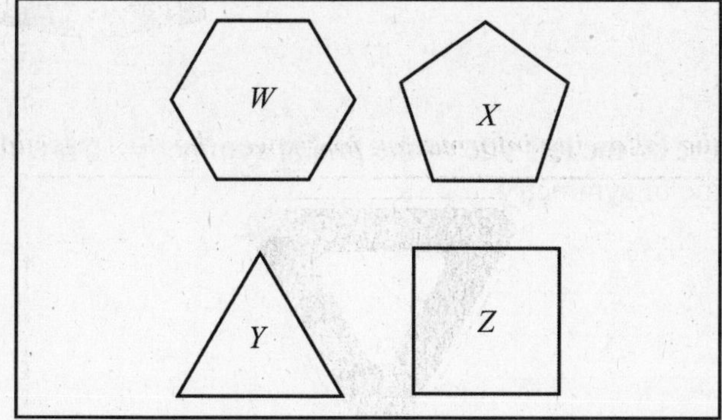

6. Order the given regular polygons from the fewest lines of symmetry to the most lines of symmetry.

Use the following information to answer the next question.

Sasha sorts the following regular polygons into two groups according to the following rules.

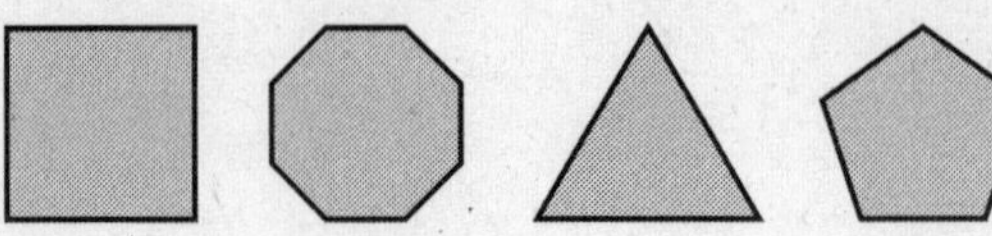

Group 1: Fewer than 4 lines of symmetry
Group 2: More than 3 lines of symmetry

7. What shapes belong to each group? Explain your answer.

Use the following information to answer the next question.

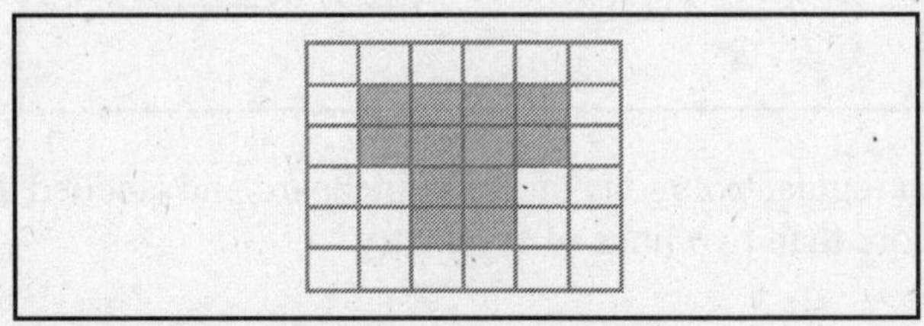

8. How many lines of symmetry does the shape have?

9. Ken draws half of a picture on the left side of the line of symmetry. Draw the other half of the picture on the right side of the line of symmetry.

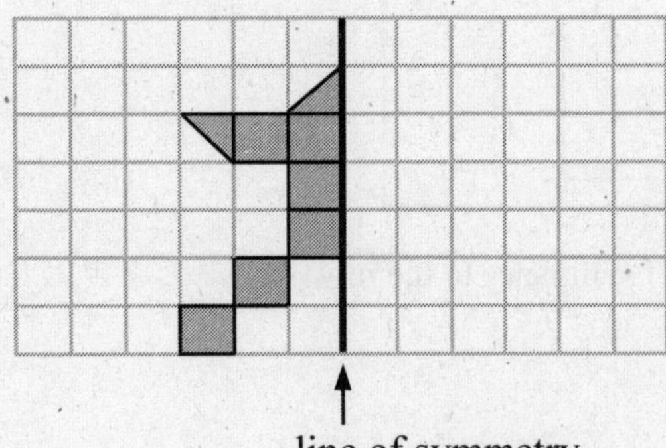

10. Shawn draws half of a picture on the bottom half of an oblique line of symmetry. Draw the other half of the image to complete the picture.

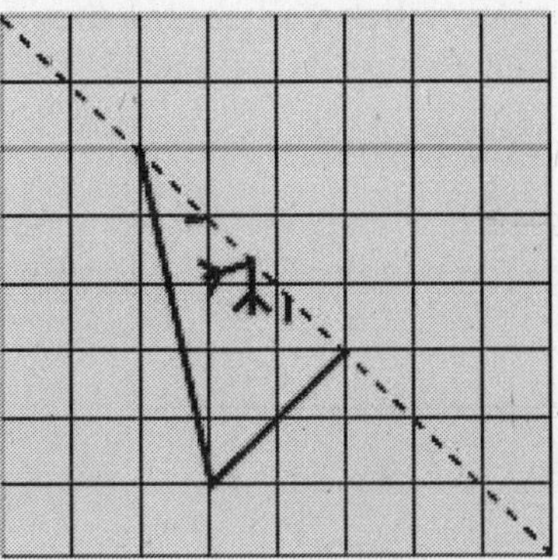

Lesson 2 ROTATION SYMMETRY

NOTES

The word "transform" means to change. A rotation is one of the transformations performed in geometry. A rotation will change the position of a geometrical shape but will not change its original size or shape.

In a **rotation**, sometimes referred to as a turn, a shape is pivoted about a point. Rotations are made clockwise (cw) or counterclockwise (ccw). Common rotation angles include:

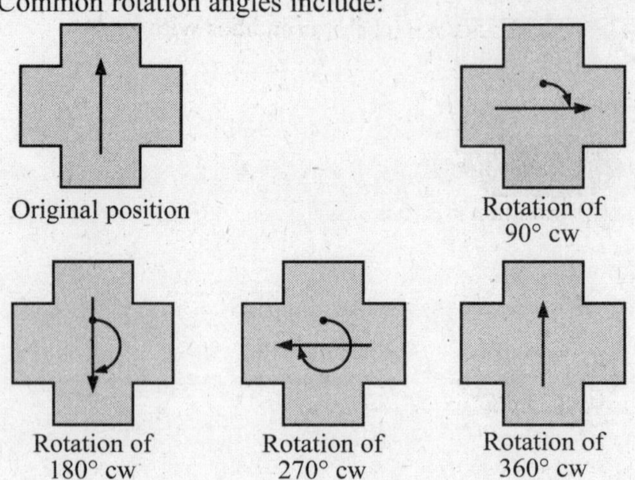

The rotated shape is called an **image**.

The easiest way to rotate a shape is to trace the shape and rotate it about a particular point as directed in the question. Then, lift up the traced image and draw the rotated image on the Cartesian plane.

The preceding image illustrated that, after each of the given rotations, the shape returns to its original position. This is called coinciding with itself.

When a shape coincides with itself after a rotation about its centre of less than 360°, the shape is said to have rotational symmetry.

The number of times a shape returns to its original position during a rotation of 360° is called the **order of rotation**. The preceding shape has an order of rotation of 4 because it returned to its original position 4 times during a rotation of 360° about its centre.

The angle of rotation can be found using the given formula:

$$\text{angle of rotation} = \frac{360°}{\text{order of rotation}}$$

For the example above, the angle of rotation will be $\frac{360°}{4} = 90°$. Since the given shape returned to its original position for each rotation of 90°, this becomes the angle of rotation.

NOTES

Example

Determine if the hexagon below has rotation symmetry about its centre. State the order and angle of rotation.

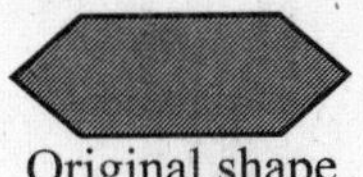

Original shape

Solution

Step 1

Rotate the original shape clockwise until it coincides with itself.

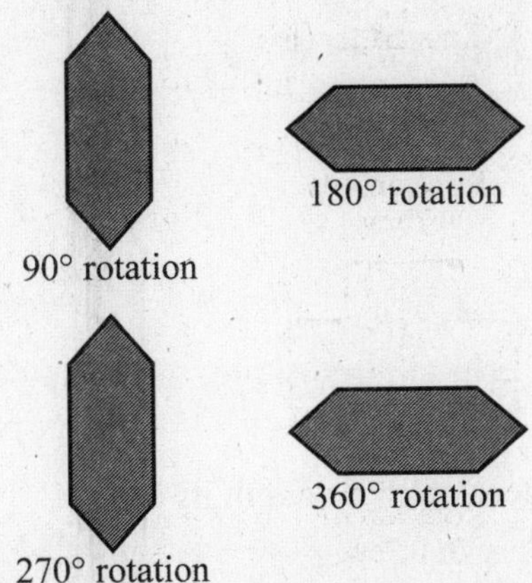

Step 2

State the order of rotation.

The hexagon has rotational symmetry because it coincides with itself after a rotation of less than 360°. The order of rotation is 2, since the hexagon returned to its original position twice.

Step 3

Determine the angle of rotation.

Apply the angle of rotation formula.

The angle of rotation is $\frac{360°}{2} = 180°$.

Your Turn 1

Determine if the following hexagon has rotation symmetry about its centre. State the order and angle of rotation.

Original Shape

NOTES

Example

The following shape is rotated 90° clockwise about its centre. Draw the rotated image.

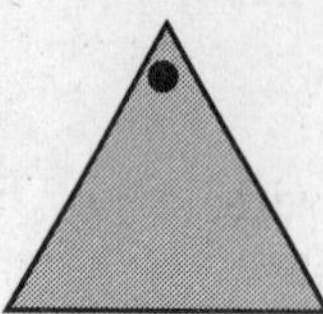

Solution

If the given shape is rotated 90° clockwise about its centre, the resulting image will be as shown.

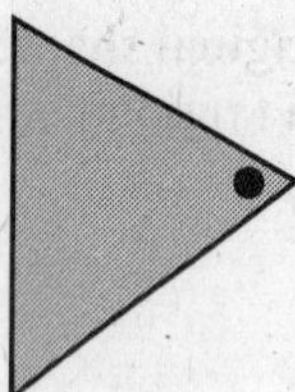

Your Turn 2

The following shape is rotated 90° counterclockwise about its centre. Draw the rotated image.

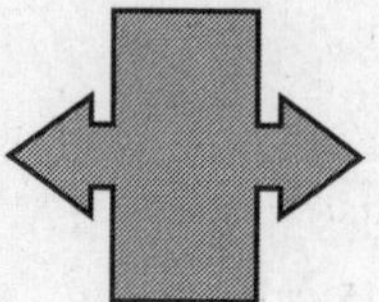

Two-dimensional shapes can also be rotated about a particular vertex of the given shape, as illustrated in the following example.

Example

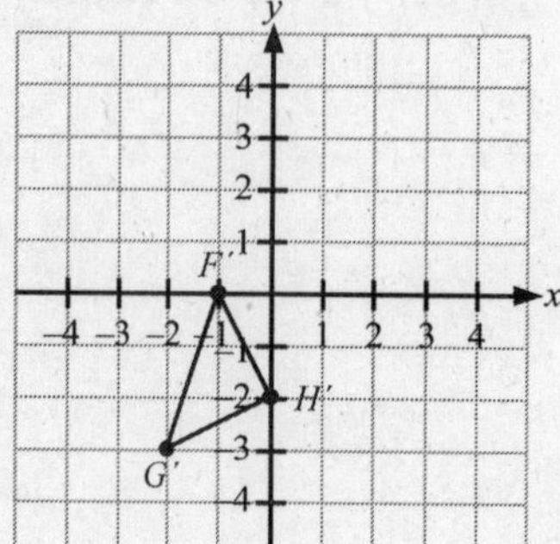

NOTES

Triangle $F'G'H'$ was drawn as shown on a Cartesian plane after a 270° clockwise rotation about the point (–1, 0). Draw the original triangle *FGH*.

Solution

Step 1

Perform the reverse transformation, which will be 270° counterclockwise. Note that point (–1, 0) coincides with point *F'*. Trace the rotated image, and rotate in the opposite direction. Place the pencil on (–1, 0), and turn the tracing paper 270° counterclockwise.

Step 2

Draw the rotated image on the Cartesian plane.
Plot and label each new point to indicate that it is the original shape. Then, connect the points with line segments to form the original triangle *FGH*. Note that points *F* and *F'* both lie at (-1, 0).

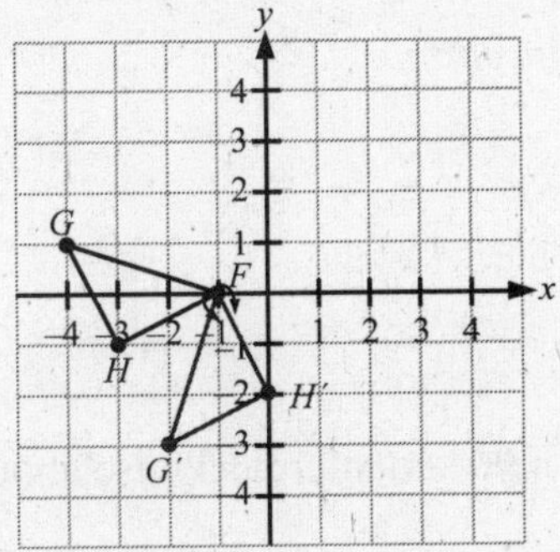

Your Turn 3

Draw triangle *DEF* with vertices $D(3, 4)$, $E(3, 1)$, $F(1, 1)$. Then, rotate it 90° counterclockwise about the point *F*. Label the image *D'E'F'*.

PRACTICE EXERCISES

1. Which of the following shapes does not have rotational symmetry?

A.
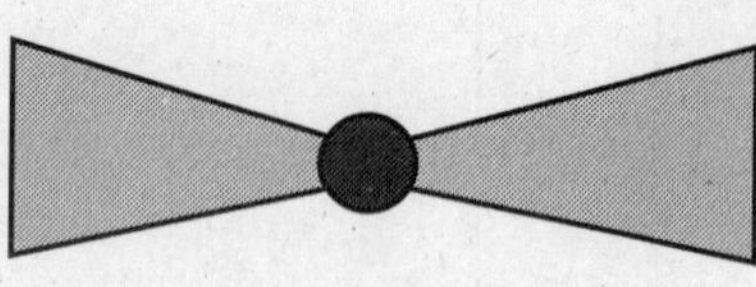

B.

C.
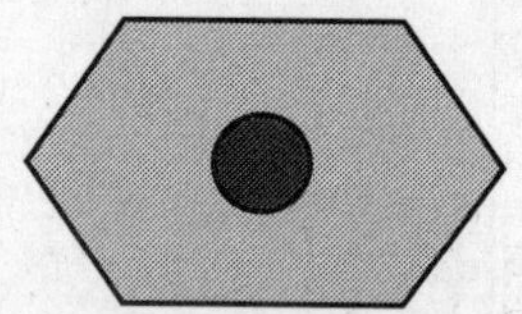

D.
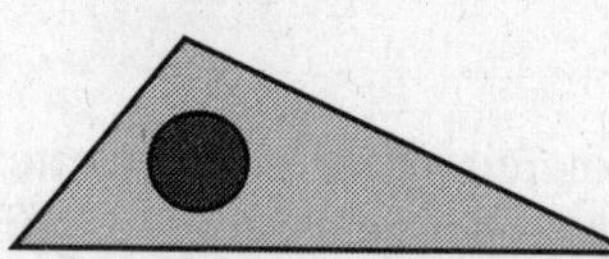

Use the following information to answer the next question.

2. Which of the given diagrams represents the given image after a rotation 90° counterclockwise about a point at the base of the cup?

A.

B.

C.
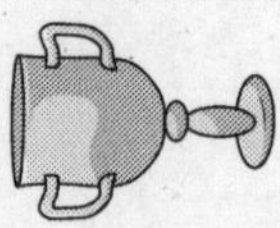

D.

Use the following information to answer the next question.

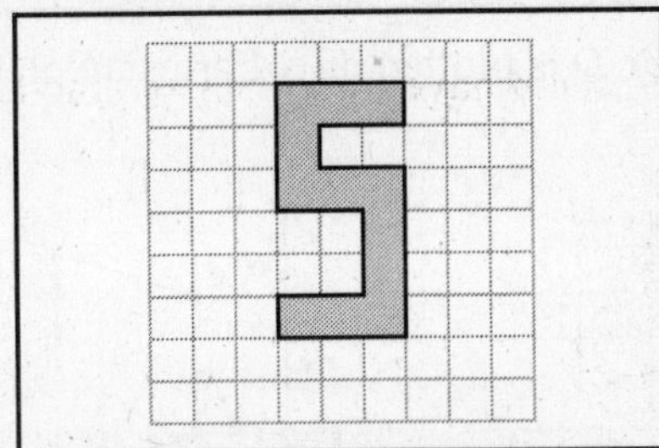

3. Which of the following diagrams shows the given shape rotated 90° clockwise?

A.

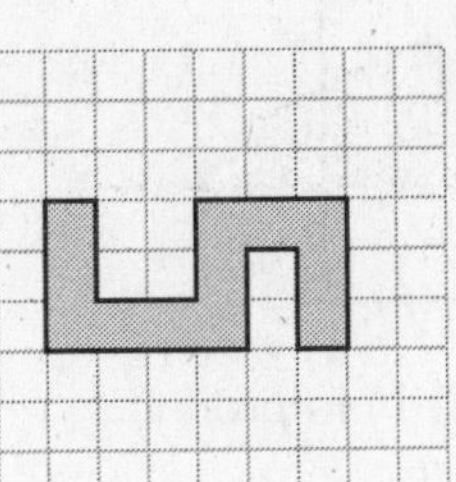

B.

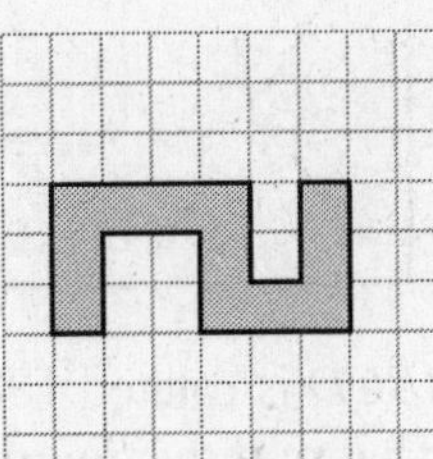

C.

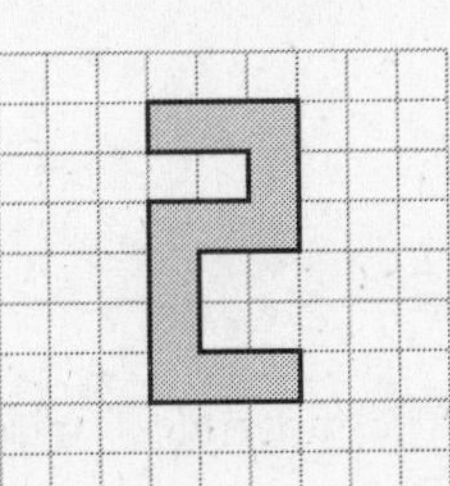

D.

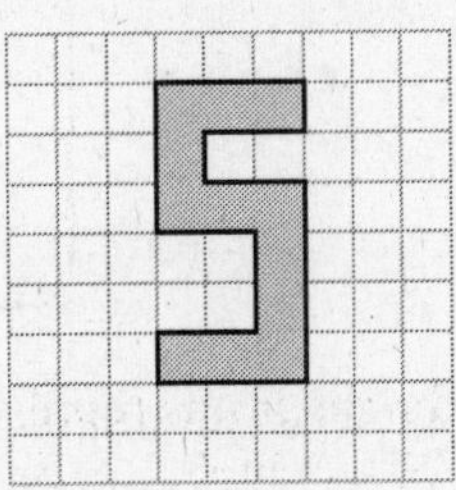

Use the following information to answer the next question.

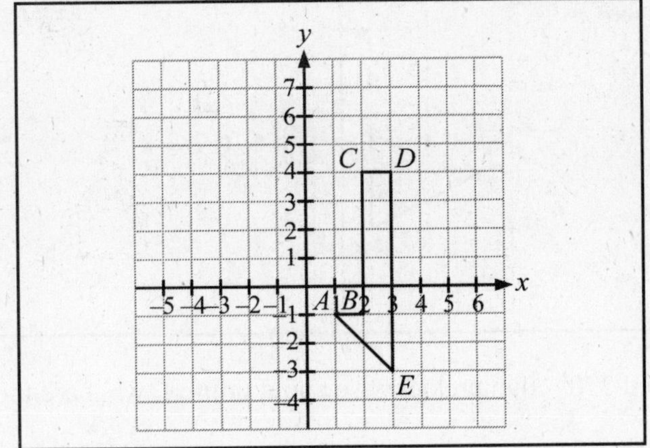

4. If the given figure *ABCDE* is rotated 90° clockwise about point *C*, what would the coordinates of *A′* be?

Use the following information to answer the next question.

Trapezoid *ABCD* is plotted on a Cartesian plane.

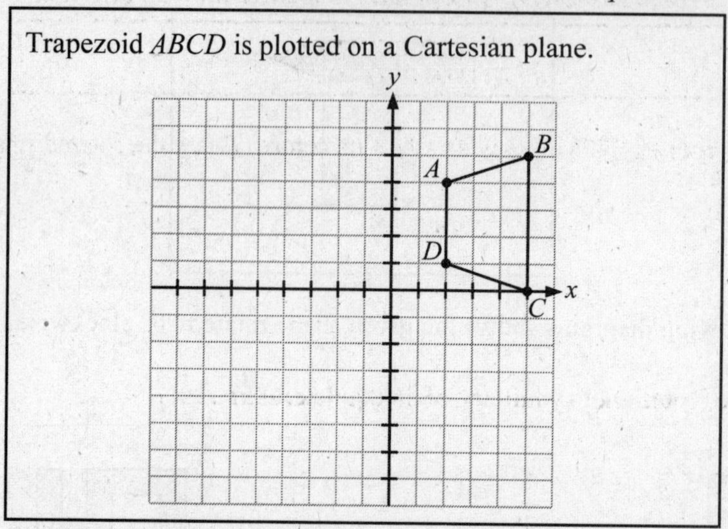

5. When trapezoid *ABCD* is rotated 180° counterclockwise about the point (2, 1) to produce shape $A'B'C'D'$, what will the coordinates of C' be?

Use the following information to answer the next question.

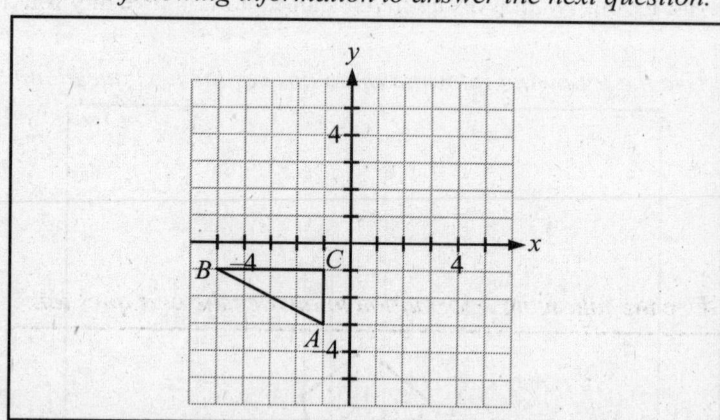

6. If triangle *ABC* is rotated 270° counterclockwise about point *A*, what are the coordinates of B'?

Use the following information to answer the next question.

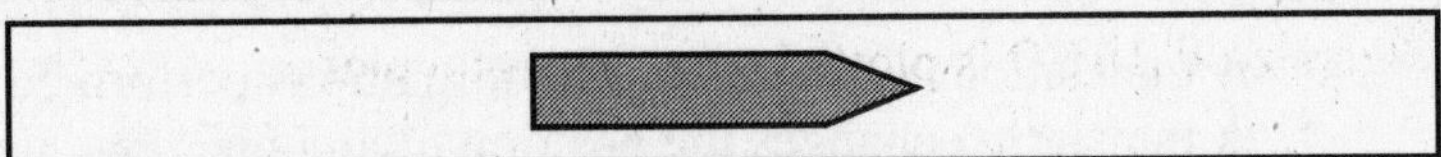

7. The given shape is rotated 270° clockwise about its centre. Draw the rotated image.

8. What is the order of rotational symmetry of an equilateral triangle?

Use the following information to answer the next question.

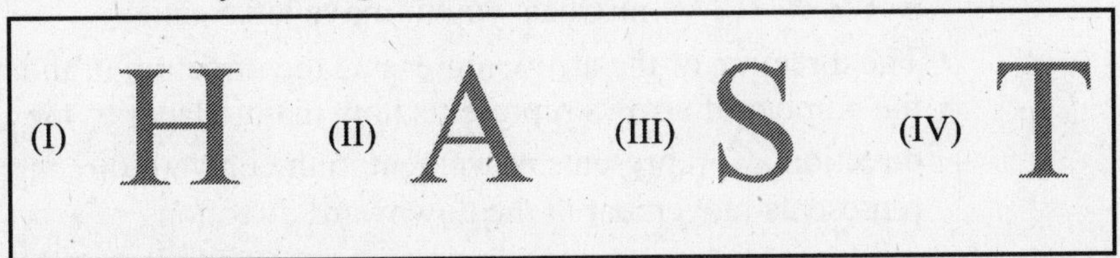

9. A set of four shapes are given. Which of the given shapes do not have any rotational symmetry?

Use the following information to answer the next question.

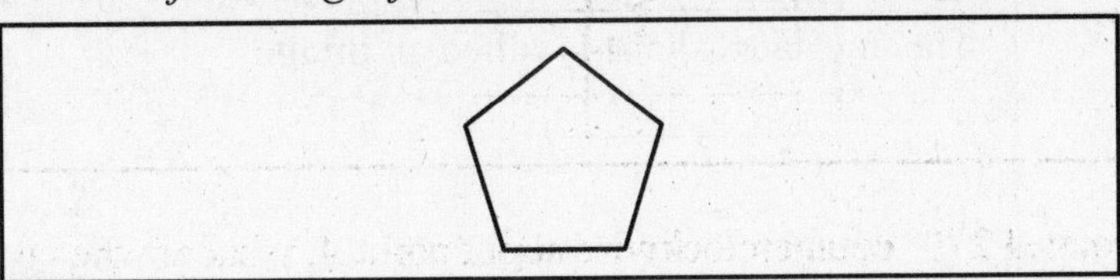

10. Determine if the given regular pentagon has rotational symmetry about its centre. State the order and angle of rotation.

Lesson 3 TRANSFORMATIONS ON THE CARTESIAN PLANE

NOTES

Recall that the word "transform" means to change.

A translation is one of the transformations performed in geometry. A translation changes the position of an object but not the size or shape of the object.

In a translation, sometimes referred to as a slide, a shape is moved up or down, right or left, or a combination of these. Translations are performed according to the instructions given in the translation rules. Rules allow you to perform the translations accurately.

Some translation rules are

- R2: tells you to move right 2 units
- L5: instructs you to move left 5 units

The letter represents the direction of the movement and the number represents how many places to move in the given direction. U represents movement in the upward direction, and D represents movement in the downward direction.

- →→: instructs you to move right 2 units.
- ←←←←←: instructs you to move left 5 units.

The direction of the arrow represents the direction of the movement, and the number of arrows represents how many places to move in the given direction. ↑ represents movement in the upward direction, and ↓ represents movement in the downward direction.

To move the shape, values are added or subtracted from the x- or y-coordinates:

- When the same value is subtracted from each x-coordinate, the shape will move to the left.
- When the same value is added to each x-coordinate, the shape will move to the right.
- When the same value is subtracted from each y-coordinate, the shape will move down.
- When the same value is added to each y-coordinate, the shape will move up.

The translated shape is called an **image**.

NOTES

Example

Draw triangle *ABC* with vertices $A(-4, 6), B(0, 4), C(-2, 2)$.

Then, translate the triangle L3 and U4. Label the image *A'B'C'*.

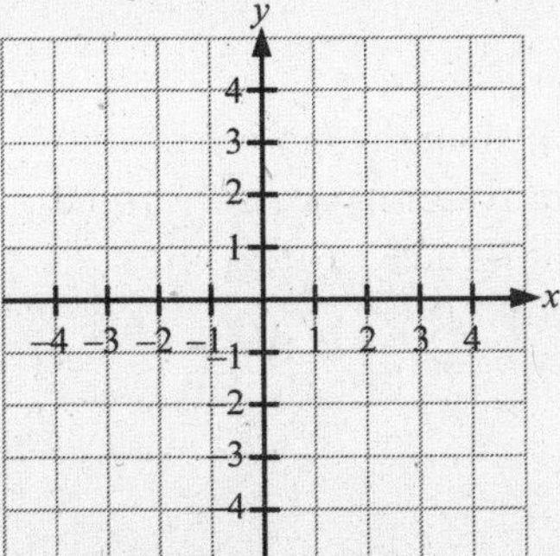

Solution

Step 1

Draw the original shape on the Cartesian plane.

Plot and label each point as given in the question. Then, connect the points with line segments.

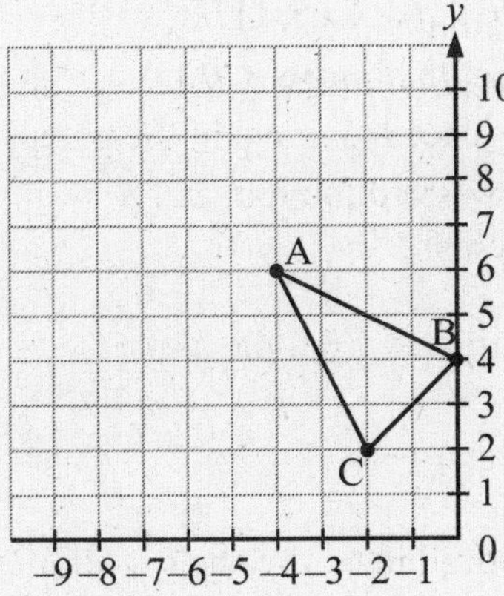

Step 2

Subtract 3 from each original *x*-coordinate because the triangle is translated 3 units to the left. Add 4 to each original *y*-coordinate because the triangle is translated 4 units up.

The resulting points are:

$A'(-4-3,\ 6+4) = (-7, 10)$

$B'(0-3,\ 4+4) = (-3, 8)$

$C'(-2-3,\ 2+4) = (-5, 6)$

NOTES

Step 3
Draw the translated image on the coordinate plane using the points A', B', and C'.

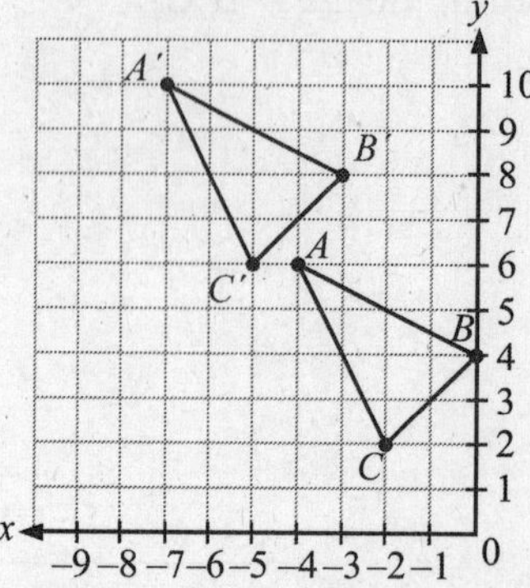

After a triangle has been translated, the lengths of the sides and the measures of the angles are unchanged. The original triangle and its translated image are congruent triangles.

Your Turn 1

Draw triangle ABC with vertices $A(2, 3), B(4, 6), C(6, 1)$.
Then, translate the triangle L4 and D3. Label the image $A'B'C'$.

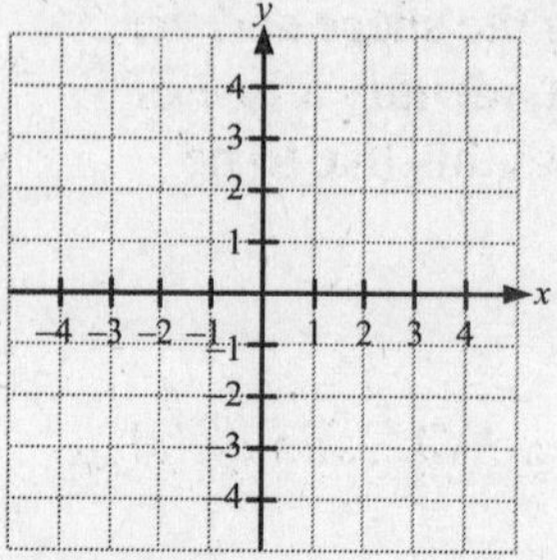

Example

Image $M'N'P'Q'$ was formed after translating the original figure ←←←, then by connecting the vertices $M'(-4, 3)$, $N'(-5, 0)$, $P'(1, -2)$, and $Q'(1, 1)$.. Draw the original shape $MNPQ$.

Solution
The translation rule of ←←← represents a translation of 3 units left. Work backward by doing the opposite translation of 3 units to the right for each of the vertices.

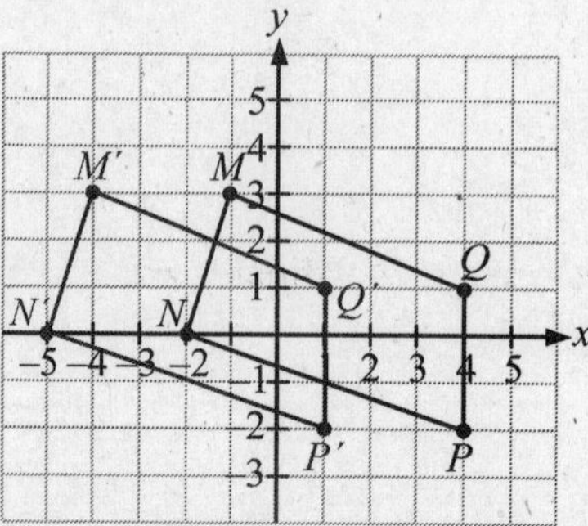

NOTES

Your Turn 2

Triangle $H'A'T'$ below was drawn after a translation of $\rightarrow$ and $\uparrow\uparrow\uparrow$. Draw the original triangle HAT.

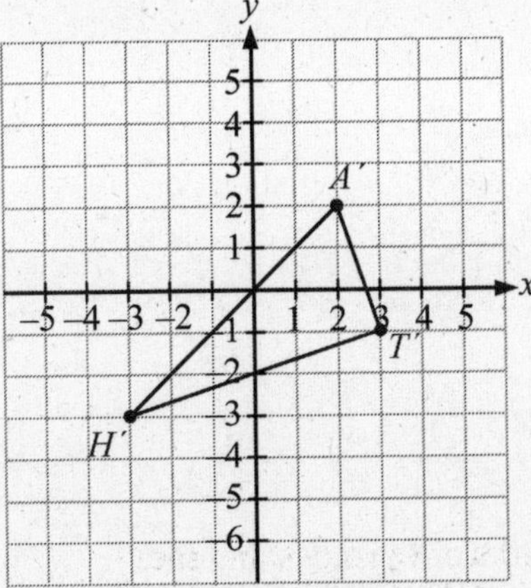

IDENTIFYING TYPES OF SYMMETRY IN TRANSFORMATIONS

After a shape has been transformed by a translation or a rotation, it is possible that the original shape and the transformed image display either line or rotation symmetry.

The type of symmetry can be identified by analysing the shape and the image after the transformation has taken place. First, identify a line of symmetry. Then, look for the images on both sides of this line to be congruent.

Example

Translate the following shape using a translation rule of D2, and identify any symmetry that may exist.

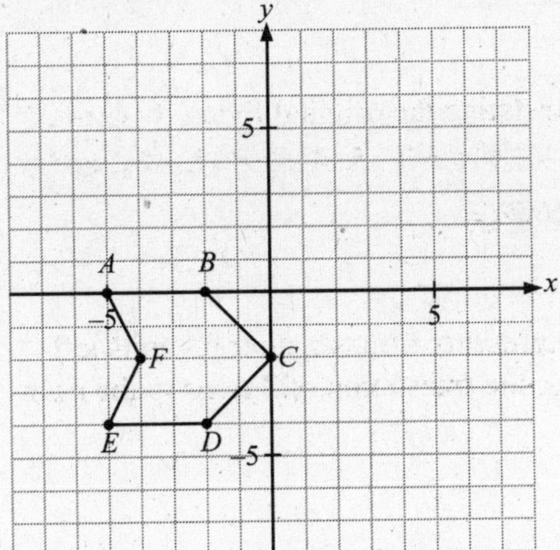

Solution

After a translation of 2 units down, the image coordinates are $A'(-5,-2)$, $B'(-2,-2)$, $C'(0, 4)$, $D'(-2,-6)$, $E'(-5,-6)$, $F'(-4,-4)$

NOTES

The resulting shape is shown in the following graph.

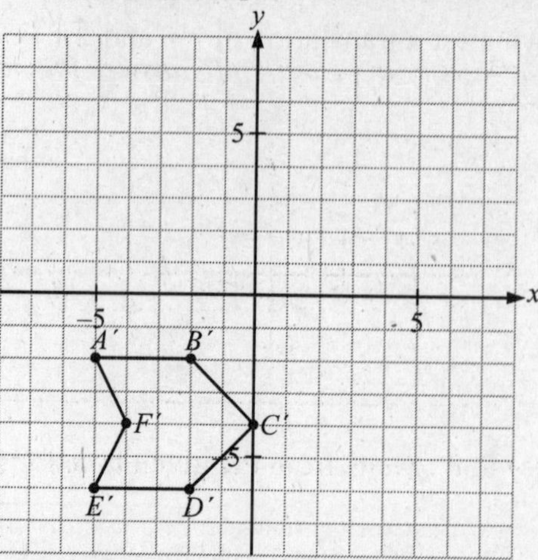

Upon analysing the original shape and the transformed image, there are no lines of symmetry because the translated image is not a mirror reflection of the original image.

Your Turn 3

Translate the following shape using a translation rule of ←← and identify any symmetry that may exist.

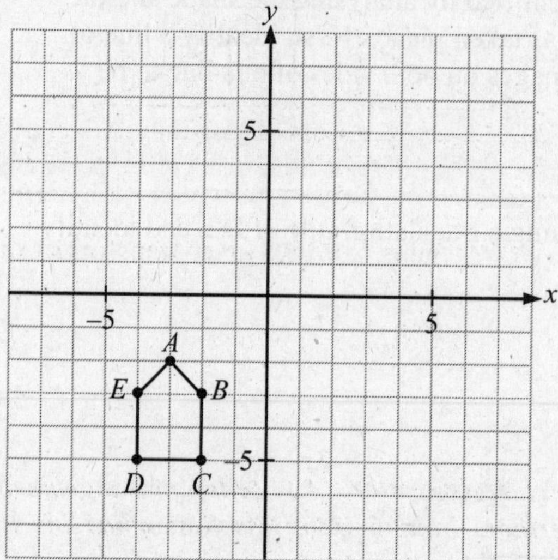

PRACTICE EXERCISES

Use the following information to answer the next question.

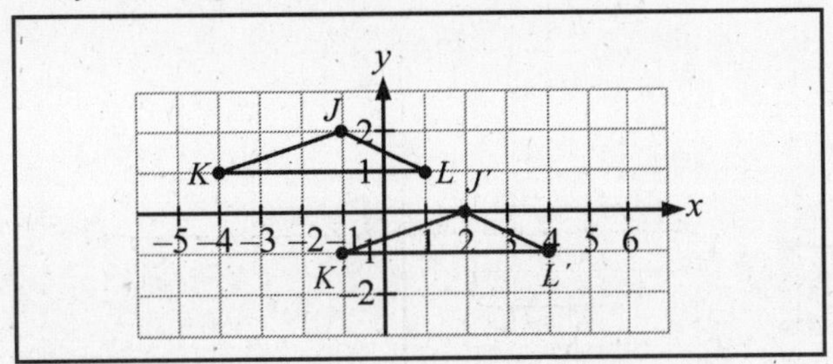

1. Identify the type of symmetry that results from the given transformation.

Use the following information to answer the next question.

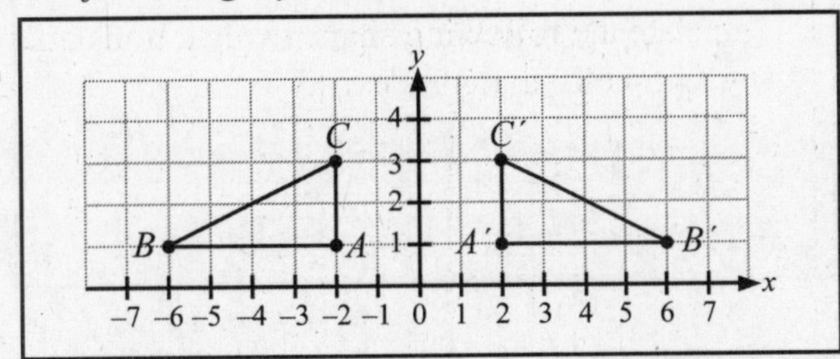

2. Identify the type of symmetry that results from the given transformation.

Each of the following diagrams is a tessellation. A tessellation is a geometric pattern that repeats itself without leaving any gaps or overlaps. Identify if the tessellation has line symmetry, rotation symmetry, or both.

3.

4.

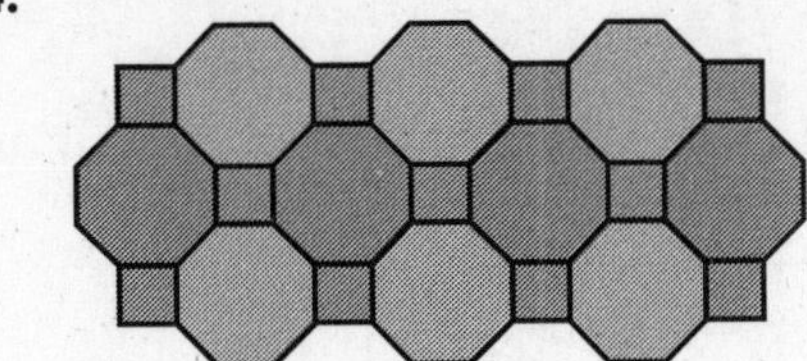

5. Draw triangle *ABC* with vertices $A(2, 3), B(4, 6), C(6, 1)$. Translate triangle *ABC* D2. Draw and label the translated image *A'B'C'*.

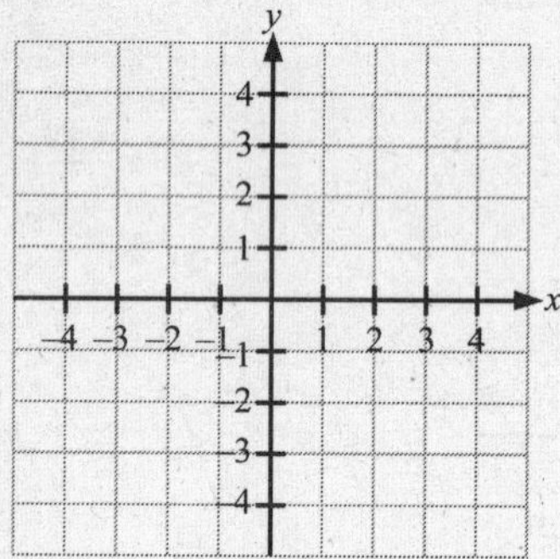

Use the following information to answer the next question.

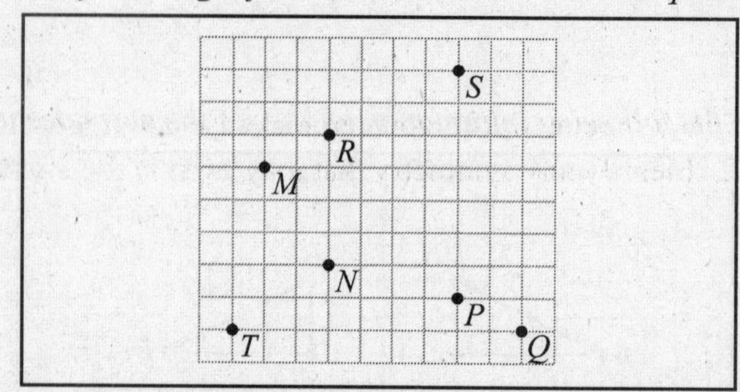

6. Point *S* is translated ←←←← and ↓↓↓↓↓↓. Which point represents its new location?

7. Triangle *ABC* has coordinates $A(3, 1), B(6, 1), C(5, 3)$. Draw triangle *ABC*. Then apply translation R2 and D4 and draw its image $A'B'C'$.

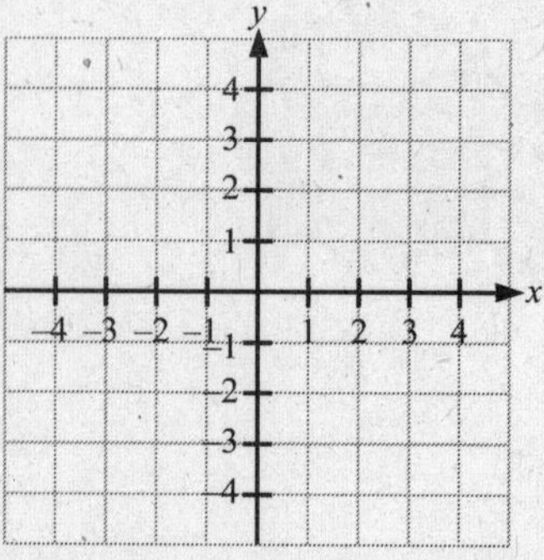

8. Triangle $L'M'N'$ was drawn after a translation ←← and ↑↑↑. Draw the original triangle *LMN*. Identify any symmetry that may exist in the transformation.

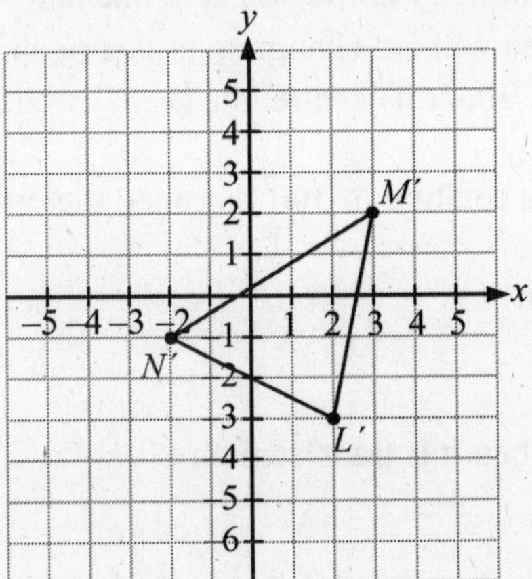

9. The given shape *ABCDEFGH* is rotated 90° counterclockwise about point *A*. Draw $A'B'C'D'E'F'G'H'$. Identify any symmetry that may exist in the transformation.

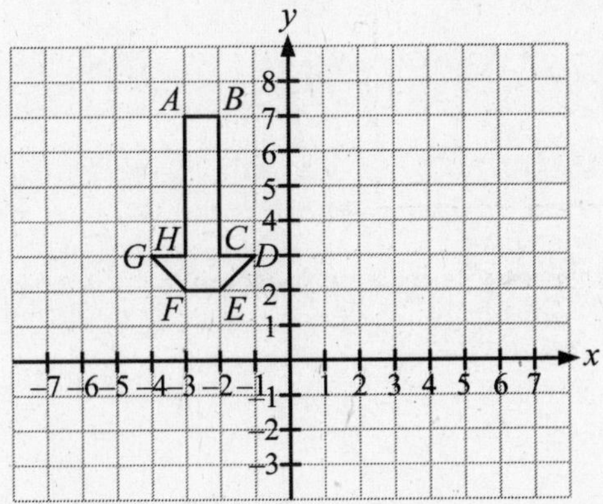

10. The coordinates of rectangle *PQRS* are $P(3, 1), Q(-4, 1), R(-4, -5), S(3, -5)$. A translation of L11 is applied to rectangle *PQRS*. Identify the coordinates of $P'Q'R'S'$ and any symmetry that may exist.

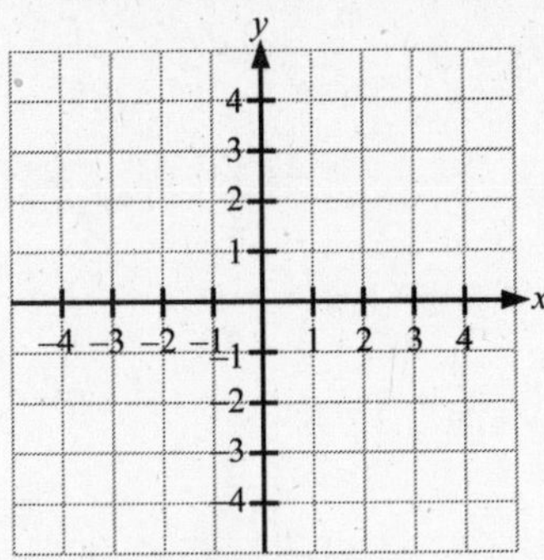

REVIEW SUMMARY

- A shape is symmetrical if the images on both sides of the line of symmetry are identical to one another.
- A rotation and a translation change the position of a geometric shape without changing its size or shape.
- When a shape coincides with itself after a rotation of less than 360° about its centre, the shape is said to have rotational symmetry.
- The number of times a shape returns to its original position during a rotation of 360° is called the order of rotation.
- The angle of rotation can be calculated using the following formula:

$$\text{the angle of rotation} = \frac{360^\circ}{\text{order of rotation}}$$

- A 2-D shape can have rotational symmetry and/or line symmetry when it is translated on a Cartesian plane.

PRACTICE TEST

Use the following information to answer the next question.

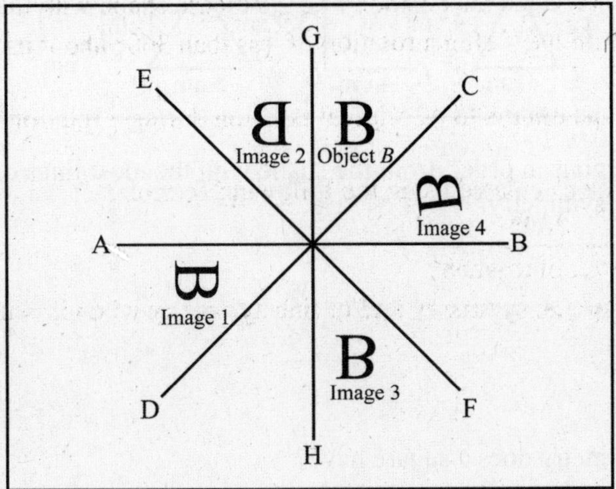

1. When Object B is reflected by mirror line EF, it becomes which Image?

Use the following information to answer the next question.

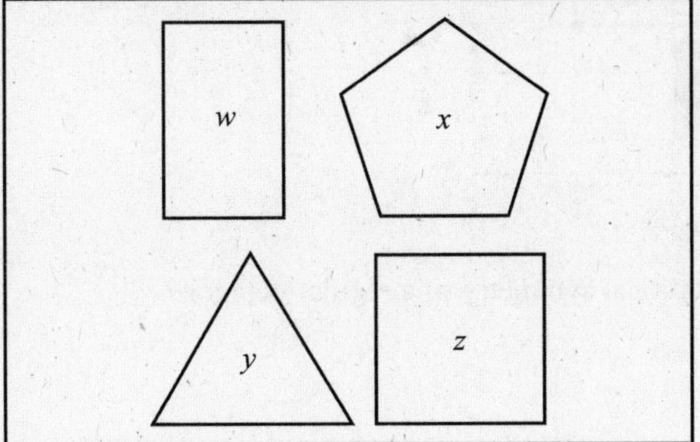

2. Sort the four given regular polygons in order, from the shape with the fewest lines of symmetry to the shape with the most lines of symmetry.

Use the following information to answer the next question.

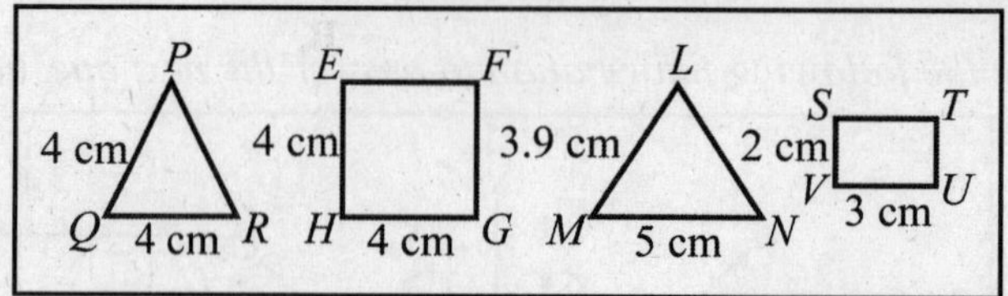

3. Sort the four given polygons in order, from the shape with the most lines of symmetry to the shape with the fewest lines of symmetry.

4. How many lines of symmetry does a square have?

5. Draw the reflection of the shape along the line of symmetry *m*.

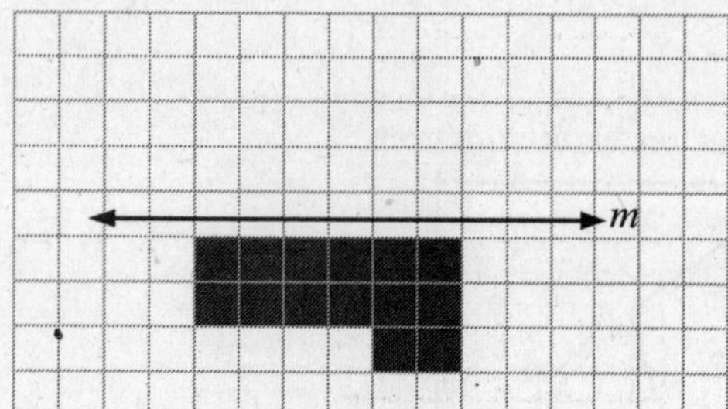

6. What is the order of rotational symmetry of a regular octagon?

7. Which of the following shapes does not exhibit rotational symmetry?

A.

B.

C.

D.

8. Which of the following shapes correctly represents a mirror image across the *y*-axis?

A.

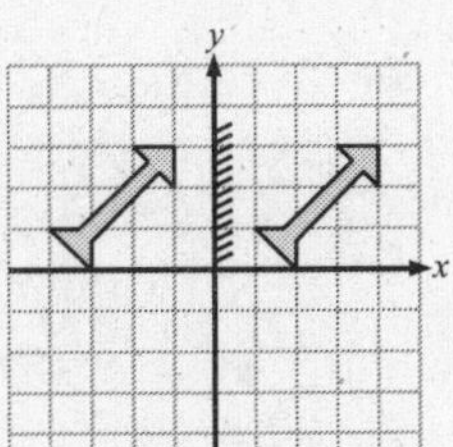

B.

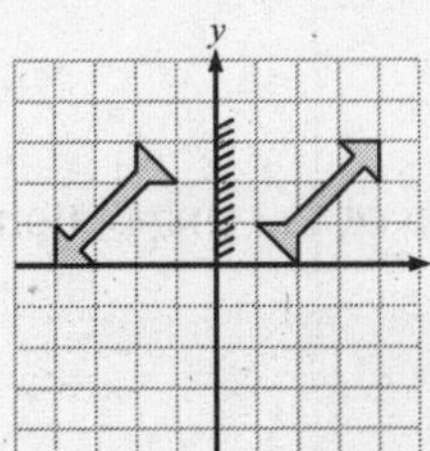

C.

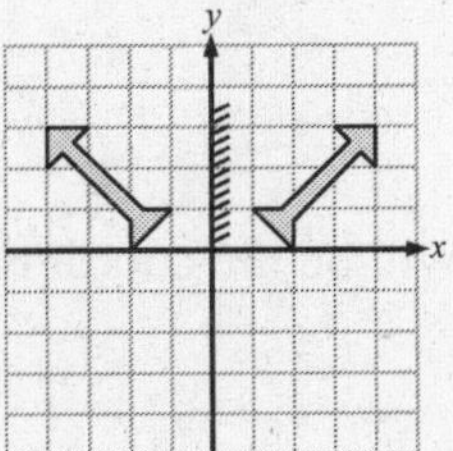

D.

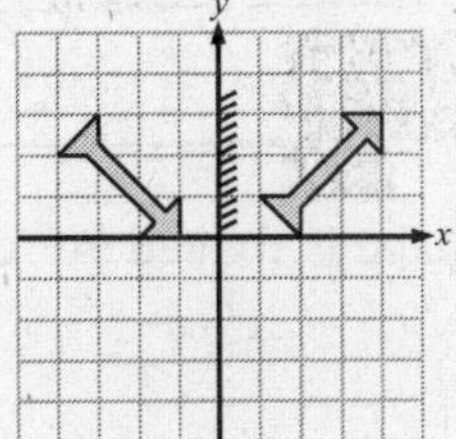

Use the following information to answer the next question.

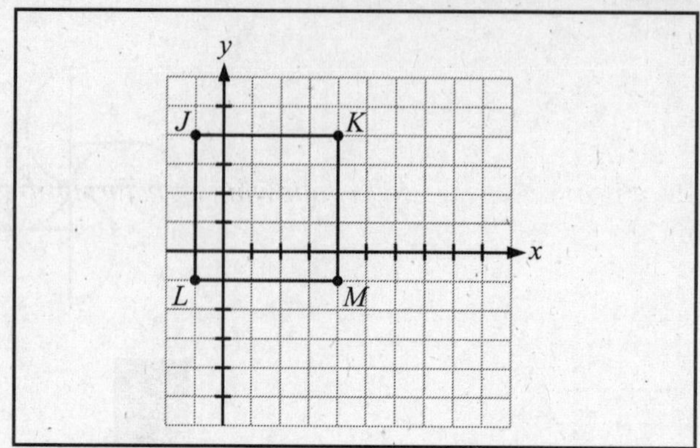

9. Square *JKML* is plotted on a Cartesian plane. If square *JKML* were rotated 90° clockwise about point *M*, what would be the coordinates of point *K'*?

Use the following information to answer the next question.

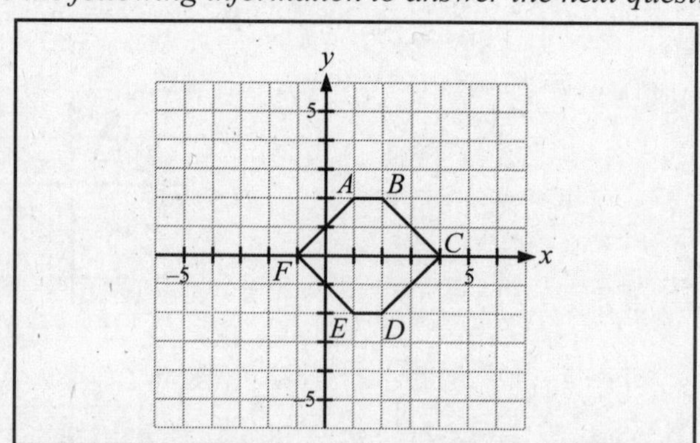

10. When the given shape is rotated 90° counterclockwise about point *A*, what will be the coordinates of *D'*?

Use the following information to answer the next question.

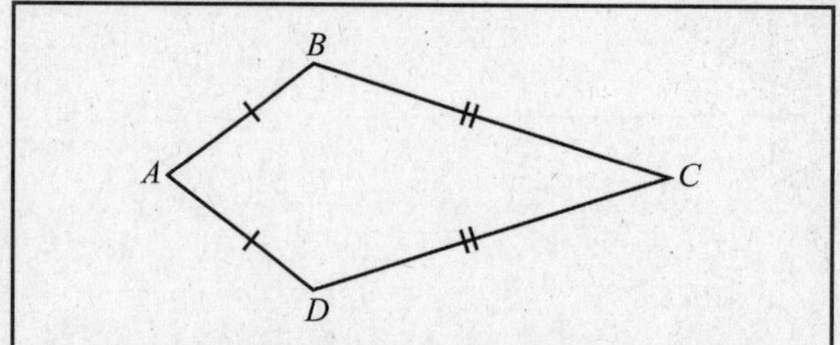

11. How many lines of symmetry does this quadrilateral have?

12. What is the order of rotational symmetry of a rectangle?

Identify the type of symmetry that is indicated from the following transformations.

13.

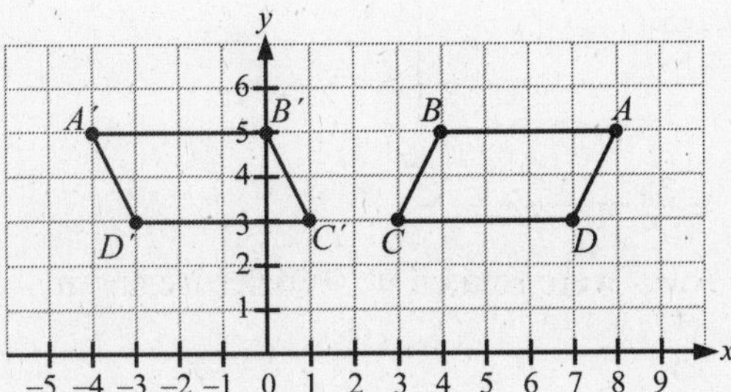

14.

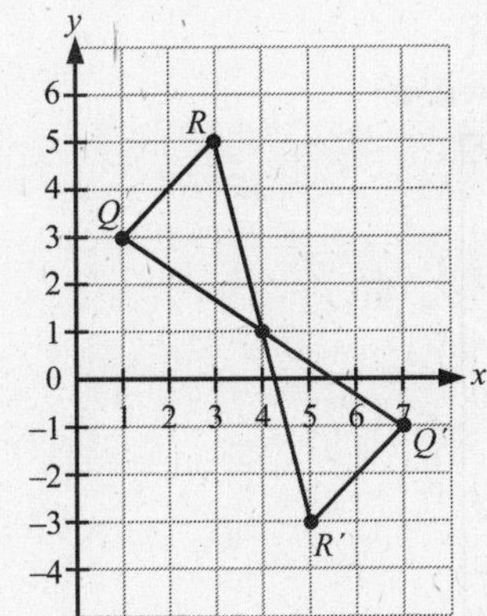

15.

16. Draw triangle ABC with vertices $A(2, 3)$, $B(4, 6)$, and $C(6, 1)$. Translate the triangle R2. Draw and label the translated image $A'B'C'$. Identify any symmetry that may exist in the transformation.

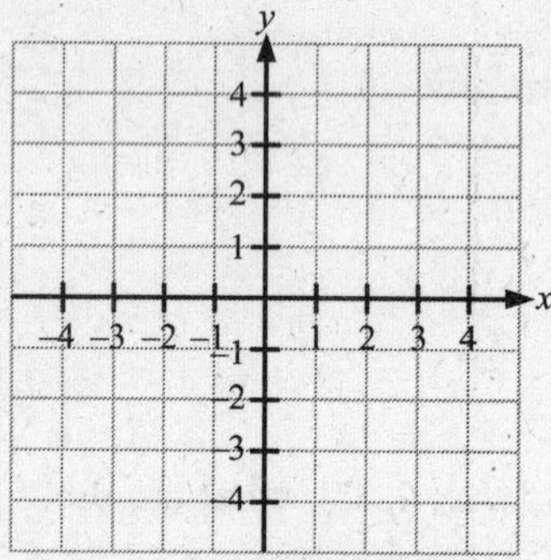

Use the following information to answer the next question.

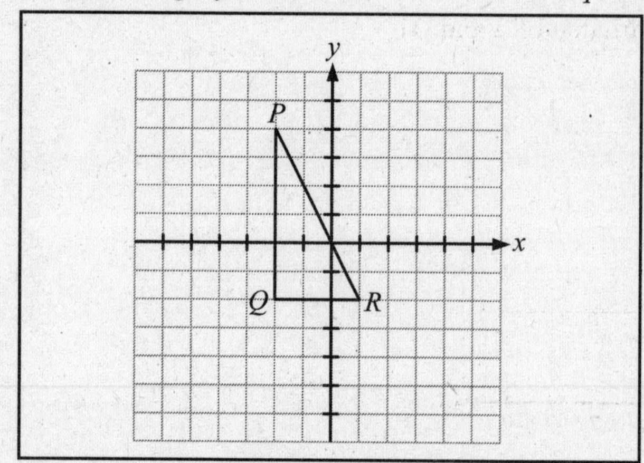

17. Triangle PQR is translated ↓↓↓ to form triangle $P'Q'R'$ and then ←← to form the triangle $P''Q''R''$. Determine the coordinates of Q'' and identify any symmetry that may exist.

Use the following information to answer the next question.

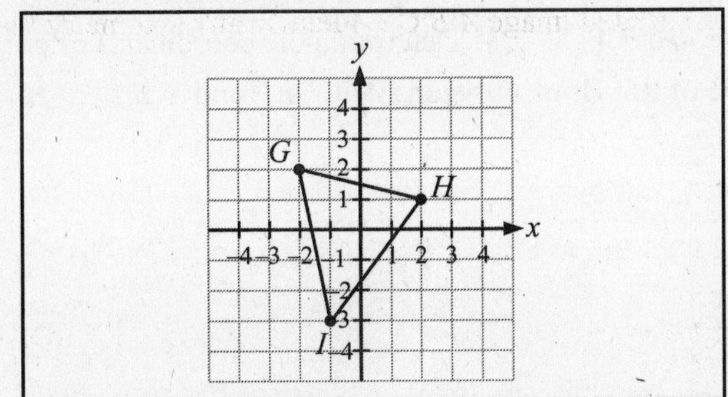

18. If triangle $G'H'I'$ is congruent to GHI and has coordinates $G'(0, 2)$ and $H'(4, 2)$, what are the coordinates of I'? Draw $G'H'I'$. Identify any symmetry that may exist in this transformation.

19. Translate the given quadrilateral R3 and D1.

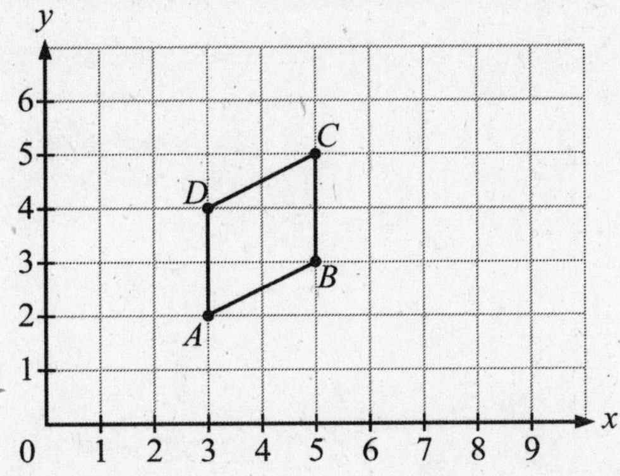

20. The coordinates of polygon *ABCDEF* are $A(-5, 0)$, $B(-1, -1)$, $C(-1, -3)$, $D(-4, -3)$, $E(-4, -2)$, and $F(-5, -2)$. Determine the coordinates of polygon $A'B'C'D'E'F'$ after a translation using a rule of R6. Draw polygons *ABCDEF* and *A'B'C'D'E'F'*.

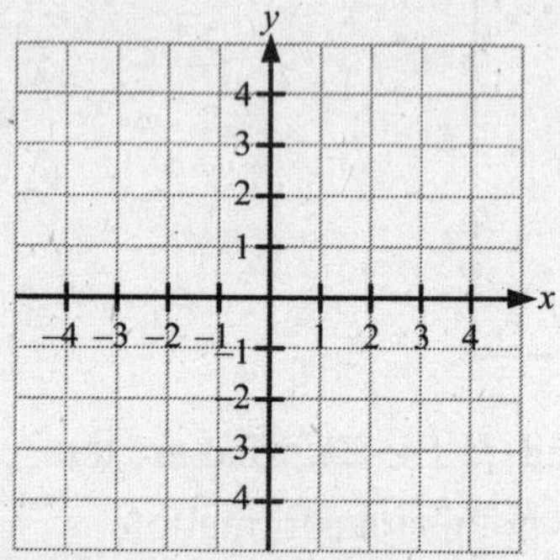

DATA ANALYSIS

When you are finished this unit, you will be able to…

- analyze a given case study and identify potential problems related to bias, use of language, ethics, cost, time and timing, privacy, or cultural sensitivity
- identify whether a given situation represents the use of a sample or a population
- provide an example of a situation in which a population may be used to answer a question, and justify the choice
- provide an example of a question where a limitation precludes the use of a population, and describe the limitation (e.g., too costly, not enough time, limited resources)
- identify and critique a given example in which a generalization from a sample of a population may or may not be valid for the population
- demonstrate the significance of sample size in interpreting data
- develop a project plan that describes
  - a question for investigation
  - the method of data collection that includes social considerations
  - the method for selecting a population or a sample
  - the methods for display and analysis of data
- create a rubric to assess a project
- identify the assumptions associated with a given probability, and explain the limitations of each assumption

PREREQUISITE SKILLS AND KNOWLEDGE

Prior to starting this unit, you should be able to…

- read a table and interpret the data
- understand the meaning of a survey, questionnaire, and interview
- solve simple probability questions
- determine the probability of independent events in a limited sample space
- use sample data to make predictions about a population

Lesson 1 FACTORS AFFECTING DATA COLLECTION

NOTES

The first step in conducting a research project is to formulate a question. The question for investigation should be well written; otherwise, it can cause the data to be misleading or inaccurate. A research question should be free from influencing factors that can negatively affect a person's response to a question. The influencing factors in a question that can lead to inaccurate data are explained in the following paragraphs.

BIAS

Bias refers to an individual's tendency to favour a particular point of view based on information that is neither impartial nor objective. Introducing bias into the survey question is done by providing the participant with some background information regarding the particular topic being studied. If the background information is negative, it will most likely illicit a negative response from the participant. If the background information is positive, it will most likely illicit a positive response from the participant.

For example, the following survey question is asked to an individual about the cost of gasoline:

"Research has shown that we pay 20% more for gas than we did 10 years ago. Do you think you pay too much for gasoline?"

The question is introducing bias by wording the question in such a way that sheds a negative light on the cost of gasoline and how it has risen over the years. This will influence a person against the rising cost of gasoline and will negatively affect the data.

USE OF LANGUAGE

A question should be worded properly so that it is easy to understand. A question should not have misleading or missing information.

For example, someone is asked, "Do you drink a 'double-double' coffee every day?"

The use of language in this question can be misunderstood because the researcher is assuming that every participant will know what the term "double-double" refers to. Not everyone knows that a "double-double" means two cream and two sugars in their coffee.

This lack of information can lead to misunderstanding and can cause the data to be inaccurate.

ETHICS

Data that is collected cannot be reused for other purposes. Using data for an unintended use is unethical.

NOTES

For example, customers at a clothing store are asked to fill out an online survey using their email addresses. They are rewarded with a 10% off coupon for their next visit. The email addresses are then used to send out information on upcoming promotions and sales. The email addresses collected are being misused and this is unethical.

COST

To perform an experiment or survey correctly, there may be costs involved. If the investigator cannot afford the cost to complete a survey, the data could be inaccurate.

For example, a restaurant owner wants to collect the opinion of all his regular customers regarding a menu change. He cannot afford to send the survey to all of them, so he asks the customers that come into his restaurant on a Monday afternoon. The restaurant owner's lack of money to complete the survey will produce inaccurate data.

TIME

Data should be collected in a proper time frame. Taking too long or not having enough time to collect the data are both instances that can lead to inaccurate conclusions about the collected data.

For example, a representative of a land development company goes door-to-door asking the community members how they would feel about the construction of future roadways in their neighbourhood. It starts to rain, so he only manages to ask half of the residents of the neighbourhood and then reports back to his supervisor.

The representative is unable to collect all the data necessary to make such an important decision. This lack of time will result in misleading data.

TIMING

Timing is important if the questions being asked are related to a particular time of day or time of the year.

For example, the following question could be posed to citizens: "Do you think our city does a good job of removing snow on city streets?" If the question is asked in July as opposed to February, the results will be very different.

PRIVACY

Privacy is a potential problem when the topic of data collection is personal or private.

For example, if someone is being asked about diet or weight issues and this is a sensitive topic, they may not give answers that are truthful. This will create inaccurate data.

NOTES

CULTURAL SENSITIVITY

Cultural sensitivity is important to consider when collecting data from people of particular religious or ethnic backgrounds.

For example, if a survey about teenage dating is being conducted in a community where teenage dating is culturally taboo, the data will be inaccurate.

Questions asked when collecting data should be free from influencing factors that may negatively affect the participant's response.

Example

Identify the potential problems in the following survey questions.

a) Players on a badminton team are asked, "Do you prefer to participate in contact sports or non-contact sports?"

Solution

The problem with this question is that badminton is a non-contact sport.

The players on a badminton team may have a bias for non-contact sports. Asking this group of people can result in inaccurate data.

b) During a time of road maintenance, a community is surveyed by the city and asked the following question: "Do you think your community is quiet and clean?"

Solution

The timing of this survey is poor. Since the roadways are under construction, there is noise and dust. Asking such a question at this particular time can cause anger and frustration from the community members resulting in misleading data.

Your Turn 1

Identify the potential problems in the following survey questions.

a) A furniture company asks customers to fill out surveys relating to their recent visit to the store. Customers are told that by completing the survey, they would automatically be entered for a chance to win a $5 000 home makeover. Later, the names and phone numbers of the customers are sold to a telemarketing company.

NOTES

b) A survey is conducted in late January to find out if people think their level of physical activity is high, medium, or low.

Example

Identify the potential problems in the following survey questions. Then, suggest ways in which the survey question or situation can be changed so the study is free of any influence.

a) A representative of a juice company asks shoppers in a supermarket the following question: "Which type of juice do you prefer to drink—apple juice or orange juice?"

Solution

The influencing factor in this question is the use of language. The shopper may not prefer either of the two choices. If the respondents are forced to choose an option, the data being collected will be inaccurate. A survey question free of any influence could be, "Which flavour of juice do you prefer to drink?"

b) People at a bus station are asked: "Do you think travelling by bus is the cheapest way to travel a long distance?"

Solution

The influencing factor is bias because someone travelling by bus could already have a preset opinion that this type of travel is the best mode of transportation. A survey question free of any influence could be, "What do you think is the most cost-effective way to travel a long distance?"

Your Turn 2

Identify the potential problems in the following survey questions. Then, suggest ways in which the survey question or situation can be changed so the study is free of any influence.

a) Grade 9 physical education students are asked, "What type of unhealthy foods do you eat the most?"

b) Free samples of sunscreen are sent to homes in the middle of winter. One week later, the sunscreen company phones the homes to see if people preferred the samples of sunscreen provided over their current brand of sunscreen.

NOTES

A survey is method of collecting data about a sample that represents the entire population.

METHODS OF DATA COLLECTION

The second step in conducting a research project is to select a method of collecting the data. In other words, you must decide on a method to use to survey the population.

Following is a list of descriptions explaining methods of data collection.

Questionnaire

A questionnaire is a series of questions asked of people to gather data on their opinions and/or personal experiences about the topic of study. This can be done through mail, online, or in person. This allows the researcher to gather the data from a large amount of people in a short period of time.

Interview

An interview is when an individual is asked questions regarding a particular topic or issue in a one-on-one setting. This can be done in person or over the phone. An interview allows the researcher to gather a large amount of data from a smaller number of people. The data collected is valuable because it provides information that cannot be communicated through paper and pencil.

Observation

Observations are when the researcher takes detailed notes about behaviour or occurrences happening around them that are related to the topic of research. This method of data collection provides the researcher with insight about the topic of study without having to interact with people directly or be exposed to their potentially biased opinions.

Example

Identify the method of data collection that should be used in the following situation.

Vanessa would like to know which brand of potting soil helps a plant grow the fastest. She purchases 5 different brands of potting soil and purchases 5 flower plants.

Solution

Vanessa should use observation to answer her research question. She is using a variety of soils to test which is the best one for her flowers. Therefore, she must observe the growth of the flowers over time and see which soil helps the plants grow the fastest.

NOTES

Your Turn 3

Identify the method of data collection that should be used in following situation.

The yearbook organizing committee would like to publish a series of questions to be printed under each graduating student's photograph in the yearbook. The committee would like to find out which questions the graduating students would like to see in the yearbook.

PRACTICE EXERCISES

Identify the potential problems in the following survey questions.

1. An inner city community would like more funding for after-school activities. The question asked to taxpayers is, "Would you support your tax dollars going toward creating more activities for inner-city youth?"

2. A survey is conducted in a local grocery store in January regarding the sale of fresh corn. Customers are asked how many times per week they purchase fresh corn.

Identify the influencing factor in the survey question and suggest ways in which the survey question or situation can be changed so the study is free of any influence.

3. A survey is conducted in a local grocery store regarding beef sales. Customers are asked, "Which cut of beef do you purchase the most?"

4. As people are entering a movie theatre to watch a horror movie, a surveyor stands outside and asks each person, "What is your favourite type of movie?"

Use the following information to answer the next 2 questions.

Ellis wants to find out which modes of transportation Grade 9 students use the most.

5. Develop a survey question free from any influence.

6. Identify who should be asked to participate in this survey.

Use the following information to answer the next 2 questions.

Maaz wants to know what type of music teenagers like.

7. Develop a survey question free from any influence.

8. Identify who should be asked to participate in this survey.

Lesson 2 SAMPLE VS. POPULATION

NOTES

The third step in conducting a research project is to decide who to collect the data from: a sample or the population.

A **population** can be defined as all the items, objects, or people being considered in an investigation.

For example, all of the parents in a school district are asked their opinion of a year-round schooling policy. All the parents in the district make up the entire population.

A sample is a smaller portion of the population. The important thing about selecting a sample is that it is representative of the population.
When collecting data from a sample, it is also important that the sample be unbiased to ensure the data is free of influence.

Surveying a population can be very costly, impractical, and time consuming. Therefore, a sample is an easier way to collect data.

There are many different types of samples that can be taken. Following are some examples:

VOLUNTARY SAMPLE

A voluntary sample is created when the entire population is invited to participate. The people who volunteer to participant make up the sample.

For example, all the people calling in to a radio talk show are asked to give their opinions on recent tax increases. Their responses make up the sample data.

CONVENIENCE SAMPLE

People from a population who are easy to access make up the sample.

For example, people eating at a particular restaurant are asked their opinion about the restaurant's service.

RANDOM SAMPLE

A specific number of people are chosen at random to participate in the investigation. In this case, each person in the population has an equal chance of being chosen.

For example, all the names of students in a class are put into a box, the teacher pulls out five names from this box, the students are chosen at random.

NOTES

STRATIFIED SAMPLE

A stratified sample is a type of random sample in which a whole population is divided into distinct groups. Then, a fixed number of people from each distinct group are chosen at random to make up the sample.

For example, a class is divided into boys and girls. Then, three people are chosen at random from each group.

SYSTEMIC SAMPLE

A systemic sample is a type of random sample in which individuals are chosen at specific points within an ordered list of the entire population.

For example, from a single soccer team roster, every fifth person is asked his opinion of a new soccer cleat.

Example

Mr. Russell would like to know how many hours per week each student in his Grade 9 Math class spends reviewing the class notes. There are 32 students in the class.

a) Identify the population in this situation.

Solution

The entire class would be the population—the 32 students in the class.

b) Identify a type of sample that can be used for collecting this data.

Solution

A systemic sample from the class could be to ask every third student.

c) Determine the best method for collecting data and explain your reasoning.

Solution

Since there are only 32 students in the class, Mr. Russell can ask each student to get accurate data.

Your Turn 1

A bag of candy guarantees 60 pieces of chocolate in each bag. Alice wants to know if a shipment of 1 000 bags would have 60 pieces of chocolate in each bag.

a) Identify the population in this situation.

b) Identify a type of sample that can be used for collecting this data.

c) Determine the best method for collecting data and explain your reasoning.

NOTES

LIMITATIONS OF USING POPULATION FOR INVESTIGATION

Sometimes, a survey can only be completed by a population in order to get accurate results. However, investigating an entire population is not always possible because of limitations. Some examples of limitations of investigating a population are that it can be too time-consuming or the investigation would be too expensive.

Example

Explain why the following situation would have limitations.

Health Canada would like to research food allergies in Canadian children. A Canada-wide telephone survey is conducted to collect the data.

Solution

This situation would have limitations because a nationwide telephone survey would be time-consuming and expensive. However, in order to get accurate data, the best method of data collection would be to survey the population.

Your Turn 2

Explain why the following situation would have limitations.

A high school counsellor would like to organize a post-secondary information fair. She would like to survey all the students in the school to see what their plans are after high school. She wants to cater the fair to meet all the students' needs and requirements.

LIMITATIONS OF USING A SAMPLE FOR INVESTIGATION

A good sample will result in data that is unbiased and accurately reflects the views of an entire population.

Sometimes, the data collected from a sample is not a reflection of the population. Consequently, the data taken from a sample may yield results that are not valid.

NOTES

Example

A camp counsellor wants to find out what type of movie to play for movie night. There are 300 campers ranging in age from 9 to 15 years. The camp counsellor decides to ask the first 20 campers that walk into the dining hall that night for dinner what movie they would like to watch.

Explain why the sample is invalid.

Solution

The sample is not representative of the population because the campers' ages range from 9 to 15 years. The first 20 children being asked will not be an accurate representation of all the age groups. If the first 20 children are 13 to 15 years, their choice of movie will be much different from a camper aged 9 or 10 years.

Your Turn 3

A television network would like to know what types of reality television shows are most popular. To collect this data, the network puts a survey in a travel and adventure magazine for people to complete and mail back. Explain why the sample is invalid.

EFFECTS OF SAMPLE SIZE IN INTERPRETING DATA

Sample size refers to the number of people, objects, or items used in an investigation. Determining sample size is an important aspect of data collection. The questions an investigator should ask when deciding sample size are

- Do I have enough time to complete the investigation with this sample size?
- Do I have the financial resources to complete the investigation with this sample size?
- Is the method of sampling the best choice for this sample size?
- Is the sample size representative of the population?

Depending on the goals of the investigation, the sample size can result in a successful or an unsuccessful final result. If the sample size is large, the data collected will be more accurate. If the sample size is too small, the data collected may be misleading or inaccurate.

NOTES

Example

The Vancouver 2010 Olympic committee surveyed Canadians who watched the opening ceremonies of the Winter Olympic Games. They asked each person the following question: "Do you feel there was enough aboriginal representation in the opening ceremonies of the 2010 Olympic Games in Vancouver?"

The surveyors asked a sample of the population in the following proportions:

- 21% Asian-Canadian
- 40% Indo-Canadian
- 33% Caucasian
- 6% Native-Canadian

Identify the potential problem with the sample size in this situation.

Solution

The potential problem with this sample size is that it is not representative of the entire population of Canada. The percentage of citizens from each cultural group does not accurately represent the cultural diversity of Canada. The surveyor's sample will result in misleading data.

Your Turn 4

A coffee shop owner wants to know if customers would use pre-paid coffee cards to make coffee purchases instead of counting change every time they purchase a coffee. The owner decides to give a complimentary ten-dollar coffee card to every fifth customer for a one-week period. Then, he will record how often they use the coffee card after they receive it.

Identify the potential problems with the sample size in this situation.

PRACTICE EXERCISES

Identify the sample type in the following situations.

1. All of the people leaving a children's clothing store are given a survey and asked to mail it back.

2. From a voter registration list, every ninth person is asked the name of the candidate for whom they would vote for.

Use the following information to answer the next 3 questions.

Scientists attempt to collect data on the average health of migrating humpback whales in the Pacific Ocean.

3. What is the population?

4. What type of sample could be used?

5. Which is the best method for data collection and why?

Use the following information to answer the next 3 questions.

Parents at the local playground on a Sunday afternoon are asked if they prefer driving a car, SUV, or minivan.

6. What is the population?

7. What type of sample could be used?

8. Which is the best method for data collection and why?

Use the following information to answer the next 3 questions.

The manager of a software company wants to build a workout facility in the office building. He wants to find out what percentage of people would be interested in this service for employees. He sends out an inter-office email survey.

9. What is the population?

10. What type of sample could be used?

11. Which is the best method for data collection and why?

Use the following information to answer the next question.

A new fitness facility would like to know if the women currently using the weightlifting area would like a "Women's Only" area for weightlifting. The facility owner decides to do a random sample of women in the fitness facility on a Wednesday evening.
The owner asks a sample in the following proportions:

- 5 women finishing a yoga class
- 5 women running on the treadmills
- 5 women in the weightlifting area
- 5 women in the children's play area

12. Identify the potential problem with the sample size in the given situation.

Lesson 3 DEVELOPING A PROJECT PLAN AND CREATING A RUBRIC

NOTES

The government conducts a census to count the number of people in the country. At the same time, they often ask questions to collect other data about the population.

From the information covered in previous lessons, it is clear that investigating a research question requires careful planning. The best way to organize an investigation is to construct a project plan. A project plan should be a map followed by the investigator to collect, analyse, and assess an investigation. A project can be assessed using a rubric.

DEVELOPING A PROJECT PLAN

Step 1

Formulate a question for investigation that is free from any influence.
The question should be free from the following influencing factors:

- Bias
- Use of Language
- Ethics
- Cost
- Time
- Timing
- Privacy
- Cultural Sensitivity

Step 2

Select and identify a method of collecting data.
Some examples of data collection methods are listed:

- Questionnaire
- Census
- Observation

Step 3

Select and identify a sample or population to be surveyed.
The samples used should be representative samples. Choose from the following:

- Population
- Voluntary Sample
- Random Sample
- Convenience Sample
- Systemic Sample
- Stratified Sample

Step 4

Collect and record the data.
Administer the survey to the sample or population.
Record the data in a spreadsheet or tally chart.

Step 5
Display and analyse the data.
A graph can be used to display the data. Some examples of graphs are listed:

- Bar Graph: best used when data is a comparison of different categories.
- Circle Graph or Pie Chart: best used for comparing smaller categories to the whole.
- Line Graph: best used for showing how data changes over time.
- Pictograph: best used to show data using symbols.

A combination of display methods can be used, such as written or oral reports, PowerPoint presentation, or other technology.

Analyse the data and draw a conclusion, or make a prediction from the data. When analysing the data, ask the following questions:

- Does the data answer the research question? Do I need to do further research?
- Is the data biased? How could this be avoided in further research?

Step 6
Design a rubric and evaluate the investigation.
A rubric will help evaluate important aspects of the investigation.

CREATING A RUBRIC

A rubric is a system designed to help evaluate and assess the work completed on an investigation. A rubric is usually set up in a chart form and lists all criteria necessary to make a task successful. The criteria in a rubric should represent the following areas:

- Planning
- Performing
- Recording
- Analysing
- Presenting

A rubric should be a balanced assessment, focusing on the knowledge, understanding, and skill of each area of the investigation. A rubric shows an investigator their current level of understanding and clearly shows the areas of improvement required to progress the investigation to a higher level.

NOTES

The type of data collected will determine the best method of displaying the data.

NOTES

A rubric uses levels of progress to assess all criteria. The levels of progress represent the rules and guidelines used to score the work. As the levels increase, the investigation reaches a level of excellence. The levels are explained as follows:

Level 1 would represent an investigation that is not adequate and needs improvement. An investigation that is evaluated as Level 1 will produce results that are not clear or are misleading.

Level 2 would represent an investigation that is adequate and needs some improvement. The results of an investigation that is evaluated at Level 2 will produce results that are somewhat clear with some areas needing further clarity.

Level 3 would represent an investigation that is proficient and needs minimal improvements. The results of an investigation that is evaluated at Level 3 will produce results that are mostly, but not entirely, accurate. The investigation will need slight improvement to get to a level of excellence.

Level 4 would represent an investigation that is at a level of excellence. The results of an investigation that is evaluated as Level 4 will produce clear and completely accurate results.

See the following page for an example of a rubric an investigator may use. All criteria should be assigned a level.

Criteria	Level 1	Level 2	Level 3	Level 4
PLANNING • Formulating a question • Choosing a data collection method that includes social considerations • Choosing population or a sample	• Not adequate • Needs improvement • Misleading and unclear	• Adequate • Needs some improvement • Needs further clarification	• Proficient • Needs minimal improvement • Results are not fully accurate	• Excellent • Clear results • Accurate results
PERFORMING & RECORDING • Collecting data and recording findings	• Not adequate • Needs improvement • Misleading and unclear	• Adequate • Needs some improvement • Needs further clarification	• Proficient • Needs minimal improvement • Results are not fully accurate	• Excellent • Clear results • Accurate results
RECORDING • Displaying data in an appropriate manner	• Not adequate • Needs improvement • Misleading and unclear	• Adequate • Needs some improvement • Needs further clarification	• Proficient • Needs minimal improvement • Results are not fully accurate	• Excellent • Clear results • Accurate results
ANALYSING & PRESENTING • Analysing data and drawing conclusions to answer the question	• Not adequate • Needs improvement • Misleading and unclear	• Adequate • Needs some improvement • Needs further clarification	• Proficient • Needs minimal improvement • Results are not fully accurate	• Excellent • Clear results • Accurate results

NOTES

This sample rubric is only a blueprint for what an investigator can use to assess performance levels. For example, if a student wants to asses her level of readiness for an exam, she may change the description of Level 1 to the following statement:

- "Homework was completed 3 out of 5 days and class notes were not reviewed."

In other words, investigators can personalize their rubric to a description of performance levels that match their needs, thereby ensuring a successful research project.

Example

An ice cream store in the local mall is considering adding a new flavour of ice cream to their menu. The company has created two possible new flavours.

Complete the following tasks for the given situation:

a) Create a project plan.

Solution

Step 1

Formulate a survey question that is free from any influence."Given the following two new potential flavours of ice cream, which flavour of ice cream would you prefer?"
This question does not have bias, cultural sensitivity, or any other influencing factor.

Step 2

Select and identify a method of collecting data.
A questionnaire can be used to collect the data. It is cost efficient and the data can be collected quickly.

Step 3

Select and identify a sample or population to be surveyed.
A systemic sample can be used by asking every fifth customer to try a sample of both flavours and answer the survey question. This can be carried out for one entire business day.

Step 4

Collect and record the data.
The data can be collected and recorded on a tally chart by the surveyor.

Step 5

Display and analyse the data.
Data should be displayed on a bar graph showing the two flavours of ice cream and the frequency of customers who liked each flavour.

b) Create a rubric to assess the investigation.

Solution

A potential rubric that can be used for the investigation is outlined on the next page.

Criteria	Level 1	Level 2	Level 3	Level 4
PLANNING • Formulating a question • Choosing a data collection method that includes social considerations • Choosing population or a sample	• The question has many influencing factors • Data collection method is not adequate • The wrong choice was made	• The question has some influencing factors • Data collection method is weak • The choice is weak	• The question has one influencing factor • Data collection method is adequate • The choice may result in inaccurate data	• The question has no influencing factors • Data collection method is appropriate • The choice will result in accurate data
PERFORMING & RECORDING • Collecting data and recording findings	• The data was collected but not recorded accurately	• The collection and recording of data had some problems	• The collection and recording of data had one problem	• The collection and recording of data had no problems
RECORDING • Displaying data in an appropriate manner	• The data display method was not the right choice	• The display method could be clearer	• The display method is adequate	• The display method is excellent
ANALYSING & PRESENTING • Analysing data and drawing conclusions to answer the question	• The data collected does not answer the question	• The data collected is misleading and unclear	• The data collected needs some clarity	• The data collected answers the question accurately and clearly

NOTES

c) Identify strengths and weaknesses of the investigation.

Solution

Some strengths of the investigation are as follows:

- The sampling method is cost-effective
- It will not require a large time commitment
- The sample is convenient because it is surveying people who will be coming into the store
- The surveyor does not have to go anywhere to collect the data.

A weakness of the investigation is that a customer may not like either of the new ice cream flavours; the question does not address this possibility.

Your Turn 1

A local supermarket wants to start selling a new brand of hot dog. The store decides to set up a booth in the meat area for customers to sample the new hot dog and take a short survey.
Complete the following tasks for the given situation:

a) Create a project plan.

b) Create a rubric to assess the investigation.

c) Identify strengths and weaknesses of the investigation.

PRACTICE EXERCISES

Identify the best method to display data in the following situations and explain why.

1. Simon would like to display data on the battery life of 5 different battery brands.

2. Adam would like to display data on the most popular methods of communication for teenagers. His survey gave the following choices: cell phone, face to face, texting, and email.

3. Hanna is an assistant coach on the track and field team. She has collected data from daily practices for the 500-metre race. The race was timed over a five-day period.

Identify the important components of the following parts of a project plan.

4. Step 1: Formulate a survey question for investigation.

5. Step 3: Select and identify a sample or population for investigation.

Answer the following questions related to rubrics.

6. What are the two important components when creating a rubric?

7. Why is a rubric important for the success of an investigation?

Use the following information to answer the next 3 questions.

Fiona would like to investigate the length of time an insulated coffee mug keeps liquids hot. She would like to use 4 different types of insulated cups for this investigation.

8. Create a project plan.

9. Create a rubric to assess the investigation.

10. Identify strengths and weaknesses of the investigation.

Lesson 4 PROBABILITY IN SOCIETY

NOTES

Probability is the likelihood of something happening. An event with a probability of 0 means that event is impossible and will never happen. For instance, humans will never walk to the moon, so the probability of that event is 0. An event with a probability of 1 means that event is certain and will always happen. For instance, the sun will always rise in the east, so the probability of that event occurring is 1. The probability of everything else will fall in between 0 and 1, inclusive. Probability can be expressed as a ratio, fraction, or a percentage.

PROBABILITY IN MEDIA

The Internet, newspapers, and television media can use probability to impact their audiences. The media often reports data in a way that may be misleading. Sometimes, this is unintentional. When analysing data and the validity of a claim, ask yourself these important questions:

- Is there enough valid data to make a claim?
- Are assumptions being made for me?

Example

Identify what assumptions can be made reading the following advertisements:

a) "95% of mothers choose to purchase organic baby food for their babies".

Solution

The advertisement can affect consumers by creating an image in their mind that organic baby food is the best choice for their babies. Consumers may feel bad if they do not feed their child organic food.

b) A bicycle company showed the following ad to their customers: "In Edmonton last year, 83% of accidents involved cars and only 5% involved bicycles. Purchase a bike today. It could save your life!"

Solution

This is misleading because there are more people driving cars than riding bikes. An assumption can be made that more car accidents than bike accidents would be expected. The reader may get a false sense of security that riding a bike is the safest commuting alternative.

NOTES

Your Turn 1

Identify what assumptions can be made reading the following advertisements.

a) "70% of professional cleaners choose Germ-Away to clean their own homes. Germ-Away has been clinically proven to kill 99.9% of household germs"

b) Cindy would like to continue her post-secondary education in the math program. She reads in the newspaper that in the next two years, student debt will increase by 57%.

PROBABILITY TO SUPPORT OPPOSING VIEWS

Probability can be used to support or oppose a particular view.

Example

How can the following situations be used to support opposing views?

Lisa wants to go on a road trip for the upcoming long weekend. Marie doesn't think Lisa should go because of storm warnings and unsafe highway conditions. The weather report shows a 50% chance of wet snow and freezing rain resulting in possible unsafe driving conditions. Explain how Lisa and Marie can use this information to support their views.

Solution

Since there is a 50% chance of bad weather resulting in unsafe driving, Marie can claim that the danger factor is too high and Lisa should not go on the road trip. Lisa can say that 50% does not guarantee bad road conditions; in fact, she can argue that there is a 50% chance that bad weather will not occur.

Your Turn 2

Trevor feels he is ready to take his driving test since he has practised a few times with his older brother. His mother feels he should become better prepared by attending a driving school. The driving school reports that 65% of their students pass the driving test.

Explain how Trevor and his mother can use this information to support their views.

NOTES

THEORETICAL PROBABILITY, EXPERIMENTAL PROBABILITY, AND SUBJECTIVE JUDGMENT

Theoretical probability is defined as the expected probability of an event occurring. A ratio can be written for the number of favourable outcomes to the total number of possible outcomes for an event.

$$\text{Probability} = \frac{\text{number of favourable outcomes}}{\text{total number of possible outcomes}}$$

Theoretical probability is based on reasoning that each outcome has an equal chance of occurring.

Experimental probability is the probability of an event occurring based on an experiment. Experimental probability is used to predict the results of future experiences.

Subjective judgment is decisions made based on someone's feelings or emotions.

Example

The school cafeteria is introducing a new "healthy and light" menu. The cafeteria staff recorded the number of students who tried the new items the first day the menu was introduced. The results are shown on the following table.

New Lunch Item	Number of Students Purchasing New Item
Tomato Basil Soup	5
Grilled Vegetable Sandwich	12
Grilled Chicken Pizza on Multigrain Crust	22
Caesar Salad	6
Tofu Chili Dog	5

Using the table, answer the following questions:

a) What is the theoretical probability a student will choose a grilled vegetable sandwich? Express probability as a percent.

Solution

Apply the probability formula, substitute in the known values, and evaluate.

$$\begin{aligned}\text{Probability} &= \frac{\text{number of favourable outcomes}}{\text{total number of possible outcomes}}\\ &= \frac{\text{grilled vegetable sandwiches}}{\text{total number of items on the menu}}\\ &= \frac{1}{5}\\ &= 20\%\end{aligned}$$

The theoretical probability that a student will choose a grilled vegetable sandwich is 20%.

NOTES

b) From the answer to question **a)**, what assumptions have you made?

Solution

The assumption that can be made is that since there are 5 new items and one item has a probability of 20%, then each item on the list has the same chance of being selected by a student.

c) What is the experimental probability a student will choose a grilled vegetable sandwich? Express probability as a percent.

Solution

Apply the probability formula, substitute in the known values, and evaluate.

$$\begin{aligned}\text{Probability} &= \frac{\text{number of favourable outcomes}}{\text{total number of possible outcomes}}\\ &= \frac{\text{grilled vegetable sandwiches ordered}}{\text{total amount of items ordered}}\\ &= \frac{12}{50}\\ &= 24\%\end{aligned}$$

Based on experimental data, the probability that a student will choose a grilled vegetable sandwich is 24%.

d) Compare the answers from **a)** and **c)**.

Solution

The theoretical probability is 20% and the experimental probability is 24%. Therefore, theoretical probability is less than experimental probability. Both numbers are very similar; however, the experimental probability is more accurate.

e) From a survey of 500 students, how many will likely choose tomato basil soup?

Solution

Step 1

Calculate the experimental probability of a student choosing tomato basil soup.

$$\begin{aligned}\text{Probability} &= \frac{\text{number of favourable outcomes}}{\text{total number of possible outcomes}}\\ &= \frac{\text{tomato basil soup ordered}}{\text{total amount of items ordered}}\\ &= \frac{5}{50}\\ &= 10\%\end{aligned}$$

The probability that a student will choose tomato basil soup is 10%.

NOTES

Step 2
Calculate 10% of 500.
$0.10 \times 500 = 50$

Therefore, from 500 students, 50 will likely choose tomato basil soup.

Your Turn 3

Helen's Grade 9 class received the following grades on a science project.

Student Name	Grade on Science Project
Allyson	B+
Ben	A
Bruce	C–
Colin	B–
Dexter	B–
Emma	C–
Fiona	C–
Hailey	C
Henry	C+
Helen	C–
Jeffrey	A+
Kelly	A–
Karen	A
Kevin	C–
Laurie	B–
Lisa	C
Larry	C–
Melanie	C–
Matthew	A+
Melissa	C–

a) What is the theoretical probability a student will receive a grade of C–? Express the probability as a percent.

b) From the answer to question **a)**, what assumptions have you made?

c) What is the experimental probability that a student will receive a grade of C–.

d) Compare the answers from **a)** and **c)**.

e) There are three Grade 9 classes, each with 20 students. How many will likely receive a grade of A+ on the science project?

PRACTICE EXERCISES

Identify the assumptions that can be made by reading the following advertisements.

1. "75% of sales associates who take the sales training course 'Successful Sales' at the community college sell 55% more merchandise than the associates with no formal training."

2. "Bruce Williams, the candidate running for mayor, has had a 92% past success rate of fulfilling campaign promises."

3. "Smith's All Weather Tires are effective on tough winter-driving conditions 80% of the time."

Use the following information to answer the next question.

> Steven and Joel are studying for the final exam in Grade 9 Math. Steven says that the math teacher used questions from the in-class notes 50% of the time on previous exams. He is encouraging Joel to study the class notes and not the textbook to ensure he gets a passing grade on the exam.

4. How can the given situation be used to support opposing views?

Use the following information to answer the next five questions.

Olds, Alberta is a town of 7 500 people. There is an election being held for mayor. A local reporter asked a group of 60 people for whom they would vote. The results are shown in the following table.

Candidates	Preliminary Approval Rating
Candidate Peters	47%
Candidate Smith	32%
Candidate Auburn	22%

5. How many people would likely vote for Candidate Smith?

6. What is the theoretical probability that a citizen will vote for Candidate Peters? Express the probability as a percent.

7. What assumptions are made from the results of **6**?

8. Calculate the theoretical probability of Candidate Auburn winning.

9. Compare the results from **8** to the experimental probability.

10. The reporter predicts that Candidate Peters will win. Do you agree with this prediction? Justify your answer.

REVIEW SUMMARY

- Data collection can be negatively affected by factors such as: bias, use of language, ethics, cost, time and timing, privacy or cultural sensitivity.
- Sampling is a method of collecting data from a portion of a population.
- The project plan is used to develop a plan for data collection.
- A rubric is a system that can be designed to help evaluate the work completed on a survey or experiment.
- When analysing data and the validity of a claim made by the media, ask these important questions:
  - Is there enough valid data to make a claim?
  - Are assumptions being made for me?
- Probability can be used to support or oppose a particular view.
- Theoretical probability is defined as the expected probability of an event occurring. Theoretical probability is based on reasoning that each outcome has an equal chance of occurring.
- Experimental probability is the probability of an event occurring based on an experiment. Experimental probability is used to predict the results of future experiences.
- Subjective judgment is based on decisions made by someone's feelings or emotions.

PRACTICE TEST

Identify the potential problems in the following survey questions.

1. The students' union would like to introduce a food bank service for students. To identify the level of interest, a random sample of students is surveyed. The following survey question is asked: "Would you use a campus food bank?"

2. A multicultural centre is hosting a welcome night for new immigrants to Canada. They would like to know which type of services new immigrants would find most useful. The following survey question is asked: "Do you need help making a resumé?"

Use the following information to answer the next question.

A salesperson asks shoppers in a supermarket the following question: "Which type of milk do you prefer: chocolate milk or strawberry milk?"

3. Identify the potential problems in the survey question.

4. Rewrite the survey question so that it is free of any influence.

Identify the best method of data collection to be used in the following situations.

5. Susan would like to test the battery life of batteries found in children's toys.

6. A new bike path has been built in the neighbourhood of Parkland. The developer would like to know if the residents find this bike path useful or not useful.

Identify the types of samples being used in the following situations.

7. Leslie-Anne would like to choose four of her ten close friends to give their opinion on her new recipe. She puts everyone's name into a hat and pulls four names.

8. Amy would like to know if the members of the swimming team are able to swim one lap on the pool within 3 minutes. There are 30 people on the swim team. Amy tests every fifth person on the team roster.

9. All the mothers entering a stroller aerobics class are asked if they like the new stroller made especially for mothers who exercise with their children.

Use the following information to answer the next 3 questions.

Ayesha would like to know how many hours per week her teammates spend running on their own time, outside of soccer practice. There are 35 girls on her soccer team.

10. Identify the population in the situation.

11. Identify a type of sample that can be used for the collection of data.

12. Which is the best method for data collection and why?

Use the following information to answer the next question.

An airline company was having engine difficulties with its propeller jet planes. A team of mechanics came in and performed maintenance checks on all 457 planes in the fleet. The safety administrators would like to test each plane to ensure all the planes are functioning safely.

13. Explain why the given situation would have limitations.

Use the following information to answer the next question.

A local restaurant is famous for its fresh brewed coffee. The restaurant would like to switch to a cheaper coffee brand to save on supply costs. They decide to survey the first 10 people who come into the restaurant for breakfast with a free sample of the coffee.

14. Explain why the following samples are invalid.

Use the following information to answer the next 3 questions.

Anthony would like to investigate how many people choose high-grade unleaded gasoline at the local gas station.

15. Create a project plan.

16. Create a rubric to assess the investigation.

17. Identify the strengths of the investigation.

Use the following information to answer the next question.

72% of Canadians use reusable cloth bags when they go grocery shopping.

18. Identify what assumptions can be made from the given advertisement statement.

Use the following table to answer the next 4 questions.

The local gym is introducing some fitness classes. The staff recorded the number of people who tried the new fitness classes within the first month. The results are shown on the following table.

New Fitness Class	Number of People Trying New Class
Ballroom Dance	9
Power Yoga	16
Cycle for Life	19
Maximum Core Strength	10
Pilates	6

19. What is the theoretical probability that a person will choose to try the Pilates class?

20. From the answer to question **19**, what assumptions have you made?

21. What is the experimental probability that a person will choose to try the Pilates class.

22. Compare the answers from **19** and **21**.

23. From a survey of 1 000 people, how many people would be expected to choose to try the Power Yoga class?

S N A P

Student Notes and Problems

ANSWERS AND SOLUTIONS

POWERS

Lesson 1—Powers

YOUR TURN ANSWERS AND SOLUTIONS

1. The base is 6 and the exponent is 12.

2. The base is 7. The exponent is 5. The base of 7 is multiplied 5 times.

   $7^5 = 7 \times 7 \times 7 \times 7 \times 7$

   Power (the 7^5); Expanded form (the $7 \times 7 \times 7 \times 7 \times 7$)

3. The number being multiplied is 11. This value becomes the base. The number 11 is multiplied repeatedly six times. Six becomes the exponent. The power is 11^6.

4. **Step 1**
   Write the expression in expanded form.
   $8^4 = 8\times8\times8\times8$

   Step 2
   Evaluate the expression using repeated multiplication.
   $8\times8\times8\times8$
   $= 64\times8\times8$
   $= 512\times8$
   $= 4\ 096$

   $8^4 = 4\ 096$

PRACTICE EXERCISES ANSWERS AND SOLUTIONS

1. 3

3. 7

5. 4

7. **Step 1**
   Write the expression in expanded form.
   $2^5 = 2\times2\times2\times2\times2$
   Step 2
   Evaluate the expression using repeated multiplication.
   $2\times2\times2\times2\times2$
   $= 4\times2\times2\times2$
   $= 8\times2\times2$
   $= 16\times2$
   $= 32$

   $2^5 = 32$

9. **Step 1**
   Write the expression in expanded form.
   $4^2 = 4\times4$

   Step 2
   Evaluate the expression using repeated multiplication.
   4×4
   $= 16$

   $4^2 = 16$

11. The number being multiplied is 7. This value becomes the base. The number 7 is multiplied repeatedly three times. Three becomes the exponent. The power is 7^3.

Lesson 2—Negative Powers

YOUR TURN ANSWERS AND SOLUTIONS

1. The base of –3 is enclosed in brackets while the exponent 2 is outside the brackets. Since the negative is inside the brackets, it belongs to the number 3. The exponent 2 applies to everything inside the brackets. Solve the expression by multiplying the base, –3, two times.

$$\begin{aligned}(-3)^2 &= -3\times-3\\ &= 9\end{aligned}$$

2. The base and the exponent are both enclosed in brackets. The exponent 2 only applies to the base of 8. Therefore, the negative sign belongs to the numerical coefficient of 1. Solve the expression by multiplying the base, 8, two times. Then, multiply the result by –1.

$$\begin{aligned}(-8^2) &= (-1)(8\times8)\\ &= (-1)(64)\\ &= -64\end{aligned}$$

3. Since there are no brackets present, the exponent 3 only applies to the base of 6. Multiply the base, 6, three times. Then, multiply the result by –1.

$$\begin{aligned}-6^3 &= (-1)(6\times6\times6)\\ &= (-1)(36\times6)\\ &= (-1)(216)\\ &= -216\end{aligned}$$

PRACTICE EXERCISES ANSWERS AND SOLUTIONS

1. $$\begin{aligned}(-7)^3 &= -7\times-7\times-7\\ &= 49\times-7\\ &= -343\end{aligned}$$

3. $$\begin{aligned}(-9)^4 &= -9\times-9\times-9\times-9\\ &= 81\times-9\times-9\\ &= -729\times-9\\ &= 6\ 561\end{aligned}$$

5. $$\begin{aligned}(-9^2) &= (-1)(9\times9)\\ &= (-1)(81)\\ &= -81\end{aligned}$$

7. $$\begin{aligned}-2^3 &= (-1)(2\times2\times2)\\ &= (-1)(4\times2)\\ &= (-1)(8)\\ &= -8\end{aligned}$$

Lesson 3—Order of Operations

YOUR TURN ANSWERS AND SOLUTIONS

1. To solve this expression, use the order of operations.

Step 1
Perform the operations located within the brackets. Within the brackets, BEDMAS still applies. Complete the division before the addition.

$$= (\underline{15\div5}+11)+7^2$$
$$= (3+11)+7^2$$

Complete the addition next.

$$= (\underline{3+11})+7^2$$
$$= 14+7^2$$

Step 2
Perform any operations involving exponents.

$$= 14+\underline{7^2}$$
$$= 14+49$$

Step 3
Perform any addition or subtraction operations.

$$= \underline{14+49}$$
$$= 63$$

2. Locate the ( ) buttons and press the calculator keys in the following order:

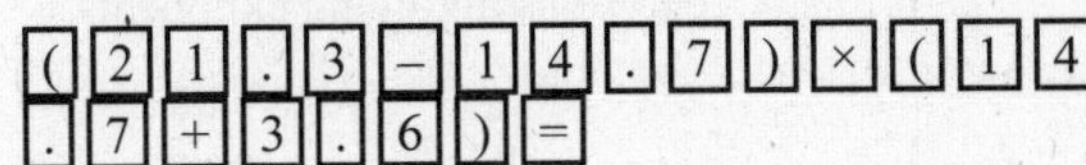
(2 1 . 3 – 1 4 . 7) × (1 4 . 7 + 3 . 6) =.

The solution is 120.78.

3.

Step 1	$=30\div(14-4)\times16-2$	Exponents were completed before brackets.
Step 2	$=30\div(14-4)\times14$	Subtraction was completed before division.
Step 3	$=30\div(10)\times14$	
Step 4	$=30\div(140)$	Multiplication was completed before division.
Step 5	$=0.214$	

The correct solution is

Step 1	$=30\div(14-4)\times4^2-2$
Step 2	$=30\div(10)\times4^2-2$
Step 3	$=30\div(10)\times16-2$
Step 4	$=3\times16-2$
Step 5	$=48-2$
Step 6	$=46$

$30\div(14-4)\times4^2-2=46$

PRACTICE EXERCISES ANSWERS AND SOLUTIONS

1. Step 1
Perform the operations located within the brackets.
$4^2+3^3\underline{(2\times9)}$
$=4^2+3^3(18)$

Step 2
Perform any operations involving exponents.
$\underline{4^2}+\underline{3^3}(18)$
$=16+27(18)$

Step 3
Perform any division or multiplication operations.
$16+\underline{27(18)}$
$=16+486$

Step 4
Perform any addition or subtraction operations.
$\underline{16+486}$
$=502$

3. Step 1
Perform the operations located within the brackets.
$5(\underline{13-3})^2$
$=5(10)^2$

Step 2
Perform any operations involving exponents.
$5\underline{(10)^2}$
$=5(100)$

Step 3
Perform any division or multiplication operations.
$5(100)$
$=500$

Answers may vary for keystroking.

5. 

The solution is 19.0.

7. 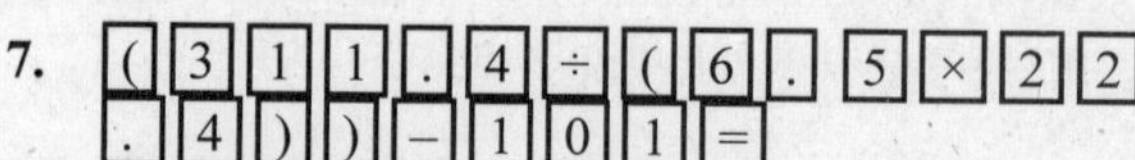

The solution is –98.9.

9.

Given Solution		Error
Step 1	$=4(15+14)-3$	Exponents were completed before brackets.
Step 2	$=4(29)-3$	
Step 3	$=4(26)$	Subtraction was completed before multiplication.
Step 4	$=104$	

The correct solution is

Step 1	$=2^2(15+14)-3$
Step 2	$=2^2(29)-3$
Step 3	$=4(29)-3$
Step 4	$=113$

$2^2(15+14)-3=113$.

Practice Test

ANSWERS AND SOLUTIONS

1. The base is 5 and the exponent is 2.

3. The base is 4 and the exponent is 3.

5. **Step 1**
Write the expression in expanded form.
$8^2=8\times8$

Step 2
Evaluate the expression using repeated multiplication.
8×8
$=64$

7. The number being multiplied repeatedly is 3. This becomes the base. The number 3 is multiplied 5 times. The number 5 becomes the exponent. The power is 3^5.

9. $(-13^4)=(-1)(13\times13\times13\times13)$
$=(-1)(169\times13\times13)$
$=(-1)(2\ 197\times13)$
$=(-1)(28\ 561)$
$=-28\ 561$

11. **Step 1**
Perform the operations located within the brackets.
$5^2+2^4\underline{(12\times9)}$
$=5^2+2^4(108)$

Step 2
Perform any operations involving exponents.
$\underline{5^2}+\underline{2^4}(108)$
$=25+16(108)$

Step 3
Perform any division or multiplication operations.
$25+\underline{16(108)}$
$=25+1\ 728$

Step 4
Perform any addition or subtraction operations.
$\underline{25+1\ 728}$
$=1\ 753$

13. Locate the [a b/c] and [^] buttons on the calculator.

Press the keys in the following order:
[(] [3] [a b/c] [4] [+] [3] [a b/c] [8] [)] [×] [2] [^] [3] [=]

The solution is 9.

15.

	Given Solution	Error
Step 1	$=45\div(15-5)\times216-21$	Exponents were completed before brackets.
Step 2	$=45\div(15-5)\times195$	Subtraction was completed before division.
Step 3	$=45\div(10)\times195$	
Step 4	$=45\div(1950)$	Multiplying was completed before division.
Step 5	$=0.023$	

The correct solution is

Step 1	$=45\div(10)\times6^3-21$
Step 2	$=45\div(10)\times216-21$
Step 3	$=4.5\times216-21$
Step 4	$=972-21$
Step 5	$=951$

$45\div(15-5)\times6^3-21=951$

EXPONENT LAW OF POWERS

Lesson 1—Multiplying and Dividing Powers

YOUR TURN ANSWERS AND SOLUTIONS

1. **Step 1**
Verify that the bases of the powers are the same.
The base of both the powers is 6.

Step 2
Add the exponents: $6^4 \times 6^2 = 6^{4+2}$
$= 6^6$

2. **Step 1**
Verify that the bases of the powers are the same.
The base of all the powers is 5.

Step 2
Add the exponents: $5^5 \times 5^2 \times 5^3 = 5^{5+2+3}$
$= 5^{10}$

3. **Step 1**
Verify that the bases of the powers are the same.
The base of both the powers is –4.

Step 2
Add the exponents: $(-4)^2 \times (-4)^{10} = (-4)^{2+10}$
$= (-4)^{12}$

4. **Step 1**
Verify that the bases of the powers are the same.
The base of all the powers is –7.

Step 2
Add the exponents:
$(-7)^3 \times (-7)^2 \times (-7)^4 = (-7)^{3+2+4}$
$= (-7)^9$

5. **Step 1**
Verify that the bases of the powers are the same.
The base of both the powers is 10.

Step 2
Subtract the exponents: $\frac{10^5}{10^3} = 10^{5-3}$
$= 10^2$

6. **Step 1**
Verify that the bases of the powers are the same.
The base of both the powers is 6.

Step 2
Subtract the exponents: $6^{14} \div 6^8 = 6^{14-8}$
$= 6^6$

7. **Step 1**
Verify that the bases of the powers are the same.
The base of both the powers is –3.

Step 2
Subtract the exponents: $(-3)^{12} \div (-3)^6 = (-3)^{12-6}$
$= (-3)^6$

8. **Step 1**
Verify that the bases of the powers are the same.
The base of all the powers is –7.

Step 2
Subtract the exponents: $\frac{(-7)^7}{(-7)^4} = (-7)^{7-4}$
$= (-7)^3$

PRACTICE EXERCISES ANSWERS AND SOLUTIONS

1. $4^4 \times 4^3 = 4^{4+3}$
$= 4^7$

3. $12^4 \times 12^8 = 12^{4+8}$
$= 12^{12}$

5. $\frac{10^5}{10^3} = 10^{5-3}$
$= 10^2$

7. $\frac{6^8 \times 6^4}{6^3} = 6^{(8+4)-3}$
$= 6^9$

9. $\frac{2^5 \times 2^3}{2} = 2^{(5+3)-1}$
$= 2^7$

Lesson 2—Power Laws

YOUR TURN ANSWERS AND SOLUTIONS

1. The pattern is dividing the equation by 5.

Step 1
Divide each side of the equation by 5.
$$5^3 = 125$$
$$5^3 \div 5^1 = 125 \div 5$$
$$5^{3-1} = 25$$
$$5^2 = 25$$

Step 2
Divide each side of the equation by 5 again.
$$5^2 \div 5^1 = 25 \div 5$$
$$5^{2-1} = 5$$
$$5^1 = 5$$

Step 3
Divide each side of the equation by 5 again.
$$5^1 \div 5^1 = 5 \div 5$$
$$5^{1-1} = 1$$
$$5^0 = 1$$

This pattern verifies the exponent of zero law.

2. Multiply the exponents to reduce the expression to a single power.
$$(3^4)^3 = 3^{4\times3}$$
$$= 3^{12}$$

3. Multiply the exponents to reduce the expression to a single power.
$$((-2)^3)^4 = (-2)^{3\times4}$$
$$= (-2)^{12}$$

4. **Step 1**
Distribute the exponent 3 located outside the brackets to each term located inside the brackets.
$$(2^2 6)^3 = (2^2)^3(6)^3$$

Step 2
Apply the power of a product law.
$$(2^2)^3(6)^3 = 2^{2\times3}6^{1\times3}$$
$$= 2^6 6^3$$

Step 3
Evaluate the expression.
$$2^6 6^3 = 64\times216$$
$$= 1\ 3824$$

5. **Step 1**
Distribute the exponent 2 located outside the brackets to each term located inside the brackets.
$$(7^2(-2)^5)^2 = (7^2)^2 \times ((-2)^5)^2$$

Step 2
Apply the power of a product law.
$$(7^2)^2 \times ((-2)^5)^2 = 7^{2\times2} \times (-2)^{5\times2}$$
$$= 7^4 \times (-2)^{10}$$

Step 3
Evaluate the expression.
$$7^4 \times (-2)^{10} = 2\ 401 \times 1\ 024$$
$$= 2\ 458\ 624$$

6. **Step 1**
Distribute the exponent 4 located outside the brackets to each term located inside the brackets.
$$(-8\times10)^4 = (-8)^4 \times 10^4$$

Step 2
Apply the power of a product law.
$$(-8)^4 \times 10^4 = (-8)^{1\times4} \times 10^{1\times4}$$
$$= (-8)^4 \times 10^4$$

Step 3
Evaluate the expression.
$$(-8)^4 \times 10^4 = 4\ 096 \times 10\ 000$$
$$= 40\ 960\ 000$$

7. **Step 1**
Distribute the exponent 2 located outside the brackets to each term located inside the brackets.
$$((-13)^2 \times (-4))^2 = ((-13)^2)^2 \times (-4)^2$$

Step 2
Apply the power of a product law.
$$((-13)^2)^2 \times (-4)^2 = (-13)^{2\times2} \times (-4)^{1\times2}$$
$$= (-13)^4 \times (-4)^2$$

Step 3
Evaluate the expression.

$$(-13)^4 \times (-4)^2 = 28\ 561 \times 16$$
$$= 456\ 976$$

8. Step 1
Distribute the exponent 3 located outside the brackets to each term located inside the brackets.

$$\left(\frac{5}{8}\right)^3 = \frac{5^3}{8^3}$$

Step 2
Evaluate the expression by using repeated multiplication.

$$\frac{5^3}{8^3} = \frac{5\times5\times5}{8\times8\times8}$$
$$= \frac{125}{512}$$

9. Step 1
Distribute the exponent 2 located outside the brackets to each term located inside the brackets.

$$\left(\frac{5^2}{9^3}\right)^2 = \frac{(5^2)^2}{(9^3)^2}$$

Step 2
Apply the power of a power law.

$$\frac{5^{2\times2}}{9^{3\times2}} = \frac{5^4}{9^6}$$

Step 3
Evaluate the expression by using repeated multiplication.

$$\frac{5^4}{9^6} = \frac{5\times5\times5\times5}{9\times9\times9\times9\times9\times9}$$
$$= \frac{625}{531\ 441}$$
$$\doteq 0.001\ 18$$
$$\doteq 0.001$$

10. Step 1
Distribute the exponent 2 located outside the brackets to each term located inside the brackets.

$$\left(\frac{-5}{-11}\right)^2 = \frac{(-5)^2}{(-11)^2}$$

Step 2
Evaluate the expression by using repeated multiplication.

$$\frac{(-5)^2}{(-11)^2} = \frac{-5\times-5}{-11\times-11}$$
$$= \frac{25}{121}$$

11. Step 1
Distribute the exponent 2 located outside the brackets to each term located inside the brackets.

$$\left(\frac{(-3)^2}{(-4)^3}\right)^2 = \frac{\left((-3)^2\right)^2}{\left((-4)^3\right)^2}$$

Step 2
Apply the power of a power law.

$$\left(\frac{(-3)^2}{(-4)^3}\right)^2 = \frac{(-3)^{2\times2}}{(-4)^{3\times2}}$$
$$= \frac{(-3)^4}{(-4)^6}$$

Step 3
Evaluate the expression by using repeated multiplication.

$$\frac{(-3)^4}{(-4)^6} = \frac{-3\times-3\times-3\times-3}{-4\times-4\times-4\times-4\times-4\times-4}$$
$$= \frac{81}{4\ 096}$$
$$= 0.0198$$
$$= 0.020$$

PRACTICE EXERCISES ANSWERS AND SOLUTIONS

1. $(1^2 4^3)^4 = 1^{2\times4} 4^{3\times4}$
$= 1^8 4^{12}$

3. $(13^4)^6 = 13^{4\times6}$
$= 13^{24}$

5. $(8\times2^4)^6 = 8^{1\times6}\times2^{4\times6}$
$= 8^6\times2^{24}$

7. $\left(\dfrac{5}{8^2}\right)^3 = \dfrac{5^3}{8^{2\times 3}}$
$= \dfrac{5^3}{8^6}$

9. $\left((-2)^8 \div (-2)^4\right)^2 = (-2)^{8\times 2} \div (-2)^{4\times 2}$
$= (-2)^{16} \div (-2)^8$
$= (-2)^{16-8}$
$= (-2)^8$

or

$\left((-2)^8 \div (-2)^4\right)^2 = \left((-2)^{8-4}\right)^2$
$= \left((-2)^4\right)^2$
$= (-2)^{4\times 2}$
$= (-2)^8$

Lesson 3—Sum and Difference of Powers

YOUR TURN ANSWERS AND SOLUTIONS

1. **Step 1**
Solve the first exponential expression by using repeated multiplication.
$3^2 = 3\times 3$
$= 9$

Step 2
Solve the second exponential expression by using repeated multiplication.
$8^4 = 8\times 8\times 8\times 8$
$= 4\ 096$

Step 3
Add the two values together.
$9 + 4\ 096 = 4\ 105$

2. **Step 1**
Solve the first exponential expression by using repeated multiplication.
$(-8)^3 = (-8)\times(-8)\times(-8)$
$= -512$

Step 2
Solve the second exponential expression by using repeated multiplication.
$(-2)^5 = (-2)\times(-2)\times(-2)\times(-2)\times(-2)$
$= -32$

Step 3
Add the two values together.
$(-512) + (-32) = -544$

3. **Step 1**
Solve the first exponential expression by using repeated multiplication.
$4^3 = 4\times 4\times 4$
$= 64$

Step 2
Solve the second exponential expression by using repeated multiplication.
$2^2 = 2\times 2$
$= 4$

Step 3
Subtract the two values.
$64 - 4 = 60$

4. **Step 1**
Solve the first exponential expression by using repeated multiplication.
$(-5)^2 = (-5)\times(-5)$
$= 25$

Step 2
Solve the second exponential expression by using repeated multiplication.
$(-9)^4 = (-9)\times(-9)\times(-9)\times(-9)$
$= 6\ 561$

Step 3
Subtract the two values.
$(25) - (6\ 561) = -6\ 536$

5. When applying the power of a product law, the powers must multiply each other. In this case, the terms are being added together. Therefore, the power of a product law cannot be applied to simplify the expression. Instead, the sum of two powers law must be applied first. Then the expression can be evaluated.

Correct Solution:

$$\begin{aligned}(3^6+3^2)^2 &= (729+9)^2\\ &= (738)^2\\ &= 544\ 644\end{aligned}$$

PRACTICE EXERCISES ANSWERS AND SOLUTIONS

1. **Step 1**
Solve the first exponential expression by using repeated multiplication.
$$\begin{aligned}(-3)^4 &= (-3)\times(-3)\times(-3)\times(-3)\\ &= 81\end{aligned}$$

Step 2
Solve the second exponential expression by using repeated multiplication.
$$\begin{aligned}(-4)^2 &= (-4)\times(-4)\\ &= 16\end{aligned}$$

Step 3
Add the two values together.
$81+16=97$

3. **Step 1**
Solve the first exponential expression by using repeated multiplication.
$$\begin{aligned}8^5 &= 8\times8\times8\times8\times8\\ &= 32\ 768\end{aligned}$$

Step 2
Solve the second exponential expression by using repeated multiplication.
$$\begin{aligned}7^4 &= 7\times7\times7\times7\\ &= 2\ 401\end{aligned}$$

Step 3
Add the two values together.
$32\ 768+2\ 401=35\ 169$

5. **Step 1**
Solve the first exponential expression by using repeated multiplication.
$$\begin{aligned}5^5 &= 5\times5\times5\times5\times5\\ &= 3\ 125\end{aligned}$$

Step 2
Solve the second exponential expression by using repeated multiplication.
$$\begin{aligned}3^2 &= 3\times3\\ &= 9\end{aligned}$$

Step 3
Subtract the two values.
$3\ 125-9=3\ 116$

7. **Step 1**
Follow the order of operations and evaluate the expression within the first set of brackets.
$$\begin{aligned}&(2^4-3^2)\\ &= (2\times2\times2\times2)-(3\times3)\\ &= (16-9)\\ &= 7\end{aligned}$$

Step 2
Evaluate the expression within the second set of brackets.
$$\begin{aligned}&(5^3+4^2)\\ &= (5\times5\times5)+(4\times4)\\ &= (125+16)\\ &= 141\end{aligned}$$

Step 3
Add the results together.
$7+141=148$

9. In this expression, the bases are the same and are being multiplied. Therefore, the product law can be applied.

Add the exponents.
$$\begin{aligned}4^2\times4^4 &= 4^{2+4}\\ &= 4^6\end{aligned}$$

Since Jana got a result of 4^8, her solution is incorrect. She multiplied the exponents instead of adding them.

Practice Test

ANSWERS AND SOLUTIONS

1. Apply the power law.
$(5^2)^3 = 5^{2\times3}$
$= 5^6$

3. **Step 1**
Apply the power of a power law in the denominator of the second term.
$\frac{5^3}{5^2}\times\frac{4^6\times4^3}{(4^2)^2} = \frac{5^3}{5^2}\times\frac{4^6\times4^3}{4^{2\times2}}$
$= \frac{5^3}{5^2}\times\frac{4^6\times4^3}{4^4}$

Step 2
Apply the product law to the second term of the expression.
$\frac{5^3}{5^2}\times\frac{4^6\times4^3}{4^4} = \frac{5^3}{5^2}\times\frac{4^{6+3}}{4^4}$
$= \frac{5^3}{5^2}\times\frac{4^9}{4^4}$

Step 3
Apply the quotient law to both terms of the expression.
$\frac{5^3}{5^2}\times\frac{4^9}{4^4} = 5^{3-2}\times4^{9-4}$
$= 5^1\times4^5$
$= 5\times4^5$

5. **Step 1**
Apply the power of a quotient law.
$\left(\frac{15^4}{11^6}\right)^3 = \frac{(15^4)^3}{(11^6)^3}$

Step 2
Apply the power of a power law.
$\frac{(15^4)^3}{(11^6)^3} = \frac{15^{4\times3}}{11^{6\times3}}$
$= \frac{15^{12}}{11^{18}}$

7. Apply the product law.
$(-8)^7\times(-8)^6 = (-8)^{7+6}$
$= (-8)^{13}$

9. **Step 1**
Apply the product law to the numerator.
$\frac{16^4\times16^8}{16^3} = \frac{16^{4+8}}{16^3}$
$= \frac{16^{12}}{16^3}$

Step 2
Apply the quotient law.
$\frac{16^{12}}{16^3} = 16^{12-3}$
$= 16^9$

11. **Step 1**
Apply the power of a power law.
$(4\times6^2)^3 = (4)^3\times(6^2)^3$
$= 4^3\times6^{2\times3}$
$= 4^3\times6^6$

Step 2
Evaluate the expression.
$4^3\times6^6 = 64\times46\ 656$
$= 2\ 985\ 984$

13. Apply the order of operations.
Step 1
Evaluate the exponents.
$-3(5)^2\times4(5)^3$
$-3(5\times5)\times4(5\times5\times5)$
$-3(25)\times4(125)$

Step 2
Multiply the terms in the expression.
$-3(25)\times4(125)$
-75×500
$-37\,500$

15. **Step 1**
Apply the quotient law.
$\frac{11^5}{11} = 11^{5-1}$
$= 11^4$

Step 2
Evaluate the expression.
$11^4 = 14\ 641$

17. Step 1
Apply the power of a product law to the numerator in the second term of the expression.

$$\frac{10^5}{10^2}\times\frac{\left(3^2\times3^3\right)^3}{\left(3^2\right)^7}=\frac{10^5}{10^2}\times\frac{\left(3^{2+3}\right)^3}{\left(3^2\right)^7}$$
$$=\frac{10^5}{10^2}\times\frac{\left(3^5\right)^3}{\left(3^2\right)^7}$$

Step 2
Apply the power of a power law to the second term in the expression.

$$\frac{10^5}{10^2}\times\frac{\left(3^5\right)^3}{\left(3^2\right)^7}=\frac{10^5}{10^2}\times\frac{3^{5\times3}}{3^{2\times7}}$$
$$=\frac{10^5}{10^2}\times\frac{3^{15}}{3^{14}}$$

Step 3
Apply the quotient law to both terms in the expression.

$$\frac{10^5}{10^2}\times\frac{3^{15}}{3^{14}}=10^{5-2}\times3^{15-14}$$
$$=10^3\times3^1$$

Step 4
Evaluate the expression.

$$10^3\times3^1=1\,000\times3$$
$$=3\,000$$

19. Step 1
Separate out the terms as follows.

$$\frac{42(4)^7(5)^5}{6(4)^4(5)}=\frac{42}{6}\times\frac{4^7}{4^4}\times\frac{5^5}{5}$$

Step 2
Apply the quotient law and simplify.

$$\frac{42}{6}\times\frac{4^7}{4^4}\times\frac{5^5}{5}=7\times4^{7-4}\times5^{5-1}$$
$$=7\times4^3\times5^4$$

Step 3
Evaluate the expression.

$$7\times4^3\times5^4=7\times64\times625$$
$$=280\,000$$

RATIONAL NUMBERS AND SQUARE ROOTS

Lesson 1—Compare and Order Rational Numbers

YOUR TURN ANSWERS AND SOLUTIONS

1. Step 1
Express the rational numbers in the same format. In this case, convert the fraction into a decimal.

$$\frac{21}{4}=21\div4$$
$$=5.25$$

Now the statement becomes 5.25 ☐ 5.29.

Step 2
Compare the decimal numbers by comparing the decimals based on their place values in each number. The number 5.25 has a 5 in its hundredths position, and 5.29 has a 9 in its hundredths position. Since 9 is greater than 5, the statement becomes $5.25<5.29$ or $\frac{21}{4}<5.29$.

2. Step 1
Express the rational numbers in the same format. In this case, convert the decimal into a fraction.

$$3.8=3\frac{8}{10}$$
$$=3\frac{4}{5}$$

Now the statement becomes $3\frac{3}{4}$ ☐ $3\frac{4}{5}$.

Make equivalent fractions by using a lowest common denominator of 20.

$$3\frac{3}{4}=3\frac{15}{20},\ 3\frac{4}{5}=3\frac{16}{20}$$

3. Step 1
Change the fractions to decimals so that they are easier to put in order.

$$\frac{3}{11}=3\div11$$
$$=0.\overline{27}$$

$$\frac{4}{11}=4\div11$$
$$=0.\overline{36}$$

Step 2
Arrange the numbers in ascending order.
$0.217,\ 0.\overline{27},\ 0.\overline{36},\ 0.573,\ 2$
or
$0.217,\ \frac{3}{11},\ \frac{4}{11},\ 0.573,\ 2$

Step 3
Arrange the numbers on the number line.
The original form of fractions can be used.

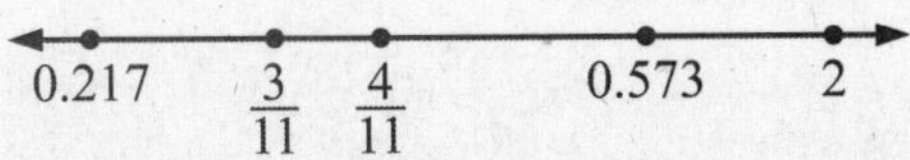

PRACTICE EXERCISES ANSWERS AND SOLUTIONS

1. Yes. It is rational because it can be written as the fraction $\frac{37\ 159}{100\ 000}$.

3. No. $\sqrt{5} = 2.236\ 067\ 977\ldots$

   It is a non-terminating number with no set pattern. It is not a rational number.

5. $\frac{1}{5}, \frac{1}{9}, \frac{207}{200}$

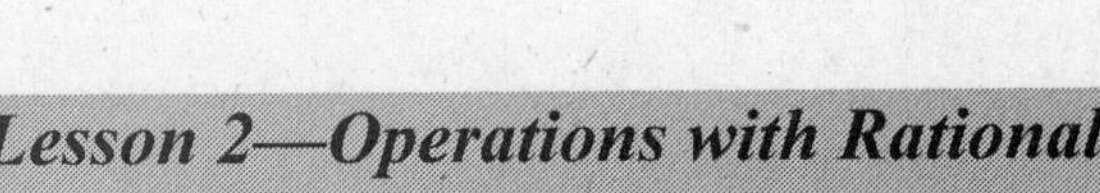

Lesson 2—Operations with Rational Numbers in Decimal Form

YOUR TURN ANSWERS AND SOLUTIONS

1. Since both signs are the same, the answer will be negative.
   $189.13 + 32.62 = 221.75$ so
   $-189.13 + (-32.62) = -221.75$

2. **Step 1**
   Rewrite the expression using the additive inverse of the second term. $68.13 + 17.87$

   Step 2
   Since both signs are the same, the answer will be positive.
   $68.13 + 17.87 = 86$ so $68.13 - (-17.87) = 86$

3. **Step 1**
   Multiply the decimal numbers.
   $3.68 \times 12.7 = 46.736$

   Step 2
   Determine the sign of the answer.
   The answer will be positive because there is an even number of negative signs.

   The answer is 46.736.

4. **Step 1**
   Divide the decimal numbers.
   $19.215 \div 9.15 = 2.1$

   Step 2
   Determine the sign of the answer.
   The answer will be negative because there are an odd number of negative signs.

   The answer is –2.1.

5. **Step 1**
   Translate the words in the problem into a mathematical expression.

   The problem is asking for the amount of change received after buying a magazine and a bag of chips and paying with a ten dollar bill.

   The magazine cost $2.55.
   The bag of chips cost $1.25.

   The keywords "how much change" imply subtraction.

   The expression that represents this problem is $10.00 - 2.55 - 1.25$.

   Step 2
   Evaluate the expression by applying the order of operations.
   $10.00 - 2.55 - 1.25$
   $= 7.45 - 1.25$
   $= 6.20$

   Justin should receive $6.20 back in change.

PRACTICE EXERCISES ANSWERS AND SOLUTIONS

1. Both signs are different, so subtract the smaller number from the larger number.
$19.16 - 3.13 = 16.03$

The sign in the answer will be the same as the sign of the larger number, which means the answer will be negative.
$3.13 + (-19.16) = -16.03$

3. **Step 1**
Rewrite the expression using the additive inverse of the second term.
$-6.17 + (+21.4)$

Step 2
Both signs are different, so subtract the smaller number from the larger number.
$21.4 - 6.17 = 15.23$

The sign in the answer will be the same as the sign of the larger number, which means the answer will be positive.
$-6.17 - (-21.4) = 15.23$

5. **Step 1**
Multiply the decimal numbers.
$25.16 \times 6.3 = 158.508$

Step 2
Determine the sign of the answer.
The answer will be positive because there is an even number of negative signs.

The answer is 158.508.

7. **Step 1**
Divide the decimal numbers.
$5.992 \div 0.7 = 8.56$

Step 2
Determine the sign of the answer.
The answer will be positive because there is an even number of negative signs.

The answer is $5.992 \div (-0.7) = -8.56$.

9. Set up the multiplication statement and evaluate.
$12 \times 0.28 = 3.36$.

The total cost was $3.36.

11. Set up the multiplication statement and evaluate.
$1.6 \times 15 = 24$

The tower is 24 cm tall.

Lesson 3—Operations with Rational Numbers in Fraction Form

YOUR TURN ANSWERS AND SOLUTIONS

1. **Step 1**
Change the mixed numbers into improper fractions.
$3\frac{5}{9} = \frac{32}{9}, \quad 2\frac{1}{2} = \frac{5}{2}$

Step 2
Find the lowest common denominator (LCD) of the fractions.

The lowest common denominator of 9 and 2 is 18.
$\frac{32}{9} - \frac{5}{2} = \frac{64}{18} - \frac{45}{18}$

Step 3
Evaluate the numerators of the fractions.
$\frac{64}{18} - \frac{45}{18} = \frac{19}{18}$

Step 4
Reduce the fraction to lowest terms.
Rewrite $\frac{19}{18}$ as a mixed number.

$\frac{19}{18} = 1\frac{1}{18}$

The answer is $3\frac{5}{9} - 2\frac{1}{2} = 1\frac{1}{18}$.

2. **Step 1**
Change the mixed numbers into improper fractions.
$-3\frac{2}{3} = -\frac{11}{3}, \quad 5\frac{4}{5} = \frac{29}{5}$

Step 2
Multiply numerator by numerator and denominator by denominator.

$$-\frac{11}{3}\times\frac{29}{5}=\frac{(-11)\times 29}{3\times 5}$$
$$=\frac{-319}{15}$$

Step 3
Reduce the fraction to lowest terms.

Rewrite $-\frac{319}{15}$ as a mixed number and reduce.

$$-\frac{319}{15}=-21\frac{4}{15}.$$

Therefore, $-3\frac{2}{3}\times 5\frac{4}{5}=-21\frac{4}{15}$.

3. **Step 1**
Change any mixed numbers to improper fractions.

$$-3\frac{4}{7}=-\frac{25}{7}$$

Step 2
Find the reciprocal of the second fraction.

The reciprocal of $-\frac{25}{7}\rightarrow-\frac{7}{25}$.

Step 3
Rewrite the expression by changing the ÷ sign to a ÷ sign.

$$\frac{6}{15}\div\left(-\frac{7}{25}\right)\rightarrow\frac{6}{15}\times\left(-\frac{7}{25}\right)$$

Step 4
Multiply the fractions, and then reduce the product into lowest terms.

$$\frac{6}{15}\times\left(-\frac{7}{25}\right)=\frac{6\times(-7)}{15\times 25}$$
$$=\frac{-42}{375}$$
$$=-\frac{14}{125}$$

Therefore, $\frac{6}{15}\div\left(-3\frac{4}{7}\right)=-\frac{14}{125}$

4. **Step 1**
Translate the words in the problem into a mathematical expression.

A race is $4\frac{1}{2}$ km long.

The track is $\frac{7}{8}$ km long.

The keywords "how many times" indicate division. The expression that represents this problem is $4\frac{1}{2}\div\frac{7}{8}$.

Step 2
Evaluate the expression by applying the order of operations.

$$4\frac{1}{2}\div\frac{7}{8}=\frac{9}{2}\div\frac{7}{8}$$
$$=\frac{9}{2}\times\frac{8}{7}$$
$$=\frac{9\times 8}{2\times 7}$$
$$=\frac{72}{14}$$
$$=5\frac{1}{7}$$

The horse will have to run around the track $5\frac{1}{7}$ times.

PRACTICE EXERCISES ANSWERS AND SOLUTIONS

1. $$\left(-\frac{1}{6}\right)-5\frac{1}{2}=-\frac{1}{6}-\frac{11}{2}$$
$$=-\frac{1}{6}-\frac{33}{6}$$
$$=\frac{-1-33}{6}$$
$$=\frac{-34}{6}$$
$$=-5\frac{2}{3}$$

3. $3\frac{6}{7}-\left(-1\frac{5}{8}\right)=3\frac{6}{7}+1\frac{5}{8}$
$=\frac{27}{7}+\frac{13}{8}$
$=\frac{216}{56}+\frac{91}{56}$
$=\frac{216+91}{56}$
$=\frac{307}{56}$
$=5\frac{27}{56}$

5. $5\frac{2}{3}\times\left(-8\frac{1}{5}\right)=\frac{17}{3}\times\left(-\frac{41}{5}\right)$
$=\frac{17\times(-41)}{3\times5}$
$=\frac{-697}{15}$
$=-46\frac{7}{15}$

7. $-\frac{2}{7}\div\frac{5}{6}=-\frac{2}{7}\times\frac{6}{5}$
$=\frac{(-2)\times6}{7\times5}$
$=-\frac{12}{35}$

9. $\left(-8\frac{2}{3}\right)\div\left(-5\frac{1}{4}\right)=\left(-\frac{26}{3}\right)\div\left(-\frac{21}{4}\right)$
$=\left(-\frac{26}{3}\right)\times\left(-\frac{4}{21}\right)$
$=\frac{(-26)\times(-4)}{3\times21}$
$=\frac{104}{63}$
$=1\frac{41}{63}$

11. Step 1
Translate the problem into a numerical expression.

Danielle has $1\frac{3}{5}$ pieces of plywood.

She wants to make 10 identical houses.

The keywords "how many" imply division.

The expression becomes $10\div1\frac{3}{5}$.

Step 2
Evaluate the numerical expression.

$10\div1\frac{3}{5}=\frac{10}{1}\div\frac{8}{5}$
$=\frac{10}{1}\times\frac{5}{8}$
$=\frac{10\times5}{1\times8}$
$=\frac{50}{8}$
$=6\frac{1}{4}$

The question asked for complete dog houses.

Since Danielle cannot make $\frac{1}{4}$ of a doghouse, she can make 6 identical dog houses with 10 sheets of plywood.

Lesson 4—Rational Numbers and Perfect Squares

YOUR TURN ANSWERS AND SOLUTIONS

1. The rational number 324 is a square number because 18 × 18 = 324.

2. To calculate the positive square root of 289, determine what number multiplied by itself results in 289.

Type in the following sequence:
[√] [2] [8] [9] or [2] [8] [9] [√] depending on your calculator.

The result of 17 will appear in your calculator screen.

3. To solve for the unknown number, multiply the square root by itself.

The square root is 0.12 so 0.12 × 0.12 = 0.0144. The unknown value is 0.0144.

4. To verify the calculation, multiply the square root by itself.
$1.45 \times 1.45 \times = 2.1025$

Since $2.1025 \neq 1.45$, the calculation is incorrect.
The correct calculation is $\sqrt{9.61} = 3.1$.

PRACTICE EXERCISES ANSWERS AND SOLUTIONS

1. In this sequence of numbers 121, 100, and 64 are square numbers because they all have square roots that are whole numbers.

3. 12

5. 9

7. Use the following relationship to check.
$b^2 = a$

$7.21^2 = 51.9841 \neq 37$, therefore, $\sqrt{37} \neq 7.21$.

The correct calculation is $\sqrt{37} \doteq 6.08$.

9. Use the following relationship to determine the value of the rational number.
$b^2 = a$

$5.48^2 = 30.0304$; therefore, $\sqrt{30.0304} = 5.48$.

Lesson 5—Rational Numbers and Non-Perfect Squares

YOUR TURN ANSWERS AND SOLUTIONS

1. The number 110 is not a perfect square.
The closest perfect squares are 100 and 121, which have square roots of 10 and 11 respectively. Since 110 is almost exactly halfway between both of these numbers, the square root of 110 will be almost exactly between 10 and 11. A good estimate for $\sqrt{110}$ is 10.5.

2. Using either method 1 or 2 (depending on your calculator), the value of $\sqrt{98} = 9.899\ 494\ 937$. The tenths place is one after the decimal.
Rounded to the nearest tenth, $\sqrt{98} \doteq 9.9$.

3. Identify any rational number between 3 and 4. In this case, you can choose 3.5.

To determine the square of 3.5, multiply 3.5 by itself using the relationship of $b^2 = a$.

$$3.5^2 = 3.5 \times 3.5 \\ = 12.25$$

Therefore, 12.25 is one number that has a square root between 3 and 4.

PRACTICE EXERCISES ANSWERS AND SOLUTIONS

1. The approximate square root of 150 can be found using the perfect squares above and below this number. The closest perfect squares above and below 150 are 144 and 169.
$12 \times 12 = 144$
$13 \times 13 = 169$

The approximate square root of 150 will be between 12 and 13.

Since 150 is closer to 144 than 169, the decimal portion of the square root will be less than 0.5. Therefore, the approximate square root of 150 is 12.2 or 12.3.

3. $\sqrt{125} = 11.18\ 033\ 989\ldots$
$\sqrt{125} \doteq 11.2$

5. $\sqrt{\frac{13}{27}} = 0.693\ 888\ 666\ldots$
$\sqrt{\frac{13}{27}} \doteq 0.7$

The area of a square is calculated by multiplying its length and its width. Since the lengths of each side of the square are the same, the square of the length is equal to the area of the square.

To calculate the side length of a square when given its area, determine the square root of the area.

7. $\sqrt{90\text{ cm}^2} = 9.4868\ldots$
$\doteq 9.5\text{ cm}$

9. $\sqrt{0.36\text{ cm}^2} = 0.6\text{ cm}$

Practice Test

ANSWERS AND SOLUTIONS

1. Square number because $\sqrt{0.16} = 0.4$

3. Square number because $\sqrt{5.29} = 2.3$

5. Not a square number because
$\sqrt{6.4} \doteq 2.529\ 822\ 128\ \ldots$

7. $4.68 + (-1.2) = 4.68 - 1.2$
$= 3.48$

9. $3.27 \times (-22.4) = -73.248$

11. $-24.4 \div 6.4 = -3.8125$

13.
$$\begin{aligned} 3 + \left(-4\frac{1}{2}\right) &= \frac{3}{1} + \left(-\frac{9}{2}\right) \\ &= \frac{6}{2} + \left(-\frac{9}{2}\right) \\ &= \frac{6 + (-9)}{2} \\ &= \frac{-3}{2} \\ &= -1\frac{1}{2} \end{aligned}$$

15.
$$\begin{aligned} 3\frac{1}{3} - 2\frac{1}{8} &= \frac{10}{3} - \frac{17}{8} \\ &= \frac{80}{24} - \frac{51}{24} \\ &= \frac{80 - 51}{24} \\ &= \frac{29}{24} \\ &= 1\frac{5}{24} \end{aligned}$$

17.
$$\begin{aligned} \frac{7}{10} \div (-5) &= \frac{7}{10} \div \left(-\frac{5}{1}\right) \\ &= \frac{7}{10} \times \left(-\frac{1}{5}\right) \\ &= -\frac{7}{50} \end{aligned}$$

19. The approximate square root of 20 can be found using the perfect squares above and below this number. The closest perfect squares above and below 20 are 16 and 25.
$4 \times 4 = 16$
$5 \times 5 = 25$

The approximate square root of 20 will be between 4 and 5.

Since 20 is almost exactly between 16 and 25, the decimal portion of the approximate square root will be around 0.5.

Therefore, the approximate square root of 20 is 4.5.

21. The area of the square garden is calculated by multiplying its length and its width. Since the lengths of each side of the square garden are the same, the square of the length is equal to the area of the square garden.
$A = s^2$

To calculate the side length of the square garden when its area is 200 m^2, determine the square root of 200.

$$\begin{aligned} 200 &= s^2 \\ \sqrt{200} &= \sqrt{s^2} \\ 14.142 &\doteq s \end{aligned}$$

Each side of the garden is approximate 14.1 m.

LINEAR RELATIONS

Lesson 1—Linear Equations

YOUR TURN
ANSWERS AND SOLUTIONS

1. **Step 1**
Write the equation in words.
Five is being subtracted from a number to equal twelve.

Step 2
Write a context.
Either of the given contexts are correct:
After Victor spends five dollars, he has twelve dollars left over.
Garrett goes down five floors in an elevator and ends up on the twelfth floor.

2. **Step 1**
Write the equation in words.
A number is being divided by nine to equal four.

Step 2
Write a context. One context could be:
Mathias has nine friends over for a sleepover. When it is time for dinner, each boy gets four cookies for dessert.

3. **Step 1**
Identify a variable to represent the unknown value.
In this case, Matt's age is the unknown value.
Let x represent Matt's age.

Step 2
Write an expression that represents other parts of the situation.
Shannon is three years older than Matt, so Shannon's age is represented by $x+3$.

The sum of their ages is thirty and is represented by $=30$.

Step 3
Write the equation.
$x+x+3=30$
Because x and x are like terms, they can be combined.

The equation that represents this situation is
$2x+3=30$

4. **Step 1**
Determine the relationship between the first set of ordered pairs.
The value of x is 2 and the value of y is 7.
The y-value is 5 more than the x-value or the y-value is 3 times plus 1 more than the x-value.

Step 2
Determine the relationship between the second set of ordered pairs.
The value of x is 1 and the value of y is 4.
The y-value is 3 more than the x-value or the y-value is 3 times plus 1 more than the x-value.

Step 3
Determine the relationship between the third set of ordered pairs just to make sure a relationship does indeed exist.
The value of x is 0 and the value of y is 1.
The y-value is 3 times plus 1 more than the x-value.

Step 4
Write the linear equation.

Since the y-value is consistently 3 times plus 1 more than the x-value, the linear equation that represents the given table of values is $y=3x+1$.

Step 5
Verify the equation by substituting ordered pairs from the table of values.

Choose an ordered pair, substitute it into the linear equation, and solve.

$$\begin{aligned} y &= 3x+1 \\ (-2) &= 3(-1)+1 \\ -2 &= -3+1 \\ -2 &= -2 \end{aligned}$$

Since both sides of the linear equation are equal, the linear equation has been verified.

PRACTICE EXERCISES ANSWERS AND SOLUTIONS

1. a number $\rightarrow x$
increased by 3 $\rightarrow +3$
the result is 21 $\rightarrow =21$
$x+3=21$

3. Step 1
Identify a variable to represent the unknown value. In this case, the number of days the DVD player was rented is the unknown value.

Let x represent the number of days Bill rented the DVD player.

Step 2
Write an expression that represents each part of the situation.

- The DVD player costs $5 per day to rent, which is represented by $5x$.
- Plus a $15 deposit is represented by $+15$.
- Bill paid $30 for his DVD player rental, which is represented by $=30$

Step 3
Write the equation.
The equation that represents this situation is $5x+15=30$.

5.
- goes down thirty-four stories $\rightarrow -34$
- ends up on the sixth floor $\rightarrow =6$
- which floor she started on $\rightarrow f$

$f-34=6$

7. Step 1
Write an expression that represents each part of the situation.

- Let x = the amount of money in Danielle's pocket $x+45$ = the amount in her bank account.
- Danielle has a total of $105 $\rightarrow =105$

Step 2
Write the linear equation
$x+(x+45)=105$
$2x+45=105$

9. Step 1
Write an expression that represents each part of the situation.

- after 3 computers are removed $\rightarrow -3$'
- 18 computers remain $\rightarrow =18$
- n = the number of computers in the classroom

Step 2
Write the linear equation
$n-3=18$

11. Step 1
Determine the relationship between the first set of ordered pairs.
The value of x is 4 and the value of y is -3.
The y-value is 7 less than the x-value.

Step 2
Determine the relationship between the second set of ordered pairs.
The value of x is 5 and the value of y is -2.
The y-value is 7 less than the x-value.

Step 3
Write the linear equation.
Since the y-value is consistently 7 less than the x-value, the linear equation that represents the given table of values is $y=x-7$.

Step 4
Verify the equation by substituting ordered pairs from the table of values.
$y=x-7$
$-1=6-7$
$-1=-1$

Lesson 2—Analysis of Linear Relations

YOUR TURN ANSWERS AND SOLUTIONS

1. **Step 1**
Make a table of values.

x	y
1	2
2	1
3	0
4	–1
5	–2

Step 2
Write the ordered pairs from the table of values.
(1, 2), (2, 1), (3, 0), (4, –1), (5, –2)

Step 3
Plot the ordered pairs on the Cartesian plane.

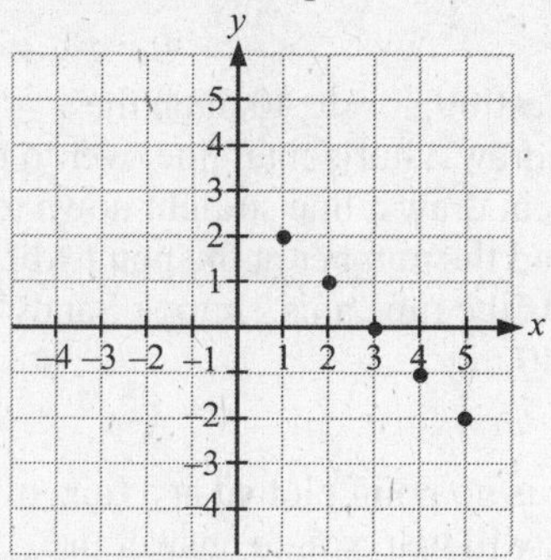

Step 4
Join the points.

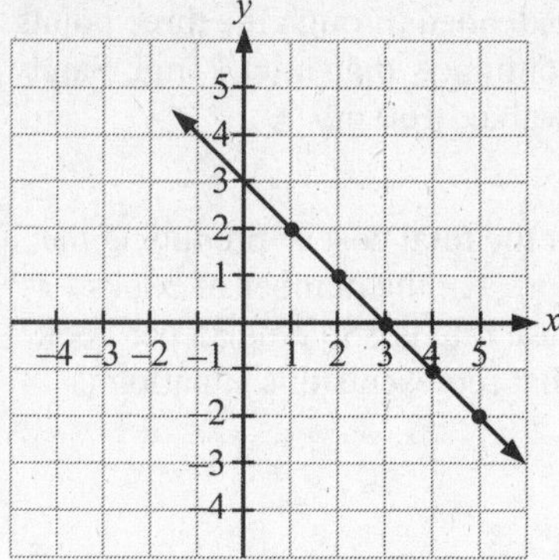

Step 5
Write the equation beside the line.

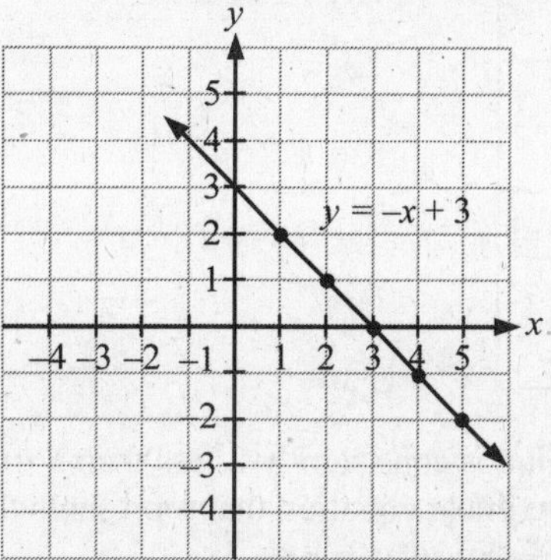

The pattern in the graph is such that the line is moving down in the negative direction. For every unit the x-value increases, the y-value decreases by 1 unit.

PRACTICE EXERCISES ANSWERS AND SOLUTIONS

1. (2, 8)
Substitute $x = 2$ into the equation and solve for y.
$y = x + 6$
$y = (2) + 6$
$y = 8$

3. (10, 16)
Substitute $x = 10$ into the equation and solve for y.
$y = x + 6$
$y = (10) + 6$
$y = 16$

5. (0, –1), (1, 0), (2, 1)

x	y
0	–1
1	0
2	1
3	2
4	3

Since the y-value is consistently 1 less than the x-value, the linear equation that represents the given table of values is $y = x - 1$.

7. (0, –2), (1, 1), (2, 4)

x	y
0	–2
1	1
2	4
3	7
4	10

Since the y-value is consistently 2 less than 3 times the x-value, the linear equation that represents the given table of values is $y = 3x - 2$.

Lesson 3—Extrapolate and Interpolate From a Graph

YOUR TURN ANSWERS AND SOLUTIONS

1. **a)** Look at the C-value on the graph when t is 3.5. The cost is 75¢.

b) Extend the line on the graph and determine what the value at $t = 8$ would be. The cost is 120¢.

2. **a)** Rahim moves half a kilometre every 10 minutes.

Let d represent the distance in km that Rahim moves after t minutes.

t	d
10	0.5
20	1.0
30	1.5

Since the d-value is consistently 0.05 times less than the t-value, the linear equation that represents the given table of values is $d = 0.05t$.

b) To determine the distance Rahim will row in one and a half hours, substitute 90 for t and solve for d.
Note: 90 minutes is equivalent to one and a half hours

$$\begin{aligned} d &= 0.05t \\ &= 0.05(90) \\ &= 4.5 \end{aligned}$$

Rahim will travel 4.5 km after rowing for an hour and a half.

PRACTICE EXERCISES ANSWERS AND SOLUTIONS

1. The total cost of landscaping done during a certain amount of time is being graphed.

3. Let C represent the total cost of the landscaping and h represent the hours worked. The base rate is \$30 per hour plus \$200. The equation that represents this situation is $C = 30h + 200$.

5. To answer this question, locate 40 m on the distance axis and draw a horizontal line over to the plotted point. Then, draw a line straight down to the time axis. Read the number at the point where your line intersects the time axis. It took Sandy's son 30 s to walk 40 m.

7. In this case, there is no point plotted at a time of 2 min (120 s) that will help you to answer the question. You must look for a pattern in the data. Draw a line through all the points to see if you can identify a pattern. In this case, a straight line can be drawn and extended through the three points. If the pattern continues, then after 2 min, Sandy's son will have walked 160 m.

9. Let C represent the total cost of producing the books and n represent the number of books ordered. The base rate is \$50 plus \$5 per book. The equation that represents this situation is $C = 50 + 5n$.

Lesson 4—Solving Linear Equations of Different Forms

YOUR TURN ANSWERS AND SOLUTIONS

1. The x is being multiplied by 6. The inverse of multiplying by 6 is dividing by 6.

$$\frac{6x}{6}=\frac{54}{6}$$

Solve for x.

$$\frac{\cancel{6}x}{\cancel{6}}=\frac{54}{6}$$
$$x=9$$

To verify the answer, substitute $x=9$ into the original equation. If both sides of the equation are equal, then the result is correct.

$$6x=54$$
$$6(9)=54$$
$$54=54$$

The solution has been verified.

2. The x is being divided by 3. The inverse of dividing by 3 is multiplying by 3.

$$3\left(\frac{x}{3}\right)=(12)3$$

Solve for x.

$$\cancel{3}\left(\frac{x}{\cancel{3}}\right)=(12)3$$
$$x=36$$

To verify the answer, substitute $x=36$ into the original equation. If both sides of the equation are equal, then the result is correct.

$$\frac{x}{3}=12$$
$$\frac{(36)}{3}=12$$
$$12=12$$

The solution has been verified.

3. **Step 1**
Remove the constant by completing the inverse operation.
The constant is 7. The inverse of subtracting 7 is adding 7.

$$-5w-7+7=23+7$$
$$-5w=30$$

Step 2
Isolate the variable by dividing both sides by the value of a.
The value of a is -5, so divide both sides of the equation by -5.

$$\frac{-5w}{-5}=\frac{30}{-5}$$
$$w=-6$$

Step 3
To verify the answer, substitute $w=-6$ into the original equation. If both sides of the equation are equal, then the result is correct.

$$-5w-7=23$$
$$-5(-6)-7=23$$
$$30-7=23$$
$$23=23$$

The solution has been verified.

4. **Step 1**
Remove the constant by completing the inverse operation.
The constant is 2. The inverse of subtracting 2 is adding 2.

$$\frac{r}{3}-2+2=-1+2$$
$$\frac{r}{3}=1$$

Step 2
Isolate the variable by multiplying both sides of the equation by the value of a.
The value of a is 3, so multiply both sides of the equation by 3.

$$\cancel{3}\left(\frac{r}{\cancel{3}}\right)=(1)3$$
$$r=3$$

Step 3
To verify the answer, substitute $r = 3$ into the original equation. If both sides of the equation are equal, then the result is correct.

$$\frac{r}{3} - 2 = -1$$
$$\frac{(3)}{3} - 2 = -1$$
$$1 - 2 = -1$$
$$-1 = -1$$

The solution has been verified.

5. **Step 1**
Move all the variables to the same side of the equation.

In this case, move $9x$ to the left side of the equation by subtracting $9x$ from both sides.

$$12x - 9x = 48 + 9x - 9x$$
$$3x = 48$$

Step 2
Isolate the variable.
Divide both sides of the equation by 3.

$$\frac{3x}{3} = \frac{48}{3}$$
$$x = 16$$

Step 3
To verify the answer, substitute $x = 16$ into the original equation. If both sides of the equation are equal, then the result is correct.

$$12x = 48 + 9x$$
$$12(16) = 48 + 9(16)$$
$$192 = 48 + 144$$
$$192 = 192$$

The solution has been verified.

6. **Step 1**
Move all the terms with x-variables to the left side by subtracting $18x$ from both sides of the equation.

$$9x - 18x + 15 = 18x - 18x + 6$$
$$-9x + 15 = 6$$

Step 2
Move the constant term to the right side of the equation by subtracting 15 from both sides of the equation.

$$-9x + 15 - 15 = 6 - 15$$
$$-9x = -9$$

Step 3
Isolate the variable by dividing both sides of the equation by -9.

$$\frac{-9x}{-9} = \frac{-9}{-9}$$
$$x = 1$$

Step 4
To verify the answer, substitute $x = 1$ into the original equation. If both sides of the equation are equal, then the result is correct.

$$9x + 15 = 18x + 6$$
$$9(1) + 15 = 18(1) + 6$$
$$9 + 15 = 18 + 6$$
$$24 = 24$$

The solution has been verified.

7. **Step 1**
Apply the distributive property to simplify the equation.

$$8(x + 4) = 72$$
$$8x + 32 = 72$$

Step 2
Move the constant to the opposite side of the equation by subtracting both sides of the equation by 32.

$$8x + 32 - 32 = 72 - 32$$
$$8x = 40$$

Step 3
Isolate the variable by dividing both sides of the equation by the numerical coefficient of x, which is 8.

$$\frac{8x}{8} = \frac{40}{8}$$
$$x = 5$$

Step 4
To verify the answer, substitute $x = 5$ into the original equation. If both sides of the equation are equal, then the result is correct.

$$8(x + 4) = 72$$
$$8(5 + 4) = 72$$
$$8(9) = 72$$
$$72 = 72$$

The solution has been verified.

8. **Step 1**
Apply the distributive property to simplify the equation.

$$3(2x + 5) = -2(-4x + 7)$$
$$6x + 15 = 8x - 14$$

Step 2
Move all the variables to one side of the equation by subtracting $8x$ from both sides of the equation.

$$6x-8x+15=8x-8x-14$$
$$-2x+15=-14$$

Step 3
Move all the constants to the opposite side of the equation by subtracting 15 from both sides of the equation.

$$-2x+15-15=-14-15$$
$$-2x=-29$$

Step 4
Isolate the variable by dividing both sides of the equation by the numerical coefficient of x, which is -2.

$$\frac{-2x}{-2}=\frac{-29}{-2}$$
$$x=14.5$$

Step 5
To verify the answer, substitute $x=14.5$ into the original equation. If both sides of the equation are equal, then the result is correct.

$$3(2x+5)=-2(-4x+7)$$
$$3(2(14.5)+5)=-2(-4(14.5)+7)$$
$$3(29+5)=-2(-58+7)$$
$$3(34)=-2(-51)$$
$$102=102$$

The solution has been verified.

9. **Step 1**
Multiply both sides of the equation by x.

$$x\left(\frac{-49.2}{x}\right)=(24.6)x$$
$$-49.2=24.6x$$

Step 2
Isolate the variable by dividing both sides of the equation by the numerical coefficient of x, which is 24.6.

$$\frac{-49.2}{24.6}=\frac{24.6x}{24.6}$$
$$-2=x$$

Step 3
To verify the answer, substitute $x=-2$ into the original equation. If both sides of the equation are equal, then the result is correct.

$$\frac{-49.2}{x}=24.6$$
$$\frac{-49.2}{(-2)}=24.6$$
$$24.6=24.6$$

The solution has been verified.

10. Shamit made his mistake in Step 4. He did not apply the inverse operations correctly.

In Step 4, he must divide both sides of the equation by 18, not just one of the sides, to isolate the variable x.

The correct solution is:

$$-4(x-18)=14x$$
$$-4x+72=14x$$
$$-4x+4x+72=14x+4x$$
$$72=18x$$
$$\frac{72}{18}=\frac{18x}{18}$$
$$4=x$$

11. **Step 1**
Draw or lay out the tiles to represent the equation.

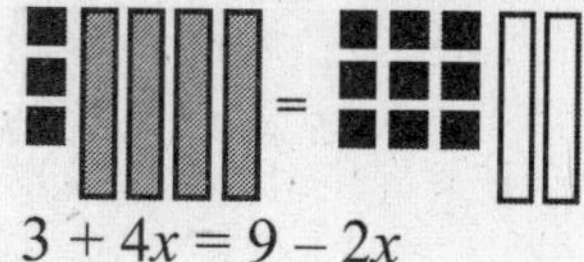

$3+4x=9-2x$

Step 2
Add three negative number tiles to both sides of the equation to cancel out the positive tiles on the left side of the equation.

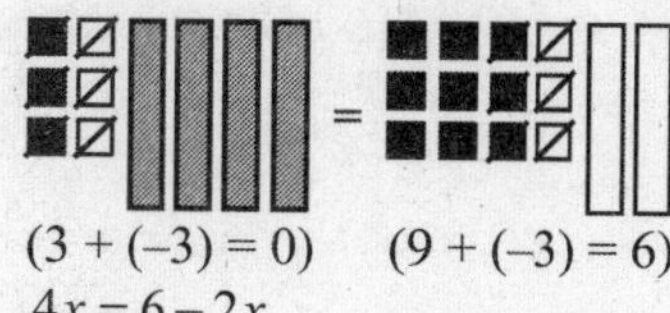

$(3+(-3)=0)$ $(9+(-3)=6)$

$4x=6-2x$

Step 3
Add two positive x-tiles to both sides of the equation to cancel out the negative x-tiles on the right side of the equation.

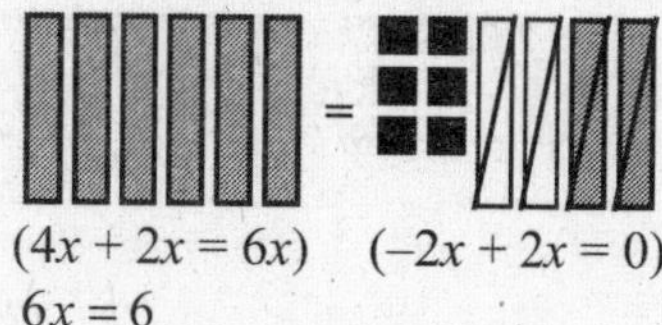

$(4x+2x=6x)$ $(-2x+2x=0)$

$6x=6$

Step 4
Share each variable tile with an equal number of number tiles.

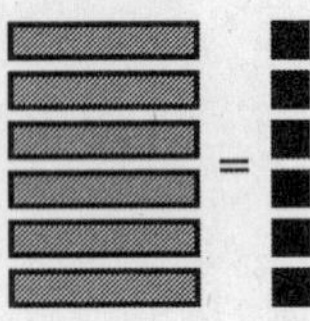

Notice each x-tile equals one unit tile. The solution is $x = 1$.

PRACTICE EXERCISES ANSWERS AND SOLUTIONS

1.
$$\begin{aligned} 3x + x &= 5x - 6 \\ 4x &= 5x - 6 \\ 4x - 5x &= 5x - 5x - 6 \\ -1x &= -6 \\ \frac{-1x}{-1} &= \frac{-6}{-1} \\ x &= 6 \end{aligned}$$

Verify
$$\begin{aligned} 3(6) + (6) &= 5(6) - 6 \\ 18 + 6 &= 30 - 6 \\ 24 &= 24 \end{aligned}$$

3.
$$\begin{aligned} 5 - 6x &= 2x + 5 \\ 5 - 6x - 2x &= 2x - 2x + 5 \\ 5 - 8x &= 5 \\ 5 - 5 - 8x &= 5 - 5 \\ -8x &= 0 \\ x &= 0 \end{aligned}$$

Verify
$$\begin{aligned} 5 - 6(0) &= 2(0) + 5 \\ 5 - 0 &= 0 + 5 \\ 5 &= 5 \end{aligned}$$

5.
$$\begin{aligned} 41 &= 0.5x + 0.7x - 7 \\ 41 &= 1.2x - 7 \\ 41 + 7 &= 1.2x - 7 + 7 \\ 48 &= 1.2x \\ \frac{48}{1.2} &= \frac{1.2x}{1.2} \\ 40 &= x \end{aligned}$$

Verify
$$\begin{aligned} 41 &= 0.5(40) + 0.7(40) - 7 \\ 41 &= 20 + 28 - 7 \\ 41 &= 41 \end{aligned}$$

7.
$$\begin{aligned} 1.2x + 3.5(2.5 - x) &= 41 \\ 1.2x + 8.75 - 3.5x &= 41 \\ -2.3x + 8.75 &= 41 \\ -2.3x + 8.75 - 8.75 &= 41 - 8.75 \\ -2.3x &= 32.25 \\ \frac{-2.3x}{-2.3} &= \frac{32.25}{-2.3} \\ x &\doteq -14.0 \end{aligned}$$

9.
$$\begin{aligned} 14 &= \frac{-3}{x} \\ 14x &= -3 \\ \frac{14x}{14} &= \frac{-3}{14} \\ x &= -\frac{3}{14} \end{aligned}$$

11. Step 1
Lay out the tiles to represent the equation.

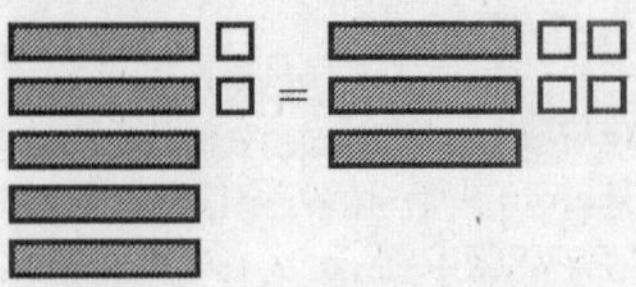

Step 2
Use inverse operations to isolate the variable. Add 2 shaded unit tiles to both sides to get all the numbers on the right side.

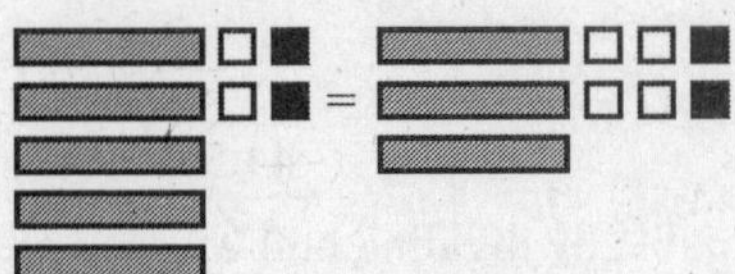

Step 3
Add 3 unshaded x-tiles to each side of the equation to get all the variables on the left side.

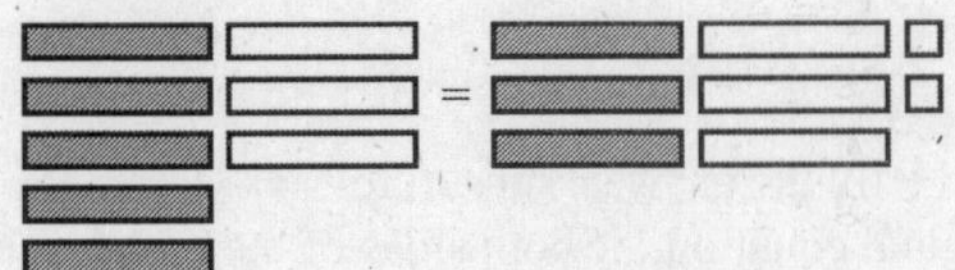

Step 4
Share each variable tile with an equal amount of number tiles.

Each variable tile is equal to 1 unshaded unit tile, so $x = -1$.

Practice Test

ANSWERS AND SOLUTIONS

1. Let x be the amount of land given to each child.
eight children equal portions of the land → $8x$
save four acres for his wife → $+4$
In total, he has twenty acres → $= 20$
$8x + 4 = 20$

3. Write the equation in words.
The sum of a number and four all multiplied by three gives a result of twenty-one.

Following is a possible context for this equation:

Dean is going to the amusement park with his family (Mom, Dad, and brother) and a number of friends. The cost of entry into the park is three dollars per person. Dean's dad pays twenty-one dollars for entry into the amusement park. Where x is the number of friends Dean can bring.

5.
$$\begin{aligned}\frac{j}{5.5} &= -8.1\\ 5.5\left(\frac{j}{5.5}\right) &= (-8.1)5.5\\ j &= -44.55\end{aligned}$$

Verify:
$$\begin{aligned}\frac{j}{5.5} &= -8.1\\ \frac{(-44.55)}{5.5} &= -8.1\\ -8.1 &= -8.1\end{aligned}$$

7.
$$\begin{aligned}3g - 9 &= 33\\ 3g - 9 + 9 &= 33 + 9\\ 3g &= 42\\ \frac{3g}{3} &= \frac{42}{3}\\ g &= 14\end{aligned}$$

9.
$$\begin{aligned}18 &= \frac{n}{4} + 3\\ 18 - 3 &= \frac{n}{4} + 3 - 3\\ 15 &= \frac{n}{4}\\ 4(15) &= \left(\frac{n}{4}\right)4\\ 60 &= n\end{aligned}$$

11.
$$\begin{aligned}2q - 35 &= 16q\\ 2q - 2q - 35 &= 16q - 2q\\ -35 &= 14q\\ \frac{-35}{14} &= \frac{14q}{14}\\ -2.5 &= q\end{aligned}$$

Verify:
$$\begin{aligned}2q - 35 &= 16q\\ 2(-2.5) - 35 &= 16(-2.5)\\ -5 - 35 &= -40\\ -40 &= -40\end{aligned}$$

13.
$$\begin{aligned}-9.2x - 16.2 &= 3.4x + 53.1\\ -9.2x - 3.4x - 16.2 &= 3.4x - 3.4x + 53.1\\ -12.6x - 16.2 &= 53.1\\ -12.6x - 16.2 + 16.2 &= 53.1 + 16.2\\ -12.6x &= 69.3\\ \frac{-12.6x}{-12.6} &= \frac{69.3}{-12.6}\\ x &= -5.5\end{aligned}$$

Verify:
$$\begin{aligned}-9.2x - 16.2 &= 3.4x + 53.1\\ -9.2(-5.5) - 16.2 &= 3.4(-5.5) + 53.1\\ 50.6 - 16.2 &= -18.7 + 53.1\\ 34.4 &= 34.4\end{aligned}$$

15.
$$\begin{aligned}\frac{222}{c} &= 74\\ c\left(\frac{222}{c}\right) &= c(74)\\ \frac{222}{74} &= \frac{74c}{74}\\ 3 &= c\end{aligned}$$

17. Let n represent the unknown number.
The product of ten and a number decreased by seven is represented by $10n-7$.
The result of forty-three means the equation becomes $10n-7=43$.

Now, solve for n:

$$\begin{aligned}10n-7&=43\\10n-7+7&=43+7\\10n&=50\\\frac{10n}{10}&=\frac{50}{10}\\n&=5\end{aligned}$$

19. Let m represent the unknown number of movies.
One seventh of the movies are comedies is represented by $\frac{1}{7}m$ or $\frac{m}{7}$.

Jason has 6 comedies means the equation becomes $\frac{m}{7}=6$.

Now, solve for m:

$$\begin{aligned}\frac{m}{7}&=6\\7\left(\frac{m}{7}\right)&=(6)7\\m&=42\end{aligned}$$

Jason has 42 movies.

LINEAR INEQUALITIES

Lesson 1—Solving Linear Inequalities

YOUR TURN ANSWERS AND SOLUTIONS

1. Let p represent the number of hours Lindsay can park after paying for the first hour.

The cost for the first hour is \$3.00.
The cost for each additional hour is \$1.25.
The maximum amount she has to spend is \$20.00.

The linear inequality can be set up as:
Cost of the first hour + Cost of each additional hour × Number of hours parked ≤ Amount of money budgeted for parking.

The algebraic expression becomes $3.00+1.25p\leq 20.00$.

2. Isolate the variable by applying inverse operations.

$$\begin{aligned}x-7&\geq 25\\x-7+7&\geq 25+7\\x&\geq 32\end{aligned}$$

Therefore, all the numbers greater than or equal to 32 will make the linear inequality a true statement.

3. Isolate the variable by applying inverse operations.

$$\begin{aligned}\frac{x}{9}&\geq 36\\9\left(\frac{x}{9}\right)&\geq 36(9)\\x&\geq 324\end{aligned}$$

Therefore, all the numbers greater than or equal to 324 will make the linear inequality a true statement.

4. Isolate the variable by applying inverse operations. When you divide by a negative, the inequality sign is reversed.

$$\frac{x}{-3} \le 27$$
$$(-3)\left(\frac{x}{-3}\right) \ge 27(-3)$$
$$x \ge -81$$

Therefore, all the numbers greater than or equal to -81 will make the linear inequality a true statement.

5. **Step 1**
Isolate the variable by applying inverse operations. Subtract 15 from each side of the inequality.

$$15-12x \ge 63$$
$$15-15-12x \ge 63-15$$
$$-12x \ge 48$$

Step 2
Divide each side of the inequality by -12.

$$-12x \ge 48$$
$$\frac{-12x}{-12} \le \frac{48}{-12}$$
$$x \le -4$$

Step 3
Verify the solution by substituting the boundary point into the inequality.
The boundary point is -4.

$$15-12(-4) = 63$$
$$15+48 = 63$$
$$63 = 63$$

Step 4
Verify the solution by substituting a value from the solution set into the inequality.

Use any number less than -4.
Use -5.

$$15-12x \ge 63$$
$$15-12(-5) \ge 63$$
$$15+60 \ge 63$$
$$75 \ge 63$$

6. **Step 1**
Isolate the variable by applying inverse operations. Add 4 to each side of the inequality.

$$8x-4 \le 6x+2$$
$$8x-4+4 \le 6x+2+4$$
$$8x \le 6x+6$$

Subtract $6x$ from both sides.

$$8x-6x \le 6x-6x+6$$
$$2x \le 6$$

Divide each side by 2.

$$\frac{2x}{2} \le \frac{6}{2}$$
$$x \le 3$$

Step 2
Verify the solution by substituting the boundary point into the inequality.

The boundary point is 3.

$$8x-4 = 6x+2$$
$$8(3)-4 = 6(3)+2$$
$$24-4 = 18+2$$
$$20 = 20$$

Step 3
Verify the solution by substituting a value from the solution set into the inequality.

Use any number less than 3.
Use 1.

$$8x-4 \le 6x+2$$
$$8(1)-4 \le 6(1)+2$$
$$8-4 \le 6+2$$
$$4 \le 8$$

PRACTICE EXERCISES ANSWERS AND SOLUTIONS

1. Let x represent the number of hair treatments Sandy can buy.

The cost of the pedicure is $60.00.
The cost of the hair treatments is $120.00 each.
The maximum amount she has to spend is $400.00.

The equation can be set up like this:
cost of the pedicure + cost of the hair treatments × number of hair treatments ≤ amount of the gift card.

The linear inequality can be expressed as $60+120x \le 400$.

3.
$$\begin{aligned} x-8&>24\\ x-8+8&>24+8\\ x&>32 \end{aligned}$$

5.
$$\begin{aligned} \frac{x}{7}&>24\\ 7\left(\frac{x}{7}\right)&>(24)7\\ x&>168 \end{aligned}$$

7.
$$\begin{aligned} \frac{x}{-6}+10&<24\\ \frac{x}{-6}+10-10&<24-10\\ \frac{x}{-6}&<14\\ (-6)\left(\frac{x}{-6}\right)&>14(-6)\\ x&>-84 \end{aligned}$$

9. **Step 1**
Isolate the variable by applying inverse operations. Subtract 12 from each side of the inequality.
$$\begin{aligned} 12-8x&\ge 60\\ 12-12-8x&\ge 60-12\\ -8x&\ge 48 \end{aligned}$$

Divide each side by -8.
$$\begin{aligned} -8x&\ge 48\\ \frac{-8x}{-8}&\le\frac{48}{-8}\\ x&\le -6 \end{aligned}$$

Step 2
Verify the solution by substituting the boundary point into the inequality.

The boundary point is –6.
$$\begin{aligned} 12-8x&=60\\ 12-8(-6)&=60\\ 12+48&=60\\ 60&=60 \end{aligned}$$

Step 3
Verify the solution by substituting a value from the solution set into the inequality.

Use any number less than. –6.
Use -10.
$$\begin{aligned} 12-8x&\ge 60\\ 12-8(-10)&\ge 60\\ 12+80&\ge 60\\ 92&\ge 60 \end{aligned}$$

Lesson 2—Graphing Linear Inequalities

YOUR TURN ANSWERS AND SOLUTIONS

1. **Step 1**
To solve this linear inequality, divide each side by 9.
$$\begin{aligned} 9x&\le 135\\ \frac{9x}{9}&\le\frac{135}{9}\\ x&\le 15 \end{aligned}$$

The solution set consists of all the values of x that are less than and equal to 15.

Step 2
Represent the solution set on a graph.
Since the solution set consists of all the values of x that are less than and equal to 15, the 15 is included in the graph. This is represented by a shaded circle, followed by all the numbers less than 15.

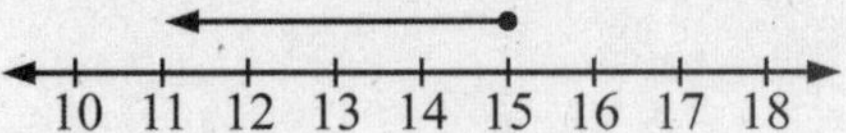

2. **Step 1**
To solve this linear inequality, multiply each side by –3.

$$\frac{x}{-3} < 6$$
$$(-3)\left(\frac{x}{-3}\right) > (6)(-3)$$
$$x > -18$$

The solution set consists of all the values of x that are greater than but not equal to -18.

Step 2
Represent the solution set on a graph.
Since the solution set consists of all the values of x that are greater than but not equal to -18, the -18 is not included in the graph. This is represented by an unshaded circle, followed by all the numbers greater than -18.

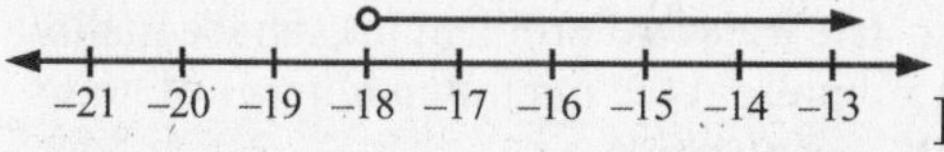

PRACTICE EXERCISES ANSWERS AND SOLUTIONS

1.
$$-4x > 4$$
$$\frac{-4x}{-4} < \frac{4}{-4}$$
$$x < -1$$

3.
$$2x+2 > x+4$$
$$2x+2-2 > x+4-2$$
$$2x > x+2$$
$$2x-x > x-x+2$$
$$x > 2$$

5. Solve the given linear inequality.
$$4x+16 \le 36$$
$$4x+16-16 \le 36-16$$
$$4x \le 20$$
$$\frac{4x}{4} \le \frac{20}{4}$$
$$x \le 5$$

This result indicates that any value less than and equal to 5 belongs to the solution set.
Therefore, –7, –6, 4 and 5 are part of the solution to the inequality.

Practice Test

ANSWERS AND SOLUTIONS

1.
$$\frac{x}{-9} \le 81$$
$$(-9)\left(\frac{x}{-9}\right) \ge (81)(-9)$$
$$x \ge -729$$

When you multiply by a negative, the sign is reversed.

3.
$$12x-6 < 30$$
$$12x-6+6 < 30+6$$
$$12x < 36$$
$$\frac{12x}{12} < \frac{36}{12}$$
$$x < 3$$

5.
$$8.2f+1.2 \ge 79.1$$
$$8.2f+1.2-1.2 \ge 79.1-1.2$$
$$8.2f \ge 77.9$$
$$\frac{8.2f}{8.2} \ge \frac{77.9}{8.2}$$
$$f \ge 9.5$$

7.
$$19x-5.22 \le 32.78$$
$$19x-5.22+5.22 \le 32.78+5.22$$
$$19x \le 38$$
$$\frac{19x}{19} \le \frac{38}{19}$$
$$x \le 2$$

Verify the solution by substituting the boundary point into the inequality.

The boundary point is 2.

$$19x - 5.22 = 32.78$$
$$19(2) - 5.22 = 32.78$$
$$38 - 5.22 = 32.78$$
$$32.78 = 32.78$$

Verify the solution by substituting a value from the solution set into the inequality.

Use any number less than 2.
Use 0.

$$19x - 5.22 \leq 32.78$$
$$19(0) - 5.22 \leq 32.78$$
$$0 - 5.22 \leq 32.78$$
$$-5.22 \leq 32.78$$

9. $x \leq 6$

11. $x > 10$

13.
$$2x - 2 \leq 3x + 1$$
$$2x - 2 + 2 \leq 3x + 1 + 2$$
$$2x \leq 3x + 3$$
$$2x - 3x \leq 3x - 3x + 3$$
$$\frac{-1x}{-1} \geq \frac{3}{-1}$$
$$x \geq -3$$

Notice that when you divide by a negative, $\leq$ is reversed to $\geq$.

Since the solution set is $x \geq -3$, the solutions are any numerical values that are greater than or equal to -3.

The graph should look like the following:

15.
$$4x - 7 \geq 5x - 9$$
$$4x - 7 + 7 \geq 5x - 9 + 7$$
$$4x \geq 5x - 2$$
$$4x - 5x \geq 5x - 5x - 2$$
$$-x \geq -2$$
$$x \leq 2$$

Since you are dividing by a negative, reverse the sign.

Since the solution set is, $x \leq 2$, the solutions are any numerical values that are less than or equal to 2.

The graph should look like the following:

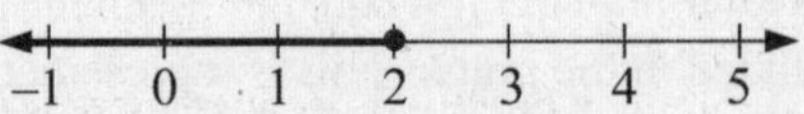

17. Step 1

Translate the word problem into an inequality. Let x represent the minimum number of hours Molly has to work.

Molly must earn at least $584.00 in order to afford the new bike. This expression can be represented by ≥ 584.

She has $62 saved and earns $8.70/hour at work. The inequality that represents this problem can be expressed as $62 + 8.70x \geq 584$.

Step 2

Solve the inequality.
Isolate the variable by applying inverse operations.

$$62 + 8.70x \geq 584$$
$$62 - 62 + 8.70x \geq 584 - 62$$
$$8.70x \geq 522$$
$$\frac{8.70x}{8.70} \geq \frac{522}{8.70}$$
$$x \geq 60$$

After at least 60 hours of work, Molly will have enough money to purchase the bike.

Step 3

Graph the solution set on a number line.

54 56 58 60 62 64 66

POLYNOMIALS

Lesson 1—Modelling and Creating Polynomial Expressions

YOUR TURN ANSWERS AND SOLUTIONS

1. The coefficient is 5.
The variable is x.
The constant is 8.
The polynomial is a binomial because there are two terms: $5x$ and 8.
The degree of the polynomial is 1.

2. The coefficients are -9 and 3.
The variable is r.
The constant is 2.
This polynomial is a trinomial because there are three terms: $-9r,\ 3r^3$, and 2.
The degree of the polynomial is 3.

3. For the polynomial expression $-3x^2+2x+5$, you need 3 negative x^2-tiles, 2 positive x-tiles, and 5 positive unit tiles. The arrangement of algebra tiles will look like the following:

4. Identify the algebra tiles that are given.
You have 3 negative x^2-tiles and 7 positive unit tiles.

The polynomial expression that represents this arrangement of algebra tiles is $-3x^2+7$.

5. Let w represent the number of wins, t represent the number of ties, and f represent the number of forfeits.

Three points are awarded for a win; hence $3\times w$ or $3w$.

A single point is earned for every tie; hence $1\times t$ or t.
Two points are deducted for every forfeit loss; hence $-2\times f$ or $-2f$.

The polynomial expression becomes $3w+t-2f$.

6. **Step 1**
Determine what the first term could represent.
Assuming the variable letter is meaningful, h could represent an hour; h is multiplied by 17.5.
The term could represent a cost of $17.50 per hour.

Step 2
Determine what the constant could mean.
10 is subtracted from the product.
This could represent a $10 discount.

Step 3
Create a context that fits with the terms.
A housecleaner charges $17.50 an hour and gives a $10.00 discount for booking in advance.

PRACTICE EXERCISES ANSWERS AND SOLUTIONS

1. The coefficients are 6 and -4.
The variable is t.
There is no constant. The constant is 0.
The polynomial is a binomial.
The degree of the polynomial is 2.

3. The coefficients are -1 and 2.
The variables are x and y.
There is no constant. The constant is 0.
The polynomial is a binomial
The degree of the polynomial is 2.

5. The coefficient is $\frac{7}{8}$.
The variable is x.
There is no constant. The constant is 0.
The polynomial is a monomial.
The degree of the polynomial is 1.

7. For the polynomial expression x^2+3x-2, you need 1 positive x^2-tile, 3 positive x-tiles, and 2 negative unit tiles. The arrangement of algebra tiles will look like the following:

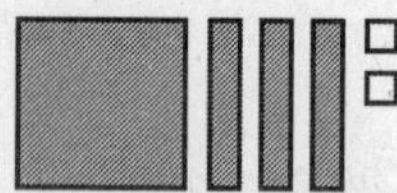

9. For the polynomial expression $4x^2+6x+3$, you need 4 positive x^2-tiles, 6 positive x-tiles, and 3 positive unit tiles. The arrangement of algebra tiles will look like the following:

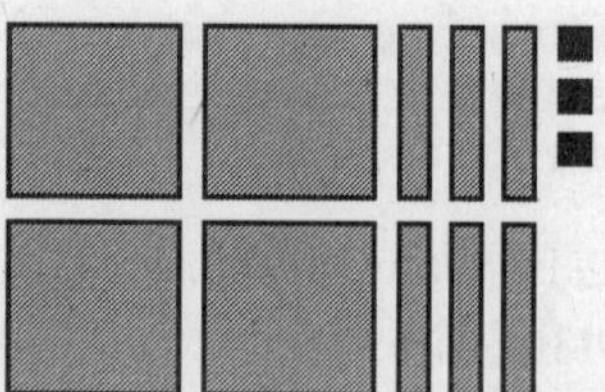

Lesson 2—Identifying Equivalent Polynomials

YOUR TURN ANSWERS AND SOLUTIONS

1. a) $2-8x^2$

   b) Any of the following answers is correct:
   $3x^2+2+4x$
   $4x+2+3x^2$
   $4x+3x^2+2$
   $2+3x^2+4x$
   $2+4x+3x^2$

2. The polynomial A has the terms $-8x^2$, $-2x$, and 6. To find the equivalent polynomial for this expression, identify another polynomial with a constant of 6. The only other polynomial with a constant of 6 is G. Therefore, A and G are equivalent.

The polynomial B has the terms $-12x^2$, $6x$, and 2. To find the equivalent polynomial for this expression, identify another polynomial with a term of $6x$. The only other polynomial with a term of $6x$ is H. Therefore, B and H are equivalent.

The polynomial C has the terms $2x^2$, $9x$, and 12. To find the equivalent polynomial for this expression, identify another polynomial with a term of $9x$. The only other polynomial with a term of $9x$ is E. Therefore, C and E are equivalent.

The polynomial D has the terms x^2, $-5x$, and 23. To find the equivalent polynomial for this expression, identify another polynomial with a term of $-5x$. The only other polynomial with a term of $-5x$ is F. Therefore, D and F are equivalent.

3. The list below shows the like terms.

$3x$	$-3x$
$-2xy$	xy
21	-5
$4y$	$2y$
$3xz$	$7xz$
z^2	z^2

4. **Step 1**
Identify the like terms.
$\underline{-12z}+\underbrace{8y^2}\boxed{+10}\underbrace{-y^2}\underline{+14z}\boxed{-7}$

Step 2
Add or subtract the like terms.
$-12z+8y^2+10-y^2+14z-7$
$=-12z+14z+8y^2-y^2+10-7$
$=2z+7y^2+3$

PRACTICE EXERCISES ANSWERS AND SOLUTIONS

1. $-8+2n$

3. $5x-4$

5. $7x^2-23$

7. Since there are no like terms overall to combine, the binomial will contribute two terms nd the trinomial will contribute three terms to the final polynomial of **five** terms.

   For example,
   $(2x+3y)+(a+2b+3c)$
   $=2x+3y+a+2b+3c$

9. Combine like terms, and add the numerical coefficients of the terms.
   $\underline{3y^2-y^2}+5y\underbrace{-9-18}$
   $=2y^2+5y-27$

   The degree of the polynomial is 2.

Lesson 3—Adding and Subtracting Polynomials

YOUR TURN ANSWERS AND SOLUTIONS

1. **Step 1**
   Model the polynomials with tiles.

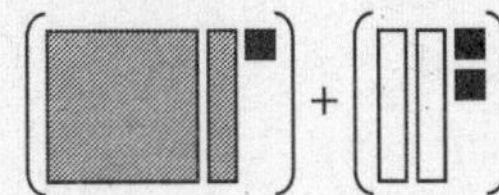

Step 2
Simplify the equation by cancelling negative and positive tiles of the same size.

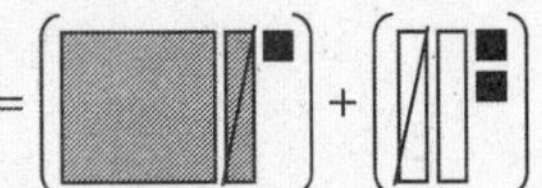

Step 3
Write the remaining tiles as the solution.

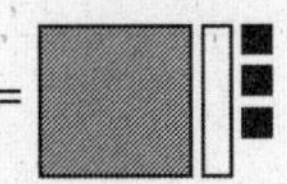

The answer is x^2-x+3.

2. **Step 1**
   Rewrite the polynomial without the brackets.
   $(2x^2+3x-5)+(9x^2+4x+2)$
   $=2x^2+3x-5+9x^2+4x+2$

   Step 2
   Gather the like terms in descending order.
   $2x^2+3x-5+9x^2+4x+2$
   $=2x^2+9x^2+3x+4x-5+2$

   Step 3
   Add the numerical coefficients of the like terms.
   $2x^2+9x^2+3x+4x-5+2$
   $=11x^2+7x-3$

3. **Step 1**
   Rewrite the polynomial without the brackets.
   $(-2x^2+2x+4)+(-8x^2+9x-3)+(5x^2+7x+4)$
   $=-2x^2+2x+4-8x^2+9x-3+5x^2+7x+4$

   Step 2
   Gather the like terms in descending order.
   $-2x^2+2x+4-8x^2+9x-3+5x^2+7x+4$
   $=-2x^2-8x^2+5x^2+2x+9x+7x+4-3+4$

   Step 3
   Add the numerical coefficients of the like terms.
   $-2x^2-8x^2+5x^2+2x+9x+7x+4-3+4$
   $=-5x^2+18x+5$

4. **Step 1**
   Model the polynomials with tiles.

Step 2
Add the opposite when subtracting polynomials. To do this, change the tiles of the second polynomial to the opposite colour.

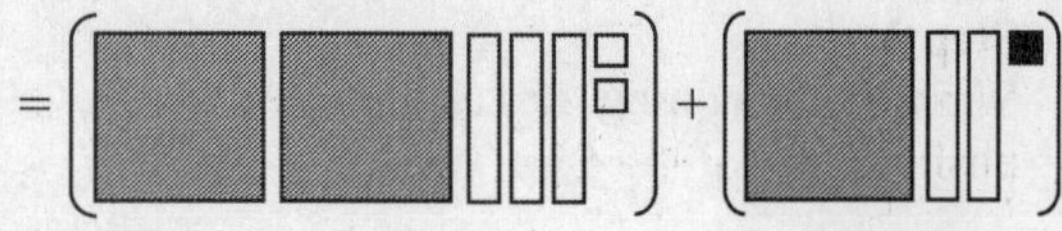

Step 3
Simplify the equation by cancelling negative and positive tiles of the same size.

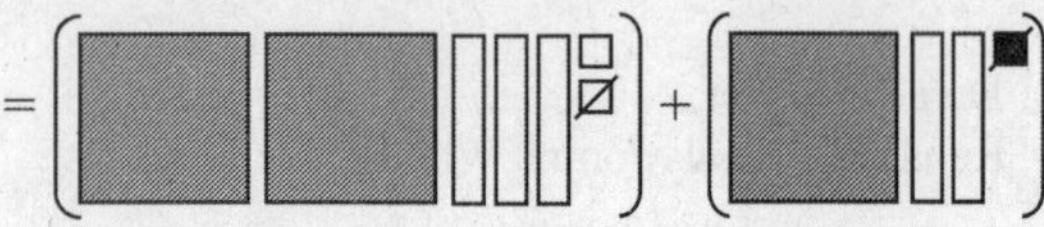

Step 4
Determine the solution by counting up the remaining tiles.

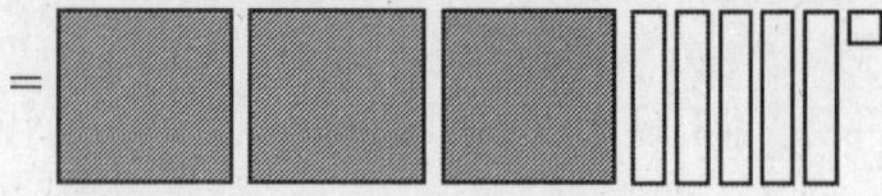

The answer is $3x^2 - 5x - 1$.

5. **Step 1**
Rewrite the polynomial by adding the additive inverse.
$(-2x^2 + x - 2) - (x + 3 - 3x^2)$
$= (-2x^2 + x - 2) + (-x - 3 + 3x^2)$

Step 2
Rewrite the polynomial without the brackets.
$(-2x^2 + x - 2) + (-x - 3 + 3x^2)$
$= -2x^2 + x - 2 - x - 3 + 3x^2$

Step 3
Gather like terms in descending order.
$-2x^2 + x - 2 - x - 3 + 3x^2$
$= -2x^2 + 3x^2 + x - x - 2 - 3$

Step 4
Add the numerical coefficients of the like terms.
$-2x^2 + 3x^2 + x - x - 2 - 3$
$= x^2 - 5$

6. **Step 1**
Rewrite the polynomial by adding the additive inverse.
$(3x^2 - 2x + 2) - (-12x^2 - 2x - 9) - (x - 3)$
$= (3x^2 - 2x + 2) + (12x^2 + 2x + 9) + (-x + 3)$

Step 2
Rewrite the polynomial without the brackets.
$(3x^2 - 2x + 2) + (12x^2 + 2x + 9) + (-x + 3)$
$= 3x^2 - 2x + 2 + 12x^2 + 2x + 9 - x + 3$

Step 3
Gather like terms in descending order.
$3x^2 - 2x + 2 + 12x^2 + 2x + 9 - x + 3$
$= 3x^2 + 12x^2 - 2x + 2x - x + 2 + 9 + 3$

Step 4
Add the numerical coefficients of the like terms.
$3x^2 + 12x^2 - 2x + 2x - x + 2 + 9 + 3$
$= 15x^2 - x + 14$

PRACTICE EXERCISES ANSWERS AND SOLUTIONS

1. **Step 1**
Model the polynomials with tiles.

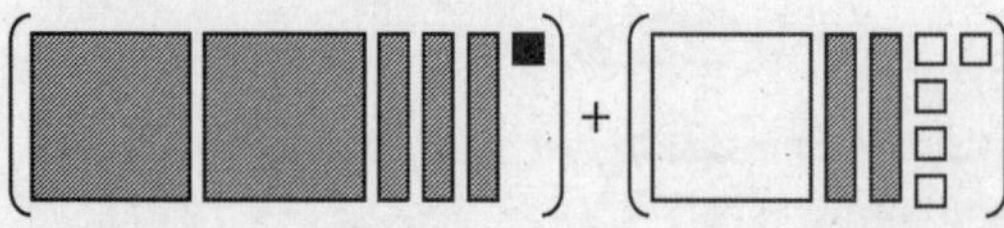

Step 2
Simplify the equation by cancelling negative and positive tiles of the same size.

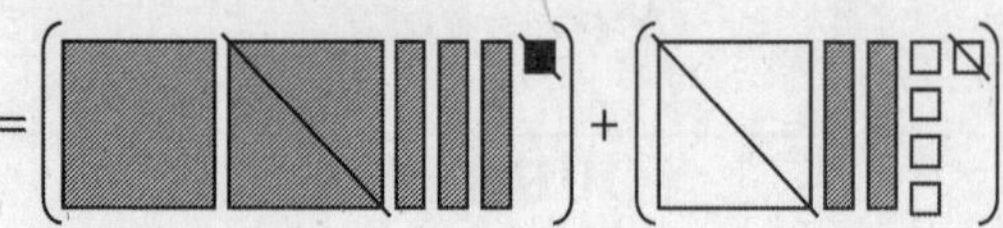

Step 3
Determine the solution by counting up the remaining tiles.

The answer is $x^2 + 5x - 4$.

3. **Step 1**
Model the polynomials with tiles.

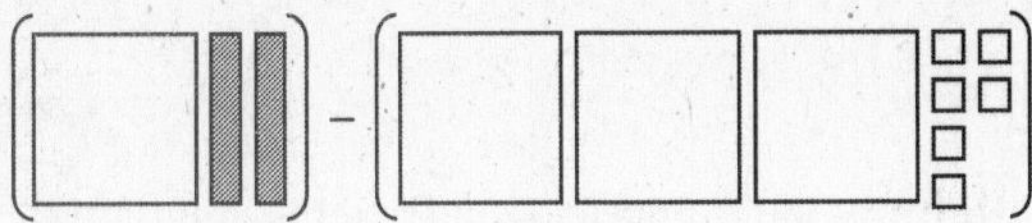

Step 2
Add the opposite when subtracting polynomials. To do this, change the tiles of the second polynomial to the opposite colour.

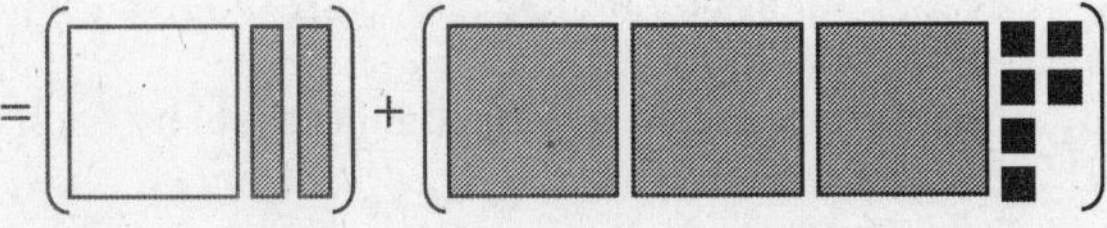

Step 3
Simplify the equation by cancelling negative and positive tiles of the same size.

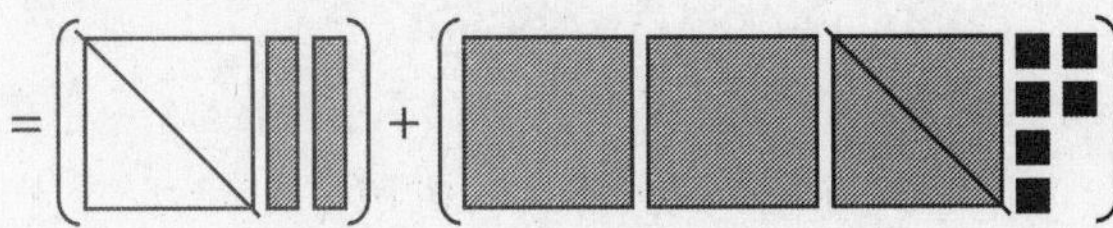

Step 4
Determine the solution by counting up the remaining tiles.

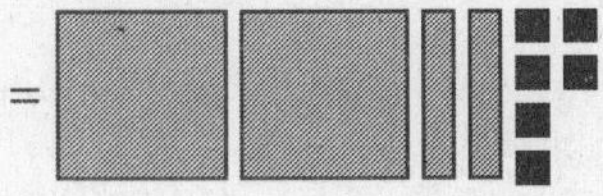

The answer is $2x^2 + 2x + 6$.

5. **Step 1**
Model the polynomials with tiles.

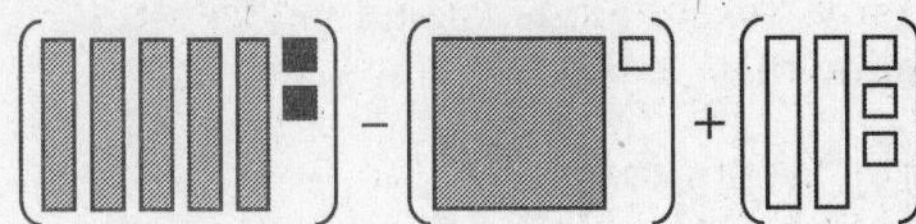

Step 2
Add the opposite when subtracting polynomials. To do this, change the tiles of the second polynomial to the opposite colour.

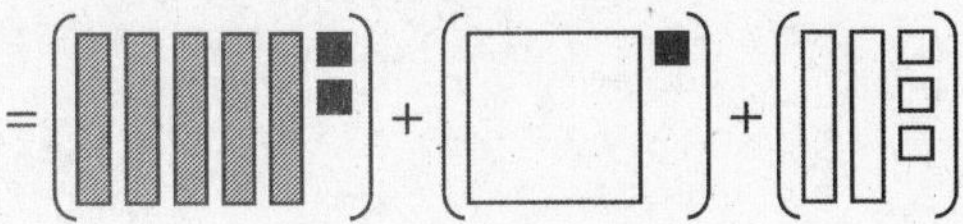

Step 3
Simplify the equation by cancelling negative and positive tiles of the same size.

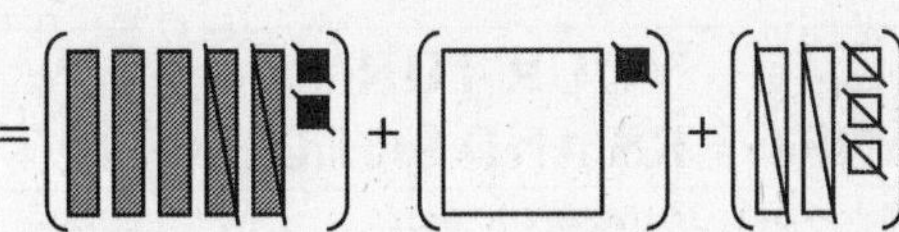

Step 4
Determine the solution by counting up the remaining tiles.

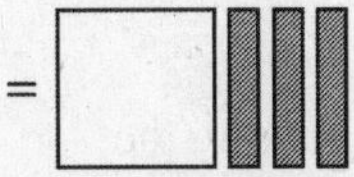

The answer is $-x^2 + 3x$.

7. **Step 1**
Rewrite the polynomial without the brackets.
$\left(x^2 - 7x - 3\right) + \left(-2x + 11\right)$
$= x^2 - 7x - 3 - 2x + 11$

Step 2
Gather the like terms.
$x^2 - 7x - 3 - 2x + 11$
$= x^2 - 7x - 2x - 3 + 11$

Step 3
Add the numerical coefficients.
$x^2 - 7x - 2x - 3 + 11$
$= x^2 - 9x + 8$

9. **Step 1**
Rewrite the polynomial by adding the additive inverse.
$(-5x^2 - 6x + 1) - (-2x^2 + 7 - 8x)$
$= (-5x^2 - 6x + 1) + (2x^2 - 7 + 8x)$

Step 2
Rewrite the polynomial without the brackets.
$(-5x^2 - 6x + 1) + (2x^2 - 7 + 8x)$
$= -5x^2 - 6x + 1 + 2x^2 - 7 + 8x$

Step 3
Gather the like terms in descending order.
$-5x^2 - 6x + 1 + 2x^2 - 7 + 8x$
$= -5x^2 + 2x^2 - 6x + 8x + 1 - 7$

Step 4
Add the numerical coefficients of the like terms.
$-5x^2 + 2x^2 - 6x + 8x + 1 - 7$
$= -3x^2 + 2x - 6$

Lesson 4—Multiplying and Dividing Polynomials

YOUR TURN ANSWERS AND SOLUTIONS

1. **Step 1**
Set up a grid using the value of the factors in the expression to represent the width and length of a rectangle.

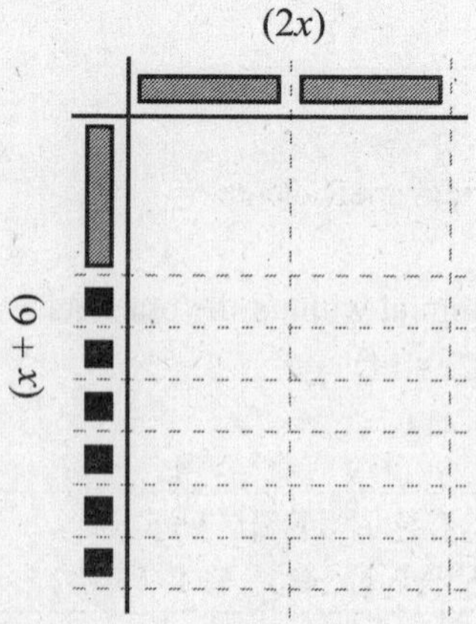

Step 2
Carry out the multiplication by filling in the area of the rectangle using algebra tiles.

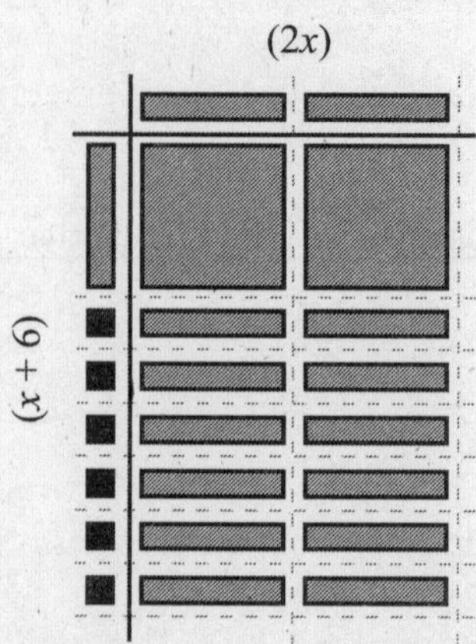

Step 3
Obtain the product by collecting like terms.

$= 2x^2$ $+ 12x$

Step 4
Write the resulting polynomial expression in degree order.
$2x^2 + 12x$

2. Multiply the numerical coefficients and then the variables together.
$(3)(5)(x)(x)$
$= 15(x)(x)$
$= 15x^{1+1}$
$= 15x^2$

3. Multiply the term outside the brackets by each term inside the brackets.
$2(4x^2 + 3x - 6)$
$= (2)(4x^2) + (2)(3x) + (2)(-6)$

Now, multiply the numerical coefficients together.
$(2)(4x^2) + (2)(3x) + (2)(-6)$
$= 8x^2 + 6x - 12$

4. Multiply the monomial by each term of the binomial inside the brackets.
$5x(x + 2)$
$= (5x)(x) + (5x)(2)$
Multiply the numerical coefficients and variables together.
$5x^{1+1} + (5)(2)(x)$
$= 5x^2 + 10x$

5. **Step 1**
Set up the grid with the divisor on the side.

Step 2
Arrange the dividend into a rectangle.

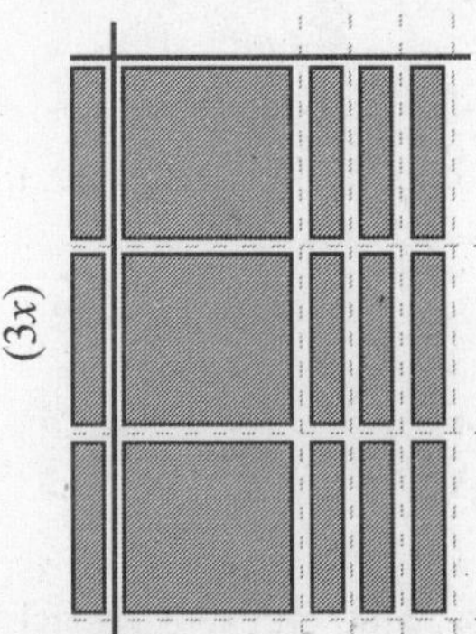

Step 3
Determine the quotient.
The quotient is the side length of each of the tiles.

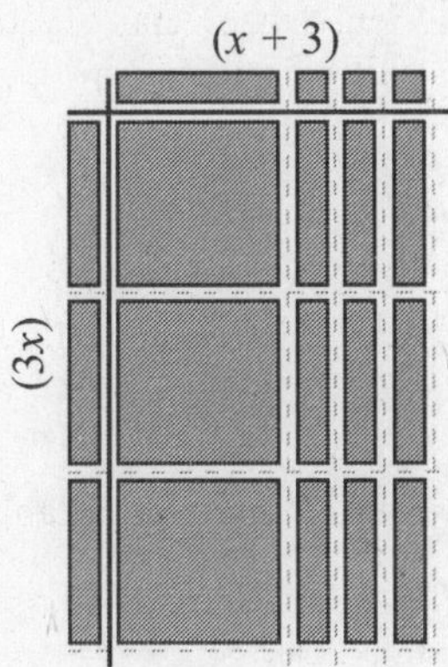

The answer is $x+3$.

6. **Step 1**
Divide each term of the numerator by the denominator.

$$\frac{15x^2+3x}{3x}$$
$$=\frac{15x^2}{3x}+\frac{3x}{3x}$$

Step 2
Divide the numerical coefficients.

$$\frac{15x^2}{3x}+\frac{3x}{3x}$$
$$=5\frac{x^2}{x}+\frac{x}{x}$$

Step 3
Divide the variables.

$$5\frac{x^2}{x}+\frac{x}{x}$$
$$=5x+1$$

7. **Step 1**
Divide each term of the numerator by the denominator.

$$\frac{8n^2+16n-20}{-2}$$
$$=\frac{8n^2}{-2}+\frac{16n}{-2}-\frac{20}{-2}$$

Step 2
Divide the numerical coefficients.

$$\frac{8n^2}{-2}+\frac{16n}{-2}-\frac{20}{-2}$$
$$=-4n^2-8n+10$$

PRACTICE EXERCISES ANSWERS AND SOLUTIONS

1. $(3x)(-4x)$
$=(3)(-4)(x)(x)$
$=-12x^{1+1}$
$=-12x^2$

3. $(-2)(x^2-x-6)$
$=(-2)(x^2)+(-2)(-x)+(-2)(-6)$
$=-2x^2+2x+12$

5. $5x(x+6)$
$=5x(x)+5x(6)$
$=5x^{1+1}+30x$
$=5x^2+30x$

7. $\frac{12x^2-8x}{4x}$
$=\frac{12x^2}{4x}-\frac{8x}{4x}$
$=3\frac{x^2}{x}-2\frac{x}{x}$
$=3x-2$

9. $\dfrac{-28+14x}{-7}$
$=\dfrac{-28}{-7}+\dfrac{14x}{-7}$
$=4-2x$

Practice Test

ANSWERS AND SOLUTIONS

1. $5y \rightarrow$ degree 1 since the exponent on the variable is 1.

3. $2x^2-6x+10 \rightarrow$ degree is 2 since $2x^2$ is the highest-degree term.

5. $(3x+7)+(2x+9)$
$=3x+7+2x+9$
$=3x+2x+7+9$
$=5x+16$

7. $(6x^2+5x+8)-(2x^2+3x+7)$
$=(6x^2+5x+8)+(-2x^2-3x-7)$
$=6x^2+5x+8-2x^2-3x-7$
$=6x^2-2x^2+5x-3x+8-7$
$=4x^2+2x+1$

9. $5(10x)$
$=(5)(10)(x)$
$=50x$

11. $3(2x^2-6x+5)$
$=3(2x^2)+3(-6x)+3(5)$
$=(3)(2)x^2+(3)(-6)x+15$
$=6x^2-18x+15$

13. The coefficients are -6 and 3.
The variables are x and y.
The constant is -8.

15. The coefficients are -7 and 10.
The variables are s and t.
The constant is 12.

17. $-5x^2(x-4)$
$=(-5x)(x)+(-5x)(-4)$
$=(-5)(x)(x)+(-5)(-4)(x)$
$=-5x^{1+1}+20x$
$=-5x^2+20x$

19. $2(4x)(3x+2)$
$=2(4)(x)(3x+2)$
$=8x(3x+2)$
$=8x(3x)+8x(2)$
$=(8)(3)(x)(x)+(8)(2)x$
$=24x^{1+1}+16x$
$=24x^2+16x$

21. $\dfrac{2a^2+15-3a}{-3}$
$=\dfrac{2a^2}{-3}+\dfrac{15}{-3}-\dfrac{3a}{-3}$
$=\dfrac{-2}{3}a^2-5+a$

CIRCLES AND 3-D COMPOSITE OBJECTS

Lesson 1—Circle Properties

YOUR TURN ANSWERS AND SOLUTIONS

1. **Step 1**
Draw the radius OB.
Notice that the radius of the circle is 9 units.
Using this value, draw radius OB on the given diagram and indicate that it is also 9 units in length.

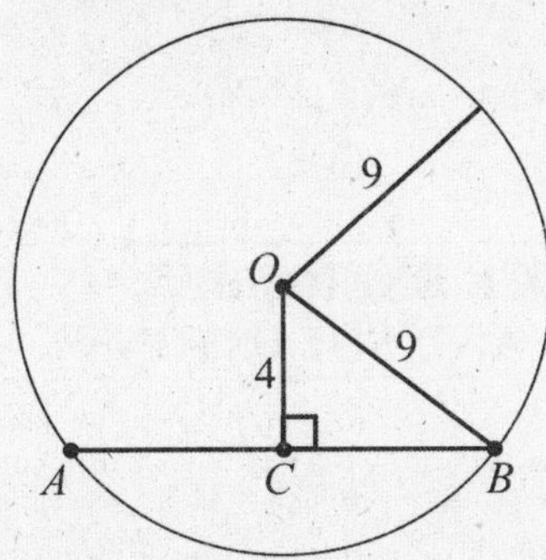

Step 2
Apply the Pythagorean theorem to the right triangle BOC in order to solve for BC.
$(BC)^2+(OC)^2=(OB)^2$

Substitute 4 for OC and 9 for OB and then solve for BC.
$$\begin{aligned}(BC)^2+(4)^2&=(9)^2\\(BC)^2+16&=81\\(BC)^2&=65\\\sqrt{BC^2}&=\sqrt{65}\\BC&\doteq 8.06\end{aligned}$$

Step 3
Since C is the midpoint of AB, AB is twice the length of BC.
$AB=2\times 8.06$
$AB=16.12$ units

2. The measure of $\angle ACB=114°$. The central angle θ is twice the measure of $\angle ACB$.
$$\begin{aligned}2\times\angle ACB&=\theta\\2\times 114°&=\theta\\228°&=\theta\end{aligned}$$

3. Inscribed angles D and C are both subtended by the same arc, arc XY. Therefore, $\angle D=\angle C$ and $\angle C=27°$.

4. **Step 1**
Determine the measure of $\angle C$.
Since $\angle C$ is inscribed in a semicircle, the measure of $\angle C=90°$.

Step 2
Determine the measure of $\angle B$.
The sum of the measures of the angles in a triangle equals 180.

Substitute 45° for $\angle A$ and 90° for $\angle C$.
$$\begin{aligned}45°+\angle B+90°&=180°\\\angle B+135°&=180°\\\angle B&=180°-135°\\&=45°\end{aligned}$$

5. $\angle T=90°$. Since TA is a tangent segment to the circle, apply the Pythagorean Theorem to solve for r.
$(OT)^2=(AT)^2+(AO)^2$

Substitute r for OT, 9 for AT, 12 for AO, and then solve for r.
$$\begin{aligned}r^2+9^2&=12^2\\r^2+81&=144\\r^2&=144-81\\r^2&=63\\\sqrt{r^2}&=\sqrt{63}\\r&\doteq 7.94\end{aligned}$$

The measure of r is approximately 7.9 units.

6. **Step 1**
Determine the measure of $\angle POB$.
Recall that the measure of the central angle is twice the measure of the inscribed angle subtended by the same arc. Therefore, $\angle POB=2\times\angle PAB$.
It follows that:
$$\begin{aligned}\angle POB&=2\times 60°\\&=120°\end{aligned}$$

Step 2
Determine the value of x.
The sum of the measures of the angles in a triangle is equal to 180°. Therefore, for triangle POB, $\angle POB+\angle OBP+\angle OPB=180°$.

Substitute 120° for $\angle POB$, x for both $\angle OBP$ and $\angle OPB$, since it is an isosceles triangle, and solve for x.

$$\begin{aligned}120°+x+x&=180°\\120°+2x&=180°\\2x&=180°-120°\\2x&=60°\\x&=30°\end{aligned}$$

Step 3
Determine the value of y.
Recall that a tangent to a circle is perpendicular to the radius at the point of tangency. Therefore, $\angle DPO = 90°$.

Also, $\angle DPO = \angle DPB + \angle BPO$.
The value of y can be determined as follows:
$\angle DPO + \angle DPB + \angle BPO = 180°$

Substitute 90° for $\angle DPO$, 30° for $\angle BPO$ (the value of x) and y for $\angle DPB$, and solve for y.

$$\begin{aligned}90°+y+30°&=180°\\y+120°&=180°\\y&=180°-120°\\y&=60°\end{aligned}$$

The measure of $\angle DPB$ is 60°.

7. **Step 1**
Draw a diagram of the situation.
The diameter of the circle is 70 m. Therefore, the radius of the circle is $70 \div 2 = 35$ m.

Recall that a line that passes through the centre of a circle and is perpendicular to a chord bisects the chord. Let x represent the shortest distance between one of the support beams and the centre of the circle, and then using the preceding information, draw a sketch similar to the one shown.

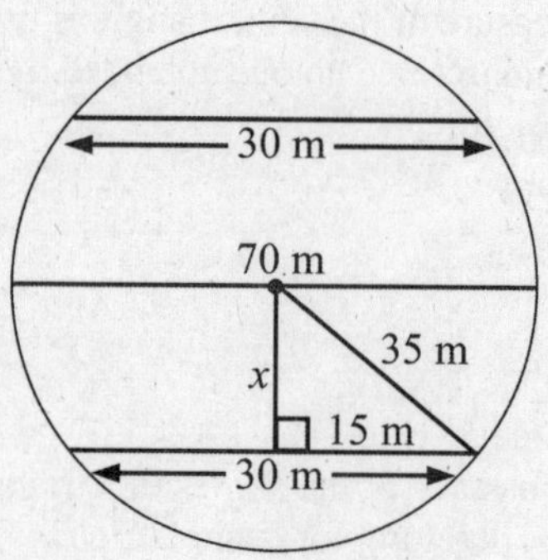

Step 2
Determine the value of x.
Apply the Pythagorean theorem.

$$\begin{aligned}x^2+15^2&=35^2\\x^2+225&=1\,225\\x^2&=1\,000\\\sqrt{x^2}&=\sqrt{1\,000}\\x&\doteq 31.6\end{aligned}$$

Step 3
Determine the distance between the two support beams.

Since each support beam is the same distance from the centre of the circle, multiply that distance by 2.
$31.6 \times 2 = 63.2$ m

The two support beams are 63.2 m apart.

PRACTICE EXERCISES ANSWERS AND SOLUTIONS

1. **Step 1**
Determine the values that represent the side lengths of the triangle. The base of the triangle is 6 units, the hypotenuse of the triangle is 10 units and x represents the height of the triangle.

Step 2
Solve for x using the Pythagorean theorem.

$$\begin{aligned}x^2+6^2&=10^2\\x^2+36&=100\\x^2&=64\\\sqrt{x^2}&=\sqrt{64}\\x&=8\end{aligned}$$

3. **Step 1**
Apply the Pythagorean Theorem, letting a represent one-half the value of x.

$$\begin{aligned}a^2+2^2&=5^2\\a^2+4&=25\\a^2&=21\\\sqrt{a^2}&=\sqrt{21}\\a&=\sqrt{21}\end{aligned}$$

Step 2
Determine the value of x.

$$\begin{aligned}x&=2a\\&=2\sqrt{21}\\&\doteq 9.17\end{aligned}$$

5. **Step 1**
Draw a diagram of the situation.

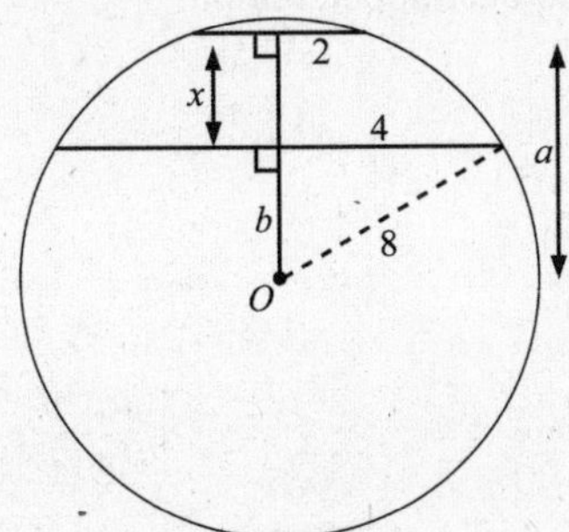

Step 2
Solve for a by applying the Pythagorean Theorem.

$$\begin{aligned} a^2 + 2^2 &= 8^2 \\ a^2 + 4 &= 64 \\ a^2 &= 60 \\ \sqrt{a^2} &= \sqrt{60} \\ a &\doteq 7.75 \end{aligned}$$

Step 3
Apply the Pythagorean Theorem in order to solve for b.

$$\begin{aligned} b^2 + 4^2 &= 8^2 \\ b^2 + 16 &= 64 \\ b^2 &= 48 \\ \sqrt{b^2} &= \sqrt{48} \\ b &\doteq 6.93 \end{aligned}$$

Step 4
Subtract the value of b from the value of a in order to determine the value of x.

$$\begin{aligned} x &= a - b \\ &= 7.75 - 6.93 \\ &= 0.82 \text{ cm} \end{aligned}$$

The distance between the chords is approximately 0.82 cm.

7. Apply the property of central angles.
The measure of the central angle is twice the measure of the inscribed angle subtended by the same arc.

$$\begin{aligned} c &= 2 \times 99° \\ &= 198° \end{aligned}$$

9. Apply the property of inscribed angles subtended by the same arc. Inscribed angles subtended by the same arc (or chord) are congruent.

$$\begin{aligned} 5x - 15 &= 2x + 30 \\ 3x &= 45 \\ x &= 15 \end{aligned}$$

Lesson 2—Surface Area of Composite 3-D Objects

YOUR TURN ANSWERS AND SOLUTIONS

1. To find the surface area of this shape, identify which faces are exposed faces and where the overlap of the objects occurs. Because this is a solid shape, find the surface area of each exposed face and then add them together.

Step 1
Break the object into two right rectangular prisms—one on the left and one on the right.

Note: It could also be broken up and down.

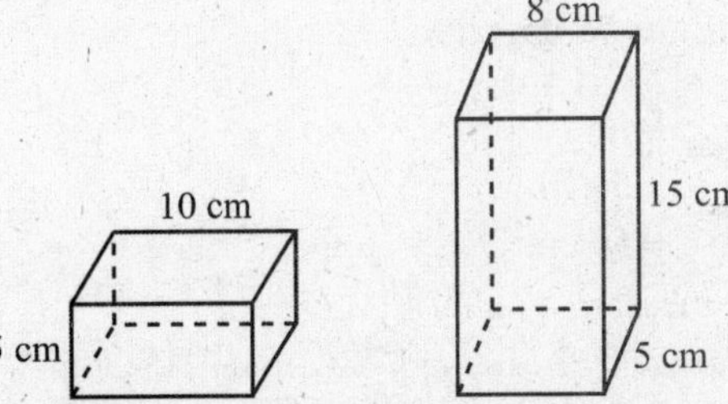

Step 2
Calculate the surface area of the right rectangular prism found on the left side of the figure.

There are five faces—front and back, top and bottom, and left side. There is no right side because it is part of the overlapped region.

$$\begin{aligned} A_{\text{front and back}} &= 2(lw) \\ &= 2(10 \times 5) \\ &= 2 \times 50 \\ &= 100 \text{ cm}^2 \end{aligned}$$

$$\begin{aligned} A_{\text{top and bottom}} &= 2(lw) \\ &= 2(10 \times 5) \\ &= 2 \times 50 \\ &= 100 \text{ cm}^2 \end{aligned}$$

$$\begin{aligned} A_{\text{left side}} &= lw \\ &= 5 \times 5 \\ &= 25 \text{ cm}^2 \end{aligned}$$

$$\begin{aligned} SA_{\text{left prism}} &= A_{\text{front and back}} + A_{\text{top and bottom}} + A_{\text{side}} \\ &= 100 + 100 + 25 \\ &= 225 \text{ cm}^2 \end{aligned}$$

Step 3
Calculate the surface area of the right rectangular prism found on the right side of the figure.

There are five faces—front and back, top and bottom, and right side. There is a partial left side because the bottom left side is part of the overlapped region.

$$\begin{aligned}A_{\text{front and back}} &= 2(lw)\\ &= 2(8\times15)\\ &= 2\times120\\ &= 240\text{ cm}^2\end{aligned}$$

$$\begin{aligned}A_{\text{top and bottom}} &= 2(lw)\\ &= 2(8\times5)\\ &= 2\times40\\ &= 80\text{ cm}^2\end{aligned}$$

$$\begin{aligned}A_{\text{right side}} &= lw\\ &= 5\times15\\ &= 75\text{ cm}^2\end{aligned}$$

$$\begin{aligned}A_{\text{left side}} &= lw\\ &= 5\times10\\ &= 50\text{ cm}^2\end{aligned}$$

$$\begin{aligned}SA_{\text{right prism}} &= A_{\text{front and back}} + A_{\text{top and bottom}} + A_{\text{right side}} + A_{\text{left side}}\\ &= 240+80+75+50\\ &= 445\text{ cm}^2\end{aligned}$$

Step 4
Calculate the total surface area of the composite object.

Add the surface area of the two rectangular prisms together.

$$\begin{aligned}SA_{\text{composite object}} &= SA_{\text{left prism}} + SA_{\text{right prism}}\\ &= 225+445\\ &= 670\text{ cm}^2\end{aligned}$$

2. **Step 1**
Calculate the surface area of the right triangular prism including the overlapped region.

$$\begin{aligned}A_{\text{front and back}} &= 2\left(\frac{bh}{2}\right)\\ &= 2\left(\frac{8\times6}{2}\right)\\ &= 48\text{ m}^2\end{aligned}$$

$$\begin{aligned}A_{\text{base}} &= lw\\ &= 8\times3\\ &= 24\text{ m}^2\end{aligned}$$

$$\begin{aligned}A_{\text{top}} &= lw\\ &= 3\times10\\ &= 30\text{ m}^2\end{aligned}$$

$$\begin{aligned}A_{\text{side}} &= lw\\ &= 3\times6\\ &= 18\text{ m}^2\end{aligned}$$

$$\begin{aligned}SA_{\text{triangular prism}} &= 48+24+30+18\\ &= 120\text{ m}^2\end{aligned}$$

Step 2
Calculate the surface area of the right rectangular prism including the overlapped region.

$$\begin{aligned}A_{\text{top and bottom}} &= 2(lw)\\ &= 2(4\times3)\\ &= 2(12)\\ &= 24\text{ m}^2\end{aligned}$$

$$\begin{aligned}A_{\text{front and back}} &= 2(lw)\\ &= 2(4\times8)\\ &= 2(32)\\ &= 64\text{ m}^2\end{aligned}$$

$$\begin{aligned}A_{\text{left and right}} &= 2(lw)\\ &= 2(3\times8)\\ &= 2(24)\\ &= 48\text{ m}^2\end{aligned}$$

$$\begin{aligned}SA_{\text{rectangular prism}} &= 24+64+48\\ &= 136\text{ m}^2\end{aligned}$$

Step 3
Calculate the areas of the overlapped regions.

The pieces that overlap are the top of the rectangular prism and the bottom of the right triangular prism. The overlapped region is rectangular in shape.

$$\begin{aligned}A_{\text{overlap}} &= 2(lw)\\ &= 2(3\times4)\\ &= 2(12)\\ &= 24\text{ m}^2\end{aligned}$$

Step 4
Calculate the total surface area of the composite object.

Add the exposed faces of the two prisms and subtract the area of overlap.

$$\begin{aligned}SA_{\text{composite object}} &= SA_{\text{triangular prism}} + SA_{\text{rectangular prism}} - A_{\text{overlap}}\\ &= 136+120-24\\ &= 232\text{ m}^2\end{aligned}$$

3. **Step 1**
Calculate the surface area of the larger figure.

The larger figure is a rectangular prism.

$$\begin{aligned}SA_{\text{rectangular prism}} &= 2(lw)+2(hw)+2(lh)\\ &= 2(11\times6)+2(9\times6)+2(11\times9)\\ &= 2(66)+2(54)+2(99)\\ &= 132+108+198\\ &= 438\text{ mm}^2\end{aligned}$$

Step 2
Calculate the area of the bases of the missing object.

The lateral faces of the smaller rectangular prism are square in shape.

$$\begin{aligned}A_{\text{bases}} &= 2(lw)\\ &= 2(2\times2)\\ &= 2(4)\\ &= 8\text{ mm}^2\end{aligned}$$

Step 3
Calculate the surface area of the lateral faces of the missing object.

The lateral faces of the rectangular prism are rectangular in shape.

$$\begin{aligned}SA_{\text{lateral faces}} &= 4(lw)\\ &= 4(2\times6)\\ &= 4(12)\\ &= 48\text{ mm}^2\end{aligned}$$

Step 4
Calculate the surface area of the entire figure including the missing piece.

Subtract the area of the bases and add the area of the lateral faces of the missing 3-D object to the surface area of the entire figure.

$$\begin{aligned}SA_{\text{entire figure}} &= SA_{\text{rectangular prism}} - A_{\text{bases}} + A_{\text{lateral faces}}\\ &= 438-8+48\\ &= 478\text{ mm}^2\end{aligned}$$

PRACTICE EXERCISES ANSWERS AND SOLUTIONS

1. **Step 1**
Calculate the surface area of the right rectangular prism.

There is no top because the triangular prism is sitting on top of the rectangular prism.

$$\begin{aligned}A_{\text{front and back}} &= 2(l\times w)\\ &= 2(12\times4)\\ &= 2\times48\\ &= 96\text{ m}^2\end{aligned}$$

$$\begin{aligned}A_{\text{sides}} &= 2(l\times w)\\ &= 2(10\times4)\\ &= 2\times40\\ &= 80\text{ m}^2\end{aligned}$$

$$\begin{aligned}A_{\text{bottom}} &= l\times w\\ &= 12\times10\\ &= 120\text{ m}^2\end{aligned}$$

$$\begin{aligned}SA_{\text{rectangular prism}} &= A_{\text{front and back}} + A_{\text{sides}} + A_{\text{bottom}}\\ &= 96+80+120\\ &= 296\text{ m}^2\end{aligned}$$

Step 2
Calculate the surface area of the right triangular prism.

There is no bottom to this figure because it sits on top of the rectangular prism; the overlapped region.

$$\begin{aligned} A_{\text{lateral faces}} &= 2(l\times w) \\ &= 2(8\times10) \\ &= 2\times80 \\ &= 160 \text{ m}^2 \end{aligned}$$

$$\begin{aligned} A_{\text{triangular bases}} &= \cancel{2}\left(\frac{b\times h}{\cancel{2}}\right) \\ &= b\times h \\ &= 12\times4 \\ &= 48 \text{ m}^2 \end{aligned}$$

$$\begin{aligned} SA_{\text{triangular prism}} &= A_{\text{lateral faces}} + A_{\text{triangular bases}} \\ &= 160+48 \\ &= 208 \text{ m}^2 \end{aligned}$$

Step 3
Calculate the total surface area of the composite object.

Add the surface area of the rectangular prism and the triangular prism together.

$$\begin{aligned} SA_{\text{composite object}} &= SA_{\text{rectangular prism}} + SA_{\text{triangular prism}} \\ &= 296+208 \\ &= 504 \text{ m}^2 \end{aligned}$$

3. **Step 1**
Calculate the surface area of the top right rectangular prism.

For this prism, there is a front and back piece, a top, and left and right pieces. There is no bottom piece.

$$\begin{aligned} SA_{\text{top prism}} &= (lw)+2(lh)+2(hw) \\ &= (8\times4)+2(8\times3)+2(3\times4) \\ &= 32+48+24 \\ &= 104 \text{ cm}^2 \end{aligned}$$

Step 2
Calculate the surface area of the bottom right rectangular prism.

For this prism, there are front and back pieces, a bottom piece, two top pieces, and left and right pieces.

$$\begin{aligned} A_{\text{front and back}} &= 2(l\times w) \\ &= 2(24\times6) \\ &= 2(144) \\ &= 288 \text{ cm}^2 \end{aligned}$$

$$\begin{aligned} A_{\text{bottom}} &= l\times w \\ &= 24\times4 \\ &= 96 \text{ cm}^2 \end{aligned}$$

$$\begin{aligned} A_{\text{top pieces}} &= 2(l\times w) \\ &= 2(8\times4) \\ &= 2(32) \\ &= 64 \text{ cm}^2 \end{aligned}$$

$$\begin{aligned} A_{\text{sides}} &= 2(l\times w) \\ &= 2(4\times6) \\ &= 2(24) \\ &= 48 \text{ cm}^2 \end{aligned}$$

$$\begin{aligned} SA_{\text{bottom prism}} &= 288+96+64+48 \\ &= 496 \text{ cm}^2 \end{aligned}$$

Step 3
Calculate the total surface area of the composite figure.

Add the surface area of the top right rectangular prism and the bottom right rectangular prism together.

$$\begin{aligned} SA_{\text{total}} &= SA_{\text{top prism}} + SA_{\text{bottom prism}} \\ &= 104+496 \\ &= 600 \text{ cm}^2 \end{aligned}$$

5. **Step 1**
Calculate the surface area of the top right cylinder including the overlap.

$SA = 2(\pi r^2)+2(\pi rh)$

Substitute 3.14 for π, $\frac{24}{2}=12$ for r, and 15 for h.

$$\begin{aligned} SA_{\text{top cylinder}} &= 2(3.14)(12^2)+2(3.14)(12)(15) \\ &= 904.32+1130.4 \\ &= 2\,034.72 \text{ cm}^2 \end{aligned}$$

Step 2
Calculate the surface area of the bottom right cylinder including the overlap.
$SA = 2(\pi r^2) + 2(\pi rh)$

Substitute 3.14 for π, $\frac{36}{2} = 18$ for r, and 32 for h.

$$\begin{aligned} SA_{\text{bottom cylinder}} &= 2(3.14)(18^2) + 2(3.14)(18)(32) \\ &= 2\,034.72 + 3\,617.28 \\ &= 5\,652 \text{ cm}^2 \end{aligned}$$

Step 3
Calculate the areas of the overlapped regions.

The area of the two overlapped regions, which are the bottom of the top cylinder and part of the top of the bottom cylinder, is

$$\begin{aligned} A_{\text{overlap}} &= 2\pi r^2 \\ &= 2(3.14 \times 12^2) \\ &= 2(452.16) \\ &= 904.32 \text{ cm}^2 \end{aligned}$$

Step 4
Calculate the total surface area of the composite object.

Add the surface area of both right cylinders and subtract the area of the overlapped regions.

$$\begin{aligned} SA_{\text{composite object}} &= SA_{\text{top cylinder}} + SA_{\text{bottom cylinder}} - A_{\text{overlap}} \\ &= 2\,034.72 + 5\,652 - 904.32 \\ &= 6\,782.4 \text{ cm}^2 \end{aligned}$$

7. **Step 1**
Calculate the surface area of the larger figure.

The larger object is a right rectangular prism.

$$\begin{aligned} SA_{\text{cylinder}} &= 2(lw) + 2(lh) + 2(hw) \\ &= 2(3 \times 2) + 2(3 \times 5) + 2(5 \times 2) \\ &= 2(6) + 2(15) + 2(10) \\ &= 12 + 30 + 20 \\ &= 62 \text{ m}^2 \end{aligned}$$

Step 2
Calculate the area of the bases of the missing 3-D object.

$$\begin{aligned} A_{\text{bases}} &= 2\left(\frac{bh}{2}\right) \\ &= 2\left(\frac{1 \times 0.75}{2}\right) \\ &= 0.75 \text{ m}^2 \end{aligned}$$

Step 3
Calculate the surface area of the lateral faces of the missing 3-D object.

The lengths of the right triangular prism are rectangular in shape.

$$\begin{aligned} A_{\text{lateral faces}} &= 3(lw) \\ &= 3(1 \times 2) \\ &= 6 \text{ m}^2 \end{aligned}$$

Step 4
Calculate the surface area of the entire 3-D composite object including the missing piece.

Subtract the area of the bases and add the area of the lateral faces of the missing object to the surface area of the entire figure.

$$\begin{aligned} SA_{\text{entire figure}} &= SA_{\text{large rectandular prism}} - A_{\text{bases}} + A_{\text{lateral faces}} \\ &= 62 - 0.75 + 6 \\ &= 67.25 \text{ m}^2 \end{aligned}$$

9. The surface area of the weight-training device is equal to the sum of the surface area of the cylindrical handle and the surface areas of the two end pieces minus the area of the overlapping regions.

Step 1
Calculate the radius of the cylindrical handle.

$$\begin{aligned} r &= \frac{d}{2} \\ &= \frac{2}{2} \\ &= 1 \text{ cm} \end{aligned}$$

Step 2
Calculate the surface area of the handle.

$$\begin{aligned} SA_{\text{handle}} &= SA_{\text{cylinder}} - A_{\text{two circular overlaps}} \\ &= (2\pi r^2 + 2\pi rh) - 2(\pi r^2) \\ &= 2\pi r^2 + 2\pi rh - 2\pi r^2 \\ &= 2\pi rh \\ &= 2(3.14)(1)(20) \\ &= 125.6 \text{ cm}^2 \end{aligned}$$

Step 3
Calculate the surface area of the two end pieces.

$$\begin{aligned} SA_{\text{end pieces}} &= 2(SA_{\text{bases}} + SA_{\text{side faces}} - A_{\text{circular overlaps}}) \\ &= 2\left[2(lw)+4(lw)-\pi r^2\right] \\ &= 2\left[2(4\times4)+4(4\times10)-(3.14\times1^2)\right] \\ &= 2\left[2(16)+4(40)-(3.14\times1)\right] \\ &= 2(32+160-3.14) \\ &= 2(188.86) \\ &= 377.72\text{ cm}^2 \end{aligned}$$

Step 4
Calculate the total surface area of the weight-training device.

Add the surface areas of the two end pieces and the handle together.

$$\begin{aligned} SA_{\text{total}} &= SA_{\text{handle}} + SA_{\text{endpieces}} \\ &= 125.6+377.72 \\ &= 503.32\text{ cm}^2 \end{aligned}$$

Rounded to the nearest tenth of a centimetre, the surface area of the weight-training device is 503.3 cm^2.

Practice Test

ANSWERS AND SOLUTIONS

1. **a)** Any one of *AO*, *CO*, *EO*, or *FO*.

   b) Any two of *AB*, *BE*, *CD*, *DF*, *AE*, *AF*, or *CF*.

   c) Many possible answers. Some examples include *ACE*, *EAB*, *FCD*, *AFC*, and *DFA*.

   d) Many possible answers. Some examples include *AB*, *CD*, *EF*, *FB*, *CE*, and *AC*.

   e) Many possible answers. Some examples include $\angle ABE$, $\angle BEA$, $\angle CDF$, and $\angle FAE$.

   f) $\angle CFD$

   g) $\angle AOE$

   h) $\angle AOE$

3. **Step 1**
Apply the Pythagorean Theorem.
Let a represent half the value of x.

$$\begin{aligned} a^2+3^2 &= 8^2 \\ a^2+9 &= 64 \\ a^2 &= 55 \\ \sqrt{a^2} &= \sqrt{55} \\ a &\doteq 7.4 \end{aligned}$$

Step 2
Determine the value of x.

$$\begin{aligned} x &= 2a \\ &= 2(7.4) \\ &= 14.8 \end{aligned}$$

5. **Step 1**
Draw a diagram of the situation.

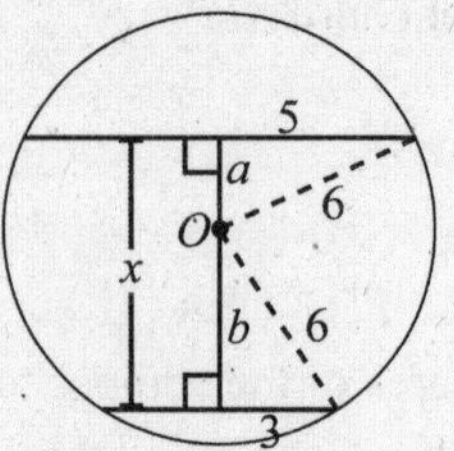

Step 2
Apply the Pythagorean Theorem and determine the value of a.

$$\begin{aligned} a^2+5^2 &= 6^2 \\ a^2+25 &= 36 \\ a^2 &= 11 \\ \sqrt{a^2} &= \sqrt{11} \\ a &\doteq 3.3 \end{aligned}$$

Step 3
Apply the Pythagorean Theorem and determine the value of b.

$$\begin{aligned} b^2+3^2 &= 6^2 \\ b^2+9 &= 36 \\ b^2 &= 27 \\ \sqrt{b^2} &= \sqrt{27} \\ b &\doteq 5.2 \end{aligned}$$

Step 4
Calculate the value of x.
Add the values of a and b together.

$$\begin{aligned} x &= a+b \\ &= 3.3+5.2 \\ &= 8.5 \end{aligned}$$

The distance between the chords is approximately 8.5 cm.

7. Step 1
Modify the diagram to include all the given information.

Draw a radius from the centre of the circle, O, to point B. Note that $OB = 7$ cm.

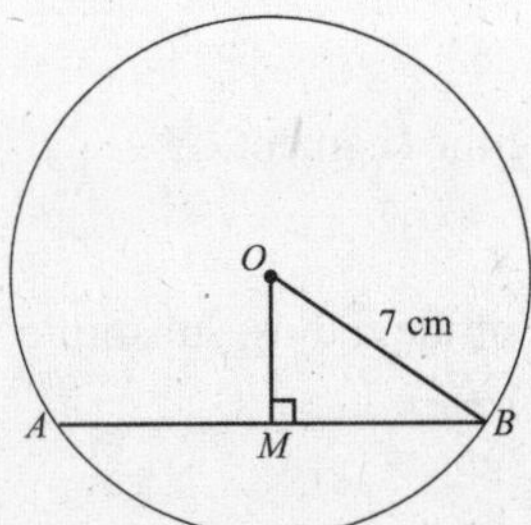

The following conclusions can be made:

- Since OM is perpendicular to AB, OM is the perpendicular bisector of chord AB.
- $$\begin{aligned} MB &= \frac{AB}{2} \\ &= \frac{10}{2} \\ &= 5 \text{ cm} \end{aligned}$$
- ΔOMB is a right triangle.
- OB is the hypotenuse of the triangle.

Step 2
Determine the length of side OM.
Apply the Pythagorean theorem.

$$\begin{aligned} (OM)^2 + (5)^2 &= (7)^2 \\ (OM)^2 + 25 &= 49 \\ (OM)^2 &= 24 \\ \sqrt{(OM)^2} &= \sqrt{24} \\ OM &\doteq 4.9 \text{ cm} \end{aligned}$$

The length of OM is approximately 4.9 cm.

9. Since a tangent to a circle is perpendicular to the radius at the point of tangency, the angle made by the tangent and the radius is a right angle.

Apply the Pythagorean theorem and solve for r.

$$\begin{aligned} 41^2 &= r^2 + 36^2 \\ 1681 &= r^2 + 1296 \\ 385 &= r^2 \\ \sqrt{385} &= \sqrt{r^2} \\ 19.62 &\doteq r \end{aligned}$$

To the nearest tenth of a centimetre, the length of the radius is approximately 19.6 cm.

11. Step 1
Calculate the measure of $\angle MON$.

$$\begin{aligned} \angle MON + 305° &= 360° \\ \angle MON &= 360° - 305° \\ &= 55° \end{aligned}$$

Step 2
Calculate the measure of $\angle x$.

Apply the property of inscribed and central angles. The measure of the central angle is twice the measure of the inscribed angle subtended by the same arc.

$$\begin{aligned} \angle x &= \frac{1}{2} \times \angle MON \\ &= \frac{1}{2} \times 55° \\ &= 27.5° \end{aligned}$$

13. Step 1
Calculate the diameter of the circle.
The diameter is equal to twice the radius.

$$\begin{aligned} d &= 2r \\ &= 2 \times 23.2 \\ &= 46.4 \text{ m} \end{aligned}$$

Step 2
Apply the property of inscribed angles in semicircles: An angle inscribed in a semicircle is a right angle.

Apply the Pythagorean Theorem to solve for x. Substitute x for a, 39 for b, and 46.4 for c.

$$\begin{aligned} a^2 + b^2 &= c^2 \\ x^2 + 39^2 &= 46.4^2 \\ x^2 + 1\,521 &= 2\,152.96 \\ x^2 &= 631.96 \\ \sqrt{x^2} &= \sqrt{631.96} \\ x &\doteq 25.14 \end{aligned}$$

Rounded to the nearest tenth of a metre, the measure of x is 25.1 m.

15. Step 1
Use the Pythagorean Theorem to determine the length of OA.

Consider the ΔOCB.

$$c^2 = a^2 + b^2$$
$$(OB)^2 = 8^2 + 13^2$$
$$(OB)^2 = 64 + 169$$
$$(OB)^2 = 233$$
$$\sqrt{(OB)^2} = \sqrt{233}$$
$$OB \doteq 15.26$$

Therefore, the radius OA, rounded to the nearest tenth, is 15.3 cm.

Step 2
Determine the length of CD.
The length OD is also the radius of the circle.

$$CD = OD - OC$$
$$= 15.3 - 8$$
$$= 7.3 \text{ cm}$$

17. The measure of a central angle is twice the measure of an inscribed angle subtended by the same arc. The measure of the central angle is $2 \times 123° = 246°$.

19. Step 1
Apply the property of tangent segments from an external point to determine the length of line segment EF.

The two tangent segments from an external point are equal in length.
$EF = CF$

Therefore, $EF = 4$.

Step 2
Apply the properties of tangents and radii at the point of tangency: A tangent to a circle is perpendicular to the radius at the point of tangency. Therefore, ΔOCF is a right-angled triangle.
Apply the Pythagorean Theorem to determine the length of segment OF.

$$(OF)^2 = (OC)^2 + (CF)^2$$

Substitute 1.5 for OC and 4 for CF.

$$(OF)^2 = 1.5^2 + 4^2$$
$$(OF)^2 = 2.25 + 16$$
$$(OF)^2 = 18.25$$
$$\sqrt{(OF)^2} = \sqrt{18.25}$$
$$OF \doteq 4.3$$

Step 3
Determine the length of the segment GF.
$GF = OF - OG$

Since OG is the length of the radius, substitute 1.5 for OG and 4.3 for OF.

$$GF = 4.3 - 1.5$$
$$= 2.8$$

Therefore, the length of segment FG, correct to the nearest tenth, is 2.8 units.

21. Step 1
Calculate the surface area of the top right cylinder including the overlap.

$$SA = 2(\pi r^2) + 2(\pi rh)$$

Substitute 3.14 for π, 5 for r, and 10 for h.

$$SA_{\text{cylinder}} = 2(3.14)(5^2) + 2(3.14)(5)(10)$$
$$= 157 + 314$$
$$= 471 \text{ mm}^2$$

Step 2
Calculate the surface area of the bottom right rectangular prism including the overlap.

$$SA_{\text{rectangular prism}} = 2(lw) + 2(lh) + 2(hw)$$
$$= 2(40 \times 25) + 2(40 \times 10) + 2(10 \times 25)$$
$$= 2(1\,000) + 2(400) + 2(250)$$
$$= 2\,000 + 800 + 500$$
$$= 3\,300 \text{ mm}^2$$

Step 3
Calculate the areas of the overlapped regions.

The area of the "two" overlapped regions, which are the bottom of the top cylinder and part of the top of the rectangular prism, is

$$A_{\text{overlap}} = 2\pi r^2$$
$$= 2(3.14 \times 5^2)$$
$$= 2(78.5)$$
$$= 157 \text{ mm}^2$$

Step 4
Calculate the total surface area of the composite 3-D object.

Add the surface area of the right cylinder and the right rectangular prism and subtract the overlapped regions.

$$\begin{aligned} SA_{\text{composite object}} &= SA_{\text{cylinder}} + SA_{\text{rectangular prism}} - A_{\text{overlap}} \\ &= 471 + 3\,300 - 157 \\ &= 3\,614 \text{ mm}^2 \end{aligned}$$

SCALING, SIMILAR TRIANGLES, AND POLYGONS

Lesson 1—Scaling

YOUR TURN ANSWERS AND SOLUTIONS

1. **Step 1**
   Pick one known length in the image diagram. Segment $M'P'$ is 5.4 cm long.

   Step 2
   Find the corresponding length in the original diagram.

   Segment MP is 1.35 cm long.

   Step 3
   Use the general formula to calculate the scale factor.

   $$\begin{aligned} \text{scale factor} &= \frac{\text{image length}}{\text{original length}} \\ &= \frac{5.4}{1.35} \\ &= 4 \end{aligned}$$

2. Side $P'Q'$ in the image diagram corresponds to side PQ in the original diagram.

   The length of side PQ is 2.6 cm and the scale factor of the image is 6.

   Multiply 2.6 by 6 to determine the length of side $P'Q'$.
   $2.6 \times 6 = 15.6$ cm

   The length of side $P'Q'$ is 15.6 cm.

3. The scale factor is 4, so the image diagram will be larger than the original diagram. This is an enlargement.

Step 1
Draw and label the original rectangle.

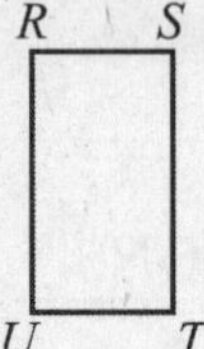

Step 2
Determine the height of each side in the image diagram.

Since $3.5\times4=14$ cm, the height of the rectangle in the image will be 14 cm long.

Since $1.5\times4=6$ cm, the length of the rectangle in the image will be 6 cm long.

Step 3
Draw the image diagram and use the ′ symbol for each letter.

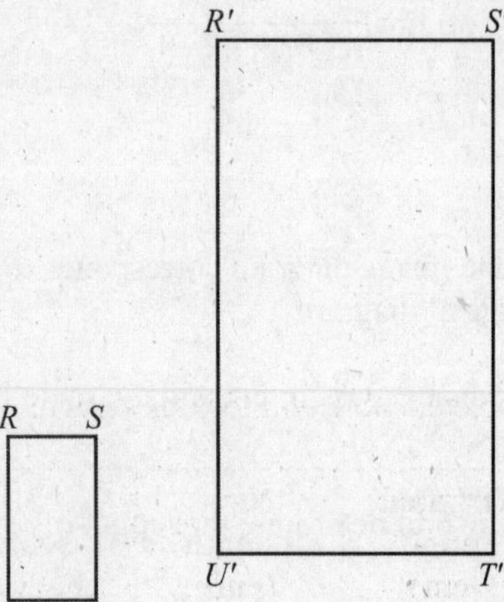

Step 4
Join each original point to its corresponding point on the image, and write the scale factor.
scale factor = 4

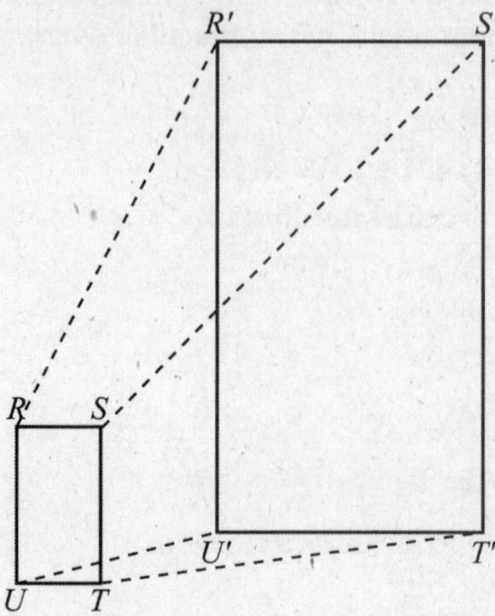

4. Given two of the three relevant numbers, you can find the remaining number by manipulating the general formula: $\text{scale factor} = \dfrac{\text{image length}}{\text{original length}}$.

Row 1

$$\begin{aligned}\text{scale factor} &= \frac{\text{image length}}{\text{original length}}\\ 32 &= \frac{\text{image length}}{7}\\ \text{image length} &= 7\times32\\ &= 224\end{aligned}$$

Row 2

$$\begin{aligned}\text{scale factor} &= \frac{\text{image length}}{\text{original length}}\\ &= \frac{15}{75}\\ &= 0.2\end{aligned}$$

Row 3

$$\begin{aligned}\text{scale factor} &= \frac{\text{image length}}{\text{original length}}\\ 2.7 &= \frac{8.1}{\text{original length}}\\ \text{original length} &= \frac{8.1}{2.7}\\ &= 3\end{aligned}$$

Row 4

$$\text{scale factor} = \frac{\text{image length}}{\text{original length}}$$

$$0.4 = \frac{\text{image length}}{14.2}$$

$$\text{image length} = 14.2 \times 0.4$$
$$= 5.68$$

Row 5

$$\text{scale factor} = \frac{\text{image length}}{\text{original length}}$$
$$= \frac{93}{0.93}$$
$$= 100$$

5. **Step 1**
Express the scale factor as a fraction.

$$1{:}2\ 000 = \frac{1}{2\ 000}$$

Step 2
Set up a proportion that represents the situation. Let d represent the height of the building in the drawing.

Since d is the height of the building in the drawing, it will represent the numerator in the second fraction.

Since 37 is the actual height of the building, it will represent the denominator in the second fraction.

$$\frac{1}{2\ 000} = \frac{d}{37}$$

Step 3
Solve for d by applying cross products.

$$d \times 2\ 000 = 1 \times 37$$
$$2\ 000d = 37$$
$$d = \frac{37}{2\ 000}$$
$$= 0.0185 \text{ m}$$

The drawing of the building is 0.0185 m in height. This measure is equivalent to 1.85 cm.

PRACTICE EXERCISES ANSWERS AND SOLUTIONS

1. **a)**

$$\text{scale factor} = \frac{\text{image length}}{\text{original length}}$$
$$= \frac{30}{10}$$
$$= 3$$

b)

$$\text{scale factor} = \frac{\text{image length}}{\text{original length}}$$
$$\frac{1}{2} = \frac{\text{image length}}{15}$$
$$\text{image length} = \frac{15}{2}$$
$$= 7\frac{1}{2}$$

c)

$$\text{scale factor} = \frac{\text{image length}}{\text{original length}}$$
$$2\frac{1}{2} = \frac{15}{\text{original length}}$$
$$\frac{5}{2} = \frac{15}{\text{original length}}$$
$$\text{original length} = \frac{15}{\frac{5}{2}}$$
$$= 15 \times \frac{2}{5}$$
$$= 6$$

The completed table will look as shown:

	Original Length (cm)	New Length (cm)	Scale Factor
a)	10	30	3
b)	15	$7\frac{1}{2}$	$\frac{1}{2}$
c)	6	15	$2\frac{1}{2}$

3. To determine the lengths of the corresponding sides in the image diagram, multiply each side length in the original diagram by 2.

$$\begin{aligned} L'M' &= LM \times 2 \\ &= 3 \times 2 \\ &= 6 \end{aligned}$$

$$\begin{aligned} M'N' &= MN \times 2 \\ &= 2 \times 2 \\ &= 4 \end{aligned}$$

$$\begin{aligned} N'L' &= NL \times 2 \\ &= 3.5 \times 2 \\ &= 7 \end{aligned}$$

5. Apply the general formula to calculate the scale factor.

$$\begin{aligned} \text{scale factor} &= \frac{\text{image length}}{\text{original length}} \\ &= \frac{0.75}{1.5} \\ &= 0.5 \end{aligned}$$

The scale factor is 0.5 or $\frac{1}{2}$.

7. **Step 1**
Express the scale factor as a fraction.

$$4{:}1 = \frac{4}{1}$$

Step 2
Set up a proportion that represents the situation.

Let d represent the length of the mosquito in the diagram.

$$\frac{4}{1} = \frac{d}{0.75}$$

Step 3
Solve for d by applying cross products.

$$\begin{aligned} d &= 0.75 \times 4 \\ &= 3 \text{ cm} \end{aligned}$$

In the drawing, the mosquito is 3 cm long.

9. **Step 1**
Express the scale factor as a fraction.

$$1{:}7\ 000\ 000 = \frac{1}{7\ 000\ 000}$$

Step 2
Set up a proportion that represents the situation.

Let m represent the distance between the two cities on the map.

$$\frac{1}{7\ 000\ 000} = \frac{m}{363}$$

Step 3
Solve for m by applying cross products.

$$\begin{aligned} 7\ 000\ 000m &= 363 \\ \frac{7\ 000\ 000m}{7\ 000\ 000} &= \frac{363}{7\ 000\ 000} \\ m &= 0.000\ 051\ 857 \end{aligned}$$

Convert the measure of the result to centimeters by multiplying by 100 000.

$$\begin{aligned} 0.000\ 0518\ 57 \text{ km} &= 0.000\ 0518\ 57 \times 100\ 000 \\ &= 5.1857 \text{ cm} \end{aligned}$$

Rounding the answer to the nearest tenth would give a final answer of 5.2 cm.

11. Apply the general formula to calculate the scale factor of each length.

$$\begin{aligned} \text{scale factor} &= \frac{\text{image length}}{\text{original length}} \\ &= \frac{108}{18} \\ &= 6 \end{aligned}$$

$$\begin{aligned} \text{scale factor} &= \frac{\text{image length}}{\text{original length}} \\ &= \frac{27}{4.5} \\ &= 6 \end{aligned}$$

13. **Step 1**
Express the scale factor as a fraction.

$$1{:}20\ 000\ 000 = \frac{1}{20\ 000\ 000}$$

Step 2
Set up a proportion that represents the situation.

Let m represent the distance between the two cities on the map.

$$\frac{1}{20\ 000\ 000} = \frac{m}{1\ 500}$$

Step 3
Solve for m by applying cross products.

$$m \times 20\ 000\ 000 = 1 \times 1\ 500$$
$$20\ 000\ 000m = 1\ 500$$
$$\frac{20\ 000\ 000m}{20\ 000\ 000} = \frac{1\ 500}{20\ 000\ 000}$$
$$m = 0.000\ 075$$

Step 4
Convert the measure of the result to centimetres by multiplying by 100 000.

$$0.000\ 075\ \text{km} = 0.000\ 075 \times 100\ 000$$
$$= 7.5\ \text{cm}$$

The cities would be 7.5 cm apart on a map.

Lesson 2—Properties of Similar Triangles

YOUR TURN ANSWERS AND SOLUTIONS

1. **Step 1**
Identify the corresponding sides.

Corresponding sides are the matching pair of sides that have the same place in both triangles.

- side AB corresponds to side DE,
- side AC corresponds to side DF, and
- side BC corresponds to side EF.

Step 2
Determine if the corresponding sides are proportional.

If the corresponding sides are proportional, then

$$\frac{AB}{DE} = \frac{AC}{DF} = \frac{BC}{EF}$$

Using the given values, write each of the preceding ratios in lowest terms or as a decimal.

$$\frac{AB}{DE} = \frac{6}{4.5} = 1.\bar{3}$$
$$\frac{AC}{DF} = \frac{10}{7.5} = 1.\bar{3}$$
$$\frac{BC}{EF} = \frac{8}{6} = 1.\bar{3}$$

Since $1.\bar{3} = 1.\bar{3} = 1.\bar{3}$, the corresponding sides are proportional and $\Delta ABC \sim \Delta DEF$.

2. **Step 1**
Draw a diagram to represent the problem.

Let x represent the height of the telephone pole.

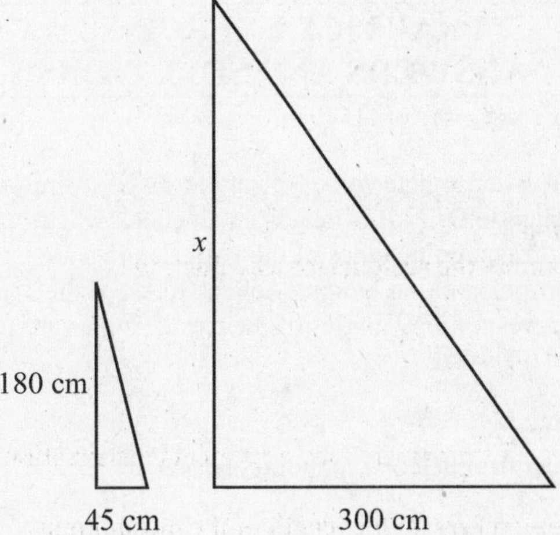

Step 2
Identify the corresponding sides in both triangles.

Corresponding sides are the matching pair of sides that have the same place in both triangles.
180 corresponds to x.
45 corresponds to 300.

Step 3
Write a proportion that represents the ratio of the corresponding sides.

$$\frac{180}{x} = \frac{45}{300}$$

Step 4
Solve for x by applying cross products.

$$\frac{180}{x}=\frac{45}{300}$$
$$180\times300=x\times45$$
$$54\,000=45x$$
$$\frac{54\,000}{45}=\frac{45x}{45}$$
$$1\,200=x$$

Convert the measure of the result to meters by dividing by 100.

$$1200\text{ cm}=\frac{1200}{100}$$
$$=12\text{ m}$$

The height of the telephone pole is 12 m.

PRACTICE EXERCISES ANSWERS AND SOLUTIONS

1. In order to determine if triangle ABC is similar to triangle DEF, it is necessary to check whether the corresponding sides of the two triangles are proportional in length or check to see if the corresponding angles of the two triangles are equal in measure.

Step 1
Identify the corresponding sides.

$$\frac{AB}{DE}=\frac{7}{3.5}$$
$$=2$$
$$\frac{BC}{EF}=\frac{9}{4.5}$$
$$=2$$
$$\frac{AC}{DF}=\frac{8}{4}$$
$$=2$$

Since $\frac{AB}{DE}=\frac{BC}{EF}=\frac{AC}{DF}$, triangle ABC is similar to triangle DEF.

Step 2
Identify the corresponding angles.

For triangle ABC, $\angle A=70^\circ$, $\angle B=60^\circ$, and $\angle C=180^\circ-(70^\circ+60^\circ)=50^\circ$.

For triangle DEF, $\angle D=70^\circ$, $\angle F=50^\circ$, and $\angle E=180^\circ-(70^\circ+50^\circ)=60^\circ$.

Since $\angle A=\angle D$, $\angle B=\angle E$, and $\angle C=\angle F$, triangle ABC is similar to triangle DEF.

Note: Recall that the sum of the measures of the angles in a triangle is equal to 180°.

3. Side RT in triangle PRT corresponds with side HG in triangle FGH.

5. Identify the corresponding sides.

$$\frac{ST}{VW}=\frac{7.5\text{ m}}{3\text{ m}}$$
$$=2.5$$
$$\frac{TU}{WX}=\frac{10\text{ m}}{4\text{ m}}$$
$$=2.5$$
$$\frac{SU}{VX}=\frac{12.5\text{ m}}{5\text{ m}}$$
$$=2.5$$

Since the given triangles have proportional sides, $\Delta STU\sim\Delta VWX$.

7. **Step 1**
Identify the corresponding sides.
3 corresponds to 19.5.
x corresponds to 32.5.
Step 2
Write the ratio of the corresponding sides.

$$\frac{3}{19.5}=\frac{x}{32.5}$$

Step 3
Solve for x using cross products.

$$\frac{3}{19.5}=\frac{x}{32.5}$$
$$3\times32.5=19.5\times x$$
$$97.5=19.5x$$
$$\frac{97.5}{19.5}=\frac{19.5x}{19.5}$$
$$5=x$$

The length of side x is 5.0 units.

9. Since both triangles are right triangles (perpendicular with the floor) and have equal angles at the top, the remaining corresponding angles will be equal. The triangles are similar.

Step 1
Draw a diagram that represents the given situation.

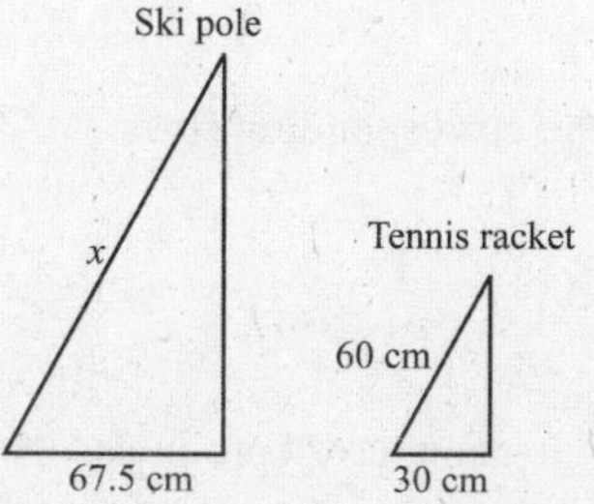

Step 2
Identify the corresponding sides.

67.5 corresponds to 30.
x corresponds to 60.

Step 3
Write the ratio of the corresponding sides.

$$\frac{67.5}{30}=\frac{x}{60}$$

Step 4
Solve for the variable using cross products.

$$\frac{67.5}{30}=\frac{x}{60}$$
$$30x=67.5\times60$$
$$30x=4\ 050$$
$$\frac{30x}{30}=\frac{4\ 050}{30}$$
$$x=135$$

The length of the ski pole is 135 cm.

Lesson 3—Similar Polygons

YOUR TURN ANSWERS AND SOLUTIONS

1. Since the length of each side of both polygons is given, it is necessary to determine whether or not the corresponding sides of the polygons are proportional in order to know if the polygons are similar.

Step 1
Identify the corresponding sides.

- Side BC corresponds to side MQ
- Side CD corresponds to side QP
- Side AD corresponds to side NP
- Side AB corresponds to side NM

Step 2
Calculate the corresponding ratios.

If the corresponding sides are proportional, then

$$\frac{BC}{MQ}=\frac{CD}{QP}=\frac{AD}{NP}=\frac{AB}{NM}$$

Using the given values, write each of the preceding ratios as a decimal.

$$\frac{BC}{MQ}=\frac{16.8}{10.5}$$
$$=1.6$$
$$\frac{CD}{QP}=\frac{8.8}{5.5}$$
$$=1.6$$
$$\frac{AD}{NP}=\frac{8.4}{5.25}$$
$$=1.6$$
$$\frac{AB}{NM}=\frac{10.4}{6.5}$$
$$=1.6$$

Since the ratios are identical, the corresponding sides are proportional. Quadrilateral $ABCD$ is similar to quadrilateral $MNPQ$.

2. **Step 1**
Identify the corresponding sides.

Since the two polygons are similar, the corresponding side must be proportional.

$$\frac{LN}{PS}=\frac{NO}{SR}$$

Step 2
Set up a proportion and solve by applying cross products.

Substitute 3.3 for *LN*, 2.2 for *PS*, and 1.2 for *NO*.

$$\frac{3.3}{2.2}=\frac{1.2}{SR}$$
$$3.3\times SR=1.2\times 2.2$$
$$3.3(SR)=2.64$$
$$\frac{3.3(SR)}{3.3}=\frac{2.64}{3.3}$$
$$SR=0.8\text{ cm}$$

PRACTICE EXERCISES ANSWERS AND SOLUTIONS

1. Choose a scale factor and then multiply each side length in quadrilateral *ABCD* by the scale factor. Construct quadrilateral *MNPQ*. (A protractor may be helpful in assisting with the construction of quadrilateral *MNPQ*.)

For example, if a scale factor of $\frac{1}{2}$ is used, quadrilateral *MNPQ* could have the following side lengths: $MN=2\times\frac{1}{2}=6\text{ cm}$, $NP=4\times\frac{1}{2}=2\text{ cm}$, and $QP=8\times\frac{1}{2}=4\text{ cm}$. Quadrilateral *MNPQ* would now appear as shown.

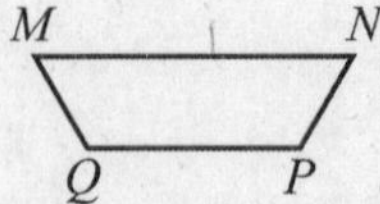

Alternate Solution
Using a protractor, measure $\angle A$, $\angle B$, $\angle C$, and $\angle D$. Next, construct quadrilateral *MNPQ* with the same angle measures. Quadrilateral *MNPQ* can be any size, however, the angle measures must be identical to those for quadrilateral *ABCD*.

3. Side *HI* in polygon *GHIJKL* matches with side *DC* in polygon *ABCDEF*. Therefore, side *HI* corresponds to side *DC*.

$\angle K$ in polygon *GHIJKL* matches with $\angle A$ in polygon *ABCDEF*. Therefore, $\angle K$ corresponds to $\angle A$.

5. **Step 1**
Write the ratio of the corresponding sides.

$$\frac{16}{x}=\frac{30}{21}$$

Step 2
Solve for the variable using cross products.

$$\frac{16}{x}=\frac{30}{21}$$
$$x\times 30=16\times 21$$
$$30x=336$$
$$\frac{30x}{30}=\frac{336}{30}$$
$$x=11.2\text{ cm}$$

The length of side *x* is 11.2 cm.

7. **Step 1**
Determine the value of *x*, given that the sum of the measures of the angles in a quadrilateral is equal to 360°.

$$112^\circ+70^\circ+x+x+8^\circ=360^\circ$$
$$2x+190^\circ=360^\circ$$
$$2x=170^\circ$$
$$x=85^\circ$$

Step 2
Determine the measure of $\angle I$.

Since $x=85^\circ$, substitute this value into $x+8^\circ$ and calculate the measure of $\angle I$.

$$\angle I=x+8^\circ$$
$$=85^\circ+8^\circ$$
$$=93^\circ$$

Step 3
Determine the measure of $\angle M$.

Observe that $\angle I$ in quadrilateral *GHIJ* corresponds to $\angle M$ in quadrilateral *KLMN*. Therefore, $\angle I=\angle M$.

The measure of $\angle M$ is 93°.

9. Step 1
Apply the property that corresponding sides of similar polygons are proportional in length.

$$\frac{AD}{MQ}=\frac{CD}{PQ}$$

Step 2
Solve for PQ by applying cross-products.

Substitute 20 for AD, 24 for MQ, 50 for CD, and then solve for PQ.

$$\begin{aligned}\frac{20}{24}&=\frac{50}{PQ}\\ 20\times PQ&=50\times 24\\ 20\times PQ&=1\,200\\ \frac{20\times PQ}{20}&=\frac{1\,200}{20}\\ PQ&=60\text{ m}\end{aligned}$$

The distance from marker Q to marker P is 60 m.

Practice Test

ANSWERS AND SOLUTIONS

1. a)

$$\begin{aligned}\text{scale factor}&=\frac{\text{image length}}{\text{original length}}\\ 6.5&=\frac{32.5}{\text{original length}}\\ \text{original length}&=\frac{32.5}{6.5}\\ &=5\end{aligned}$$

b)

$$\begin{aligned}\text{scale factor}&=\frac{\text{image length}}{\text{original length}}\\ \frac{1}{3}&=\frac{\text{image length}}{18}\\ \text{image length}&=\frac{18}{3}\\ &=6\end{aligned}$$

c)

$$\begin{aligned}\text{scale factor}&=\frac{\text{image length}}{\text{original length}}\\ &=\frac{77}{770}\\ &=\frac{1}{10}\end{aligned}$$

The completed table will look as shown:

Original Length (cm)	New Length (cm)	Scale Factor
5	32.5	6.5
18	6	$\frac{1}{3}$
770	77	$\frac{1}{10}$

3. Step 1
Use the general formula to calculate the scale factor. Use sides AE and $A'E'$.

$$\begin{aligned}\text{scale factor}&=\frac{\text{image length}}{\text{original length}}\\ &=\frac{8}{2}\\ &=4\end{aligned}$$

Step 2
To determine the measure of each of the new sides in the image, multiply each side in the original diagram by 4.

$$\begin{aligned}A'B'&=AB\times 4\\ &=1\times 4\\ &=4\text{ cm}\end{aligned}$$

Because $AB=ED=DC$, $E'D'=4$ cm and $D'C'=4$ cm.

$$\begin{aligned}B'C'&=BC\times 4\\ &=2\times 4\\ &=8\text{ cm}\end{aligned}$$

5. Step 1
Express the scale factor as a fraction.

$$1{:}50=\frac{1}{50}$$

Step 2
Set up a proportion that represents the situation.

Let s represent the actual length of the sofa.

$$\frac{1}{50}=\frac{7}{s}$$

Step 3
Solve for s by applying cross products.

$$\begin{aligned}s\times 1&=50\times 7\\ s&=350\text{ cm}\end{aligned}$$

Step 4
Convert the measure of the result to metres.

To convert centimetres to metres, divide the centimetres by 100.

$$350 \text{ cm} = \frac{350}{100} = 3.5 \text{ m}$$

The actual length of the sofa is 3.5 m.

7. Since the scale factor is 7, multiply each dimension in the drawing by 7.

$6 \times 7 = 42$ cm
$8 \times 7 = 56$ cm
$1 \times 7 = 7$ cm

The dimensions of the piano are $42 \text{ cm} \times 56 \text{ cm} \times 7 \text{ cm}$.

9. Identify the corresponding angles.

Corresponding angles have the same place in the triangles.

- $\angle A$ corresponds to $\angle D$ because both are 28°.
- $\angle B$ corresponds to $\angle E$ because both are 98°.
- $\angle C$ corresponds to $\angle F$ because both are 54°.

Since all three corresponding angles are equal, $\Delta ABC \sim \Delta DEF$.

11. Step 1
Identify the corresponding sides.

Corresponding sides have the same place in the triangle.
MO corresponds to *AC*.
MN corresponds to *AB*.

Step 2
Write the ratio of corresponding sides.

$$\frac{12}{x} = \frac{9}{6}$$

Step 3
Solve for x by applying cross products.

$$\frac{12}{x} = \frac{9}{6}$$
$$9 \times x = 12 \times 6$$
$$9x = 72$$
$$\frac{9x}{9} = \frac{72}{9}$$
$$x = 8$$

The length of side x is 8 units.

13. Step 1
Identify the corresponding sides.
1.95 corresponds to 1.50.
x corresponds to 2.

Step 2
Write the ratio of the corresponding sides.

$$\frac{1.95}{1.50} = \frac{x}{2}$$

Step 3
Solve for x by applying cross products.

$$\frac{1.95}{1.50} = \frac{x}{2}$$
$$1.50 \times x = 1.95 \times 2$$
$$1.50x = 3.9$$
$$\frac{1.50x}{1.50} = \frac{3.9}{1.50}$$
$$x = 2.6$$

The length of x is 2.6 m.

15. Step 1
Draw a diagram to visualize the problem.

Use a variable to identify the unknown side.
Write an equation using proportional sides to solve the problem. Use meters for all units.

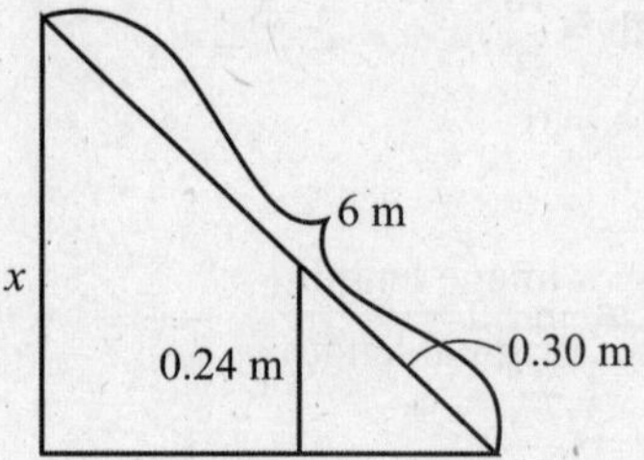

Step 2
Identify the corresponding sides.

The smaller triangle corresponds to the entire larger triangle.

Corresponding sides have the same place in the triangle.
0.24 corresponds to x.
0.30 corresponds to 6.

Step 3
Write the ratios of the corresponding sides.

$$\frac{0.24}{x}=\frac{0.30}{6}$$

Step 4
Solve for x by applying cross products.

$$\begin{aligned}\frac{0.24}{x}&=\frac{0.30}{6}\\ 0.30\times x&=0.24\times 6\\ 0.30x&=1.44\\ \frac{0.30x}{0.30}&=\frac{1.44}{0.30}\\ x&=4.8\end{aligned}$$

The ladder will reach 4.8 m up the wall.

17. **Step 1**
Identify the corresponding sides.

$$\frac{AB}{RS}=\frac{BC}{ST}$$

Step 2
Solve for ST by applying cross products.

Substitute 24 for AB, 15 for RS, and 40 for BC.

$$\begin{aligned}\frac{24}{15}&=\frac{40}{ST}\\ 24\times ST&=40\times 15\\ 24\times ST&=600\\ \frac{24\times ST}{24}&=\frac{600}{24}\\ ST&=25\text{ cm}\end{aligned}$$

19. **Step 1**
Determine the value of the unknown side length in the top piece.

If this side length is denoted by the variable y, then $6+y+6=21$. Solve for y to find the length of the unknown side.

$$\begin{aligned}6+y+6&=21\\ y+12&=21\\ y&=9\text{ cm}\end{aligned}$$

Step 2
Determine the value of x.

Apply the property that the corresponding sides in similar polygons are proportional in length. Solve for x by applying cross products.

$$\begin{aligned}\frac{9}{4.5}&=\frac{6}{x}\\ 9\times x&=6\times 4.5\\ 9x&=27\\ \frac{9x}{9}&=\frac{27}{9}\\ x&=3\end{aligned}$$

The length of side x is 3 cm.

ROTATION SYMMETRY AND TRANSFORMATIONS OF 2-D SHAPES

Lesson 1—Classify and Complete 2-D Shapes

YOUR TURN ANSWERS AND SOLUTIONS

1. Four possible lines of symmetry are shown.

2. These shapes have one line of symmetry.

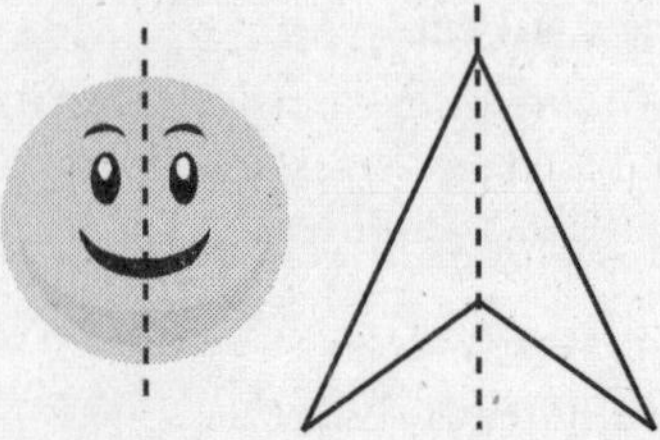

These shapes have four lines of symmetry.

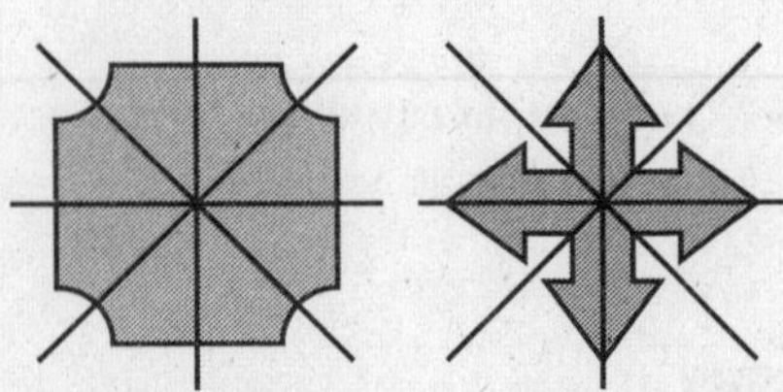

3. Draw the identical image on the other side of the line of symmetry.

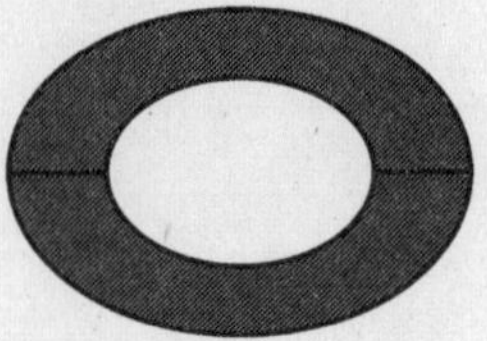

PRACTICE EXERCISES ANSWERS AND SOLUTIONS

1. A figure and its reflected mirror image in this case have the same shape, size and orientation about the line of symmetry. The only diagram that illustrates this concept is diagram **B**.

3. The yield sign can be divided into two congruent parts in 3 different ways. Therefore, the sign has 3 lines of symmetry.

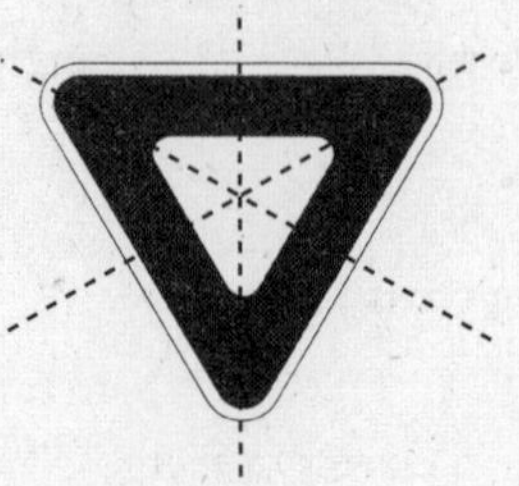

5. A regular pentagon (**A**) has five equal sides and five equal angles. It has five lines of symmetry.

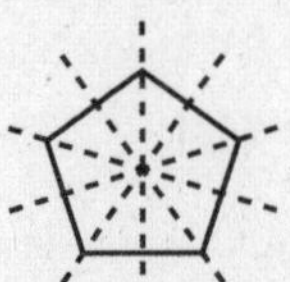

A rhombus (**B**) has four equal sides and two pairs of equal angles. It has two lines of symmetry.

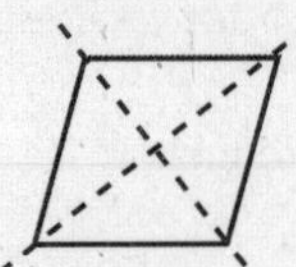

A regular hexagon (**C**) has six equal sides and six equal angles. It has six lines of symmetry.

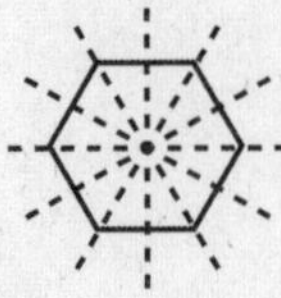

An equilateral triangle (**D**) has three equal sides and three equal angles. It has three lines of symmetry.

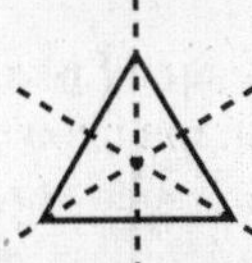

The polygons that have more than two lines of symmetry are A, C, and D.

7. Group 1: Fewer than 4 lines of symmetry
Only the triangle fits into this group.
The equilateral triangle has 3 lines of symmetry.

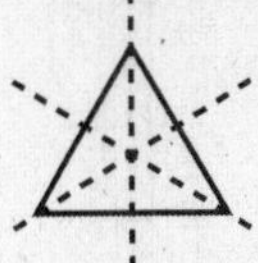

Group 2: More than 3 lines of symmetry
The square, octagon, and pentagon fit into this group. The square has 4 lines of symmetry, the octagon has 8 lines of symmetry, and the pentagon has 5 lines of symmetry.

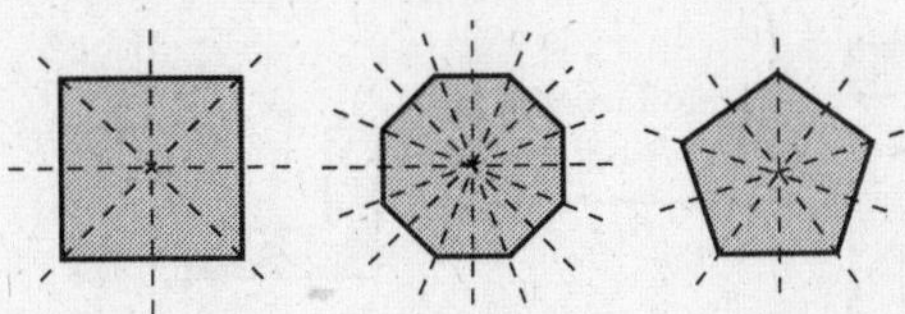

9. Draw the identical image on the other side of the line of symmetry.

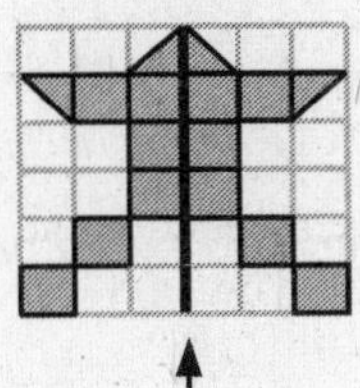

Lesson 2—Rotation Symmetry

YOUR TURN
ANSWERS AND SOLUTIONS

1. **Step 1**
Rotate the original shape clockwise until it coincides with itself.

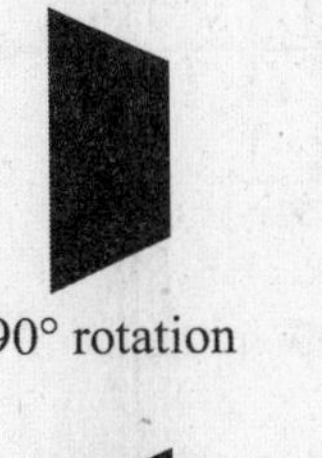

90° rotation

180° rotation

270° rotation

360° rotation

Step 2
State the order of rotation.
The hexagon has rotational symmetry about its centre because it coincides with itself after a rotation of 360°. The order of rotation is 1.
Step 3
Determine the angle of rotation.
Apply the angle of rotation formula.

The angle of rotation is $\frac{360°}{1} = 360°$.

2. If the given shape is rotated 90° counterclockwise, the resulting image will be as shown.

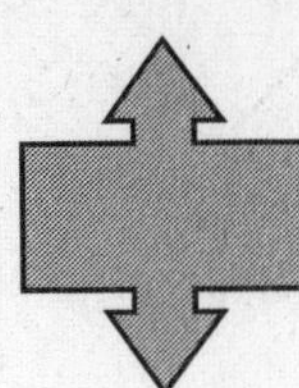

3. **Step 1**
Draw the triangle on a Cartesian Plane.

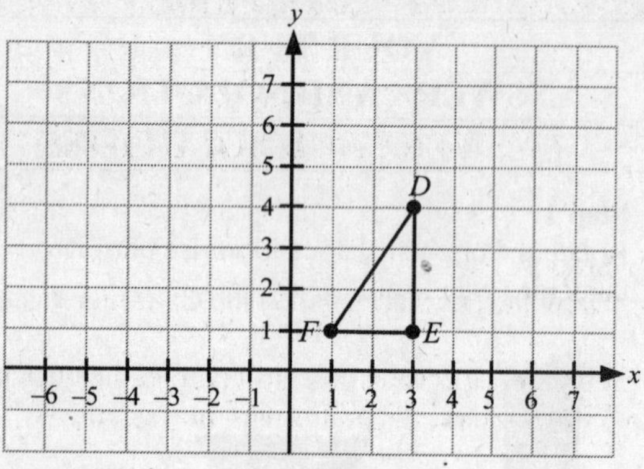

Step 2
Trace the shape, and rotate it 90° in the counterclockwise direction.
Make sure the traced image is directly on top of the shape. Place the pencil on point *F*, which is at $(1, 1)$, and turn the tracing paper counterclockwise.

Step 3
Draw the rotated shape on the Cartesian plane. Plot and label each new point. Then, connect the points with line segments to form the rotated triangle *D'E'F'*.

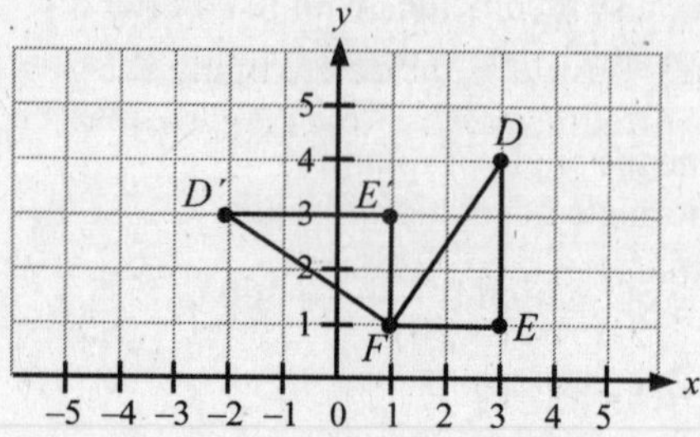

PRACTICE EXERCISES ANSWERS AND SOLUTIONS

1. Alternatives A and C will both look exactly like the original figures when they rotate 180° and 360°. Since they both have two lines of symmetry, their orders of rotational symmetry will be 2.

   Alternative B has 5 equally spaced points and 5 lines of symmetry. The star can be rotated 5 times. Each time it is rotated, it will look exactly like the original figure. Therefore, its order of rotational symmetry is 5.

   This figure is a scalene triangle.

   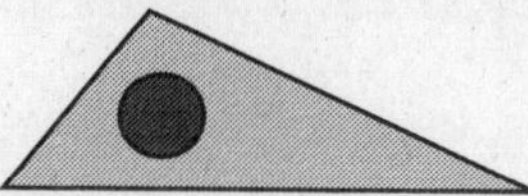

   Since it does not have any equal sides, it does not have symmetry. When it is rotated, it will not have rotational symmetry. The correct solution is **D**.

3. 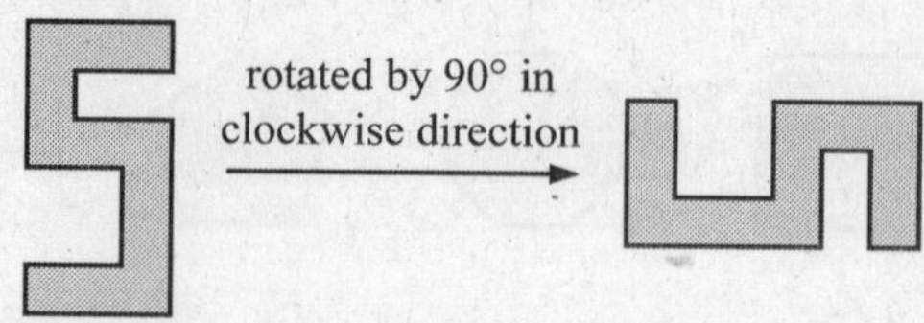

   The correct solution is **A**.

5. **Step 1**
Trace the original shape and rotate it 180° counterclockwise about $(2,1)$.
Place the pencil on $(2,1)$ and turn the tracing paper 180° counterclockwise.

Step 2
Draw the rotated image on the Cartesian plane. Plot and label each new point with a prime on the point to indicate it is the image of trapezoid *ABCD*.

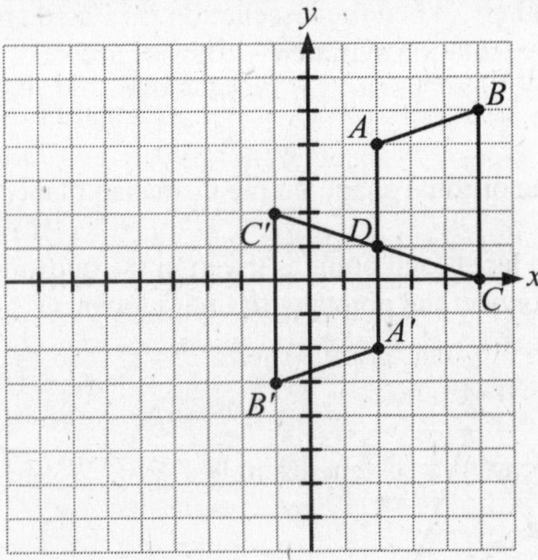

Step 3
Determine the coordinates of C' from the plotted image.
The coordinates of C' are $(-1, 2)$.

7. If the given shape is rotated $270°$ clockwise about its centre, the resulting image will be as shown.

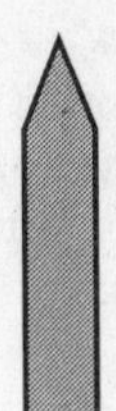

9. If an image looks exactly the same after it is rotated, then the figure is said to show rotational symmetry. Letters A and T do not have any rotational symmetry. Letters H and S both have an order of rotational symmetry of 2.

Lesson 3—Transformations on the Cartesian Plane

YOUR TURN ANSWERS AND SOLUTIONS

1. **Step 1**
Draw the original shape on the Cartesian plane.

Plot and label each point as given in the question. Then, connect the points with line segments.

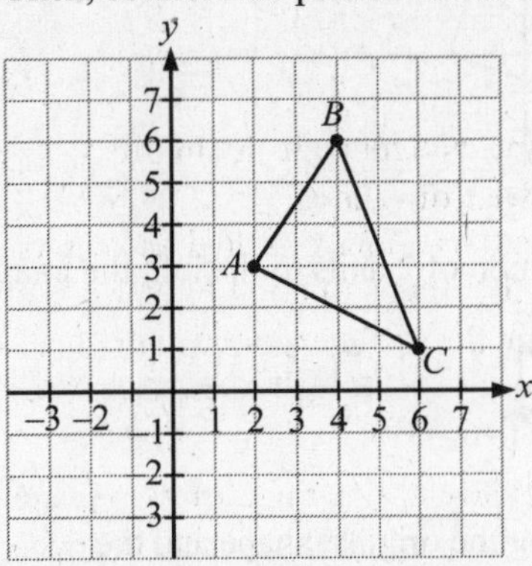

Step 2
Subtract 4 from the *x*-coordinate since the triangle is translated 4 units to the left, and subtract 3 units from the *y*-coordinate since the triangle is translated 3 units down. Label the translated points with primes.

The resulting points are:
$A'(2-4,\ 3-3)=(-2,0)$
$B'(4-4,\ 6-3)=(0,3)$
$C'(6-4,\ 1-3)=(2,-2)$

Step 3
Draw the translated image on the Cartesian plane using the translated points.

The original triangle ABC and the translated triangle $A'B'C'$ are as shown.

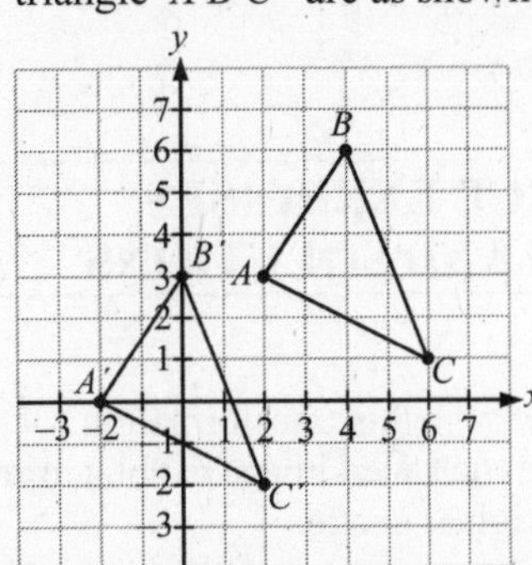

2. The translation rule of → and ↑↑↑ represents a translation of 1 unit right and 3 units up.

The opposite of this translation is to translate the image 1 unit left and 3 units down.

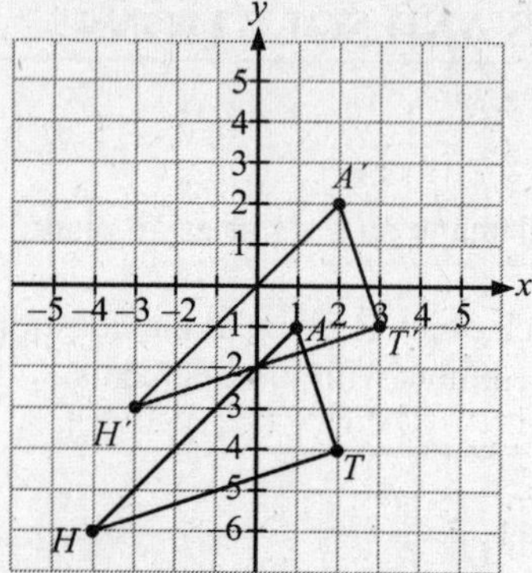

3. After a translation of 2 units to the left, the image coordinates are
$A'(-5,-2), B'(-4,-3), C'(-4,-5),$
$D'(-6,-5), E'(-6,-3)$

Upon analysing the original shape and the transformed image, there is one line of symmetry because the shapes are congruent and each one is the same distance from the line of symmetry.

The translated image is a mirror reflection of the original image.

The resulting shape is as shown.

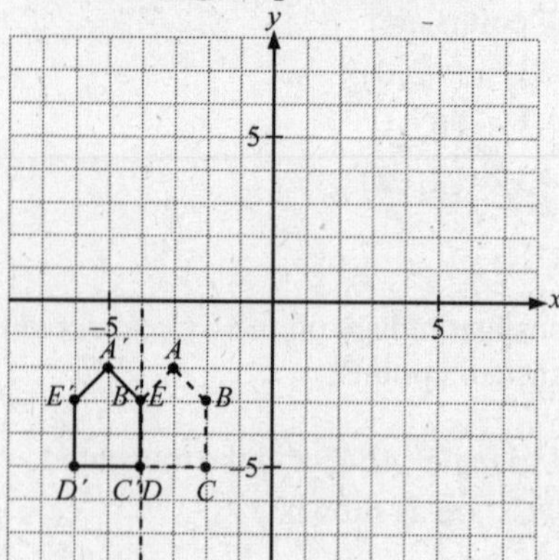

PRACTICE EXERCISES ANSWERS AND SOLUTIONS

1. There is no symmetry in this transformation. This is because the translated image is not a mirror reflection of the original image.

3. This tessellation has both line symmetry and rotational symmetry. When a line is drawn directly down the centre of the tessellation, both images on either side of the line of symmetry are identical to one another. When the tessellation is rotated about its centre, rotation symmetry exists of order 3.

5. **Step 1**
Draw the original shape on the Cartesian plane.

Plot and label each point as given in the question. Then, connect the points with line segments.

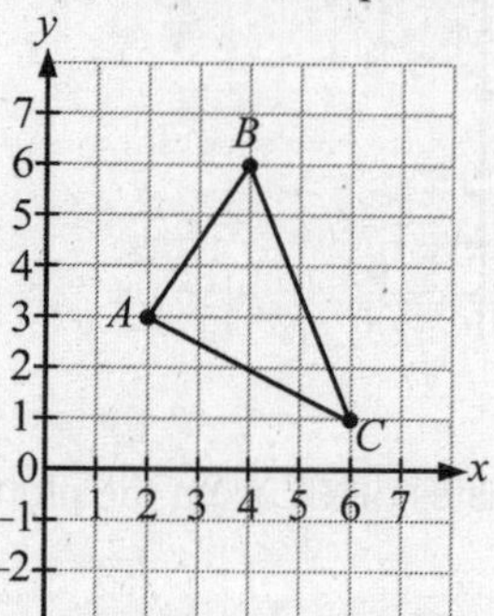

Step 2
Add or subtract, from the original coordinates of the vertices, the number of units the image will move horizontally or vertically.

The image is moving down. Downward motion affects the y-coordinate. Subtract 2 from each of the given y-coordinates. There is no right or left movement, so the x-coordinates stay the same.

$A'(2, 3-2) = (2, 1)$

$B'(4, 6-2) = (4, 4)$

$C'(6, 1-2) = (6, -1)$

Step 3
Draw the translated image on the Cartesian plane.

Plot and label each new point, then connect the new points with line segments to form the translated triangle $A'B'C'$.

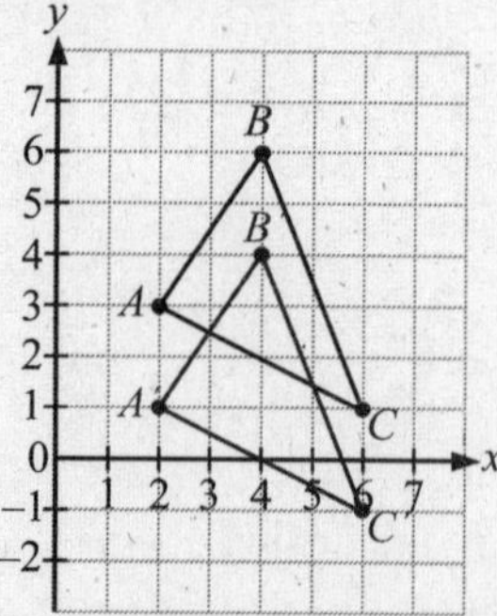

7. **Step 1**
Draw the original shape on the Cartesian plane.

Plot and label each of the coordinates.
Then, connect the points with line segments.

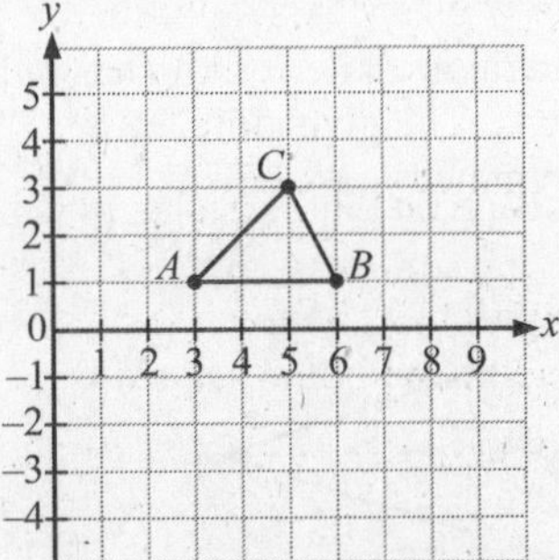

Step 2
Add or subtract the number of units the image will move on each axis.

The image is moving right and down. Left and right motion affects the *x*-coordinate. Add 2 to each *x*-coordinate. Up and down motion affects the *y*-coordinate. Subtract 4 from each *y*-coordinate.

$A'(3+2, 1-4) = (5, -3)$,
$B'(6+2, 1-4) = (8, -3)$
$C'(5+2, 3-4) = (7, -1)$

Step 3
Draw the translated image on the Cartesian plane.

Plot and label each new coordinate with a prime on the letter to indicate that it is the translated image of the original shape. Then, connect the points with line segments.

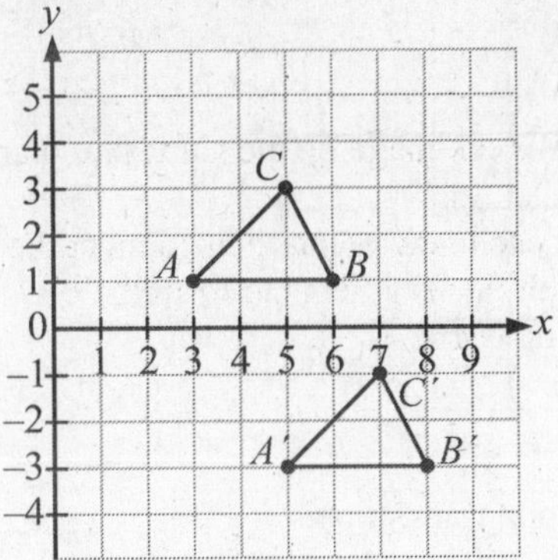

9. **Step 1**
Trace the original shape and rotate it 90° counterclockwise about point *A*. Place your pencil on $(-3, 7)$, and turn the tracing paper 90° counterclockwise.

Step 2
Draw the rotated image on the Cartesian plane.

Plot and label each new point with a prime on the point to indicate it is the image of the shape.

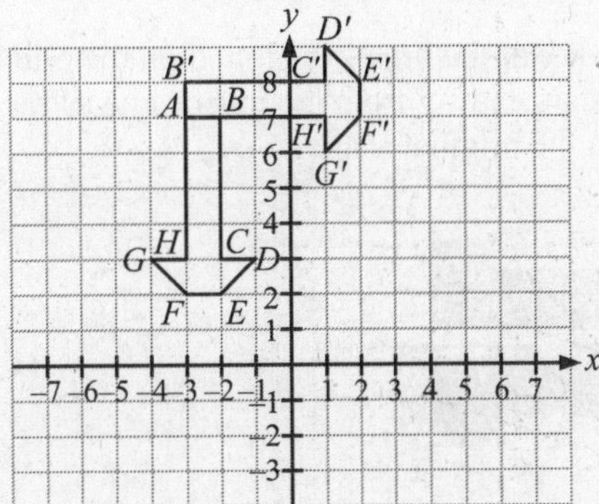

Step 3
Identify if any symmetry exists.

There is no symmetry in this because the translated image is not a mirror reflection of the original image.

Practice Test

ANSWERS AND SOLUTIONS

1. When the mirror line is *EF*, then the image of Object *B* is Image 1, which is shown in the figure.

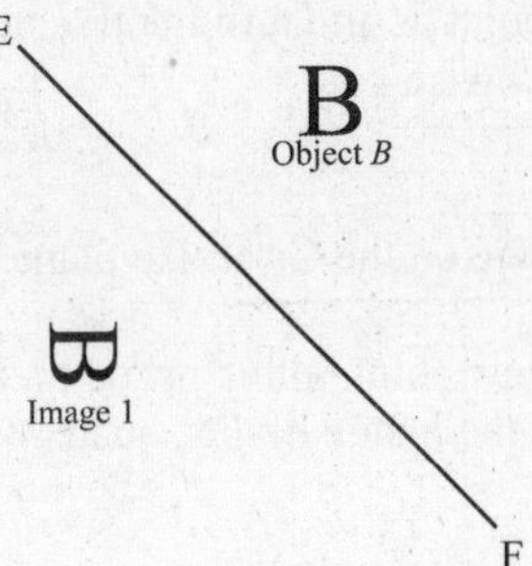

3. Figure 1 is an equilateral triangle, which has 3 lines of symmetry.

Figure 2 is a square, which has 4 lines of symmetry.

Figure 3 is an isosceles triangle, which has 1 line of symmetry.

Figure 4 is a rectangle, which has 2 lines of symmetry.

The correct arrangement is Figure 2, Figure 1, Figure 4, Figure 3.

5. Each vertex of the image is plotted on the grid the same distance away from the mirror line as each vertex in the original shape.

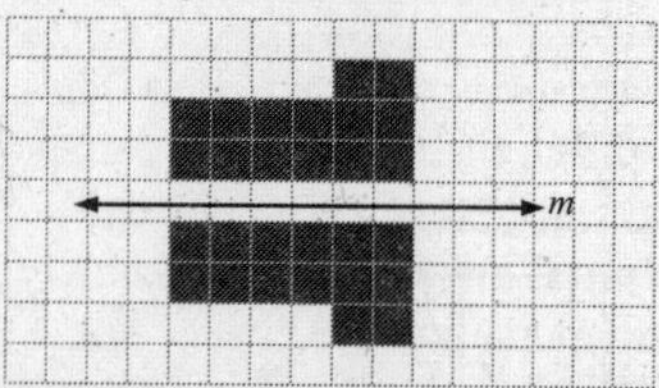

7. Rotational symmetry is symmetry with respect to some or all rotational axes.

Clearly, the figure shown above has no rotational symmetry. The correct answer is **D**.

9. **Step 1**
Trace the original shape and rotate it 90° clockwise about point *M*.

Place the pencil on point *M* and turn the tracing paper 90 counterclockwise

Step 2
Draw the rotated image on the Cartesian plane.

Plot and label each new point with a prime on the point to indicate it is the image of the square *JKML*.

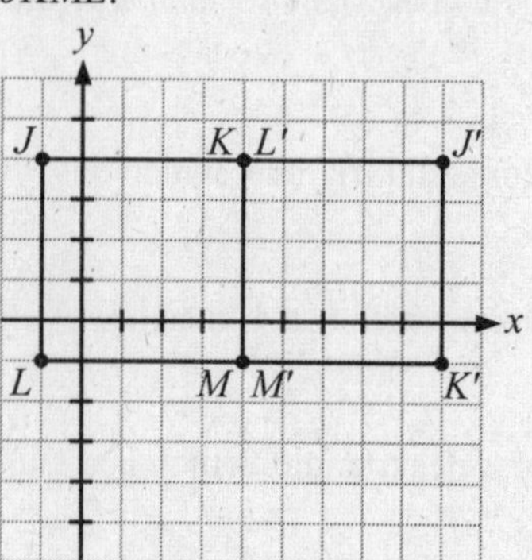

Step 3
Determine the coordinates of point *K'*..

The coordinates of point *K'* are $(9, \ -1)$.

11. The given quadrilateral is a kite. A kite has only one line of symmetry. The given kite has a horizontal line of symmetry, as shown.

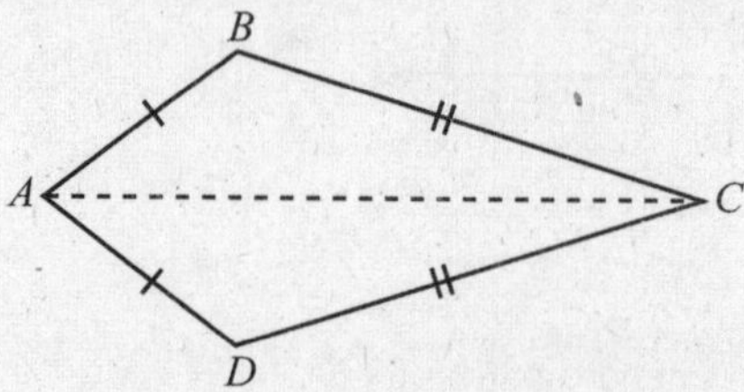

13. The transformation exhibits line symmetry because the images on both sides of the line of symmetry are congruent.

15. The transformation exhibits line symmetry. If a line is drawn directly down the centre of the shape, then line symmetry exists because the images on both sides of the line of symmetry are congruent.

17. **Step 1**
Apply the first translation.

Translate triangle *PQR* three units down to form triangle $P'Q'R'$.

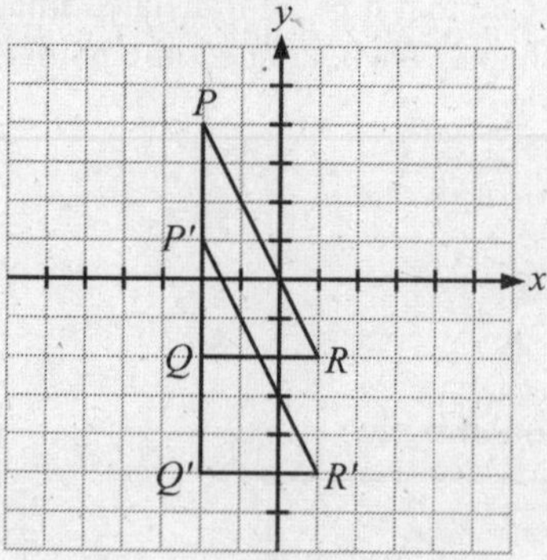

Step 2
Apply the second translation.

Translate triangle $P'Q'R'$ two units left, to form triangle $P''Q''R''$.

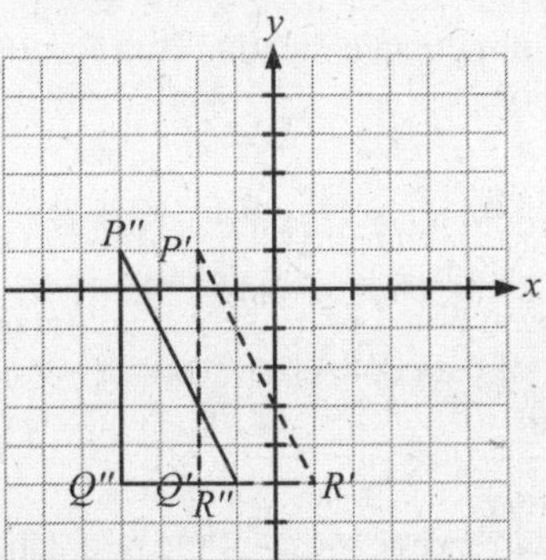

Step 3
Determine the coordinates of Q''.

The coordinates of Q'' are $(-4, -5)$.

Step 4
Identify if any symmetry exists.

There is no symmetry in this transformation because the translated image is not a mirror reflection of the original shape.

19. Step 1
Determine the coordinates of the translated image. When a quadrilateral is translated using a translation rule of R3 and D1, the x-coordinates of the vertices will increase by 3 units and the y-coordinates will decrease by 1 unit.

Thus, the coordinates of the translated image are
$A'(3+3, 2-1) = (6, 1)$
$B'(5+3, 3-1) = (8, 2)$
$C'(5+3, 5-1) = (8, 4)$
$D'(3+3, 4-1) = (6, 3)$

Step 2
Draw the translated image.

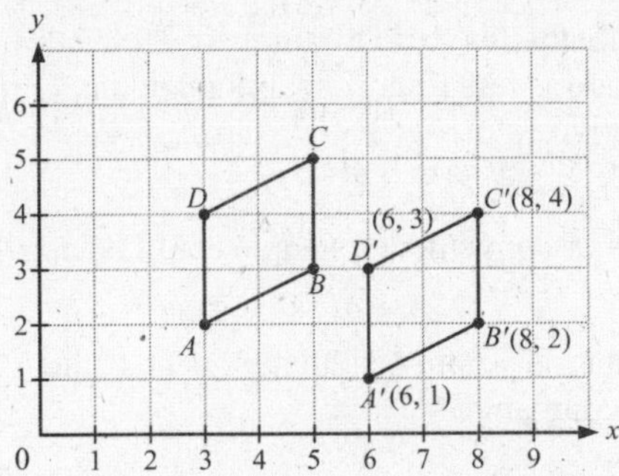

DATA ANALYSIS

Lesson 1—Factors Affecting Data Collection

YOUR TURN ANSWERS AND SOLUTIONS

1. **a)** The problem with this situation is that it is unethical. By selling the customers' phone numbers, the furniture company used the customers' personal information unethically for their own financial gain.

   b) The timing of this survey is poor. Late January is cold, and people are usually indoors and less physically active during this time of year.

2. **a)** The influencing factor is privacy. Some people may consider eating habits to be private information. They may not be willing to share a truthful answer.

   A survey question free of any influence could be, "What are some unhealthy food items you encounter in your daily life?"

   b) The influencing factor is timing. The timing of this survey is poor because most people do not use sunscreen during the winter season.

   A more suitable time to conduct the survey would be in the summertime. People are more likely to be outdoors and in the sun. Thus, they are more likely to use sunscreen.

3. The yearbook committee can use a questionnaire to collect this data. The questionnaire can be given to a random sample of graduating students.

PRACTICE EXERCISES ANSWERS AND SOLUTIONS

1. The problem with this question is bias and use of language.

   Some people may have a preset bias regarding inner-city youth and may react negatively to their tax dollars going toward inner-city projects for youth.

   Use of language is a problem because this question should not focus on the words "tax dollars" and "inner-city youth." These words can cause the respondent to have a negative or angry reaction to the question.

3. The influencing factor is cultural sensitivity. Cultural sensitivity is an issue with this survey because there are some cultures that do not eat meat or, if they eat meat, they do not eat beef specifically.

   A question free of any influence could be: "Do you purchase beef?" If yes, "Which cut of meat do you purchase the most?"

5. A question free from influence could be: "Which mode of transportation do you use the most:"
   - Car
   - Bus
   - Walking
   - Bicycle

7 A question free from any influence could be, "What genre of music do you like the best?"

Lesson 2—Sample vs. Population

YOUR TURN ANSWERS AND SOLUTIONS

1. **a)** The population would be all the 1 000 bags.

   b) A random sample could be used to count the number of chocolates from a randomly pulled sample of 100 bags.

   c) Taking a sample of 100 bags would give accurate results and a good representation of the population. Taking a sample is less time-consuming than collecting data from the population.

2. This situation would have limitations because surveying all the students would be time consuming. However in order to get accurate data the best method of data collection would be to survey the population.

3. The sample is not representative of the population because asking people who read travel and adventure magazines would create data that is influenced by bias. People who read adventure magazines may also watch travel or adventure reality shows. This sample is not a valid reflection of all reality show watchers.

4. The problems with the sample size are the finances, method, and representation. Giving a $10 coffee card to every fifth person will add up to hundreds of dollars for this investigation. Patrons are likely to use the coffee card because it means free coffee. Thus, their use of the card does not indicate whether they would use a coffee card if they had to buy one.

PRACTICE EXERCISES ANSWERS AND SOLUTIONS

1. This is an example of a convenience sample because the people leaving the children's clothing store are easy to access.

3. The population consists of all migrating humpback whales in the Pacific Ocean.

5. The best method is to do a sample of 20 whales. This method is less time consuming and is cost effective.

7. A random or convenience sample could be used.

9. The population would be all employees at the software company.

11. For more accurate data, asking the entire population would be best. Sending out an inter-office email survey would be cost-effective and a time saving way to collect data.

Lesson 3—Developing a Project Plan and Creating a Rubric

YOUR TURN ANSWERS AND SOLUTIONS

1. a) **Step 1**
Formulate a survey question that is free from any influence.
"Do you like the new brand of hot dogs?"

Step 2
Select and identify a method of collecting data.
A questionnaire can be used to collect the data. It is cost efficient and data can be collected quickly.

Step 3
Select and identify a sample or population to be surveyed.
A random sample of customers can be asked to try the new hot dogs and give their opinion. This can be carried out between the hours of 12 P.M. and 3 P.M. for one day.

Step 4
Collect and record the data.
The data can be collected and recorded on a tally chart by the surveyor.

Step 5
Display and analyse the data.
Data should be displayed on a circle graph because it can show the comparison of people who liked and disliked the new product.

b) A potential rubric that can be used for the investigation is outlined on page 311 of the text.

c) Some strengths of the investigation are listed below:

- The sampling method being used is cost effective and will not require a large time commitment.
- The sampling method will be convenient because it is surveying people who will be coming into the store. The surveyor does not have to go anywhere to collect the data.

Some weaknesses of the investigation are listed below:

- The question does not consider the influence of cultural sensitivity because some cultures do not eat meat. Therefore, if a person who does not eat meat is approached to take the survey, they may become angry or offended.
- The question does not consider the influence of timing. Only those shoppers in the store between the survey times and on that particular day will be included in the survey. Therefore, it is not a fair representation of the population of people who shop at the supermarket.

PRACTICE EXERCISES ANSWERS AND SOLUTIONS

1. A bar graph is the best choice because it can show a comparison of the different battery brands and the battery life of each brand.

3. A line graph is the best choice because it shows how the data changes over a period of time.

5. An important component for Step 3 is to ensure that any sample used is representative of the population.

7. The levels show the current level of understanding and the areas of improvement required to progress the investigation to a higher level.

9. A potential rubric that can be used for the investigation is outlined on page 305 of the text.

Lesson 4—Probability in Society

YOUR TURN
ANSWERS AND SOLUTIONS

1. a) The advertisement can affect a consumer by creating an image of a germ-infested home that can only be cured by this particular product. The consumer may assume they are protecting their loved ones by using this product.

   b) The reader will assume that becoming a student results in financial stress for an extended period of time. This is misleading because student debt can be based on a variety of factors. Just because a student is enrolled in post-secondary education does not automatically mean they will accumulate a 57% increase in debt.

2. Trevor can argue that the driving school does not guarantee that he will pass the test. He can argue that 35% of the driving school students fail the test. He feels he has a good chance of passing the test without going to the driving school. Trevor's mother can argue that by going to the driving school, he can increase his chances of passing the test because the school has an above average success rate.

3. a) Apply the probability formula, substitute in the known values, and evaluate.

$$\begin{aligned}\text{Probability} &= \frac{\text{\# of favourable outcomes}}{\text{total \# of possible outcomes}}\\ &= \frac{\text{mark of C–}}{\text{total \# of marks possible}}\\ &= \frac{1}{8}\\ &= 0.125\end{aligned}$$

$0.125\times100 = 12.5\%$

The theoretical probability that a student will receive a grade of C– is about 12.5%.

   b) The assumption that can be made is that since there are 20 students in the class and the probability of receiving a grade of C– is 12.5%, then 2 students on the list have a chance of receiving a grade of C–.

   c) Apply the probability formula, substitute in the known values, and evaluate.

$$\begin{aligned}\text{Probability} &= \frac{\text{\# of favourable outcomes}}{\text{total \# of possible outcomes}}\\ &= \frac{\text{mark of C–}}{\text{total \# of marks given}}\\ &= \frac{8}{20}\\ &= 0.40\end{aligned}$$

$0.40\times100 = 40\%$

Based on experimental data, the probability that a student will receive a grade of C– is 40%.

   d) The theoretical probability is 12.5% and the experimental probability is 40%. Therefore, theoretical probability is much less than experimental probability. The experimental probability is more accurate.

   e) **Step 1**
Calculate the experimental probability of a student receiving a mark of A+.

The experimental probability that a student will receive a grade of A+ from a total of 60 students is

$$\begin{aligned}\text{Probability} &= \frac{\text{\# of favourable outcomes}}{\text{total \# of possible outcomes}}\\ &= \frac{\text{mark of A+}}{\text{total \# of marks given}}\\ &= \frac{2}{20}\\ &= 0.10\end{aligned}$$

$0.10\times100 = 10\%$

The experimental probability that a student will receive a grade of A+ from a total of 60 students is 10%.

Step 2
Calculate 10% of 60.
$0.10\times60 = 6$

Therefore, from 60 students, 6 will likely receive a grade of A+.

PRACTICE EXERCISES ANSWERS AND SOLUTIONS

1. The advertisement can affect a reader by causing them to believe that taking the training course is the only way to become a successful sales associate.

3. The advertisement can affect a reader by causing them to believe this particular brand of all weather tires is the best item to buy during the winter season for safety on the roads. There are other brands of tires that may be just as effective and perhaps more cost effective.

5. There were 60 people polled and 32% chose Candidate Smith.

   Calculate 32% of 60.
   $0.32 \times 60 = 19.2$

   Therefore, out of 60 polled, 19 of them will likely vote for Candidate Smith.

7. The assumption is that each candidate has the same chance of being selected.

9. The experimental probability given in the table (22%) is less than the theoretical probability.

Practice Test

ANSWERS AND SOLUTIONS

1. The problem with this question is that it has the influencing factor of privacy. Students may not want to disclose that they would like to use the food bank. Consequently, when asked the survey question, they may not give a truthful answer.

3. The influencing factor in this question is use of language. The shopper may not prefer either of the two choices. If the respondents are forced to choose an option, the data being collected will be inaccurate.

5. The data collection method used for this investigation should be experiment and observation.

7. This is an example of a random sample.

9. This is an example of a convenience sample.

11. A systemic sample from the team could involve asking every third girl.

13. This situation could have limitations because a test of all 457 planes would be time-consuming and expensive. However, in order to get accurate data, the best method of data collection would be to survey the entire population of propeller planes. Surveying a sample would result in some planes not being tested and potentially harming a passenger.

15. **Step 1**
    Formulate a question for investigation that is free from any influence.

    "When you fill up your vehicle, which type of fuel do you choose?"
    a) Premium Gold Unleaded
    b) Silver Standard Unleaded
    c) Regular Unleaded

    This question does not have bias, cultural sensitivity, or any other influencing factor.

    Step 2
    Select and identify a method of collecting data.

    An observation can be used to carry out the investigation. A survey can also be used.
    Both options are good ways to collect data that can answer the question under investigation.

    Step 3
    Select and identify a sample or population to be investigated.

    This would be a convenience sample because the customers are coming to the gas station to fill their vehicles with gasoline. Data can be gathered for one business day.

    Step 4
    Collect and record the data.

    The data can be collected and recorded on a tally chart by the surveyor.

Step 5
Display and analyse the data.

Data should be displayed on a bar graph showing the three gasoline choices and the preference of the customers surveyed.

17. Some strengths of the investigation are listed:
- The sampling method being used is cost effective and will not require a large time commitment.
- The sampling will be convenient because it is done with people who will be coming into the store.
- The surveyor does not have to go anywhere to collect the data.

19. Apply the probability formula, substitute in the known values, and evaluate.

$$\begin{aligned}\text{Probability} &= \frac{\text{\# of favourable outcomes}}{\text{total \# of possible outcomes}}\\ &= \frac{\text{Pilates class}}{\text{total \# of classes}}\\ &= \frac{1}{5}\\ &= 0.20\end{aligned}$$

$0.20 \times 100 = 20\%$

The theoretical probability that a person will choose to try the Pilates class is 20%.

21. Apply the probability formula, substitute in the known values, and evaluate.

$$\begin{aligned}\text{Probability} &= \frac{\text{\# of favourable outcomes}}{\text{total \# of possible outcomes}}\\ &= \frac{\text{people who tried Pilates}}{\text{total \# of people trying new classes}}\\ &= \frac{6}{60}\\ &= 0.10\end{aligned}$$

$0.10 \times 100 = 10\%$

The experimental probability that a person will choose to try the Pilates class is 10%.

23. Step 1
Calculate the experimental probability of a person trying out the Power Yoga class. The experimental probability that a person will try the Power Yoga class is

$$\begin{aligned}\text{Probability} &= \frac{\text{\# of favourable outcomes}}{\text{total \# of possible outcomes}}\\ &= \frac{\text{people who tried Power Yoga}}{\text{total \# of people trying new classes}}\\ &= \frac{16}{60}\\ &= 0.2666666667\\ &= 0.27\end{aligned}$$

$0.27 \times 100 = 27\%$

Step 2
Calculate 27% of 1 000.
$1000 \times 27\% = 270$

Therefore, out of 1 000 people, 270 would be expected to choose Power Yoga.

Credits

NOTES

NOTES

NOTES

ORDERING INFORMATION

SCHOOL ORDERS

Schools and school jurisdictions are eligible for our educational discount rate. Contact Castle Rock Research for more information.

***THE KEY* Study Guides** are specifically designed to assist students in preparing for unit tests, final exams, and provincial examinations.

***THE KEY* Study Guides**—$29.95 each plus G.S.T.

Senior High		Junior High	Elementary
Biology 30	Biology 20	English Language Arts 9	English Language Arts 6
Chemistry 30	Chemistry 20	Mathematics 9	Mathematics 6
English 30-1	English 20-1	Science 9	Science 6
English 30-2	Mathematics 20-1	Social Studies 9	Social Studies 6
Mathematics 30-1	Physics 20	Mathematics 8	Mathematics 4
Mathematics 30-2	Social Studies 20-1	Mathematics 7	English Language Arts 3
Physics 30	English 10-1		Mathematics 3
Social Studies 30-1	Mathematics 10 Combined		
Social Studies 30-2	Science 10		
	Social Studies 10-1		

Student Notes and Problems (SNAP) Workbooks contain complete explanations of curriculum concepts, examples, and exercise questions.

SNAP Workbooks—$29.95 each plus G.S.T.

Senior High		Junior High	Elementary
Biology 30	Biology 20	Mathematics 9	Mathematics 6
Chemistry 30	Chemistry 20	Science 9	Mathematics 5
Mathematics 30-1	Mathematics 20-1	Mathematics 8	Mathematics 4
Mathematics 30-2	Physics 20	Science 8	Mathematics 3
Mathematics 31	Mathematics 10 Combined	Mathematics 7	
Physics 30	Science 10	Science 7	

Class Notes and Problem Solved—$19.95 each plus G.S.T.

Senior High		Junior High
Biology 30	Biology 20	Mathematics 9
Chemistry 30	Chemistry 20	Science 9
Mathematics 30-1	Mathematics 20-1	Mathematics 8
Mathematics 30-2	Physics 20	Science 8
Mathematics 31	Mathematics 10 Combined	Mathematics 7
Physics 30		Science 7

Visit our website for a tour of resource content and features or order resources online at
www.castlerockresearch.com/store/

#2410, 10180 – 101 Street NW
Edmonton, AB Canada T5J 3S4
e-mail: learn@castlerockresearch.com

Phone: 780.448.9619
Toll-free: 1.800.840.6224
Fax: 780.426.3917

ORDER FORM

THE KEY	QUANTITY
Biology 30	
Chemistry 30	
English 30-1	
English 30-2	
Mathematics 30-1	
Mathematics 30-2	
Physics 30	
Social Studies 30-1	
Social Studies 30-2	
Biology 20	
Chemistry 20	
English 20-1	
Mathematics 20-1	
Physics 20	
Social Studies 20-1	
English 10-1	
Math 10 Combined	
Science 10	
Social Studies 10-1	
Social Studies 9	
English Language Arts 9	
Mathematics 9	
Science 9	
Mathematics 8	
Mathematics 7	
English Language Arts 6	
Mathematics 6	
Science 6	
Social Studies 6	
Mathematics 4	
Mathematics 3	
English Language Arts 3	

Student Notes and Problems Workbooks	QUANTITY SNAP Workbooks
Mathematics 31	
Biology 30	
Chemistry 30	
Mathematics 30-1	
Mathematics 30-2	
Physics 30	
Biology 20	
Chemistry 20	
Mathematics 20-1	
Physics 20	
Mathematics 10 Combined	
Science 10	
Mathematics 9	
Science 9	
Mathematics 8	
Science 8	
Mathematics 7	
Science 7	
Mathematics 6	
Mathematics 5	
Mathematics 4	
Mathematics 3	

Problem Solved and Class Notes	QUANTITY	
	Class Notes	Problem Solved
Mathematics 31		
Biology 30		
Chemistry 30		
Mathematics 30-1		
Mathematics 30-2		
Physics 30		
Biology 20		
Chemistry 20		
Mathematics 20-1		
Physics 20		
Mathematics 10 Combined		
Mathematics 9		
Science 9		
Mathematics 8		
Science 8		
Mathematics 7		
Science 7		

Total Cost

Subtotal 1	
Subtotal 2	
Subtotal 3	
Cost Subtotal	
Shipping and Handling*	
G.S.T	
Order Total	

*(Please call for current rates)

School Discounts

Schools and school jurisdictions are eligible for our educational discount rate. Contact Castle Rock Research for more information.

PAYMENT AND SHIPPING INFORMATION

Name: ______________________

School Telephone: ______________________

SHIP TO

School Code: ______________________

School: ______________________

Address: ______________________

City: ____________ Postal Code: ______

PAYMENT

□ By credit card VISA/MC

Number: ______________________

Expiry Date: ______________________

Name on card: ______________________

□ Enclosed cheque

□ Invoice school P.O. number: ______

#2410, 10180 – 101 Street NW, Edmonton, AB T5J 3S4 **Phone:** 780.448.9619 **Fax:** 780.426.3917
Email: learn@castlerockresearch.com **Toll-free:** 1.800.840.6224
www.castlerockresearch.com

CASTLE ROCK
RESEARCH CORP